# MAXON
# Cinema 4D R20
## A Detailed Guide to Modeling, Texturing, Lighting, Rendering, and Animation

*Pradeep Mamgain*

PADEXI

**MAXON Cinema 4D R20**

*A Detailed Guide to Modeling, Texturing, Lighting, Rendering, and Animation*

## NOTICE TO THE READER

### Examination Copies

### Electronic Files

### Disclaimer

**Book Code:** PDX014P

**ISBN:** 9781092900355

*For information about the books, eBooks, and video courses published by PADEXI ACADEMY, visit our website: **www.padexi.academy***

# Contents

# Acknowledgments

I would like to express my gratitude to the many people who saw me through this book; to all those who provided support, offered comments, and assisted in the editing, proofreading, and design.

Thanks to:

Parents, family, and friends.

Teachers and mentors: Thank you for your wisdom and whip-cracking--they have helped me immensely.

I am grateful to my many students at the organizations where I've taught. Many of them taught me things I did not know about computer graphics.

Everyone at MAXON Computer [**www.maxon.net**].

Finally, thank you for picking up the book.

# About the Author

I'll keep this short, I am a digital artist, teacher, consultant, and founder of Padexi Academy [**www.padexi.academy**]. I am self-taught in computer graphics, Internet has been the best source of training for me [thanks to those amazing artists, who share the knowledge for free on YouTube]. I have worked with several companies dealing with animation and VFX. I love helping young aspiring 3D artists to become professional 3D artists. I helped my students to achieve rewarding careers in 3D animation and visual effects industry.

I have more than ten years of experience in CGI. I am passionate about computer graphics that helped me building skills in particles, fluids, cloth, RBD, pyrotechnics simulations, and post-production techniques. The core software applications that I use are: Maya, 3ds Max, Cinema 4D, Photoshop, Nuke, After Effects, and Fusion. In addition to the computer graphics, I have keen interest in web design/development, digital marketing, and search engine optimization.

You can contact me by sending an e-mail to **pradeepmamgain@gmail.com**.

# Introduction

The **MAXON Cinema 4D R20: A Detailed Guide to Modeling, Texturing, Lighting, Rendering, and Animation** book aims to help you become the best Cinema 4D artist you can be. This book will help you get started with modeling, texturing, lighting, rendering, and animation in Cinema 4D and you will learn some important concepts as well as some of the popular techniques which you can utilize to create any scene in Cinema 4D.

Using a structured and pragmatic approach, this guide begins with basics of modeling, then builds on this knowledge using practical examples to enhance your texturing, lighting, rendering, and animation skills. Each unit builds on the knowledge gained in the previous unit, showing you all the essentials of modeling, texturing, lighting, rendering, and animation with Cinema 4D. As you go from hands-on exercise to hands-on exercise, you'll develop a strong arsenal of skills that combined will form a complete end to end process to creating high quality projects using Cinema 4D.

This book shares tips, tricks, notes, and cautions throughout, that will help you become a better Cinema 4D artist and you will be able to speed up your workflow. This book is aimed to be a solid teaching resource for learning Cinema 4D. It avoids any jargon and explains concepts and techniques in an easy-to-understand manner. The first page of the every unit summarizes the topics that will be covered in the unit. Hands-on exercises in this book instruct users how things can be done in Cinema 4D step-by-step.

Practicing is one of the best ways to improve skills. This book contains practice activities which you are highly encouraged to complete and gain confidence for real-world projects. By completing these activities, you will be able to master the powerful capabilities of Cinema 4D. By the time you're done, you'll be ready to model, illuminate, and render any scene in Cinema 4D.

If you buy this book, you'll also get access to all Cinema 4D files, texture files, and any other resource used in the book. You are free to use these resources in your own projects personal or commercial. These working files allow you to follow along with the author throughout the units.

## What are the key features of the book?

- Covers Cinema 4D's updated user interface, navigation, tools, functions, and commands.
- Covers all the basics as well as advanced topics using easy to follow, hands-on exercises. Detailed coverage of tools and features.
- Covers polygon, subdivision, spline, and volumetric modeling techniques.
- Explains the **Standard, Physical, Hardware OpenGL,** and **Software OpenGL** renderers.
- Explains global illumination, ambient occlusion, color mapping, and other post effects. Covers the process of rendering flicker free animation.
- Explains the depth-of-field and motion blur effects.
- Covers Cinema 4D lights.
- Covers the product visualization and interior rendering techniques.
- Covers UV mapping.
- Explains the process of creating various materials.
- Covers the **Node Editor** and nodes in detail.
- Features **85** hands-on exercises – complete with before and after files.
- Features **26** practice activities to test the knowledge gained.
- Additional guidance is provided in the form of tips, notes, and cautions.
- Important terms are in bold face so that you never miss them.
- The content under **"What just happened?"** heading explains the working of the instructions.
- The content under **"What next?"** heading tells you about the procedure you will follow after completing a step(s).
- Includes an ePub file that contains the color images of the screenshots/ illustrations used in the textbook. These color images will help you in the learning process. This ePub file is included with the resources.
- Tech support from the author.
- Access to each exercise's initial and final states along with the resources used in hands-on exercises.
- Quiz to assess the knowledge.

## Who this book is for?

- Beginners and intermediate users of Cinema 4D
- Digital artists
- Motion graphics artists
- Indie game developers
- And anyone who wants to learn Cinema 4D

## What are the prerequisites?

- Before you start this book, you should have Cinema 4D Studio R20 installed on your system.
- You should have the desire to learn.
- Willingness to be awesome.

## What you will learn?

- Polygon, subdivision, spline, and volumetric modeling techniques.
- Use various renderers available in Cinema 4D.
- Work with post effects such as global illumination, ambient occlusion, and so on.
- Illuminate and render any scene in Cinema 4D.
- Create the depth-of-field and motion blur effects.
- Use the new node-based material system and various nodes.
- Speedup your workflow.
- Create cool looking renders.

## How this book is structured?

This book is divided into following units:

**Unit CM1: Introduction to Cinema 4D R20**, introduces you to Cinema 4D interface and primitive objects available in the Object command group. You will learn about Cinema 4D unit system, coordinate system, interface elements, and how to customize the interface. You will also create models using primitives.

**Unit CM2: Tools of the Trade**, walks you through some of the important tools that you will use in the modeling process. These tools are used to create guides in the editor view, interactively placing lights and adjusting their attributes in the scene, measure angles and distances, arrange/duplicate/randomize objects, correct lens distortions, and create virtual walkthroughs.

**Unit CM3: Spline Modeling**, introduces you to the spline modeling tools, concept, and techniques.

**Unit CM4: Polygon Modeling**, introduces you to the polygon modeling tools, concepts, and techniques. This unit talks about polygons components, selection tools, polygons structure tools, modeling objects, and deformers.

**Unit CMP: Practice Activities [Modeling]**, contains practice activities which you are highly encouraged to complete.

**Unit CV1: Volumes - I,** covers the Volume Builder and Volume Mesher functions. You will learn how to quickly create 3D models with ease using boolean operations with voxels.

**Unit CV2: Volumes - II,** covers volume filters, volume group, and the Volume Loader object.

**Unit CVP: Practice Activities [Volumes]**, contains practice activities which you are highly encouraged to complete.

**Unit CR1: Standard Renderer,** introduces you Standard renderer and its settings. You will also learn about various post effects such as global illumination, ambient occlusion, and so on. In addition, you will learn how to create dynamic depth-of-field effect.

**Unit CR2: Other Renderers,** introduces you to the Physical, Hardware OpenGL, and Software OpenGL renderers. You will also learn how to create depth-of-field and motion blur effects. Moreover, this unit covers the process of illuminating a scene using only polygon lights.

**Unit CR3: Lighting,** introduces you to Cinema 4D lights, you will learn various lighting techniques.

**Unit CT1: Introduction to UV Mapping,** introduces you to UVs, the UV Manager, and UV Projection techniques.

**Unit CT2: Material Presets,** introduces you to some of the material presets available in Cinema 4D. You will learn how to create these presets from scratch.

**Unit CT3: Creating Materials,** covers material creation process. You will learn how to create various materials. In addition, you will learn about the reflectance model of Cinema 4D.

**Unit CT4: Node-Based Materials,** covers the new node-based system introduced in R20. You will learn about various nodes and how to use them to create node graphs.

**Unit CNA: Understanding Animation and Keyframes,** introduces you to the fundamentals of animation in Cinema 4D. You will learn how to record and edit animation in Cinema 4D. In addition, you will learn to use Cinema 4D's Motion System.

**Unit CMA: Appendix - Quiz Answers [Modeling],** contains quiz answers.
**Unit CVA: Appendix - Quiz Answers [Volumes],** contains quiz answers.
**Unit CRA: Appendix - Quiz Answers [Rendering],** contains quiz answers.
**Unit CTA: Appendix - Quiz Answers [Texturing],** contains quiz answers.
**Unit CAA: Appendix - Quiz Answers [Animation],** contains quiz answers.

| Icon | Description |
|------|-------------|
| | **Tip:** A tip tells you about an alternate method for a procedure. It also show a shortcut, a workaround, or some other kind of helpful information. |
| | **Note:** This icon draws your attention to a specific point(s) that you may want to commit to the memory. |
| | **Caution:** Pay particular attention when you see the caution icon in the book. It tells you about possible side-effects you might encounter when following a particular procedure. |
| | **What just happened?:** This icons draws your attention to working of instructions in a hands-on exercise. |
| | **What next?:** This icons tells you about the procedure you will follow after completing a step(s). |
| | **Parameter:** This icons tells you about the functioning of a parameter. |

Given below are some examples with these icons:

*Note: Refraction index*
*Materials such as glass and water look realistic when they are rendered with refraction index but they increase the render time. However, note that if the scene does not contain materials that reflect light, no additional render time will be added if the* **Refraction** *check box is selected.*

*Tip: Rendering transparency*
*If the transparent objects that lie behind other transparent objects are rendered black, increase the value of the* **Ray Depth** *parameter. The default value for the* **Ray Depth** *parameter is* **15**.

? *What just happened?*
*When we apply a material to an object, a texture tag is automatically assigned to the object. The texture tag controls how the texture is mapped or placed on the object. The settings appear in the **Attribute Manager**.*

→ *What next?*
*Now, we already have the scene with optimized shadows. Before we apply the **Global Illumination** settings, we need to make sure that our materials are looking right. If you find any issue, you need to fix it before you proceed. In next steps, we will apply materials and also specify the optimized render settings.*

**Parameter: Exit Reflections**
When reflection rays meet a surface after being refracted, two types of reflections can be calculated: one when rays enter the medium and the other when they exit the medium. A single reflection is visually more appealing than the double reflection. To achieve single reflection, clear the **Exit Reflections** check box.

## Important Words
Important words such as menu name, tools' name, name of the dialogs/windows, button names, and so on are in bold face. For example:

Create an area light and then position it, as shown in Fig. E4. Rename the light as **Fill Light**. In the **General** tab, change **Intensity** to **3** and on the **Details** tab, select the **Z Direction Only** check box.

## Unit Numbers
The following table shows the terminology used for the unit numbers:

| No. | Description |
| --- | --- |
| Unit CM1 ... CM4 | CM stands for (**C**)inema 4D (**M**)odeling |
| Unit CMP | CMP stands for (**C**)inema 4D (**M**)odeling (**P**)ractice Activities |
| Unit CV1 ... CV2 | CV stands for (**C**)inema 4D (**V**)olumes |
| Unit CVP | CVP stands for (**C**)inema 4D (**V**)olumes (**P**)ractice Activities |
| Unit CR1 ... CR3 | CR stands for (**C**)inema 4D (**R**)endering |
| Unit CT1 ... CT4 | CT stands for (**C**)inema 4D (**T**)exturing |
| Unit CAN | CAN stands for (**C**)inema 4D (**AN**)imation |

| No. | Description |
|-----|-------------|
| Unit CMA | CMA stands for (C)inema 4D (M)odeling (A)ppendix |
| Unit CVA | CVA stands for (C)inema 4D (V)olumes (A)ppendix |
| Unit CRA | CRA stands for (C)inema 4D (R)endering (A)ppendix |
| Unit CTA | CTA stands for (C)inema 4D (T)exturing (A)ppendix |
| Unit CAA | CAA stands for (C)inema 4D (A)nimation (A)ppendix |

This approach helps us better organize the units when multiple modules/books are included in a textbook. For example, XPresso units will be numbered as **CX1**, **CX2**, **CX3**, and so on; dynamics units will be numbered as **CD1**, **CD2**, and so on.

### Figure Numbers
In theory, figure numbers are in the following sequence **Fig. 1**, **Fig. 2**, and so on. In hands-on exercises, the sequence is as follows: **Fig. E1**, **Fig. E2**, and so on. In hands-on exercises, the sequence restarts from number **E1** for each exercise.

## Naming Terminology
### LMB, MMB, and RMB
These acronyms stand for left mouse button, middle mouse button, and right mouse button.

### MEV Menu
This acronym stands for **Menu in editor view**. It represents the menubar located in each viewport of Cinema 4D.

### Tool
If you click an item in a palette, toolbar, manager, or browser and a command is invoked to create/edit an object or perform some action then that item is termed as tool. For example: **Move** tool, **Rotate** tool, **Loop Selection** tool.

### Right-click Contextual Menus
The right-click menus [see Fig. 1] are the contextual menus in Cinema 4D that provide quick access to the commands/functions/tools related to the currently selected entities.

### Hidden Menus
There are several hidden menus available in Cinema 4D. These menus quickly allow you to select tools, command, and functions. For example, the **M** menu lets you quickly access the modeling tools. Now, if you want to invoke the **Extrude** tool, press **MT** [see Fig. 2].

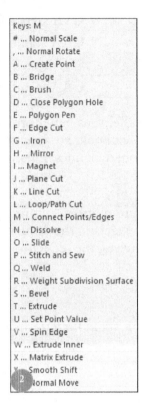

## Check Box

A small box [labelled as 1 in Fig. 3], when selected by the user, shows that a particular feature has been enabled or a particular option chosen.

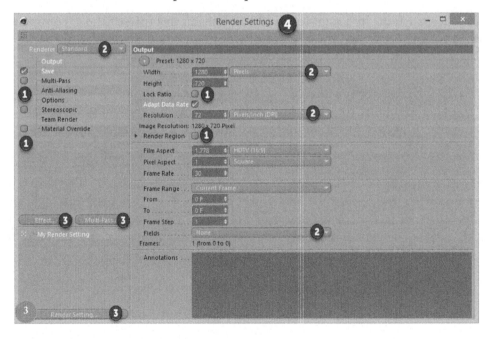

### Drop-down

A drop-down (abbreviated drop-down list; also known as a drop-down menu, drop menu, pull-down list, picklist) is a graphical control element [labelled as 2 in Fig. 3], similar to a list box, that allows the user to choose one value from a list.

### Button

The term button (sometimes known as a command button or push button) refers to any graphical control element [labelled as 3 in Fig. 3] that provides the user a simple way to trigger an event, like searching for a query, or to interact with dialog boxes, like confirming an action.

### Window

A window [labelled as 4 in Fig. 3] is a separate viewing area on a computer display screen in a system that allows multiple viewing areas as part of a graphical user interface (GUI).

### Dialog Box

An area on screen [see Fig. 4] in which the user is prompted to provide information or select commands.

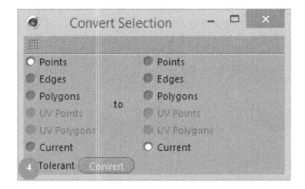

### Trademarks

**Windows** is the registered trademarks of **Microsoft Inc. Cinema 4D** is the registered trademarks of **MAXON Computer.**

### Access to Electronic Files

This book is sold via multiple sales channels. If you don't have access to the resources used in this book, you can place a request for the resources by visiting the following link: *http://www.padexi.academy/contact.* Fill the form under the **Book Resources [Electronic Files]** section and submit your request.

### Customer Support

At **PADEXI Academy,** our technical team is always ready to take care of your technical queries. If you are facing any problem with the technical aspect of the textbook, please send an email to author at the following email address: **pradeepmamgain@gmail.com**

## Errata

We have made every effort to ensure the accuracy of this book and its companion content. If you find any error, please report it to us so that we can improve the quality of the book. If you find any errata, please report them by visiting the following link: *http://www.padexi.academy/errata.*

This will help the other readers from frustration. Once your errata is verified, it will appear in the errata section of the book's online page.

- Navigating the workspace
- Customizing the interface
- Understanding UI components
- Setting preferences
- Understanding layouts
- Moving, rotating, and scaling objects
- Managers and Browsers
- Getting help

# Unit CM1: Introduction to Cinema 4D R20

Welcome to the latest version of Cinema 4D. In any 3D computer graphics application, the first thing you see is interface. Interface is where you view and work with your scene.

Cinema 4D's interface is intuitive and highly customizable. You can make changes to the interface and then save multiple interface settings using the **Layout** feature. You can create multiple layouts and switch between them easily.

## Cinema 4D Interface Elements

You can start Cinema 4D by using one of the following methods:

- Double-click on the Cinema 4D icon on the desktop
- Double-click on a Cinema 4D scene file
- Clicking Cinema 4D entry from the **Start** menu
- Dragging a **.c4d** file from **Windows Explorer** to the program icon
- Running it from **Command Prompt**
- Running **Cinema 4D Lite** from After Effects

When you first time open Cinema 4D, you are presented with the UI, as shown in Fig. 1. I have labeled various elements of the interface using numbers.

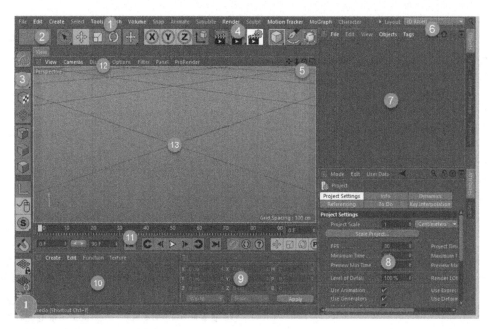

The following table summarizes the main UI elements.

| Table 1: The Cinema 4D Interface Elements | | |
|---|---|---|
| **No.** | **Name** | **Description** |
| 1 | Menubar | The menubar contains the Cinema 4D commands and functions. |
| 2 | Standard palette | It is located below the menubar. This palette hosts tools, commands, and functions. |
| 3 | Tools Palette | This palette contains most commonly used commands and tools. |
| 4 | Command Groups | The command groups are the collection of tools and commands. |
| 5 | Navigation Buttons | You can use these buttons to navigate in a scene. |
| 6 | Layout drop-down list | The options in this drop-down list are used to switch between layouts. |
| 7 | Object Manager | This manager contains all objects present in the scene. |
| 8 | Attribute Manager | It displays the properties and settings of the selected objects. |
| 9 | Coordinate Manager | It contains fields that you can use to precisely model and manipulate an object in the scene. |
| 10 | Material Manager | It contains all the materials available in the scene. |
| 11 | Animation Toolbar | This toolbar contains controls for recording and playing animation. |

| Table 1: The Cinema 4D Interface Elements | | |
|------|------|------|
| No. | Name | Description |
| 12 | Menu in editor view | This menu is available in every viewport and used to set various tasks related to the viewports. In later units, I've referred to it as **MEV** menubar. |
| 13 | View Panel | The view panel is collection of upto four viewports where you build and animate 3D models. |

The Cinema 4D interface is highly configurable. You can dock and undock windows in the main window. When you move a docked window, the surrounding windows are resized automatically. You can also display windows as tabs to save the screen real-state. You can define the arrangements of elements as layouts and freely switch between them. The fastest way to switch between the layouts is the **Layout** drop-down list [labeled as 6 in Fig. 1] located on the top-right corner of the interface.

Let's explore various components of the Cinema 4D interface.

## Title Bar

The title bar is the first element of the interface and located at the top of the UI. It displays name and version of the software as well as the name of the currently opened file.

## Menubar

The menubar is located below the tile bar. It hosts almost all important commands, tools, and functions that Cinema 4D offers. You can tear-off a menu [or sub-menu] from the menubar by clicking on the corrugated line located at the top of the menu or sub-menu [see Fig. 2].

## Standard Palette

The **Standard** palette is located below the menubar and it hosts various tools, commands, and groups of commands. Some of the icons on the palette have a black triangle on the bottom-right corner that indicates a folded group of tools/commands.

To access the folded group of commands, hold LMB on the icon and then choose the desired command from the displayed flyout.

The table given next summarizes the tools available in the **Standard** palette:

**Table 2:** The tools and commands available in the **Standard** palette

| Name | Icon | Shortcut | Description |
|------|------|----------|-------------|
| Undo | | Ctrl+Z | This tool undoes the last change. It restores scene to the previous state. By default, you can restore up to **30** previous states. If you want to change the undo depth, choose **Preferences** from the **Edit** menu to open the **Preferences** window or press **Ctrl+E**. Choose **Memory** from the list of categories and then set a new value for the **Undo Depth** parameter in the **Project** area. |
| Redo | | Ctrl+Y | This tool redoes a change. It restores the changes you made in the scene. |
| Live Selection | | 9 | It is like a paint brush type of selection tool. To change the brush size, change the value of the **Radius** parameter in **Attribute Manager**. To interactively change the radius, hold MMB and drag. To select entities, paint over the objects' points, edges, or polygons. You can quickly select the elements when the **Rotate, Move,** or **Scale** tool is active by RMB dragging over the objects. You can press **Spacebar** to toggle between the **Live Selection** tool and previously selected tool. |
| Rectangle Selection | | 0 | This tool allows you to select the objects by dragging a selection frame [like marquee selection in Photoshop] over the elements. To add an element to the selection, hold **Shift** while you select. To deselect an element, hold **Ctrl** while you select. |
| Lasso Selection | | 8 | This tool behaves like a lasso. You can use it to draw a loop around elements to select them. |

**Table 2:** The tools and commands available in the **Standard** palette

| Name | Icon | Shortcut | Description |
|---|---|---|---|
| Polygon Selection |  | - | This tool allows you to draw a n-sided shape to frame the elements to select them. To complete the loop, click on the starting point or RMB click. |
| Move |  | E/4/7 | Allows you to place the selected object or component in the viewport. You can also use it to select points, edges, and polygons. The selection can also be drawn using RMB. You can press the **4** key and drag the mouse to move the objects. Press **7** and drag the mouse to move the objects without child objects.<br><br>You can also use the **Axis Extension** feature to accurately position the objects. You need to **Ctrl+RMB** click on an axis handle to enable the **Axis Extension** feature. |
| Scale |  | T | Allows you to resize the selected objects or components. The **Axis Extension** function is also available for the **Scale** tool. |
| Rotate |  | R | Allows you to rotate the selected objects or components. |
| Active | 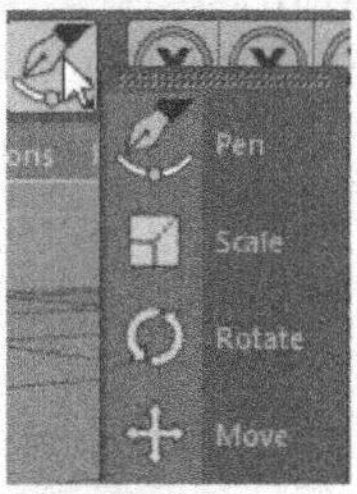 | | A list of last used 8 tools is displayed here when you click and hold on it. |
| X-Axis / Heading |  | X | This tool locks or unlocks the transformation along the X-axis. |
| Y-Axis / Pitch |  | Y | This tool locks or unlocks the transformation along the Y-axis. |
| Z-Axis / Bank |  | Z | This tool locks or unlocks the transformation along the Z-axis. |

**Table 2:** The tools and commands available in the **Standard** palette

| Name | Icon | Shortcut | Description |
| --- | --- | --- | --- |
| Coordinate System | | W | This tool is a toggle switch that allows you to switch between the local and world coordinate systems. |
| Render View | | Ctrl+R | Renders the current active view. |
| Render to Picture Viewer | | Shift+R | Renders the active view in the **Picture Viewer** window. |
| Edit Render Settings | | Ctrl+B | Opens the **Render Settings** window from where you can specify settings for rendering the scene. |
| Cube | | | Hold **LMB** on this tool to reveal the **Objects** command group. This group holds the geometric primitives that Cinema 4D offers. |
| Pen | | | Hold **LMB** on this tool to reveal the **Spline** command group. This group holds the spline primitives and other spline tools Cinema 4D offers. |
| Subdivision Surface | | | Hold **LMB** on this tool to reveal the **Generators** command group. This group holds the generators that Cinema 4D offers. |
| Array | | | Press and hold LMB on this tool to reveal the **Modeling** command group. This group holds various modeling commands. |
| Bend | | | Hold **LMB** on this tool to reveal the **Deformer** command group. This group holds the deformer functions Cinema 4D offers. |
| Floor | | | Hold **LMB** on this tool to reveal other environment tools available in the **Environment** command group. |
| Camera | | | Hold **LMB** on this tool to reveal other camera tools available in the **Camera** command group. |
| Light | | | Hold **LMB** on this tool to reveal other light tools available in the **Light** command group. |

## Tools Palette

The **Tools** palette is the vertical toolbar located on the extreme left of the standard interface. It contains various tools. The following table summarizes these tools:

**Table 3:** The tools and commands available in the **Tools** palette

| Name | Icon | Shortcut | Description |
|------|------|----------|-------------|
| Make Editable | | C | The primitive objects in Cinema 4D are parametric. They have no points or polygons and are instead created using math. This tool allows you to convert the parametric objects to editable objects with polygons and points. When you make an object editable, you lose its parametric creation parameters. |
| Model | | | If you want to move, rotate, or scale an object, use this mode. |
| Object | | | This icon is available when you press and hold the left mouse button on the **Model** icon. The **Object** mode is suited when you are working with an animation. When you scale an object using the **Scale** tool, only the object axes are scaled not the surfaces themselves. If you scale an object non-uniformly, the child objects get squashed and stretched when you rotate them. You can avoid this problem by working in the **Object** mode. The rule of thumb is when modeling, use the **Model** mode, use the **Object** mode for animation. |
| Animation | | | This icon is available when you press and hold the left mouse button on the **Model** icon. This mode allows you to move, scale, or rotate the entire animation path of an object. |
| Texture | | | This mode allows you to edit the active texture. Only one texture can be edited at a time. Also, note that the projection type is also taken into consideration in this mode. |

**Table 3:** The tools and commands available in the **Tools** palette

| Name | Icon | Shortcut | Description |
|------|------|----------|-------------|
| Workplane | | | Workplanes are explained in detail in Unit **CM2**. |
| Points | | | Select this tool to enable the **Points** mode. Once enabled, you can use various tools to edit the points of an object. |
| Edges | | | Click this tool to enable the **Edges** mode and edit the edges of an object. |
| Polygons | | | Click this tool to enable the **Polygons** mode and edit the polygons of an object. |
| Enable Axis | | L | This tool allows you to move the origin of the object. |
| Tweak | | | This tool works with the **Polygon Pen** tool. You can tweak points, edges, and polygons using the **Polygon Pen** tool in this mode. |
| Viewport Solo Mode | | | This mode is useful when you are working on a complex scene and you want to concentrate on a specific area of the scene. The **Viewport Solo Off** option is a toggle switch that you can use to turn on or off the **Viewport Solo** mode.<br><br>In the **Viewport Solo Single** mode, all objects are hidden except the currently selected objects. The **Viewport Solo Hierarchy** mode displays only the selected objects, including their child objects.<br><br>When the **Viewport Solo Selection** option is selected, the visibility of the objects will be defined automatically when they are selected. |
| Enable Snap | | Shift+S | It is a toggle switch that lets you enable or disable snapping. |
| Locked Workplane | | Shift+X | This tool disables any defined automatic **Workplane** modes and fixes the **Workplane**. |
| Planar Workplane | | | Depending on the angle of view of the camera, one of the world coordinate planes will be automatically displayed as the **Workplane**. |

## Navigation Tools

The navigation tools are located on the top-right corner of each viewport. Click-drag the first icon to pan the view [move the camera], click-drag second icon to zoom in or out [move the camera in the direction of view] of the viewport. Click-drag the third icon to rotate [rotate the camera] the view. Click the forth icon to maximize the view. You can also maximize a viewport by **MMB** clicking on it. You can also use hotkeys to navigate the view. To use a hotkey, hold down the key on the keyboard and drag the mouse.

The following table summarizes these hotkeys:

| Table 4: The navigation hotkeys | |
|---|---|
| **Key** | **Description** |
| 1 | Move camera |
| 2 | Move camera in the direction of view |
| 3 | Rotate Camera |

The viewports with the orthogonal view can be rotated around their orthographic axis. If you hold **Shift**, you can rotate the view in **15** degrees increments.

## Menu In Editor View

The **Menu in editor view** [**MEV** menubar] is located on the top of each viewport. It hosts command, tools, and functions corresponding to the views. The **MEV** menubar contains seven menus. The following tables summarizes the options available in these menus:

| Table 5: The **View** menu | | | |
|---|---|---|---|
| **Option** | **Icon** | **Shortcut** | **Description** |
| Use as Render View | | | When enabled, the active camera will be used for the rendering in **Picture Viewer**. |
| Undo View/ Redo View | | Ctrl+Shift+Z Ctrl+Shift+Y | These tools only work in the viewports. The main **Undo/Redo** tools do not affect the cameras. |
| Frame All | | | Centers all objects including lights and cameras to fill the view. |
| Frame Geometry | | Alt+H H | Centers all objects excluding lights and cameras to fill the view. |
| Frame Default | | | Resets the viewport to the default values. |

**Table 5:** The **View** menu

| Option | Icon | Shortcut | Description |
|--------|------|----------|-------------|
| Frame Selected Elements | 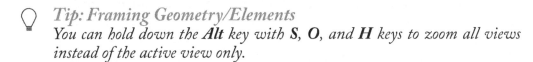 | Alt+S S | Centers all selected elements [objects, polygons] to fill the view and are centered. |
| Frame Selected Objects | | Alt+O O | Centers all active objects to fill the view. |
| Film Move | | | The functioning of this tools is similar to that of the first icon in the navigation tools, refer to Table 4. |
| Redraw | | A | Redraws the scene. By default, Cinema 4D updates the scene automatically. If it does not happen, use this function to redraw the scene. |
| Send to Picture Viewer | | | Sends the current viewport picture to **Picture Viewer**. |

*Tip: Framing Geometry/Elements*
*You can hold down the **Alt** key with **S**, **O**, and **H** keys to zoom all views instead of the active view only.*

**Table 6:** The **Cameras** menu

| Option | Icon | Description |
|--------|------|-------------|
| Cursor Mode | | Every viewport has a default camera called **Editor Camera**. This camera is active by default. The options available in the **Navigation** sub-menu define how camera is rotated. If you have defined a camera and using it, the camera will be always rotated around its origin independent of **Camera Mode**. The **Cursor** mode is the default mode. In this mode, the camera rotates around the selected object point. If you click on an empty area of the viewport, the camera will rotate around the screen center at the depth of the last defined point of interest. |
| Center Mode | | In this mode, the camera will rotate around the center of the screen. |
| Object Mode | | In this mode, the camera will rotate around the center of the selected objects/elements. |

| Table 6: The Cameras menu | | |
|---|---|---|
| **Option** | **Icon** | **Description** |
| Camera Mode | | In this mode, the camera will rotate around its own axis. |
| Default Camera | | This command activates the default camera. |
| Set Active Object as Camera | | You can use this function to view the scene from the origin of the active object. Your view will point in the direction of the object's Z axis. This command can be useful, among other things, for checking which objects a light source can see. |
| Camera 2D Mode | | When this mode is active, 3D object will be displayed in 2D. You can navigate as usual using the hotkeys and navigation icons. This is a temporary mode, which can be used to precisely examine parts of the scene. This mode is designed for use in the perspective view. |
| Perspective | | This is the default projection mode for the viewport [see Fig. 3]. You see the scene as if you are looking through a conventional camera. |
| Parallel | | All lines are parallel. The vanishing point is infinitely distant [see Fig. 4]. |
| Left | | The YZ view [see Fig. 5]. |
| Right | | The ZY view [see Fig. 6]. |
| Front | | The XY view [see Fig. 7]. |
| Back | | The YX view [see Fig. 8]. |
| Top | | The XZ view [see Fig. 9]. |
| Bottom | | The ZX view [see Fig. 10]. |

| Table 6: The **Cameras** menu | | |
|---|---|---|
| **Option** | **Icon** | **Description** |
| Axonometric | | There are six more **Axonometric** views available. The **Axonometric** projection is a type of parallel projection used for creating a pictorial drawing of an object, where the object is rotated along one or more of its axes relative to the plane of projection. |

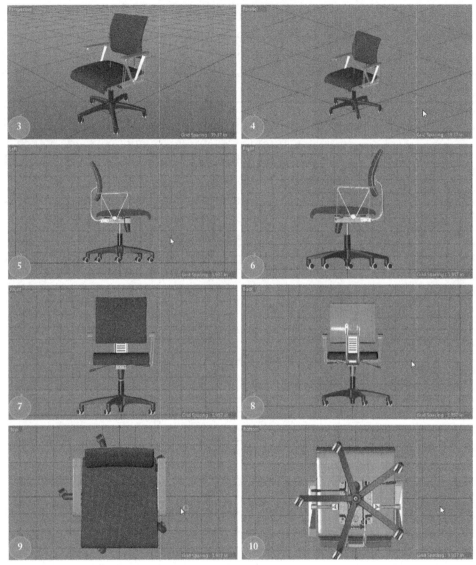

**Table 7:** The **Display** menu

| Option | Icon | Shortcut | Description |
|--------|------|----------|-------------|
| Gouraud Shading | | N~A | This is the high quality display mode for viewports [see Fig. 11]. The object smoothing and lights are taken into consideration. |
| Gouraud Shading (Lines) | | N~B | Adds wireframes or isoparms to the shading [see Fig. 12]. |
| Quick Shading | | N~C | Identical to **Gouraud Shading**, however, the auto light is used instead of scene's lights. |

| 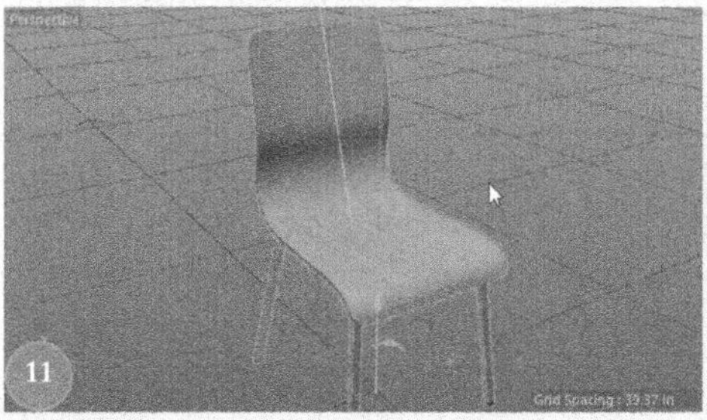 Option |  Icon | Shortcut | Description |
|--------|------|----------|-------------|
| Quick Shading (Lines) | | N~D | In this mode, you can add wireframes or isoparms to the quick shading by choosing **Wireframe** or **Isoparms** from the **Display** menu. |
| Constant Shading | | N~E | Shows constant shading on the objects. |
| Constant Shading (Lines) | | | Shows constant shading with lines on the objects. |
| Hidden Line | | N~F | The hidden lines are not displayed. |
| Lines | | N~G | Displays complete mesh including hidden lines. |
| Wireframe | | N~H | Draws lines on objects. |

| Table 7: The **Display** menu | | | |
|---|---|---|---|
| **Option** | **Icon** | **Shortcut** | **Description** |
| Isoparms | | N~I | This mode displays isoparm lines for objects that use them such as **Generators**. |
| Box | | N~K | Displays each object as box. |
| Skeleton | | N~L | This is the fastest display mode. It is only suitable for hierarchical structures. |

| Table 8: The **Options** menu | | | |
|---|---|---|---|
| **Option** | **Icon** | **Shortcut** | **Description** |
| [Level of Detail] Low Medium High | | | These options define level of detail in the viewport. The **Low**, **Medium**, and **High** options set the level of detail in the viewport to **25%,50%**, and **100%**, respectively. |
| Use Render LOD for Editor Rendering | | | Using this option, you can define LOD detail for each view. This option lets you use the LOD settings defined in the respective settings such as subdivision surfaces or metaballs. |
| Stereoscopic | | | Enables the stereoscopic display in the view. |
| Linear Workflow Shading | | | If you are considering a stereoscopic view, the color and shaders can be turned off using this option. |
| Enhanced OpenGL | | | Defines whether the viewport should use the **Enhanced OpenGL** quality for display. |
| Transparency | | | Defines whether or not **Enhanced OpenGL** should display transparency in high quality. |
| Shadows | | | Defines whether or not **Enhanced OpenGL** should display shadows. |
| Post Effects | | | Defines whether or not **Enhanced OpenGL** should display post effects. |

| Table 8: The **Options** menu | | | |
|---|---|---|---|
| **Option** | **Icon** | **Shortcut** | **Description** |
| Noises | | | Toggles the display of the **Noise** shader for **Enhanced OpenGL**. |
| Reflections | | | Defines whether or not **Enhanced OpenGL** should display reflections. |
| SSAO | | | Defines whether or not an **Ambient Occlusion** approximation should be rendered in the Viewport. |
| Tessellation | | | Defines whether or not tessellation should be displayed for respective objects in the Viewport. |
| Depth of Field | | | Defines whether or not the depth of field should be rendered in the editor view. |
| Backface Culling | | N~P | Toggles backface culling on or off when in the **Lines** mode. With backface culling, all concealed surfaces are hidden from the camera improving the performance. |
| Isoline Editing | | Alt+A | It projects all **Subdivision Surfaces** cage object elements onto the smoothed surface. As a result, these elements can be selected directly on the smoothed object. |
| Layer Color | | | This option lets you view which objects have been assigned to which layer. The objects are displayed in the color assigned to their respective layer. |
| Polygon Normals | | | Toggles the display of normals in the polygon mode. |
| Vertex Normals | | | Toggles the display of normals in the vertex mode. |
| Tags | | N~O | If enabled, the objects will use the display mode defined in their **Display** tags. |
| Textures | | N~Q | Allows you to see textures in the view panel in real-time. |
| X-Ray | | N~R | Enables the X-Ray effect. The object becomes semi-transparent so that you can see its concealed points and faces. |

| Table 8: The **Options** menu | | | |
|---|---|---|---|
| **Option** | **Icon** | **Shortcut** | **Description** |
| DefaultLight | 💡 | | Opens the **Default Light** manager that you can use to quickly light the selected objects from any angle. Click-drag on the sphere to set the angle of light. |
| Configure | | Shift+V | The **Configure** option is used to specify the viewport settings. The settings are displayed in **Attribute Manager**. The options and parameters displayed in bold face in **Attribute Manager** are saved globally and these options are used when you create a new scene or restart Cinema 4D.<br><br>All non-bold parameters and options are saved with the file locally. The local options and parameters affect the active view or the selected view. You can select multiple views by clicking on the blank gray area of their headers with **Shift** held down. You can make an option or a parameter global or local. To do this, select the element by clicking on it in **Attribute Manager** and then RMB click. Choose **Make Parameter Global/Make Parameter Local** from the popup menu. |
| Configure All | | Alt+V | This option affects all existing views. |

---

📝 *Note: Reflection*

*If no sky is present in the scene, an internal substitute object will be reflected onto the scene. However, it will not be rendered. This applies to the **Sky** object, **HDRI** textures, and **Physical Sky**. The most of settings will be reflected in the scene but few settings are not supported such as **Roughness**, **Bump Strength**, and **Refraction Index**. The following reflection models are supported: **Beckmann**, **GGX**, **Phong**, **Ward**, **Oren-Nayar (Diffuse)**, and **Lambert (Diffuse)**.*

📝 *Note: Reflectance channel*

*Now, if you are using the **Reflectance** channel, Cinema 4D can display physically correct shading in the editor view without rendering the scene. The **Sky** objects and rectangular area lights can be correctly reflected in the viewport. Also, the simplified version of other objects will be reflected. With all these new enhancement, viewport display come closer to the rendered results. For the non-complex scenes, you can use the **Renderer Hardware OpenGL** option to skip the test renderings.*

The options in the **Filter** menu allow you to define which types of objects are displayed in the views. By default, all types are displayed. Choose **All** from the menu to enable all types. Choose **None** to disable all types.

*Tip: Filters*
*To enable one option and disable all others, choose the desired filter from the* ***Filter*** *menu with* ***Ctrl*** *held down.*

*Note: Hidden Objects*
*If you select a hidden object from* ***Object Manager****, the axis system of the object appears in the viewport.*

Each view in Cinema 4D can have upto four view panels. The options available in the **Panel** menu allow you to choose a different mode [arrangement of viewports] for the view panel. Fig. 13 shows the viewport arrangement when I chose **Arrangement >** **4 Views Top Split** from the **Panel** menu.

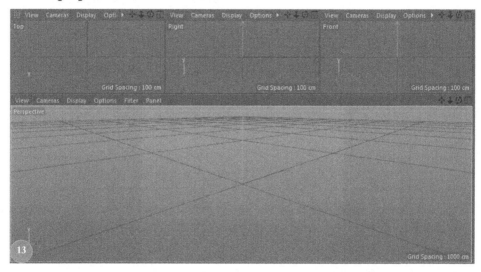

You can use the **Function** keys to toggle between the full-screen and normal size. You can also access the corresponding functions from the **Panel** menu. The following table summarizes these keys:

| Table 9: The **Function** keys | |
|---|---|
| **Key** | **Description** |
| View 1 (F1) | Maximizes the **Perspective** view. |
| View 2 (F2) | Maximizes the **Top** view. |
| View 3 (F3) | Maximizes the **Right** view. |
| View 4 (F4) | Maximizes the **Front** view. |
| View 5 (F5) | Restores four viewports. |

| Table 10: The **ProRender** menu | | |
|---|---|---|
| **Option** | **Icon** | **Description** |
| Use as ProRender View | | Use this option to set the current view as the preview view. You can select ProRender options only if you have set **Renderer** to **ProRender** in the **Render Settings** window. Any view can be defined as an interactive preview renderer. You can also navigate in the view and reduce resolutions to achieve faster results interactively. The changes that you make to materials or cameras will be immediately visible in the ProRender view.

When you select the **Use as ProRender View** option, a small HUD will be displayed at the bottom of the ProRender view to start/stop the rendering or select the render settings. |
| Start ProRender | | Use this option to start rendering in the preview view. The speed of the rendering depends on the complexity of the scene. Select this option again to switch back to the normal OpenGL view. |
| Use Offline Settings | | These two options are used to select the settings to be used for the ProRender view to be rendered. |
| Use Preview Settings | | |
| Camera Updates | | These update options are used to define if the preview render should be updated if one the elements such as camera, light, material, or geometry is modified. |
| Material Updates | | Normally, all elements are updated by default. Due to technical reasons, the rendering can occasionally be restarted without ending while you are working on **MoGraph**, **Hair**, or **XPresso**. If you disable **Geometry Updates**, that will help you in preventing constant updating. |
| Light Updates | | |
| Geometry Updates | | |
| Synchronize Viewport | | This option is useful when you are working in two views. For example, one ProRender view and one OpenGL view. In such cases, if you move the camera in the OpenGL view, the camera movement will be carried over to the ProRender view. |

**Note: Highlight feature**

*The highlight feature helps you in discovering new features in Cinema 4D. The menu items, icons, and parameters in **Attribute Manager** will be color coded for easy recognition [see Fig. 14]. When you first time call a new feature, its color will be slightly dimmed but if you call a feature **5** times, the color will change to the normal interface color.*

*If you don't want this color transition, press **Ctrl+E** to open the **Preferences** window and then select **Interface** from the left pane. Now, expand the **Highlight Features** option from the right pane and then clear the **Fading** check box. You can click on the **Reset Highlights** button to reset the highlights. As a result, all highlighted features will remain so until they have been used **5** times once again.*

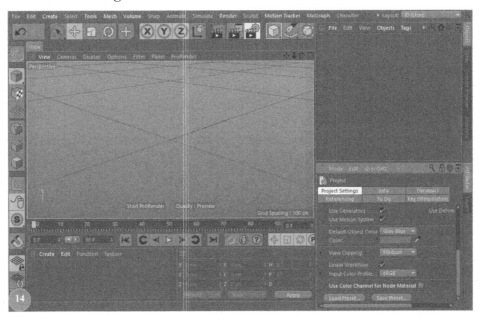

## HUD

The term HUD is taken from the aviation industry. In aircraft, HUD refers to the projection of reading on a screen so that the pilot can read the values without looking down. HUD in Cinema 4D does the same function. The HUD can be switched on and off from the **Filter** tab of the **Viewport** settings. To access this tab, choose **Configure** from the **MEV's Options** menu. Now, in **Attribute Manager**, choose the **Filter** tab.

From this tab, you can toggle HUD using the **HUD** check box. Now, choose the **HUD** tab and select the checkboxes as per the requirement. For example, if you want to see HUD for the number of polygons in the scene, select the **Total Polygons** check box. If you want to see number of the selected polygons as well, select the **Selected Polygons** check box, refer to Fig. 15.

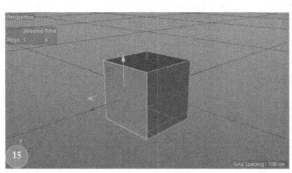

You can also add objects parameters to the HUD. To do so, select the parameter(s) in **Attribute Manager** and then RMB. Choose **Add to HUD** from the popup menu to add selected parameters to the HUD. You can also drag and drop parameters from **Attribute Manager** to editor view. Now, you can click drag a parameter to adjust its value.

You can use the following keys with HUD:

- Use **Shift** to select multiple HUD elements.
- Use **Ctrl** to move HUD elements.
- Double-click on a HUD element to open a text field that allows you to enter a new value for the element.

## Managers and Browsers
There are variety of managers, explorers, and browsers that Cinema 4D offers. Given below is a quick rundown:

### Object Manager
**Object Manager** is the nerve center for all objects and their corresponding tags in a scene. This manager allows you to manage object's name, hierarchy, visibility, and so on. It also allows you to manage tags that have been assigned to the objects. Some of the functions of **Object Manager** are given next:

- To select an object, click on it. To select multiple objects, click with **Ctrl** held down. You can use **Shift** to select an entire range of objects. You can also select multiple objects by holding down **Shift** and using the **Up** and **Down** arrow keys. The objects can also be selected by drawing a marquee selection. When you select an object, its settings are displayed in **Attribute Manger**. When you select multiple objects, common settings are displayed in **Attribute Manager**.
- **MMB** click on an object to select the object including all its children.
- **Alt+MMB** click selects the object you click and all objects on the same hierarchy level except children.
- The selected items are color highlighted. The last selected object highlighted in slightly lighter color. Child objects of the selected objects are also highlighted in a lighter color.

- To open and close branches in **Object Manager,** click + or - sign. If you want to open or close the entire hierarchy, click + or - sign with **Ctrl** held down.
- Press the left or right arrow key to close or open the active branches.
- To make copies of an object, drag it with **Ctrl** held down.
- You can rearrange items in the manager by dragging and dropping.
- To rename items, double-click on their names. You can also select an item and press **Enter** to enable a rename field in which you can type the new name. When rename field appears, you can use the up and down arrow keys to quickly rename the items.

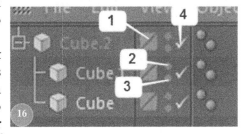

- The second column in **Object Manager** [see Fig. 16] contains some switches labeled from 1 to 4 in Fig. 16 [sometimes also referred to as **Traffic Lights**]. The **Layer color** switch, labeled as 1, displays color of the layer. Click on this switch to open a popup menu. You can add the object to a layer or open **Layer Manager** to have a greater control on layers and objects they host.
- The switch labeled as 2, is the **Editor On/Off** switch. It allows you to control the visibility of the object in the editor view. By default, the color of this switch is gray, which is the default behavior. Click on it to override the default behavior and turn the visibility of the object on. The color of the switch turns green. Click one more time to hide the object from the editor view. On doing so, the color of the switch turns red. The green dot enforces the visibility of an object. If you have grouped several objects [Hotkey: **Alt+G**] and now you turn off the visibility of the group using red dots, you can still make the objects visible from the group by using the green dots.
- The switch labeled as 3 allows you to visibility of the objects in renders.
- The switch labeled as 4 affects the object in the editor view as well as in the renderer. It is essentially a way to turn off an object completely.
- The right side of the switches column is the area where you will find the tags associated with the objects.

You can use the modifier keys for object insertion in Cinema 4D to better organize hierarchies. Using these keys, will save you lot of time. When an object is selected in **Object Manager** and you create a new object [such as generators], you can affect where that object will be placed in the hierarchy by holding down the modifiers keys. These keys will also work on multiple objects. The functions of the modifier keys is given next:

- **Alt:** It makes the new object parent of the selected object. Works on multiple objects as well [see Fig. 17].
- **Shift:** It makes new object child of the selected object. If multiple child and parent objects are selected, only a single object can be created [see Fig. 18].
- **Shift+Alt:** It makes the selected object a child object of the newly created object [see Fig. 19].

- **Ctrl+Alt:** It groups the objects like the **Group Objects** command but instead of a **Null** object an arbitrary object will be used as parent [see Fig. 20].
- **Ctrl:** It places the new object on the same hierarchical level as the selected object. The new object will be placed behind the selected object.
- **Ctrl+Shift:** It places the new object on the same hierarchical level as the selected object. The new object will be placed in front of the selected object.

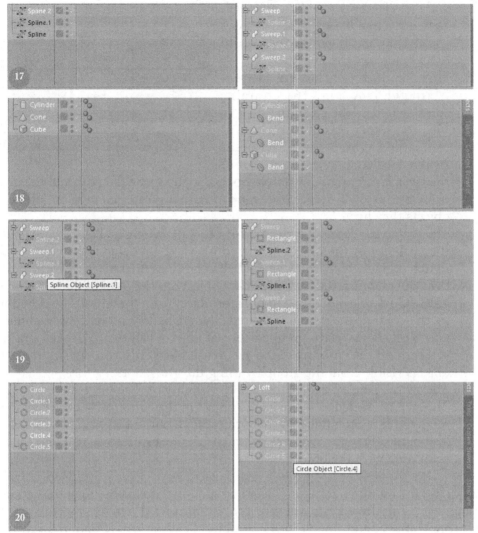

## Rearranging Objects

There are many ways for rearranging objects in **Object Manager**. When you drag the objects, different icons appear on the mouse pointer indicating what action Cinema 4D will take once you drop them.

The table given next summarizes these icons.

| Table 11: Rearranging objects | |
|---|---|
| **Icon** | **Description** |
| | Drag an object between two other objects or to the end of the list. |
| | **Ctrl+Drag** to create a copy. |
| | Makes the dragged object a child of the other. |
| | Use **Ctrl+drag** and move the mouse pointer over an object to create a copy and make it a child of another object. |
| | You can also drag-and-drop tags. To transfer a tag from one object to another, drag the tag icon on to the line of the other object. |
| | If you want to create a copy, use **Ctrl+Drag**. |
| | No operation is available. |

## Attribute Manager

**Attribute Manager** allows you to specify value for almost every parameter in Cinema 4D. You can access parameters for objects, tools, materials, and so on from this manager. You can also animate parameters using **Attribute Manager**. By default, it displays parameters of the selected object. If you are using an object frequently, you can create a copy of **Attribute Manager** and then lock it to that object. To create a new copy, click on the + icon [▦] located on the top-right corner of the title bar. To lock the manager, click the lock icon [🔒] on the manager's title bar.

## Coordinate Manager

**Coordinate Manager** allows you to manipulate objects numerically. It displays fields for editing position, scale, and rotation values. You can also use it as a reference when you are scaling objects interactively in the editor view. The values are displayed in conjunction with the tool you are using. For example, if you are using the **Move** tool; the position, size, and rotation values of the selected element are shown in the fields.

> *Note: Scaling objects*
> *Scale the objects only when there is no other way. For example, if you want to make a sphere bigger, use its **Radius** parameter instead of scaling it up. Also, see the **Object** mode description in Table 3.*

## Material Manager

**Material Manager** allows you to create materials and apply them onto the objects in the scene. The thumbnail of each material you create is displayed in the manager. When you select an object in **Object Manager**, the thumbnails of the materials applied to that object appear depressed. To apply a material to an object, drag the material's thumbnail from **Material Manager** and drop it on an object(s) in **Attribute Manager** or in the editor view.

## Take Manager

When you are working on a complex project that contains various animations, render settings, cameras, and so on, you will have to prepare and maintain several project files. Working on different files wastes a lot of time and effort. **Take Manager** [see Fig. 21] allows you to overcome this issue by saving multiple settings in one file and then that file can be rendered with powerful variable file and path names (**Tokens**). **Take Manager** lets you save the initial state as the master take and then you can create new animations to fine-tune and test the scene.

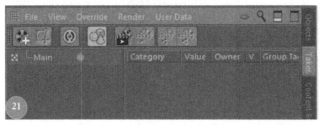

## Content Browser

**Content Browser** [see Fig. 22] allows you to navigate through the content libraries that come with Cinema 4D. You can easily import additional content and presets into your projects. You can use this manager to manage scenes, images, materials, shaders, and presets. This browser lets you manage file structure of the scene.

## Structure Manager

**Structure Manager** [see Fig. 23] shows the data related to an object if the selected object is editable. This manager shows data like a spreadsheet. It contains cells that are divided into rows and columns. The data shown in the cells depends on the mode you are in. The following data is shown in **Structure Manager**:

- Points
- Polygons
- UVW Coordinates
- Bezier Spline Tangents
- Weight Vertices
- Normal Vector Coordinates

The values shown in the cells can be directly edited. You can also drag and drop the lines. The editing functions such as cut, copy, and paste are also supported.

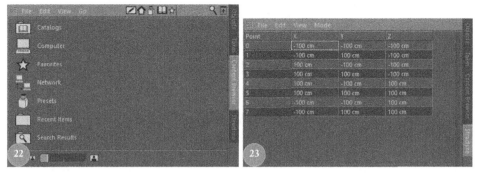

## Layer Manager

The **Layer Manager** [see Fig. 24] displays all layers that you have created. It is very useful when you are working on a complex scene. It lets you manage a complex scene easily. You can assign a custom color to the layer that also appears in **Object Manager**. You can drag and drop a layer onto an object to assign that object to the dragged layer. If you hold down the **Ctrl** key while dragging and dropping a layer onto an item, the layer is assigned to the item's children as well.

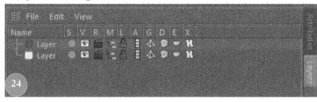

## Project Settings

You can use **Project Settings** [see Fig. 25] to define standard values such as animation time, scene scale, and so on for the current scene. These are the settings that affect the scene globally. You can open **Project Settings** by choosing **Project Settings** from the **Edit** menu. Alternatively, you can press **Ctrl+D**. You can also open it by choosing **Mode > Project** from the **Attribute Manager's** menu bar.

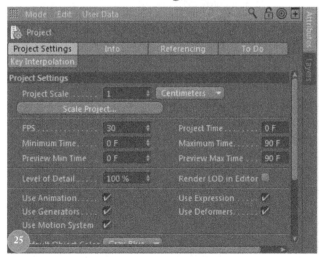

## Help

The Cinema 4D help documentation can be accessed by choosing **Help** from the **Help** menu. Like any other window in Cinema 4D, the help window can be docked anywhere in the interface. Cinema 4D also supports context sensitive help. If you want to access help for a button, tool, icon, and so forth, hover the mouse pointer on the element and then press **Ctrl+F1**. You can also RMB click on a parameter's label and then choose **Show Help** from the popup menu to see help documentation about that parameter.

If you hover the mouse pointer over almost any item in Cinema 4D, a brief description about the item appears in the bottom-most window of the interface.

## Commander

The **Commander** window in Cinema 4D is used to call up commands, objects, tools, and tags without using any manager. You can invoke the **Commander** window by clicking on the magnifying glass icon located next to the **Layout** drop-down list in the top-left corner of the interface. Alternatively, you can press **Shift+C** to open it. Type the name of the entity you are looking for; Cinema 4D will display a list of matching commands [see Fig. 26]. Select the desired option from the list. You can press **Esc** to close the **Commander** window.

## Hidden Menus

There are several hidden menus available in Cinema 4D. These menus quickly allow you to select tools, command, and functions. The **V** menu [see Fig. 27] provides a useful shortcut to quickly switch between the view, selection, tools/modes, plugins, and snapping options.

The **M** menu [see Fig. 28] lets you quickly access the modeling tools. For example, if you want to invoke the **Extrude** tool, press **M+T**. The **N** menu [see Fig. 29] clones the options from the **Display** menu of the editor's menubar. The **P** menu allows you to access snapping functions and commands [see Fig. 30].

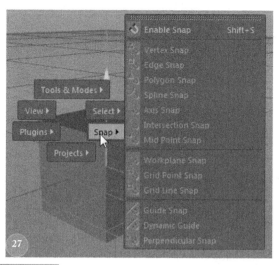

27

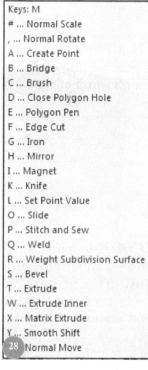

Keys: M
# ... Normal Scale
, ... Normal Rotate
A ... Create Point
B ... Bridge
C ... Brush
D ... Close Polygon Hole
E ... Polygon Pen
F ... Edge Cut
G ... Iron
H ... Mirror
I ... Magnet
K ... Knife
L ... Set Point Value
O ... Slide
P ... Stitch and Sew
Q ... Weld
R ... Weight Subdivision Surface
S ... Bevel
T ... Extrude
W ... Extrude Inner
X ... Matrix Extrude
Y ... Smooth Shift
28 Normal Move

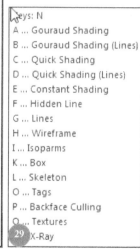

Keys: N
A ... Gouraud Shading
B ... Gouraud Shading (Lines)
C ... Quick Shading
D ... Quick Shading (Lines)
E ... Constant Shading
F ... Hidden Line
G ... Lines
H ... Wireframe
I ... Isoparms
K ... Box
L ... Skeleton
O ... Tags
P ... Backface Culling
Q ... Textures
29 X-Ray

30

## Exercise 1: Creating a Sofa

In this exercise, we will model a sofa using the **Cube** primitive [see Fig. E1]. Table E1 summarizes the exercise.

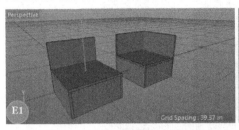 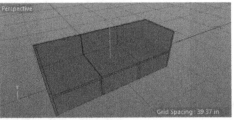

| Table E1 | |
|---|---|
| Skill level | Beginner |
| Time to complete | 30 Minutes |
| Topics | • Getting Your Feet Wet<br>• Creating One Seat Section of the Sofa<br>• Creating Corner Section of the Sofa |
| Resources folder | **unit-cm1** |
| Units | **Inches** |
| Final file | **sofa-finish.c4d** |

### Getting Your Feet Wet

Follow these steps:

1. Choose **File > New** from the main menubar or press **Ctrl+N** to start a new scene. Choose **Object > Cube** from the **Create** menu to create a cube at the center of the **Perspective** view. Ensure any selection tool is active in the **Standard** palette and then click and drag the green handle [along +Y-axis]; notice that the new **Y** position value is displayed in **Coordinate Manager** and **Status Bar** at the bottom of the UI [see Fig. E2].

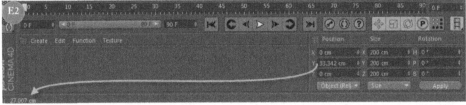

2. In the **Coordinate Manager > Position [Y]** field, enter **0** to place the cube back at the origin.

3. Choose **World** from the drop-down list located below the **Position** fields in the **Coordinate Manager** and then enter **100** in the **Position [Y]** field. The cube now sits at a distance of **100** units from the origin.

4.  In **Object Manager,** double-click on the text **Cube** to enable the edit field and then rename it as **myCube.** Notice the name is displayed in **Attribute Manager** as well.

5.  In **Attribute Manager,** ensure **Coord** tab is selected [see Fig. E3] and then in **Freeze Transformation** area, click **Freeze P.**

    *What just happened?*
*Freezing transformations in Cinema 4D freezes [zero out, also referred to as dual transformation] the coordinates of all selected objects. When you freeze coordinates, the local position and rotation coordinates will each be set to 0 and scale to 1 without changing position or orientation of the object.*

*Freezing transformations is particularly useful in animations using parent-child relationships. When you rotate a child object around an axis, all three axes are affected because the parent object's coordinate system has a different orientation from the local coordinates. You can avoid this scenario by freezing the coordinates before animating.*

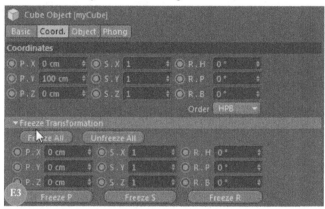

   *Tip: Parameter groups/tabs*
*The parameters of an object are categorized in different groups or tabs in* ***Attribute Manager.*** *Notice in Fig. E3 there are four groups or tabs:* ***Basic,*** ***Coord, Object,*** *and* ***Phong.*** *The selected group button appears in the light blue color [****Coord*** *in this case]. If you want to display parameters from different groups in* ***Attribute Manager.*** *Click on the parameter buttons with* ***Shift*** *or* ***Ctrl*** *held down. You can also click-drag on the buttons to display parameters from different groups/tabs.*

6.  Choose **Object (Rel)** from the first drop-down list in **Coordinate Manager** and then enter **50** in the **Position [Y]** field. Notice now the cube moves **50** units up from its current position.

**What just happened?**

*Object (Rel) defines the relative object location without frozen coordinates. This is same as the main coordinates in the **Coord** tab of the **Attribute Manager**. **Object (Abs)** defines the relative object location as a combination of frozen coordinates and **Object (Rel)** coordinates. **World** defines the object location in world units.*

7. In **Object Manager**, drag **myCube** with **Ctrl** held down to create a copy of the cube with the name **myCube.1**. In the editor view, drag the green handle in the positive Y-axis to display both cubes [see Fig. E4].

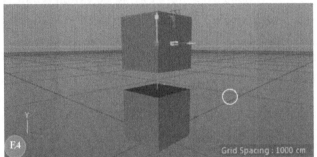

8. In **Object Manager**, drag **myCube.1** onto the **myCube** and release the mouse button when an icon similar to the one shown in Fig. E5 to make **myCube.1** child of **myCube** [see Fig. E6].

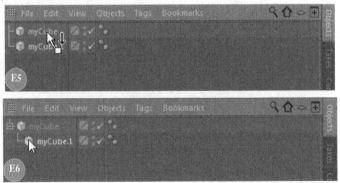

9. Select **myCube** in **Object Manager**. Choose **Size+** from the middle drop-down list in **Coordinate Manager**. Notice that the size of the parent+child is displayed in the **Scale** fields.

**What just happened?**

*The middle drop-down list in **Coordinate Manager** specifies which object size is shown in the **Scale [XYZ]** fields. **Size** shows the size of the object without considering children [see Fig. E7] whereas **Size+** considers the children as well [see Fig. E8]. Scale shows the axis length of the object coordinate system. Default value is 1:1:1 [see Fig. E9].*

 *Note: Scale and parent-child relationship*
*When you create a child–parent relationship, the scale of the child axis is adjusted according to the parent so that the child appears normal with respect to world axes. For example, if scale of the parent object is **4:1:1**, when you create a child for this object, the scale of the child axes will be **0.25:1:1**.*

10. Choose **Close** from the **File** menu or press **Ctrl+F4** to close the scene. Do not save the file.

*What next?*
*Now, we understood Cinema 4D's coordinate system therefore now let's move ahead and build the sofa. Before we jump into modeling, let's first set the units for the project.*

## Specifying Units

You can define units for the project from two locations in Cinema 4D: **Preferences** window and **Project Settings**. Choose **Preferences** from the **Edit** menu or press **Ctrl+E**. Choose **Units** from the list of categories and then choose **Inches** from the **Unit Display** drop-down list of the **Units > Basic** area. Close the **Preferences** window.

*What just happened?*
*Here, I chose **Inches** as units for this project. This setting does not affect the scene parameters [scale]. It just converts the values in the fields. For example, if you have defined a value of **20 cm** and you switch units to **Meters**, the filed will display the value **0.2m**. However, if you want to change the scale of the scene, you can do so from the **Project Settings** by adjusting the **Project Scale** parameter. If you change units to meters, a **20cm** wide object will be scaled to **20m** wide object.*

*Tip: Project settings*
*You can open **Project Settings** in **Attribute Manager** by choosing **Project Settings** from the **Edit** menu, or by pressing **Ctrl+D**. To change scale of the scene, click **Scale Project** from **Attribute Manager** to open the **Scale Project** dialog box. In this dialog box, set the **Target Scale** and then click **OK** to change the scale. This feature is specifically useful when you are importing an object created in an external application and does not have a correct scale.*

Press **Ctrl+S**, the **Save File** dialog box appears. Save the file.

*Note: Saving files*
*I highly recommend that you save your work at regular intervals by pressing* **Ctrl+S**.

## Creating One Seat Section of the Sofa
Follow these steps:

1. In the **Standard** palette, click **Cube** 🔲 to create a cube in the editor view. In the **Attribute Manager > Object** tab, enter **25.591, 1,** and **25.591** in the **Size X, Size Y,** and **Size Z** fields, respectively.

2. Press **Alt+O** to frame the cube in all views. Press **NB** to enable **Gouraud Shading (Lines)** display mode [see Fig. E10]. Create another cube and then set cube's **Size X, Size Y,** and **Size Z** fields to **25.591, 11.417,** and **1**, respectively.

3. Press **Ctrl+A** to select both the cubes. Choose **Arrange Objects > Center** from the **Tools** menu. In the **Attribute Manager > Options** tab, choose **Negative** from the **Z Axis** drop-down list. Click **Apply** in the **Tool** tab to align objects [see Fig. E11].

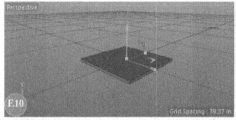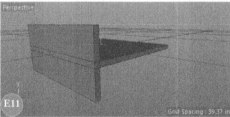

4. In the **Tool** tab, click **New Transform** and then in the **Options** tab, choose **----, Positive,** and **----** from the **X Axis, Y Axis,** and **Z Axis** drop-down lists, respectively to align the two objects [see Fig. E12].

5. Select **Cube.1** from **Object Manager** or in the editor view and then align it with the bottom face of the cube using the **Move** tool [see Fig. E13]. You can switch to the **Right** viewport to align the cubes accurately.

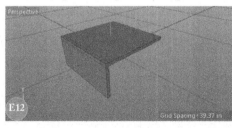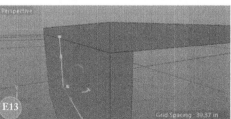

6. Make sure **Cube.1** is selected and then choose **Arrange Objects > Duplicate** from the **Tools** menu. In the **Attribute Manager > Duplicate** tab, enter **1** [i.e. type **1** and then press **Enter**] in the **Copies** field to create one duplicate of the cube.

7.  Select **Linear** from the **Mode** drop-down list in the **Options** tab. In the **Position** area, clear the X and Y checkboxes. Enter **24.591** in the **Move [Z]** field to move the duplicate on the other side [see Fig. E14].

 **What next?**
Next, we need to create the back support for the seat.

8.  Create another cube in the editor view and then set its **Size X, Size Y**, and **Size Z** fields to **1, 25.591**, and **25.591**, respectively. Align the cube to the back of the seat using the process described above [see Fig. E15]. Similarly, create a cube for the font section and align it [see Fig. E16].

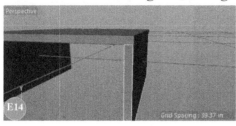

9.  Press **Ctrl+A** to select all objects and then choose **Objects > Group Objects** from the **Object Manager's** menu. You can also press **Alt+G** to group the objects. In **Object Manager**, double-click on **Null** and rename it as **oneSeat**.

 **What just happened?**
Here, I've grouped objects [all cubes] in **Object Manager**. A **Null** object is created and selected objects are placed inside **Null**. Groups help you in better organizing your scene and keep **Object Manager** neat and tidy. When you group objects with children, child objects are also placed inside **Null** and object hierarchies are maintained. You can expand a group using the **Shift+G** hotkeys. The objects that are one level below the parent are moved to the same level as the parent and the existing hierarchies are preserved.

## Creating Corner Section of the Sofa
Follow these steps:

1.  Make sure **oneSeat** is selected and then create a copy of **oneSeat** in **Object Manager** or editor view [see Fig. E17].

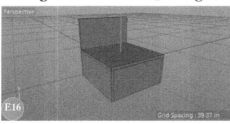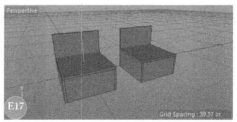

2. Rename the new group **Null** as **cornerSeat** in **Object Manager**. In **Object Manager**, select **cornerSeat > Cube.1_copies > Cube.1.0**. In the **Attribute Manager > Object** tab of **Cube.1.0**, set **Size X** and **Size Y** to **27.591** and **25.591**, respectively. Now, align the cube [see Fig. E18]. Similarly, create **cornerSeat** for the other end [see Fig. E19].

## Exercise 2: Creating a Coffee Table

In this exercise, we will model a coffee table using the **Cylinder** and **Torus** primitives [see Fig. E1].

The following table summarizes the exercise:

| Table E2 | |
| --- | --- |
| Skill level | Beginner |
| Time to complete | 30 Minutes |
| Topics | • Getting Started<br>• Creating the Coffee Table |
| Resources folder | **unit-cm1** |
| Units | **Inches** |
| Final file | **coffee-table-finish.c4d** |

### Getting Started
Start a new scene in Cinema 4D and set units to **Inches**.

### Creating the Coffee Table
Follow these steps:

1. Press and hold the LMB on **Cube** 🔲 in the **Standard** palette and then click **Cylinder** 🔲 . Press **NB** to enable **Gouraud Shading (Lines)** display mode. In the **Attribute Manager > Cylinder > Object** tab, set **Radius, Height,** and **Rotation Segments** to **37.5, 2,** and **60**, respectively. Press **Alt+O** to frame the object.

2. Press and hold the LMB on **Cube** in the **Standard** palette and then click **Torus** . In the **Attribute Manager > Torus > Object** tab, set **Ring Radius, Ring Segments, Pipe Radius** to **37.5, 60,** and **1.521,** respectively. Align the two objects [see Fig. E2]. Select both objects and then press **Alt+G** to group the two objects and rename the group's **Null** to **tableTop.**

*What next?*
*Now, we will create a clone of **tableTop** to create the bottom part of the table.*

3. Invoke the **Move** tool and ensure that **tableTop** is selected. Choose **Enable Quantizing** from the **Snap** menu or press **Shift+Q.** Drag the green Y-axis handle about **30** units in positive Y direction with **Ctrl** held down [see Fig. E3]. To enter accurate value, enter **30** in the **Position [Y]** field of **Coordinate Manager.** In **Object Manager,** rename the group as **tableBottom.** Press **Shift+Q** to disable the quantizing function.

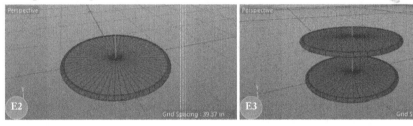

*What just happened?*
*Here, I have used the quantizing function. This function restricts stepless movement to a defined grid. For example, instead of a stepless rotation, you can allow rotation on **45** degrees increment. This function is primarily intended to use with the **Move** , **Scale** , and **Rotate** tools. However, you can use it with other tools such as **Polygon Pen** .*

*You can specify settings for the quantizing function from the modeling settings. In **Attribute Manager,** choose **Modeling** from the **Mode** menu and then choose the **Quantize** tab. Select the **Enable Quantizing** check box and specify the quantizing settings using the **Movement, Scaling, Rotation,** and **Texture** parameters.*

4. Press and hold the LMB on **Cube** in the **Standard** palette and then click **Cylinder** . Rename the cylinder as **leg.** In the **Attribute Manager > leg > Object** tab, set **Radius,** and **Height** to **2** and **50,** respectively. In **Coordinate Manager,** set **Position [Y]** and **Position [Z]** fields to **10,** and **40,** respectively to align leg with **tableBottom** and **tableTop** [see Fig. E4].

*What next?*
*Now, its time to create two more copies of the leg.*

5.  Ensure leg is selected in **Object Manager** and then **Alt** click on **Array** in the **Standard** palette to add an **Array**  object. By default, the **Array** object creates 7 copies [see Fig. E5]. Also, notice that the **Array** object has used center of leg as a pivot to arrange the copies. Next, we will fix it.

> *What just happened?*
> *If you press **Alt** while selecting an object from the **Standard** palette, the selected object will become child of the new object. Otherwise, both objects will be at the same level in **Object Manager**.*

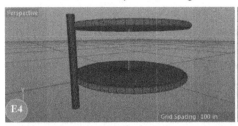
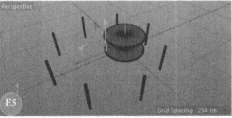

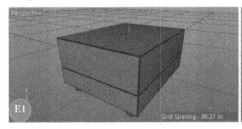

6.  In the **Attribute Manager** > **Array** > **Coord** tab, set **P.Z** to **0**. In the **Attribute Manager** > **Array** > **Object** tab, set **Copies** and **Radius** to **2** and **40.5**, respectively.

## Exercise 3: Creating a Foot Stool

In this exercise, we will model a foot stool using the **Cube** and **Cylinder** primitives [see Fig. E1].

The following table summarizes the exercise:

| Table E3 | |
| --- | --- |
| Skill level | Beginner |
| Time to complete | 30 Minutes |
| Topics | • Getting Started<br>• Creating the Foot Stool |
| Resources folder | **unit-cm1** |
| Units | **Inches** |
| Final file | **foot-stool-finish.c4d** |

## Getting Started

Start a new scene in Cinema 4D and set units to **Inches**.

Follow these steps:

1. Press **NB** to enable the **Gouraud Shading (Lines)** mode. Click **Cube** on the **Object** command group to add a cube to the editor view. Rename **Cube** as **baseGeo**. In the **Attribute Manager** > **baseGeo** > **Object** tab, set **Size X, Size Y**, and **Size Z** to **31.5, 5**, and **24.8**, respectively. Select the **Fillet** check box and set **Fillet Radius** and **Fillet Subdivision** to **0.2** and **3**, respectively [see Fig. E2].

2. Create another copy of the **baseGeo** by **Ctrl** dragging. Rename it as **topGeo** and place it on top of **baseGeo** [see Fig. E3]. Select **topGeo** and then in the **Attribute Manager** > **topGeo** > **Object** tab, set **Size Y** to **8**. Align the two objects [see Fig. E4].

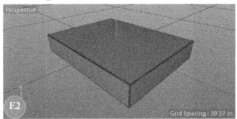
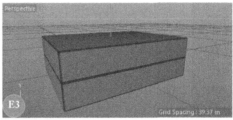

*What next?*
*Now, we will create legs for the foot stool.*

3. Click **Cylinder** in the **Object** command group to add a cylinder in the editor view. Rename it as **legGeo**. In the **Attribute Manager** > **legGeo** > **Object** tab, set **Radius** and **Height** to **1.5** and **4**, respectively. In the **Attribute Manager** > **legGeo** > **Caps** tab, select the **Fillet** check box and then set **Segments** and **Radius** to **3** and **0.5**, respectively. Align, **legGeo** with **baseGeo** [see Fig. E5]. Create three more copies of **legGeo** and align them.

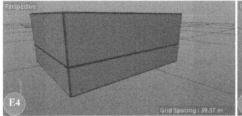
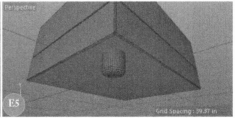

*What next?*
*Let's now arrange objects in layers.*

4. Click **Layer** switch on the right of the **topGeo** and choose **Add to New Layer** [see Fig. E6] from the popup menu; a new layer is created with the name **Layer** and **topGeo** is added to it. Also, Cinema 4D assigns a color to the layer.

5. Press **Shift+F4** to open the **Layer Manager**. In **Layer Manager**, double-click on **Layer** and rename it as **mainGeoLayer**. Drag **baseGeo** from **Object Manager** to the **mainGeoLayer** layer on **Layer Manager**. The **baseGeo** is now part of the layer **mainGeoLayer**.

6. Choose **File > New Layer** from the **Layer Manager's** menubar and rename the new layer as **legGeoLayer** [see Fig. E7]. Drag **legGeoLayer** from **Layer Manager** to the **legGeo** in the editor view to make **legGeo** part of the layer. Notice that the color of layers is now reflected [make sure you have selected **Options > Layer Color** from the MEV menubar] in the editor view which helps in identifying which object is part which layer. Now, drag **legGeoLayer** on **legGeo.1**, **legGeo.2**, and **legGeo.3**. Double-click on the color swatches in the **Layer Manager** to change the color of the layers.

In **Layer Manager**, there are many toggle switches on right of the layer name. The following table summarizes these switches:

| Table E3.1 | |
|---|---|
| Icon | Description |
| S | Solo objects |
| V | Visible in editor |
| R | Visible in render |
| M | Show in managers |
| L | Lock layer |
| A | Animation on/off |
| G | Generators on/off |
| D | Deformers on/off |
| E | Switches XPresso, C.O.F.F.E.E. tags, etc. on or off. |
| X | Update/load XRefs |

## Exercise 4: Creating a Bar Table

In this exercise, we will model a bar table using the **Cube** and **Cylinder** primitives [See Fig. E1].

The following table summarizes the exercise:

| Table E4 | |
|---|---|
| Skill level | Beginner |
| Time to complete | 35 Minutes |
| Topics | • Getting Started<br>• Creating the Bar Table |
| Resources folder | **unit-cm1** |
| Units | **Inches** |
| Final file | **bar-table-finish.c4d** |

## Getting Started

Start a new scene in Cinema 4D and set units to **Inches**.

## Creating the Bar Table

Follow these steps:

1. Press **NB** to enable the **Gouraud Shading (Lines)** mode. Click **Cylinder** ⬚ in the **Object** command group to add a cylinder in the editor view. Rename it as **topGeo**. In the **Attribute Manager > topGeo > Object** tab, set **Radius**, **Height**, and **Rotation Segments** to **13.78**, **1.5**, and **50**, respectively. In the **Attribute Manager > topGeo > Caps** tab, select the **Fillet** check box and then set **Segment** and **Radius** to **5** and **0.15**, respectively.

2. Create another cylinder for the central part and rename it as **centerGeo**. In the **Attribute Manager > centerGeo > Object** tab, set **Radius**, **Height**, and **Rotation Segments** to **1.3**, **38**, and **18**, respectively. Align the two cylinders [see Fig. E2].

3. Click **Tube** in the **Object** command group to add a tube in the editor view. Rename the tube as **tubeGeo**. In the **Attribute Manager > tubeGeo > Object** tab, set **Inner Radius**, **Outer Radius**, **Rotation Segments**, and **Height** to **1.3**, **4**, **50**, and **2**, respectively. Align the **tubeGeo** at the bottom of the **centerGeo** [see Fig. E3].

*What next?*
*Now, we are going to create support for the table.*

4. Create a cube in the viewport and then rename it as **supportGeo**. In the **Attribute Manager > supportGeo > Object** tab, set **Size X, Size Y, Size Z** to 1.6, 12.8, and **2.1**, respectively. Also, select the **Fillet** check box and then set **Fillet Radius** and **Fillet Subdivisions** to **0.1** and **3**, respectively. Now, align **supportGeo** with **tubeGeo** [refer to Fig. E4]

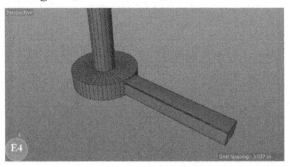

5. Ensure **supportGeo** is selected in **Object Manager** and then in the **Standard** palette > **Deformer** command group, press and hold **LMB** on **Bend** 🢂. Click **Taper** 🞄 with the **Shift** held down.

> ❓ *What just happened?*
> *Here, I have applied the **Taper** deformer to **supportGeo**. Holding down **Shift** ensures that the **Taper** object will be child of **supportGeo**. Otherwise, it will be added to the same level as **suppportGeo**. Deformer objects modify the geometry of the other objects. You can use deformer objects with primitive objects, generators, polygon splines, and splines.*
>
> *Keep the following in mind while working with deformers:*
>
> - *The deformer object only affects its parent.*
> - *You can apply a number of deformer objects to an object.*
> - *The order of the deformers is also important.*
> - *Deformer objects are evaluated from top to bottom.*
> - *Deformer objects have its origin and orientation.*
> - *All deformers are activated automatically when you create them. A deformer object has no effect if it is deactivated.*

6. In the **Attribute Manager > Taper > Object** tab, click **Fit To Parent**. Set **Strength** to **40** and select the **Fillet** check box [see Fig. E5]

> 💡 *Tip: Taper strength*
> *You can interactively change the strength in the viewport by dragging the orange line [refer to Fig. E6].*

> ⊖ *What next?*
> *Now, we will work on the roller.*

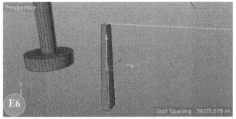

7. Create a cube and then set its **Size X, Size Y, Size Z** to **0.3**, **0.926**, and **0.6**, respectively. Set **Segment Y** to **15**. Apply a **Bend**  deformer to the cube using the **Shift** key.

8. In the **Attribute Manager > Bend > Object** tab, click **Fit to Parent** and then set **Strength** to **180**. Now, align the cube [see Fig. E7]. Now, create a cylinder and align it [see Fig. E8]. Group the cube and cylinder that you just created with the name **rollerGrp**. Group **rollerGrp** and **supportGeo** with the name **baseGrp**.

9. Switch to the **Top** view and ensure the **baseGrp** is selected. Press **L** to invoke the **Enable Axis** mode and then move the axis at the center of the **topGeo** using the **Move** tool [see Fig. E9]. Press **L** again to disable the **Enable Axis** mode. Enable snapping for easily aligning axis.

> **(?)** *What just happened?*
> *Here, I've moved the origin of the group to the center of the model so that when I create copies of the **baseGrp**, they are rotated correctly around the new axis center. You can quickly enable/disable the **Enable Axis** mode using the **L** key. Keep the following in mind:*
>
> - *When you rotate or move axes of a hierarchical object, all axes of the child objects will also get affected.*
> - *Before animating objects, ensure that you define the axis because if you rotate the parent, error will occur in the animation tracks of the child. The error occurs because of the change in the axes of the parent object.*
> - *You cannot move axis while working with primitive objects. You need to make the object editable [first selecting it and then pressing **C**]. The workaround for primitive is that you make it child of a **Null** object and then move axis. The quickest way to enclose an object inside a **Null** is that, select the object and then press **Alt+G**.*
> - *Do not make multiple selections in **Object Manager** when you are temporarily making axis changes.*

10. Now, using the **Array** object ![array icon] from the **Modeling** command group to create four more copies of the **baseGrp** [see Fig. E10].

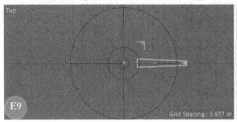

# Quiz

Evaluate your skills to see how many questions you can answer correctly.

**Multiple Choice**
Answer the following questions:

1.  Which of the following keys is used to invoke the **Live Selection** tool?

    [A] 8                              [B] 9
    [C] 6                              [D] 1

2.  Which of the following mouse-drag operations is used to interactively change the size of the **Live Selection** tool's brush size?

    [A] LMB                            [B] MMB
    [C] RMB                            [D] Ctrl+RMB

3.  Which of the following key combinations is used to render the current active view?

    [A] Ctrl+R                         [B] Alt+Shift+R
    [C] Shift+R                        [D] None of these

4.  Which of the following key combinations is used to render the active view in the **Picture Viewer** window?

    [A] Ctrl+R                         [B] Ctrl+Alt+R
    [C] Shift+R                        [D] Alt+R

5.  Which of the following key combinations is used to invoke the **Render Settings** window?

    [A] Ctrl+A                         [B] Ctrl+B
    [C] Shift+A                        [D] Alt+B

## Fill in the Blanks

Fill in the blanks in each of the following statements:

1. The **X-Axis / Heading, Y-Axis / Pitch**, and **Z-Axis / Bank** tools are used to _____ or _____ the transformations along the X, Y, and Z axes, respectively.

2. The _____ key is used to make an object editable.

3. The _____ key combination is used to enable snapping.

4. The _____ key combination is used to display the project settings.

5. You can also maximize a viewport by _____ clicking on it.

6. The _____ key combination is used to invoke the **Commander** window.

7. The _____ key combination is used to invoke **Layer Manager**.

8. You can expand a group using the _____ hotkeys.

## True or False

State whether each of the following is true or false:

1. When you resize a docked window, the surrounding windows are resized automatically.

2. You can select multiple views by clicking on the blank gray area of their headers with **Shift** held down.

3. The **Configure** option in the **MEV > Options** menu is used to specify the viewport settings.

4. The **Alt+G** key combination is used to group objects.

5. If you hold down the **Shift** key while dragging and dropping a layer onto an item in **Layer Manager**, the layer is assigned to the items children as well.

## Summary

This unit covered the following topics:

- Navigating the workspace
- Customizing the interface
- Understanding UI components
- Setting preferences
- Understanding layouts
- Moving, rotating, and scaling objects
- Managers, and Browsers
- Getting help

- Creating guides in the editor view
- Interactively placing lights and adjusting their attributes in the scene
- Measuring angles and distances
- Working with Workplanes
- Arranging, duplicating, and randomizing objects
- Correcting lens distortions
- Creating virtual walkthroughs

# Unit CM2: Tools of the Trade

In the last unit, we learned how to create and place objects in the scene view. In this unit, I will describe how we can place and arrange these objects accurately using arrange tools, guides, and **Workplanes**. You will learn to add annotations to the objects in the editor view so that you can mark objects in a complex scene for easy identification. Moreover, you will learn to create the virtual walkthrough. Cinema 4D offers many tools that let you accomplish complex challenges with ease. These tools are available in the **Tools** menu of the menubar. This unit deals with these tools.

## Guide Tool

 **Guide Tool** allows you to interactively create guidelines in the viewports. You can use handles of these guidelines to snap other entities such as vertices to them. You can create guidelines in one of the following ways:

Click on a viewport to create a handle, click again to create the second handle, and then press **Esc** to create a guide [see Fig. 1]; a red line appears. Now, you can click-drag the red line to create a guide surface perpendicular the view [see Fig. 2].

Click on a viewport to create a handle, click again to create the second handle. Don't release the mouse button and drag the mouse pointer and then click to create the guide surface.

To create a segmented guideline, click on a viewport to create a handle, click again to create the second handle. Now, a clicking within these handles creates a segmented guide [see Fig. 3]. To create a duplicate guide, click-drag one of the handles of the guide with **Ctrl** held down [see Fig. 4].

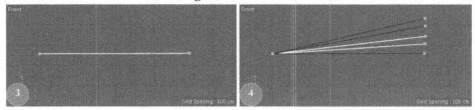

Tip: *The Delete Enabled Guides tool*
The **Delete Enabled Guides** *tool deletes all guidelines which are active in* **Object Manager**. *The active guidelines have green tick mark next to them [see Fig. 5]. No prior selection is required to delete the active guidelines.*

Tip: *Guides and Snaps*
*The guides work in combination with all* **Snap** *options.*

## Lighting Tool

This tool allows you to interactively create, select, and place a light object in the viewports. Also, it allows you to adjust the brightness of the lights without using **Attribute Manager**. The process is given next:

Invoke **Lighting Tool** from the **Tools** menu. Click on the empty area of the editor view to create a light source. Each click in the empty area of the editor will create a new light. Each new light will inherit the properties of the previously created light.

If lights already exist in the scene, most relevant light for a surface will automatically be marked when you place the mouse pointer on a surface.

While manipulating the light, you can:

- Press **Shift** to move the light source in the direction of the current normals. You can control the distance between the light and surface using **Shift**.
- Press **Ctrl** to adjust the brightness of the light source.
- Press **Ctrl+Shift** to adjust the cone of the spot light.
- During manipulating light, press **Alt** to temporarily switch to the **Target** mode to adjust the target of the spot lights. For example, if you are using **Shift** to move the light along the direction of the current normals, you can press **Alt** while moving to temporarily switch to the **Target** mode and adjust the target of the light.

*Caution: Lighting Tool*
*The functionality of this tool is limited with the generators such as **Arrays** and **Cloners** unless you make the objects editable. When deformer objects are used, it might be cumbersome to locate the surface. In such cases, hide the **Deformer** object in the view.*

## Naming Tool

T  This tool allows you to efficiently rename object hierarchies in your scene. Although, this tool is specifically built for naming character rigs. However, you can use it to rename tag, material, layer, and take names. You can also use this tool to save already corrected named hierarchies as a preset and then use the preset to rename other hierarchies.

To understand working of this tool, create a series of five joints in the scene using **Joint Tool** and then rename them as **Hip, Knee, Foot, Ball,** and **Toe** [see Fig. 6]. Now, select **Hip** from **Object Manager** and then choose **Naming Tool** from the **Tools** menu. In **Attribute Manager**, click **Add** from the **Options** group. The **Name** dialog box appears. In this dialog box, type name as **leg** and click **OK**. Now, select **leg** from the **Type** drop-down list. Enter **L_** in the **Prefix** field and **_$N** in the **Suffix** field. Now, click **Apply Name** to rename the objects [see Fig. 7]. The **$N** string is used to number objects automatically.

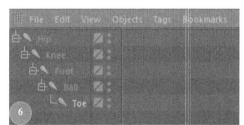  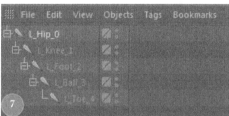

Now, for example, if you want to rename the hierarchy for the right leg, select all joints in **Object Manager** and then invoke **Naming Tool**. In the **Attribute Manager** > **Replace** area, enter **L_** in the **Replace** field and **R_** in the **With** field. Click **Replace Name** to rename the objects [see Fig. 8].

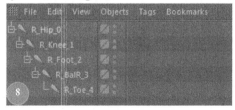

# Measure & Construction Tool

You can use this tool to measure distance and angle between two objects. The measurement can be stored in a measurement object for later use. You can also adjust the distance and angles numerically after taking the measurement. To measure distance, choose the **Measure & Construction** tool from the **Tools** menu and enable snapping. Press and hold **Ctrl+Shift** and drag the mouse pointer from one point to another point to measure distance [refer to Fig. 9].

To measure a new distance, click **New Measure** on the **Attribute Manager**. Repeat the process to measure the new distance. To measure an angle, create a second measurement line by **Ctrl** clicking on a point [see Fig. 10]. Now, you can change distance and angle directly in the viewport by dragging the value labels or from **Attribute Manager** using the **Distance 1**, **Distance 2**, and **Angle** attributes.

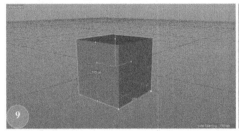

To move arrowheads, drag them with **Shift** [red arrowheads] or **Ctrl** [green arrowheads] held down. You can also use this tool to move individual points, edges, and polygons of an object.

# Annotation Tool

This tool is used to interactively create annotation tags in the viewports [see Fig. 11]. These tags are very useful in adding object-specific comments to the objects in a complex scene. The text fields move with the corresponding object. If the object is not visible, the corresponding text fields will also not be visible in the viewport.

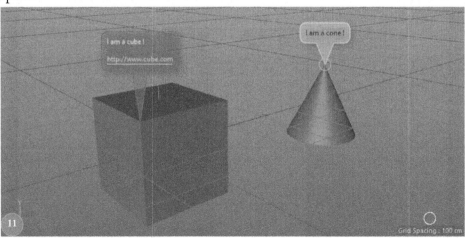

To create a tag, invoke **Annotation Tool** from the **Tools** menu and then press and hold the LMB on the object, a green cursor appears. This cursor snaps to the valid object points. If you release the mouse button without snapping the cursor, the annotation is snapped to the center point of the object. You can press **Esc** to abort the creation process. When you create an annotation, an **Annotation** tag is applied to the object. Once you create an annotation, you can change the text and URL from the **Attribute Manager > Annotation** tab. Make sure the tag is selected in the **Object Manager**.

If you hover the mouse pointer on the annotations, the folded and scaled down boxes will be maximized temporarily. You can double-click on a field, to unfold as well as activate it.

 *Note: The WWW tag*
*The older **WWW** tag will be automatically converted to the **Annotation** tags when loaded in Cinema 4D.*

## Workplanes

**Workplanes** are primarily designed for use in the technical modeling in which elements are arranged along perpendicular axis. They are generally used in the **Perspective** view. You can use **Workplanes** to place and arrange objects across a plane. However, the position, scale, and rotation will always be according to the world coordinate system. This system always remains visible as a light gray grid in a viewport.

 *Tip: Default workplane settings*
*To switch back to default settings [the world grid], choose **Workplane > Align Workplane to Y***  *from the **Tools** menu.*

### Align Workplane to X, Align Workplane to Y, Align Workplane to Z

 You can use these commands to arrange the workplane to the respective axis. The normals will be always oriented along the Y-axis. The **Align Workplane to Y** mode is the most commonly used command, as it resembles the world grid.

### Align Workplane to Selection

 This command rotates the **Workplane** according to the currently selected element.

### Align Selection to Workplane

This command positions the selected elements on the **Workplane**.

# Arranging Objects

Cinema 4D offers many tools to arrange objects in a scene. Let's explore them.

## Arrange

This command allows you to arrange, scale, or rotate selected objects. When you change the attributes in **Attribute Manager**, real-time feedback is displayed in the viewports. To arrange objects, select objects and then choose **Arrange Objects** > **Arrange** from the **Tools** menu. In **Attribute Manager**, set the desired **Mode** and then click **Apply** if the objects are not instantly arranged in the viewport. Now, adjust the settings in **Attribute Manager** as long as the **Arrange** function is active, see Figs. 12 and 13.

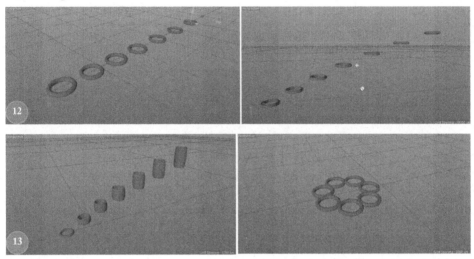

## Center

This command allows you to center objects in 3D space in viewports. This command is applied to all selected objects in **Object Manager**. However, the children of the selected objects are not affected. An object in Cinema 4D is enclosed inside a cuboid of bounding box. The axis system used for alignment considers the center of the axis at the center of the bounding box. Refer to **Exercise 1** of **Unit CM1** to understand functioning of this tool.

## Duplicate

This command allows you to create as many as duplicates you want to create depending on the RAM available. You can also transform duplicates using this command. Most of the options available for this command are similar to that of the **Arrange** command. Refer to **Exercise 1** of **Unit CM1** to understand functioning of this tool.

## Transfer

 This command allows you to copy the **PSR** values [position, rotation, and scale] from one object to another. To transfer values, select the object[s] you want to modify and then execute the **Transfer** command. Now, hover the mouse over the source object, a white line appears. Click to transfer values.

## Randomize

 You can use this function to randomly place objects in 3D space. You can also randomize the scale and rotation of the objects. To randomize objects, select them and then execute the **Randomize** command [see Fig. 14].

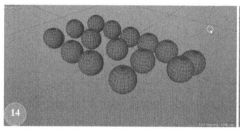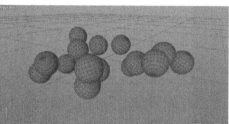

# Lens Distortion

The **Lens Distortion** tool allows you to deal with the lens distortion effects in Cinema 4D. You can correct the distortion in the image, shot with the small focal lengths [shot with wide angles]. This distortion can be problematic while motion tracking a footage. Motion tracking produces better results when used with the distortion free footage. The distortions can be classified as barrel distortion, pincushion distortion, and mustache distortions. Fig. 15 shows the barrel, pincushion, and mustache distortion. The live footage generally have the barrel shaped distortions. You can use the **Lens Distortion** tool to create a lens profile that you can use later when tracking a live footage.

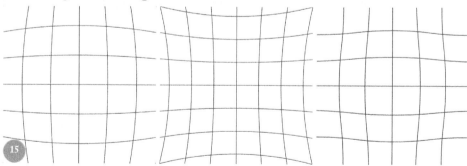

There are two algorithms that you can use to solve the distortion: **Manual** and **Automatic**. The **Manual** method is for the experienced users in which the tool's settings are manually adjusted. The **Automatic** method is the recommended method and works well in most of the situations.

You can use the **Lens Distortion** tool to create guides in the image. Try to match the guides with the curved lines [the lines that should be straight] on the image. You can **Ctrl+Drag** a guide to create duplicates. **Ctrl+Click** once on a guide to create a new point on the line. You can delete the selected point by using **Backspace** or **Del**.

Keep the following in mind while creating lens profiles:

- Place guides precisely. The more guides [precise] you use, the better result you get.
- The lens distortion is calculated accurately where the density of guide is more. However, the areas with low number of guides can be calculated incorrectly. Therefore, you need to place and spread out guides strategically.
- To restore the size of the original image after correction, you can modify the scale of the image as well as its offset values.

## Doodle

The options available for **Doodle** allow you to sketch in the editor view. You can use this tool to mark corrections, make notes, load bitmaps, and so on. These options work well with a tablet, however, you can use a mouse as well. When you draw in the editor view, each drawing is saved in the doodle object for each frame.

 *Tip: Rendering Doodle*
*By default, the **Render Doodle** option is active in **Render Settings > Options**. As a result, the doodles appear in the render output and this is the reason you can only draw doodle in the **Render Safe** area of the viewport.*

## Virtual Walkthrough

There are two tools available that allow you to walk or fly through the Cinema 4D scenes. This experience is similar to a third-person shooter game where you can walk or fly though the scene. The camera path can be recorded or can be output as spline. A virtual walkthrough can be created in Cinema 4D using one of the following methods:

- Use the **Virtual Walkthrough** tool to fly freely through the scene. To exit this mode, select any other tool.
- Use the **Collision Orbit** tool to define an orbital path around an object.
- Use the **Collision Detection** tag to exclude specific objects such as doors from the collision detection.

Keep in mind the following while working with these tools:

- If you stuck somewhere in the scene [due to collision detection] and not able to move, press **Ctrl** to temporarily deactivate the detection.
- These tools work with the polygonal objects. If you face any issue with the geometry, make it editable by first selecting it and then pressing **C**.
- These tools behave correctly if a floor [polygonal object] is used in the scene.

### Collision Orbit Tool

 You can use this tool in conjunction with **Target Camera** to orbit around an object. The camera will automatically avoid the obstacles. To understand working of this tool:

- Create a **Target Camera** in the scene.
- Target the object [around which you want to orbit] using **Camera's Null**.
- Switch to the target camera.
- Invoke the **Collision Orbit** tool and move the mouse in the 3D view with LMB held down. The **HP** rotation values will be displayed in **HUD** in the viewport. The motion path can be recorded.

The collision is detected when the camera's z-axis [path of the view] intersects with the given object. A green icon appears when this happens.

### Virtual Walkthrough Tool

 You can use this tool to fly around the scene. The mouse and keyboard can be used to navigate the scene as you do in a 3D third person shooter game.

## 3D Connexion

The options available for **3D Connexion** work with the 3D mouse, sometimes also referred to as **Spacemouse**. This mouse offers six directions for movement. Cinema 4D uses the 3DxWare driver to operate the **Spacemouse**. It is must that you install the driver before starting the 3D mouse.

## Quiz

Evaluate your skills to see how many questions you can answer correctly.

**Multiple Choice**
Answer the following questions:

1. Which of the following tools is used to create guides interactively in the editor view?

   [A] Guide Tool                    [B] Create Guide Tool
   [C] A and B                       [D] None of these

2. Which of the following key combinations along with LMB is used to create distance arrow while measuring distances using the **Measure & Construction** tool?

   [A] Ctrl+Shift                    [B] Ctrl
   [C] Alt                           [D] Ctrl+Alt

## Fill in the Blanks

Fill in the blanks in each of the following statements:

1. _____ are primarily designed for use in the technical modeling in which elements are arranged along perpendicular axis.

2. The _____ command allows you to center objects in the 3D space in the viewports.

3. The _____ command allows you to copy the PSR values [position, rotation, and scale] from one object to another.

4. You can use the _____ tool to create a lens profile that you can use later when tracking a live footage.

5. The _____ feature allows you to sketch in the editor view.

## True or False

State whether each of the following is true or false:

1. You can create a segmented guide by using the **Alt** key.

2. **Guide Tool** works in combination with all **Snap** options.

3. **Lighting Tool** allows you to interactively create, select, and place a light object in the viewports.

4. **Naming Tool** allows you to efficiently rename object hierarchies in the scene.

5. The measurement computed using the **Measure & Construction** tool can not be stored in a measurement object for later use.

## Summary

This unit covered the following topics:

- Creating guides in the editor view
- Interactively placing lights and adjusting their attributes in the scene
- Measuring angles and distances
- Working with Workplanes
- Arranging, duplicating, and randomizing objects
- Correcting lens distortions
- Creating virtual walkthroughs

- Splines tools
- Splines functions
- Generators command group

# Unit CM3: Spline Modeling

A spline is a sequences of vertices, connected by lines [segments] lying in 3D space. However, a spline has no 3-dimnesional depth. Splines are infinitely thin entities and are not visible during rendering. However, if you are using Studio version of Cinema 4D, you can render splines using Hair and Sketch & Toon features. The shape of these lines is defined by the interpolation method. The interpolation method defines whether the shape of the line is curved or straight. The curved splines have a soft leading edge without any sharp corner. In this unit, I will cover the spline modeling tools and techniques.

A spline is made up of several partial curves called lines or segments. You can create holes using splines, when a spline lies completely inside another spline and both splines are closed. If two segments overlap, no 3D surface will be created or you will see strange results.

Cinema 4D offers a number of predefined parametric spline curves known as spline primitives. These primitives are calculated using the mathematical formulae and therefore they have no points [vertices] to edit. However, you can convert a parametric spline primitive to an editable spline by first selecting it and then pressing **C**.

To adjust vertices using the **Pen** tool [I will discuss is shortly], you must make the spline editable. However, you can apply **Deformers** to a spline even if the spline has not been made editable. You can access spline primitives from the **Spline** sub-menu of the **Create** menu or from the **Spline** command group from the **Standard** palette [see Fig. 1].

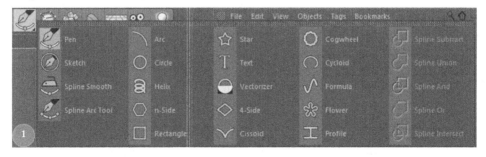

# Working with Spline Tools

Cinema 4D offers four tools for drawing splines: **Pen**, **Sketch**, **Spline Smooth**, and **Spline Arch Tool**.

## Sketch Tool

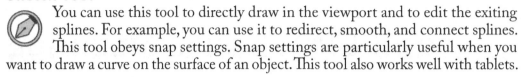 You can use this tool to directly draw in the viewport and to edit the exiting splines. For example, you can use it to redirect, smooth, and connect splines. This tool obeys snap settings. Snap settings are particularly useful when you want to draw a curve on the surface of an object. This tool also works well with tablets.

*Note: Bezier spline*
*Whenever a new spline is created, the **Bezier** spline will be created by default. When you edit the exiting splines, the original spline type is preserved.*

*Tip: Drawing on 3D Objects*
*This tool observes the snap settings, you can use the 3D snapping function to draw a spline directly onto an object surface. You define the radius of the brush interactively by MMB dragging.*

To draw a spline using this tool, invoke it, and then click and drag in the editor view. As soon as you release LMB, spline will be created. Some of the functions of this tool are given below:

- You can grab a spline from any location and edit it from that location.
- You can connect two splines [connected at their ends] or two segments of the same spline. If you connect the start and end points of a spline, the spline will be closed. You can also connect two splines or two segments of the same spline anywhere along the spline.
- You can temporarily switch to the **Spline Smooth** tool by pressing the **Shift** key. The previously defined settings of the **Spline Smooth** tool will be used.
- If you want to unify spline segments or two separate splines, select the splines first. MMB drag to specify the radius of the brush interactively, and then drag in the view to connect the splines. Two separate splines will be combined into one.

## Spline Smooth Tool

This tool not only allows you to smooth the splines but also offers a number of other features [works as a shaping brush] that can be combined seamlessly. You can adjust the strength and radius of this tool interactively by dragging the mouse pointer vertically or horizontally. This tool can create lots of points on the spline when you are using feature such as random. You can fix this by switching to the **Smooth** mode.

*Note: Spline types*
*This tool works with all types of splines.*

### Spline Arch Tool

 You can use this tool to create variety of arc shapes and soft connections between segments. This tool creates 3 point circle and obeys snap settings. To create an arch three points are required: start point, middle point, and end point.

### Pen Tool

 This tool is used to create or edit splines. It replaces the previous **Bézier**, **B-Spline**, **Linear** and **Akima Spline** tools and provides a wide variety of new functions. To create a spline, invoke the tool and then click on the view to create a point. If you drag the mouse pointer, a tangent is created to produce a curved section. A ghost preview of the next segment is shown before you create the next point. It helps in visualizing the next segment that will be created if you click to create next point.

Some of the functions of this tool are given below:

- This tool obeys snapping settings.
- The points created using this tool can be selected and moved without need of selecting them.
- If you click on a segment using this tool, the neighboring points will be selected.
- You can make multiple selections using **Shift**.
- When you click on a point or segment, the tangents are displayed and can be edited.
- If you want to extend a spline at the beginning or at the end, select the respective point and then click to create a new point. If a point is selected along the spline [other than the end point], press **Ctrl** to continue at the spline's end.
- If you position the mouse pointer on a segment, it will be highlighted. RMB click shows a menu with number of options that you can use to edit splines.
- Splines points and segments can be moved by clicking and dragging on them. If you press **Shift** and then drag the tangent handles, the tangents will be broken and the selection will be manipulated between the neighboring points.
- Double-clicking on a point toggles between the soft tangent [both halves have same length] and null tangent.
- If you hover mouse over the spline with **Ctrl** held down, a preview appears that shows where a matching tangent will be inserted.
- If you connect the start and end points of a spline, the spline will be closed.
- You can also connect sections of a single spline. If the spline contains other open sections, a new spline will be created.

As mentioned above, if you RMB click on a point or segment, a popup appears with several options. The table given next summarizes these options.

| Table 1: The context popup options | |
|---|---|
| Option | Description |
| Delete Point | Deletes the selected point. You can also delete a point by **Ctrl** clicking on it. |
| Disconnect Point | Disconnects the spline at the selected point. If spline is a closed spline, the spline will be separated at the selected location and both end points will have the same shared location. |
| Hard Tangents | Creates an angular point by setting tangent length of the **Bezier** splines to **0**. |
| Soft Tangents | Sets equal length for the both halves of the tangent and creates a soft curve. |
| Kill Edge | Deletes the spline section. |
| Add Point | Adds a new point at the clicked location. |
| Split Point | Adds two new, non-coherent, congruent points at the clicked location of the segment. The spline will be split into sections. |
| Hard Edge | Tangents' length will be set to zero thus the spline will be made linear. Double-clicking on a point do the same. |
| Soft Edge | The spline will be made curve. Double-clicking on a point do the same. |

## Working with Generators

The tools available in the **Generators** command group are some of the most powerful tools of Cinema 4D that allow you to create surfaces quickly, see Fig. 2. The **Generators** are interactive and they use other objects to generate their surfaces. You can also access these tools from the **Generators** sub-menu  of the **Create** menu. The following table summarizes the generators.

| Table 2: The generators | | |
|---|---|---|
| Option | Icon | Description |
| Subdivision Surface | | This tool is one of the most powerful sculpting tools offered by CIENMA 4D to a digital artist. You can create almost any shape using the point weighting, and edge weighting. This tool uses an algorithm to subdivide and round the object. You can use any kind of object with this tool, however, most of the times, you will work with polygons. |

| Table 2: The generators | | |
|---|---|---|
| Option | Icon | Description |
| Extrude | | You can use this tool to extrude a spline to create an object with depth. |
| Lathe | | When you apply this tool on a spline, it rotates the spline about the Y axis of the local axis system of the generator object to generate a surface of revolution. |
| Loft | | Use this tool to stretch a skin over two or more splines. |
| Sweep | | This tool works with two or three splines. The first spline referred to as contour spline, defines the cross section and is swept along the second spline, referred to as path. The optional third spline, referred to as rail spline, controls the scale of the contour spline over the object's length. |
| Bezier | | This tool stretches a surface over Bezier curves in the X and Y directions. |

## Options in the Mesh Menu

Some of the spline tools, commands, and options are available in the **Mesh** menu. These can be accessed from the **Mesh > Spline** sub-menu and are discussed next:

### Hard Interpolation

This command changes all selected points to hard interpolation. If no points are selected, all points on the spline are changed to hard interpolation, see Fig. 3. When you execute this command, Cinema 4D essentially sets the length of the tangents to **0**.

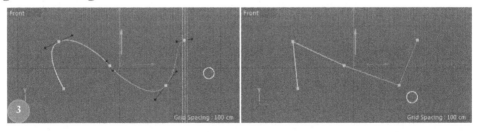

### Soft Interpolation

This command changes all selected points to soft interpolation, see Fig. 4.

### Equal Tangent Length

When you execute this command, the shorter tangent handle is set to the length to that of the second associated tangent, see Fig. 5.

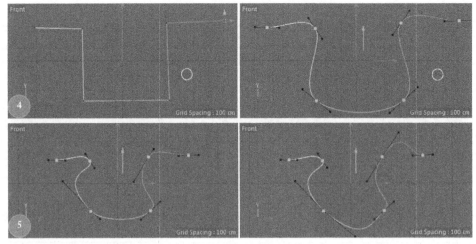

## Equal Tangent Direction

This command is used to restore the smoothness of the broken tangents, see Fig. 6.

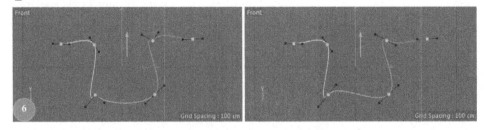

*Tip: Breaking Tangents*
*You can use the **Move** tool with the **Shift** key to break the tangent's handles association and move one tangent handle while leaving the other unchanged.*

## Join Segment

You can use this command to connect several unconnected segments. To connect segments, select one or more points of each segment and then use the **Join Segment** command, see Fig. 7.

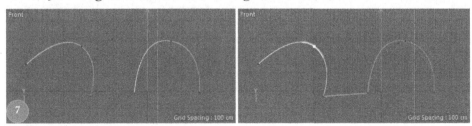

## Break Segment

This command is used to create a new spline segment. To break spline, select one of the points and execute this command, a new segment appears and all points on either side of the separated segment will become a new segment, see Fig. 8. Note that this command works in the **Points** mode only.

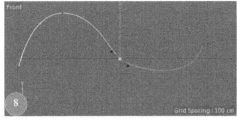

## Explode Segments

 You can use this command to split a spline into separate objects. For this command to work, you don't need to have a selection or the **Points** mode active. New spline objects become child of the original spline.

## Set First Point

 You can use this command to make the selected point first point of a spline. Note that the start of a spline is displayed in white color whereas the end displayed in the blue color. This command needs a point selection and it works in the **Points** mode only.

## Reverse Sequence

 Use this command to reverse the point order of a segment. This command can be applied to several segments of a spline by **Shift** selecting various segments.

## Move Down Sequence

 When you use this command, the sequence number of each point is incremented and the last point of the original sequence becomes the first point in the new sequence.

## Move Up Sequence

 When you use this command, the sequence number of each point is decremented and the last point of the original sequence becomes the first point in the new sequence.

## Chamfer

 This tool is an interactive tool that you can use to convert a selected point to two points with soft-interpolation between them, see Fig. 9. If no points are selected, the entire points on the spline will be chamfered.

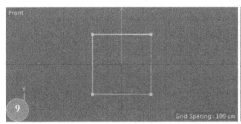
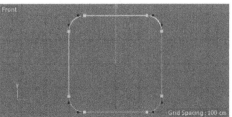

## Create Outline

 This tool is also an interactive tool and is used to create outline around the original spline, see Fig. 10.

 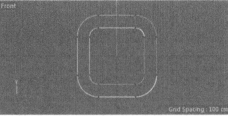

## Cross Section

 This tool is used to create a cross section for a group of spline, see Fig. 11. Before you use this tool, the splines must be selected in **Object Manager**.

## Line Up

Use this command to align sequentially selected points to a straight line, see Fig. 12.

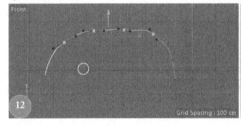 

## Project

You can use this command to project a spline onto surfaces of the other objects, see Fig. 13. To understand the working of this command, create a sphere and a helix. Make helix spline primitive editable. Execute the **Project** command. From the **Options** tab in **Attribute Manager**, select **Spherical** from the **Mode** drop-down list and then from the **Tool** tab, click **Apply**.

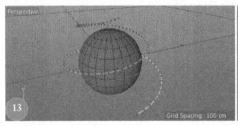 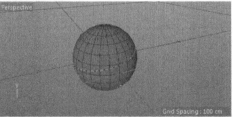

## Round

 You can use this command to round and subdivide the sequentially selected points of a spline, see Fig. 14.

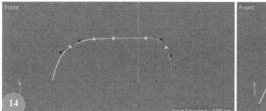

## Spline Subtract

 This command is used for subtract boolean operations. The surfaces that overlaps the target spline will be cut out, see Fig. 15.

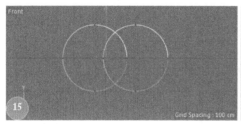

## Spline Union

 When you use this command, the splines are unified and overlapping surfaces are removed, see Fig. 16.

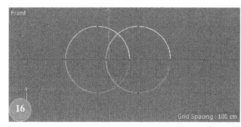

## Spline And

 When you use this command, a new spline is created out of the overlapping regions of all splines that are included in the operation, see Fig. 17.

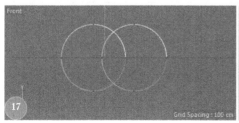

## Spline Or

The opposite of the **Spline And** function, see Fig. 18.

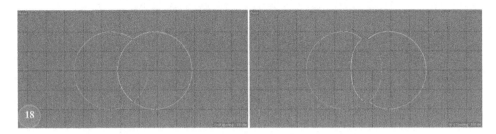

## Spline Intersect

This command is a combination of the results of the **Spline And** and **Spline Or** commands, see Fig. 19.

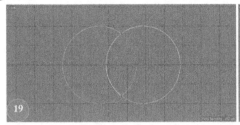
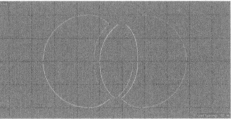

# Hands-on Exercises

### Exercise 1: Creating Model of a Pear

In this exercise, we will model a pear using splines and **Lathe** generator [Fig. E1].

The following table summarizes the exercise:

| Table E1 | |
|---|---|
| Difficulty level | Beginner |
| Estimated time to complete | 20 Minutes |
| Topics | • Getting Started<br>• Creating the Pear Model |
| Resources folder | **unit-cm3** |

| Table E1 | |
| --- | --- |
| Units | Centimeters |
| Final file | pear-finish.c4d |

## Getting Started

Ensure that you have access to **pear.jpg** in the **unit-cm3** folder. Start a new scene in Cinema 4D and set units to **Centimeters**.

## Creating the Pear Model

Follow these steps:

1. Open **Windows Explorer** and drag **pear.jpg** to the **Front** view. Press **Shift+V** to open **Viewport [Front]** options in **Attribute Manager**. In the **Attribute Manager > Back** tab, set **Transparency** to **65%** and **Offset Y** to **435** so that bottom of the pear sits on the origin [Fig. E2].

2. Choose **Pen** ✐ from the **Standard** palette > **Spline** command group and then click and drag at the origin to create the first point. Follow the pear shape to create a profile curve [Fig. E3] and then press **Esc** to complete the creation of the curve. Don't worry about the exact placement of the points. You can always come back and adjust the points using the **Pen** tool.

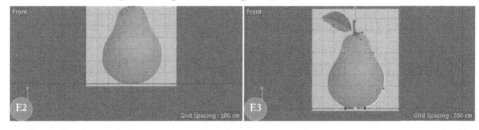

3. Select the bottom point and then enter **0** in the **Position [X]** and **Position [Y]** fields in **Coordinate Manager** to place the point at the origin point. Similarly, select the top point and set its **Position [X]** to **0**.

 *What just happened?*
*By positioning the points, we have ensured that both points are in a line in 3D space. It will ensure that there will be no hole in the geometry when we will apply the **Lathe** generator in the next step.*

4. Ensure spline is selected and then click **Standard** palette > **Generators** command group > **Lathe** 🝆 with **Alt** held down to connect **Lathe** object to the **Spline**. Switch to the **Perspective** view to see the shape of the pear. Press **NB** to enable the **Gouraud Shading (Lines)** mode [Fig. E4].

5. Select **Spline** in **Object Manager** and then in the **Attribute Manager > Object** tab, choose **Natural** from the **Intermediate Points** drop-down list. Now, set **Number** to **10** [Fig. E5].

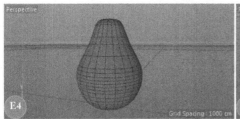
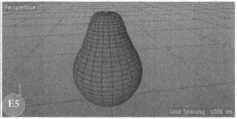

*What just happened?*
*The options in the **Intermediate Points** drop-down list define how the spline is further subdivided with the intermediate points. This setting only affects when spline is used with the generators. When you select the **Natural** method for interpolation, the **Number** field corresponds to the number of intermediate points between vertices. The points on the curvature are positioned closer together where the spline has more curvature.*

6. Ensure **Lathe** is selected in **Object Manager** and then click **Bend** 🝁 from the Standard palette > **Deformer** command group, to add a **Bend** object. Ensure the order of the objects, as shown in Fig. E6. In the **Attribute Manager** > **Bend** > **Object** tab, click **Fit to Parent**. Set **Size [Y]** to **430** and **Strength** to **-16** [Fig. E7].

*What next?*
*Now, we will create a stem for the pear.*

7. Create a **Cylinder** ⬚ primitive. In the **Attribute Manager** > **Cylinder** > **Object** tab, set **Radius, Height, Height Segments**, and **Rotation Segments** to **6, 79, 24**, and **24**, respectively. Align it to the top of the cylinder [Fig. E8]. Apply a **Bend** deformer to it and then on the **Attribute Manager** > **Bend** > **Object** tab, click **Fit to Parent**. Set **Strength** to **-120** to bend the stem [Fig. E9].

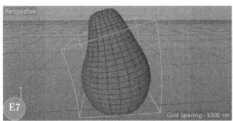
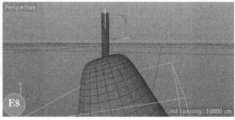

*Note: Subdivisions*
*If you want to increase the number of subdivisions along the rotation of the curve, select the **Lathe** object and then in the **Attribute Manager** > **Lathe** > **Object** tab, change the value of the **Subdivision** field.*

*You can use the **Isoparm Subdivision** parameter to define the number of isoparms used to display the **Lathe** object when the **Isoparms** display mode is active. Press **NI** to activate this mode. Fig. E10 shows the pear model with **Isoparm Subdivision** set to **12**.*

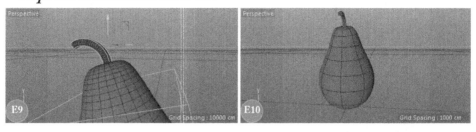

## Exercise 2: Creating a Glass Bottle and Liquid

In this exercise, we will model a glass bottle and liquid using the **Lathe** generator [Fig. E1].

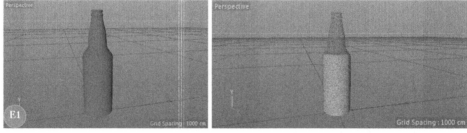

The following table summarizes the exercise:

| Table E2 | |
| --- | --- |
| Difficulty level | Intermediate |
| Estimated time to complete | 35 Minutes |
| Topics | • Getting Started<br>• Creating the Bottle<br>• Creating the Liquid |
| Resources folder | **unit-cm3** |
| Units | **Centimeters** |
| Final file | **bottle-liquid-finish.c4d** |

### Getting Started

Ensure that you have access to **beer.jpg** in the **unit-cm3** folder. Start a new scene in Cinema 4D and set units to **Centimeters**.

### Creating the Bottle

Follow these steps:

1. Open **Windows Explorer** and drag **beer.jpeg** to the **Front** view. Press **Shift+V** to open **Viewport [Front]** options in **Attribute Manager**. In the **Attribute**

**Manager > Back** tab, set **Size X** and **Size Y** to **400**. Also, set **Transparency** to **65%** and **Offset Y** to **188** so that bottom of the bottle sits on the origin. Create a shape using the **Pen** tool [Fig. E2]. Rename the spline as **bottle**. Select the bottom point and set its X and Y positions to **0**. Select the top point and set its X position to **0**.

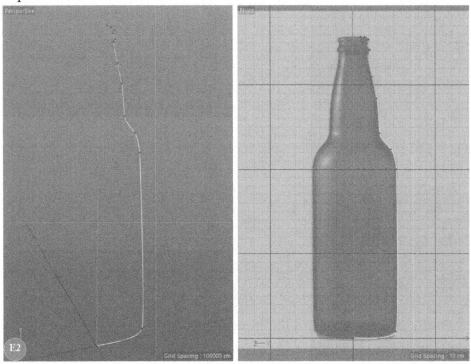

2. Make sure the **Pen** tool is active and then RMB click in the editor view. Choose **Create Outline** from the menu and then drag the spline to create an outline [Fig. E3]. Notice that the **Create Outline** function created a closed spline. *In the* **Attribute Manager > bottle > Object** tab, clear the **Close Spline** check box. Select the second point from the bottom and make sure its X position is set to **0** [Fig. E4].

3. Select the points at the top [Fig. E5] and then press **Delete** to make a straight shape inside of the bottle. Now, apply a **Lathe** generator to create shape of the bottle [Fig. E6].

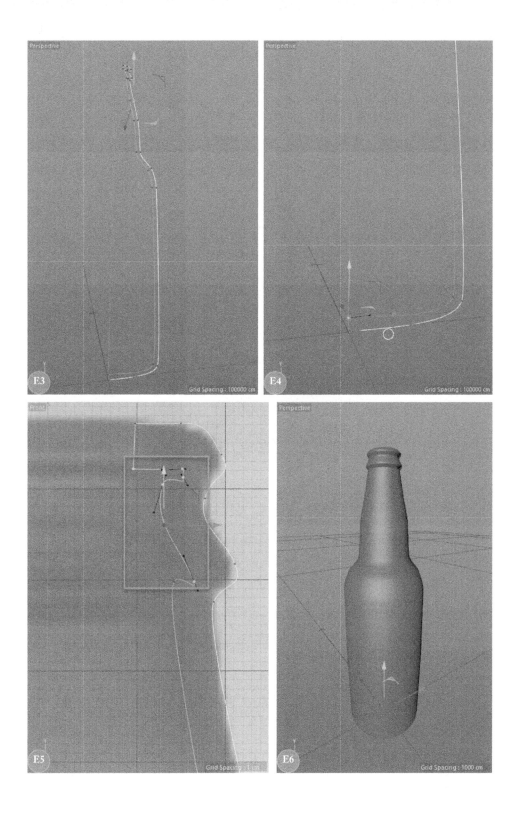

## Creating the Liquid
Follow these steps:

1.  Turn off the **Lathe** object  . Select inside points of the bottle [Fig. E7]. RMB click in the editor view and then choose **Split** from the menu to create a new spline. In **Object Manager**, drag the new spline out of the **Lathe** group and rename it as **liquid**.

> ### Tip: Liquid level
> *If you want to create a different height for the liquid, RMB click on the spline and then choose* **Line Cut** *from the menu. You can also press* **MK**. *Now, create a cut on the spline on the desired height and delete the points. The* **Line Cut** *tool lets you to cut polygon and spline objects. The tool works in all three modes:* ***point, edge*** *and* ***polygon***.

2.  Make sure **liquid** is selected in **Object Manager** and then in the **Attribute Manager > Object** tab, clear the **Close Spline** check box.

3.  Using the **Pen** tool , click on the top point of the liquid and then extend the curve to the vertical green line [Fig. E8]. Adjust the shape of the liquid, as shown in Fig. E9. Now, create the liquid geometry by applying a **Lathe** generator object to the **liquid** spline. Turn on the **Lathe** object corresponding to **bottle**.

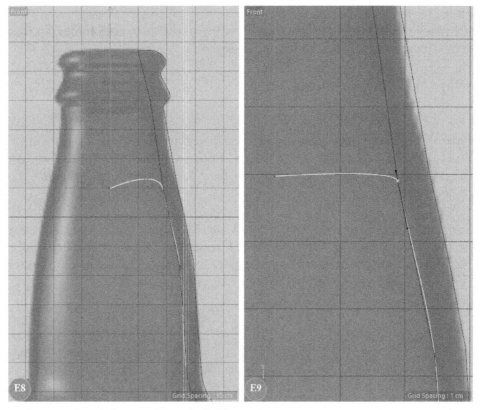

## Exercise 3: Creating a Martini Glass

In this exercise, we will model a martini glass using the **Lathe** generator [Fig. E1].

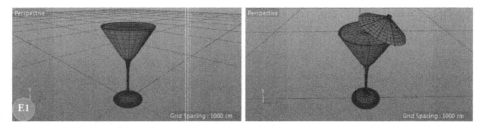

The following table summarizes the exercise:

| Table E3 | |
|---|---|
| Difficulty level | Intermediate |
| Estimated time to complete | 45 Minutes |
| Topics | • Getting Started<br>• Creating the Glass and Liquid<br>• Creating the Umbrella |
| Resources folder | **unit-cm3** |
| Units | **Centimeters** |
| Final file | **martini-glass-finish.c4d** |

## Getting Started

Ensure that you have access to **martini-glass.jpg** in the **unit-cm3** folder. Start a new scene in Cinema 4D and set units to **Centimeters**.

## Creating the Glass and Liquid

Follow these steps:

1.  Open **Windows Explorer** and drag **martini-glass.jpg** to the **Front** view. Press **Shift+V** to open the **Viewport [Front]** options in the **Attribute Manager**. In the **Attribute Manager > Back** tab, set **Size X** and **Size Y** to **300** and **456.472**, respectively.

2.  Set **Transparency** to **65%** and **Offset Y** to **194** so that bottom of the bottle sits on the origin. Also, set **Offset X** to **2**. Create a shape using the **Pen** tool [Fig. E2]. Now, create the geometry for the glass and liquid, as described in **Exercise 2** [Fig. E3]. You can also open the **martini-glass-liquid.c4d**.

## Creating the Umbrella

Follow these steps:

1.  Create a cone object in the scene. In the **Attribute Manager > Cone > Object** tab, set **Top Radius, Bottom Radius,** and **Height** to **10, 100,** and **57**, respectively. In the **Caps** tab, clear the **Caps** check box. Create a cube and then in the **Attribute Manager > Cube > Object** tab, set **Size X, Size Y,** and **Size Z** to **120, 8,** and **8,** respectively. Align it with the cone [Fig. E4].

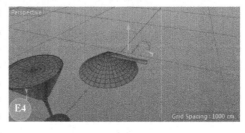

2.  Select cube in **Object Manager** and press **Alt+G** to group it inside a **Null** object. Press **L** and then move the axis to the center of the cone [Fig. E5]. Press **L** again to disable **Enable Axis** mode.

3.  Ensure **Null** is selected in **Object Manager** and then click **Array** on the **Standard** palette with **Alt** held down. In the **Attribute Manager > Array > Object** tab, set **Radius** to **0** and **Copies** to **8**. Select **Cube** on **Object Manager** and then press the **R** key to activate the **Rotate** tool. Now, rotate the objects along **Z**-axis

[Fig. E6]. You can now modify the dimensions of the cube and cone so that they better fit with each other.

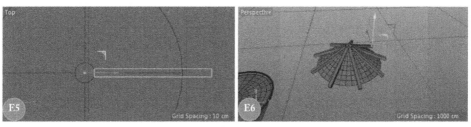

4. Using a **Cube** primitive, create the stick and then align the stick with the umbrella.

## Exercise 4: Creating the Apple Logo
In this exercise, we will create apple logo in 3D [see Fig. E1].

The following table summarizes the exercise:

| Table E4 | |
|---|---|
| Difficulty level | Beginner |
| Estimated time to complete | 40 Minutes |
| Topics | • Getting Started<br>• Creating the Logo |
| Resources folder | **unit-cm3** |
| Units | **Centimeters** |
| Final file | **apple-logo-finish.c4d** |

## Getting Started
Follow these steps:

1. Start a new scene in Cinema 4D and set units to **Centimeters**. Maximize the **Front** viewport and then press **Shift+V** to open the viewport settings.

2. In the **Attribute Manager** > **Back** tab, assign **apple-logo.jpg** to the **Image** parameter. Also, set **Offset X**, **Offset Y**, and **Transparency** to **8**, **398**, and **90**, respectively.

## Creating the Logo
Follow these steps:

1.  Create a shape using the **Pen** tool in the **Front** view [Fig. E2]. Make sure that the X coordinate value of the two end points is **0**. Press **Ctrl+A** to select all points and then choose **Transform Tools** > **Mirror** from the **Mesh** menu.

2.  Click drag towards the left in **Front** view; a line appears in the view. Snap the line to the two end vertices [Fig. E3] and then release the mouse button to create the mirror copy [Fig. E4].

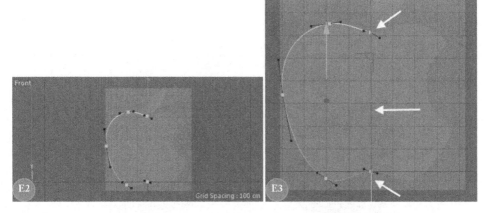

3.  Select the top points [Fig. E5], RMB click and then choose **Soft Interpolation** from the popup menu. Weld the two points using the **Weld** command. Make sure **Spline** is selected in **Object Manager** and then in the **Attribute Manager** > **Object** tab, select the **Close Spline** check box.

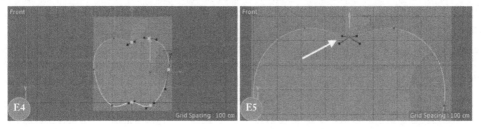

> ✎ *Note: Gap in spline*
> *If you see a weird looking spline around the bottom points [see Fig. E6], use the **Pen** tool to select them. RMB click on them and then choose **Delete Point** from the shortcut menu.*

4.  Create a **Circle** object, align it with the **Spline** [Fig. E7] and then press **C** to make it editable. In **Object Manager**, select **Circle** and then select **Spline** [select them in the correct order]. Choose **Spline** > **Spline Subtract** from the **Mesh** menu to create the shape shown in Fig. E8.

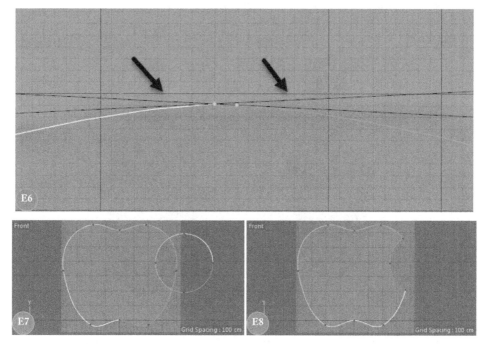

5. Create two circles, make them editable and then align, as shown in Fig. E9. Select the two circles and then choose **Spline** > **Spline And** from the **Mesh** menu to create the shape shown in Fig. E10.

6. Select both splines in **Object Manager** and then choose **Conversion** > **Connect Objects + Delete** from the **Mesh** menu to combine them. Now, connect the unified spline with the **Extrude** generator.

7. In the **Attribute Manager** > **Object** tab, set **Movement** Z to **30**. In the **Caps** tab, set **Start** and **End** to **Fillet Cap**. Also, set **Step** and **Radius** for **Start** and **End** to **3** and **1.5**, respectively.

## Exercise 5: Creating a Whiskey Bottle

In this exercise, we will create a whiskey bottle using the **Loft** generator [Fig. E1].

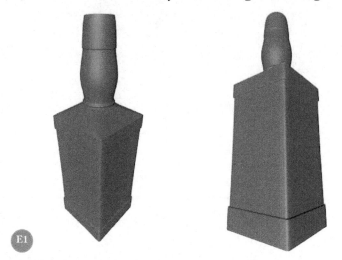

E1

The following table summarizes the exercise:

| Table E5 | |
| --- | --- |
| Difficulty level | Beginner |
| Estimated time to complete | 40 Minutes |
| Topics | • Getting Started<br>• Creating the Bottle |
| Resources folder | **unit-cm3** |
| Units | **Centimeters** |
| Final file | **whiskey-finish-finish.c4d** |

### Getting Started
Follow these steps:

1.  Start a new scene in Cinema 4D and set units to **Centimeters**. Maximize the **Front** viewport and then press **Shift+V** to open the viewport settings.

2.  In the **Attribute Manager** > **Back** tab, assign **whiskey.jpg** to the **Image** parameter. Also, set **Offset X**, **Offset Y**, and **Transparency** to **0**, **381**, and **90**, respectively.

### Creating the Bottle
Follow these steps:

1.  Choose **Rectangle** from the **Standard** palette > **Spline** command group to create a rectangle in the editor view. In the **Attribute Manager** > **Rectangle** > **Object** tab, set **Width** and **Height** to **232** each.

2. Select the **Rounding** check box and then set **Radius** to **8.248** and **Plane** to XZ. Align the rectangle in the **Front** view [Fig. E2]. Create a copy of the rectangle and align it [Fig. E3].

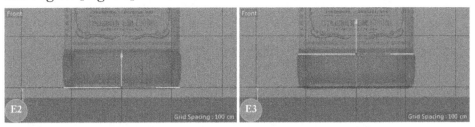

3. Similarly, create five more rectangles and align them [Fig. E4]. You need to adjust the size of the rectangles to get the shape you are looking for.

4. Choose **Circle** from the **Standard** palette > **Spline** tab to create a circle in the editor view. In the **Attribute Manager** > **Circle** > **Object** tab, set **Radius** to **54**, **Plane** to XZ, and then align it [Fig. E5]. Similarly, create more circles, adjust their radii and then align them [Fig. E6]. Fig. E7 shows all the rectangles and circles in the scene.

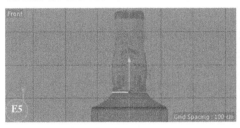 

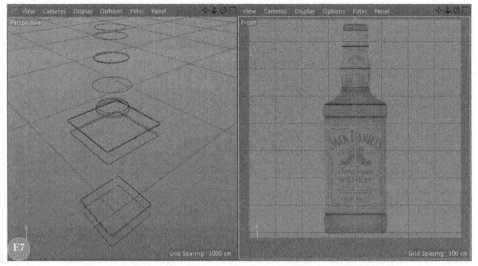

5. Now, connect all shapes with the **Loft** generator to create shape of the bottle.

# Quiz

**Multiple Choice**
Answer the following questions:

1. Which of the following tools uses an algorithm to subdivide and round the objects?

   [A] Extrude            [B] Lathe
   [C] Loft               [D] Subdivision Surface

2. Which of the following tools is used to stretch a skin over two or more splines?

   [A] Extrude            [B] Lathe
   [C] Loft               [D] Subdivision Surface

3. Which of the following key combinations is used to activate the isoparm display mode?

   [A] NI                 [B] NP
   [C] NB                 [D] ND

4. Which of the following key combinations is used to activate the **Line Cut** tool?

   [A] MI                 [B] MP
   [C] MK                 [D] MD

5. Which of the following keys is used to activate the **Enable Axis** mode?

[A] E                    [B] A
[C] C                    [D] L

**Fill in the Blanks**
Fill in the blanks in each of the following statements:

1. You can convert a parametric spline primitive to an editable spline by first selecting it and then pressing _____.

2. _____ creates 3 point circle and obeys snap settings.

3. The options in the _____ drop-down list define how the spline is further subdivided with the intermediate points.

**True or False**
State whether each of the following is true or false:

1. Whenever a new spline is created, the **Bezier** spline type will be created by default.

2. The **Extrude** tool is used to extrude a spline to create an object with depth.

**Summary**
This unit covered the following topics:

- Splines tools
- Splines functions
- Generators command group

This page is intentionally left blank

- Polygons components
- Polygon modeling techniques
- Selection tools
- Polygons structure tools
- Modeling objects
- Deformers

# Unit CM4: Polygon Modeling

Polygons are a type of geometry that you can use to create 3D models in Cinema 4D. Polygons represent and approximate surfaces of a 3D model. Many 3D modelers use the primitive objects [discussed in **Unit CM1**] as the basic starting point for creating models and then create complex geometries using sub-object levels [components] such as points, edges, and polygons. You can also apply commands such as **Bevel**, **Extrude**, **Bridge**, and so on, on a primitive's polygon mesh in order to modify the primitive's shape.

Closed shapes in a plane with three or more sides are called polygons. The endpoints of the sides of polygons are called points or vertices. The line connecting two points is called an edge. Polygons are classified by how many sides or angles they have. The following list shows types of polygons based on number of sides they have:

- A triangle is a three sided polygon.
- A quadrilateral is a four sided polygon.
- A pentagon is a five sided polygon.
- A hexagon is a six sided polygon.
- A septagon or heptagon is a seven sided polygon.
- An octagon is an eight sided polygon.
- A nonagon is a nine sided polygon.
- A decagon is a ten sided polygon.

There are a variety of techniques that you can use to create 3D polygonal models in Cinema 4D but before we start creating models, let's first understand the tools, commands, modes, and options that are required to build a 3D model. Let's first start with different modes used in polygonal modeling in Cinema 4D.

## Working with Modes

Cinema 4D provides three modes for polygonal modeling. These modes are: **Points**, **Edges**, and **Polygons** and you can access them from the **Tools** palette. Before you use these modes, you need to make a primitive object editable. To do so, ensure that the object is selected and then press **C**. When you make an object editable, you loose its parametric creation attributes.

## Points

Use the **Points** mode when you want to edit points of an object. When this mode is active, the points appear as small squares. Hover the cursor on the points to highlight them. To select points, you can use the selection tools. You can also select them by clicking on points one by one. The selected points appear in yellow.

To add points to the selection, click on them with **Shift** held down. To remove points from selection, **Ctrl** click on them. To select all points, choose **Select All** from the **Edit** menu or press **Ctrl+A**. To de-select all points, choose **Deselect All** from the **Edit** menu or press **Ctrl+Shift+A**. To delete selected points, choose **Delete** from the **Edit** menu. Alternatively, you can press the **Backspace** or **Delete** key.

## Edges

Use this mode to edit the edges of the polygons, selected edges are highlighted in color. You can select edges much the same way as you select points.

## Polygons

In Cinema 4D, you can work on three types of polygons: triangles, quadrangles, and n-gons. You can select polygons much the same way as you select points or edges.

 *Note: Using transformation tools*
*You can also use the **Move**, **Scale** and **Rotate** tools to edit the selected edges, points, or polygons. To add to the selection, hold **Shift** while you make selection. To remove from selection, click on the object with **Ctrl** held down.*

# Selecting Objects and Components

In order to make models in any 3D application, you should be able to select objects or sub-objects/components [points, edges, and polygons]. Cinema 4D offers various tools and commands for making selections. Let's explore these tools and commands available in the **Select** menu. These options are also available in the **U** hidden menu.

## Selection Filter

The options in the **Selection Filter** sub-menu allow you to choose which types of object can be selected in the viewport. By default, all objects in the viewport are selectable. These options are very useful in scenes where you have many lights, cameras, bones, and so on. For example, if you are working on the lighting of the scene, you can make only light selectable and disable all other by first choosing **Selection Filter > None** from the **Select** menu and then choosing **Selection Filer > Light** from the **Select** menu.

## Loop Selection
**Hotkey: U~L**

 Loops are elements that are connected in a shape of a loop. The **Loop Selection** tool allows you to quickly select the loops. Fig. 1 shows the loop selection in **Polygons**, **Edges**, and **Points** modes.

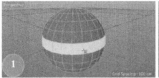 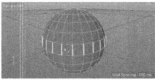 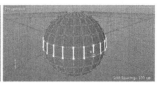

*Tip: Loop Selection*
*If you are in the **Edges** mode, you can quickly select a loop by double-clicking on an edge using the **Move**, **Select**, or **Rotate** tool. If a point or polygon is already selected in one of the modes, press **Ctrl+Shift** and then click on the next element to create a selection between it and the already selected element.*

*Tip: Handling*
*You can influence of the length of the loop by dragging instead of clicking when the **Loop Selection** tool is active. If you just want to select boundary loops, select the **Select Boundary Loop** check box from **Attribute Manager**. If you select the **Stop at Boundary Edges** check box, the loop will stop at boundary edges [it works in the **Points** and **Edges** modes].*

## Ring Selection
**Hotkey: U~B**

The function of this tool is similar to that of the **Loop Selection** tool, however, it select the elements that form a broad ring-shape.

## Outline Selection
**Hotkey: U~Q**

In the **Polygons** mode, it selects the edges that outline the selected polygons. To select outline edges, move the mouse pointer over the polygon selection. When the edges that outline the selection change color, click to select edges, see Fig. 2. Also, the **Edges** mode gets activated. This tool also works in the **Edges** mode, existing polygon selections can be selected.

 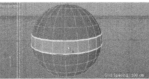 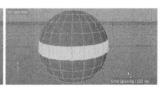

## Fill Selection
**Hotkey: U~F**

 In the **Edges** mode, this tool creates a polygon selection from an existing edge selection, see Fig. 3. To fill the selection, move the mouse pointer over the edge selection. When the polygons change color, click to select those polygons. Also, the **Polygons** mode will get activated.

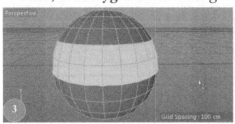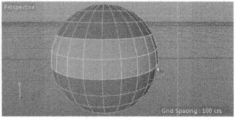

## Path Selection
**Hotkey: U~M**

 This tool lets you select polygons edges or points interactively by painting on the edges or points. This tool works only in the **Edges** or **Points** mode. Click and drag over elements to create a selection [see Fig. 4].

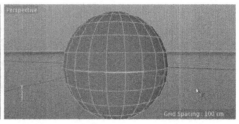

## Phong Break Selection
**Hotkey: U~N**

 This tool works with the low-res mechanical models whose edges are assigned via **Phong Break Shading**.

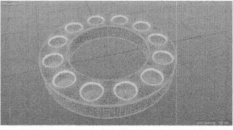

## Select All

Use this command to select all points, edges, or polygons of the currently selected object.

## Deselect All

Use this command to de-select all points, edges, or polygons of the currently selected object.

## Invert

**Hotkey: U~I**

Use this command to invert the current selection.

## Select Connected

**Hotkey: U~W**

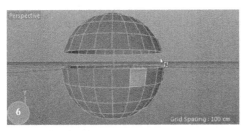 Use this command to select all points, edges, or polygons connected to the selected element, see Fig. 6.

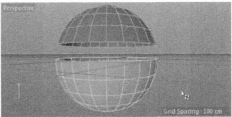

## Grow Selection

**Hotkey: U~Y**

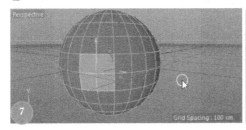 You can use this command to add to the selection. All adjacent elements (depending on the mode selected) are added to the selection, see Fig. 7.

## Shrink Selection

**Hotkey: U~K**

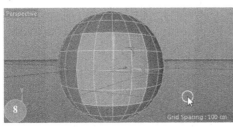 Use this command to remove from the selection, see Fig. 8.

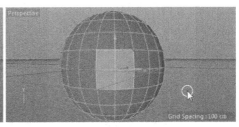

## Hide Selected

Hides the currently selected elements.

## Hide Unselected

 Hides all unselected elements.

## Unhide All

 Makes all hidden elements visible again.

## Invert Visibility

 Use this command to make visible elements hidden and hidden elements visible.

## Convert Selection

Hotkey: UX

 With this command, you can convert one type of selection to another. On executing this command, the **Convert Selection** dialog box appears. Select the desired options from the dialog box and then click **Convert** to convert the selection, see Fig. 9.

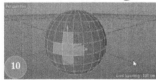

## Set Vertex Weight

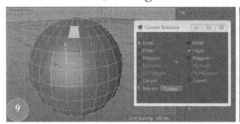 Use this tool to set the vertex weight. To create a vertex map, select the points or polygons and then execute this command, the **Set Vertex Weight** dialog box appears. In this dialog box, set the value for the **Value** parameter and then click **OK**, see Fig. 10.

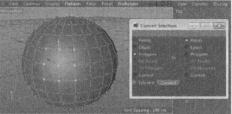

## Set Selection

 You can use the **Set Selection** command to store selection sets and then recall them later. You can create selection sets for the point, edge, and polygon selections. Make a selection and then execute this command, a tag is added to **Object Manager**. You can manipulate the selection from **Attribute Manager**, see Fig. 11.

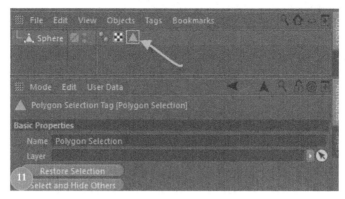

**Note: Selection Filter**

*The commands in the **Select** > **Selection Filter** submenu are used to specify which types of the object will be displayed in the viewport. By default, all objects are selectable in the viewport. Note that you can still select objects in **Object Manager**.*

**Tip: Selector**

*The **Select** > **Selection Filter** > **Selector** command allows you to select all lights, nulls, texture tags, and so on. For example, if you want to select all lights in the viewport and then want to make their **Intensity** value to **0**. Choose **Select** > **Selection Filter** > **Selector** to open the **Selector** dialog box. Now, select **Light** from the dialog box; all light objects will be selected. Now, in **Attribute Manager**, set **Intensity** to **0**. Similarly, you can select tags using the **Tags** tab of the **Selector** dialog box.*

## Adjusting Structure of the Polygonal Objects

The tools available in the **Mesh** menu are used to change the structures of the polygonal objects. Most of these tools are available in the **Points**, **Edges**, and **Polygons** modes. These tools work on the editable objects. You can make an object editable by choosing **Conversion** > **Make Editable** from the **Mesh** menu or by pressing **C**. Generally, these tools affect the selected points, edges, or polygons. However, if no component is selected, these tools affect the entire selected object.

**Note: Primitive objects**

*The primitive objects and splines objects in Cinema 4D are parametric; they have no points or polygons. They are created using parameters and math formulae. To edit these objects at component level, you need to first convert them to points or polygons. You can do so by pressing **C** from the keyboard, clicking the **Make Editable** icon on the **Tools** palette, or by choosing **Conversion** > **Make Editable** from the **Mesh** menu.*

*Note: Inactive tools*
*Any structure tool that cannot be used on the current selection will be grayed out. For example, if you make a point selection, the **Mesh** > **Create Tools** > **Edge Cut** tool will be grayed out. If you are using an interactive tool, the most recently action can be undone by pressing **Esc** as long as the mouse button is still pressed.*

*Tip: Using hotkeys*
*When you are modeling, you can temporarily activate a function using hotkeys. For example, if you select polygons using the **Live Selection** tool, press and hold **D** to temporarily activate the **Extrude** tool. Extrude the polygons and then release the hotkey to switch back to the **Live Selection** tool.*

*Tip: Modeling popup menu*
*You can also quickly access the structure tools from the RMB popup menu. The options available in the menu depend on the type of component selected. Also, you can quickly access these tools from the **U** and **M** hidden menus.*

Several tools have their own specific parameters that you can access from the **Options** tab of the tool's **Attribute Manager**, see Fig. 12. The options in the **Attribute Manager** > **Tool** tab allow you to choose whether the changes will be applied automatically in real-time or not. If you are working on a heavy scene and your system is responding slowly to the automatic updates, you can disable this feature by clearing the **Realtime Update** check box from the **Attribute Manager** > **Tool** tab, see Fig. 13.

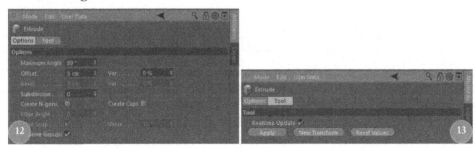

If you clear the **Realtime Update** check box, you need to click on the **Apply** button to apply the changes to the object. If you want to reapply the tool, click **New Transform**. You can also use this button to repeatedly apply changes to the object. For example, if you are using the **Extrude** tool, clicking repeatedly on this button will extrude the selected element(s) multiple times. The **Reset Values** button can be used to reset the tool to its default state. The tools, commands, and options available in the **Mesh** menu are discussed next.

## Conversion Sub-menu
The following commands are available in the **Conversion** sub-menu:

### Make Editable
**Hotkey: C**

 The primitives objects in Cinema 4D are parametric and created using math formulae. These primitive objects have no points, edges, or polygons. To create complex objects using these primitives, you need to first make the primitive objects editable. When you make an object editable, you get access to the object's components: points, edges, and polygons. You can use the **Make Editable** command to make an object editable. Note that this command is one-way. You cannot convert an editable object back to a parametric object.

### Current State to Object

 This command allows you to collapse the stack for the selected object and creates a polygon copy of the selected object. For example, if you have applied multiple deformers on an object, you can use this command to create a polygon copy of the resulting shape. If you apply this command to a parametric object, it will create a polygon copy considering all deformers.

*Caution: Child objects*
*This command ignores child objects. Therefore, you need to apply this command separately for each child object.*

*Caution: Animation data*
*The animation data is not copied to the new object when you use this command.*

### Connect Objects

 You can use this command to create a single object from multiple objects. When you connect the polygonal objects to which you have applied materials and selection tags, Cinema 4D ensures that selection tags are connected properly. Also, texture projections are restored accurately. The original objects are preserved, you can delete them if they are no longer required in the scene.

*Caution: Animation data*
*The animation data is not copied to the new object when you use this command. The original objects and their animation data is preserved.*

If you are connecting splines of different types, the new resulting spline will be a **Bezier** spline. When you use this command, not only the connected object occupies less space in **Object Manager**, it also renders quickly even though it has same number of polygons.

### Connect Objects+Delete

 The function of this command is similar to that of the **Connect Objects** command but additionally, it deletes the original objects.

### Bake as Alembic

 This command creates Alembic objects from the currently selected objects [ignoring the child object]. This command is useful to speedup a complex animation. Alembic animations can be played very quickly. When you execute this command, Cinema 4D places the Alembic files in a folder named, **alembic**. If the scene has not yet been saved, you have define a folder yourself.

### Bake as Alembic+Delete

 The function of this command is similar to that of the **Bake as Alembic** command but additionally, it deletes the selected objects. Note that the original animation will be lost.

### Polygon Groups to Objects

You can use this command to create separate polygonal objects from the non-connected surfaces [polygons groups], see Fig. 14.

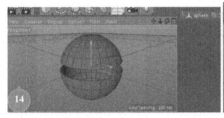

### Commands Sub-menu

The following commands are available in the **Commands** sub-menu:

### Array

This command allows you to duplicate selected elements [points or polygons] of an object and then distribute them randomly in the 3D world, see Fig. 15. You can also vary size as well as rotation of the duplicates. If no elements are selected, all points and surfaces of the selected object are duplicated. You can use this command, for example, to create a complete meadow from a single blade of polygon grass.

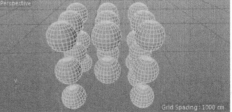

## Clone

 Use this command to create duplicate of the surface or points of an object. You can then rotate the duplicated objects along the object axis. The duplicate objects shown in the left image of Fig. 15 are created from a cube. The settings used to create the duplicate are shown in the right image of Fig. 16.

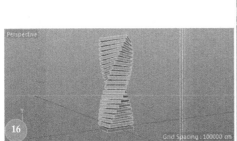 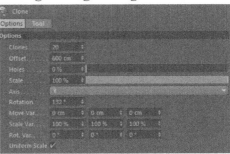

## Disconnect
**Hotkeys: U~D, U~Shift+D**

 This command is used to disconnect the selected polygons from the object or segments between the selected spline points, see Fig. 17. The disconnected surfaces will remain in place but no longer will be connected to the original element. This command can be applied on splines.

Unlike the **Break Segment** tool, the start and end points of the disconnected segments are duplicated and are not deleted from the original spline. The order of the spline remains intact both before and after the disconnection. If you press **U** followed by **Shift+D**, the **Disconnect dialog box** appears. **In this dialog box,** you can find the **Preserve Groups** setting. If you clear the check box, the elements are separated from each other as well as from the original object. If this check box is selected, the elements are disconnected from the original object in one piece.

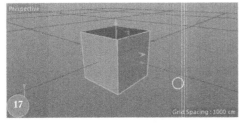 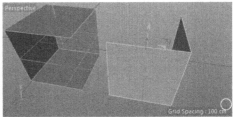

## Split
**Hotkey: U~P**

This command is little bit different than the **Disconnect** command. When you apply this command, the disconnected surfaces create a separate object leaving the original object unchanged. This tool can also be applied on splines. For splines, a point selection or **Points** mode is required.

## Collapse
**Hotkey: U~C**

This command collapses the selected points, edges, or polygons to a single center point. These points can be welded together, see Fig. 18.

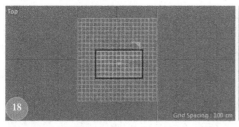
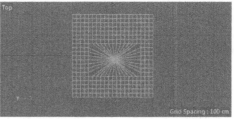

## Connect Points/Edges
### Hotkey: M~M

 This command works in the **Points** and **Edges** modes and connects points and edges, see Figs. 19 and 20.

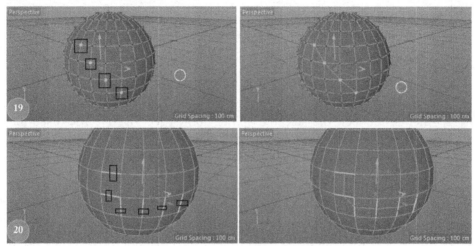

## Melt
### Hotkey: U~Z

 As name suggests, this function melts the selected points, edges, or polygons. Fig. 21 shows the melted point, edges, and polygons, respectively.

## Dissolve
### Hotkey: M~N

Use this command to delete selected edges. This command works similar to the **Melt** command. However, it deletes the unnecessary points as well. It is ideal for deleting the unnecessary edges created by the **Connect Points/Edges** command. When you delete the points the Phong angle is also taken into account. However, if you execute this command with **Shift** held down, it deletes all unnecessary points regardless of the Phong angle. In the **Points** and **Polygons** modes, this command exactly works like the **Melt** command.

## Subdivide
**Hotkeys: U~S, Shift+S**

 This command is used to subdivide polygon objects or splines, see Fig. 22. If no elements are selected, it subdivides the whole object. To define the subdivision level, click on the gear icon next to this command [or press **U**, followed by **Shift+S**], the **Subdivide** dialog box appears. In this dialog box, specify a value for the **Subdivision** parameter and then click **OK**.

## Triangulate

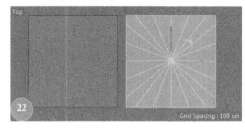 This command converts polygons into triangles, see Fig. 23. You might need this command if you are exporting mesh to an application that takes only triangulated geometry.

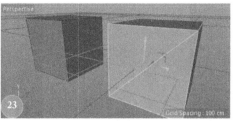

 *Note: Triangles*
*Generally, try to use quads as much as possible during the modeling process. Quads take less memory, they render faster, and produce better shading when used with the subdivision surface.*

## Untriangulate
**Hotkeys: U~U, U~Shift+U**

 If you are importing a geometry built only of triangles, you can use this command to convert the triangles into quadrangles. Triangles that cannot be converted into quads are left in their original state. You can specify the settings for this command from the **Untriangulate** dialog box that opens when you click the gear icon located next to this command. The **Evaluate Angle** check box in the dialog box lets you specify the angle using the **Angle** parameter, at which the resulting quad will be created between two triangles.

*Tip: Planar quads*
*Try to use a value like **0.00001** for the **Angle** parameter. When possible, Cinema 4D will create planar quads using this value.*

## Set Point Value
**Hotkey: M~U**

This command allows you to set values for the selected points. You can use this command to center, quantize, or crumple points. This command works on the polygon points, spline points, and FFD points.

## Spin Edge
**Hotkey: M~V**

 This command is used to spin the selected edges and then connect them to the neighboring two points, see Fig. 24.

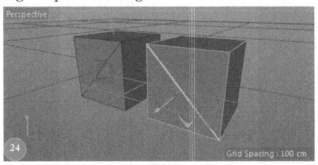

## Edge to Spline

 Use this command to create a spline from an edge selection, see Fig. 25.

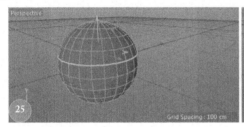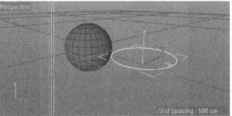

## Change Point Order

 A polygon is either a triangle or a quadrangle. A triangle has points A, B, and C whereas a quadrangle has four points A, B, C, and D. If these four points are not on the same plane, the quadrangle is a non-planar polygon. The **Change Point Order** command lets you change the order of the points of a polygon. For example, the **Matrix Extrude** tool orients itself to the coordinate system which refers to the order of the points A, B, C, and D.

## Optimize
**Hotkeys: U~O, U~Shift+O**

 When you create objects using the **Connect Objects** command, very often, some points and surface would be duplicated in the resulting geometry. You can use this command to remove these points. You can also apply this tool to spline points.

## Reset Scale

 You can use this command to restore the coordinate system of the object. You need to do this when the object's axes are not perpendicular to each other or have different lengths. Note that this type of issue occurs in Cinema 4D's versions prior to R12.

## Modeling Settings
**Hotkey: Shift+M**

When you select this option, the **Modeling Settings** section appears in **Attribute Manager**. From this section, you can specify various modeling settings such as **Snap** and **Quantize**.

## Create Tools Sub-menu

The following commands are available in the **Create Tools** sub-menu:

### Create Point
**Hotkey: M~A**

This tool allows you to add new points to the objects. There is no need to make a selection and this tool works in all three modes. To add a point on an element, move the mouse pointer over the element, the element appears highlighted. Click on element to add the point. If you don't release the mouse button, you can drag the point to change its position on the element. This tool also works with splines.

### Polygon Pen
**Hotkey: M~E**

The **Polygon Pen** tool is a super tool, it is more than just a polygon painting tool. You can use it to edit the existing geometry as well as use it as a replacement for other tools/functions such as melting points, moving and duplicating elements, minor knife functions, extruding, tweaking, and so on.

### Edge Cut
**Hotkey: M~F**

This tool allows you to interactively subdivide the selected edges, see Fig. 26. This tool works in the **Edges** mode only. You can also use the **Shift, Ctrl**, and **Ctrl+Shift** keys to adjust scale, offset, and subdivision, respectively. You can also set these properties numerically by specifying values for the **Offset, Scale**, and **Subdivision** parameters in the **Attribute Manager > Options** tab. When the **Create N-gons** check box in the **Options** tab is selected, N-gons will be created else triangles will be created.

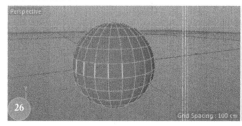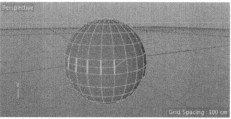

### Line Cut
**Hotkeys: K~K, M~K**

This tool has replaced the old **Knife** tool but if offers more features then the **Knife** tool. It can be used to cut polygon and spline objects. It works in all three modes: **Points, Edges**, and **Polygons**. There are many options available in the **Options** tab to control the behavior of the tool. To use this tool, click and drag to create a line or use multiple mouse clicks to create a line with multiple control points. The cut line will be projected onto the object to be cut. If you want to create additional point on the line, just click on it. The cut line will remain visible and you can edit it. Choose another tool or press **Esc** to complete the operation. You can choose the slice operation from the **Slice Mode** drop-down list available in the **Line Cut** tool's properties in **Attribute Manager**. Fig. 27 shows split operation performed using the **Line Cut** tool.

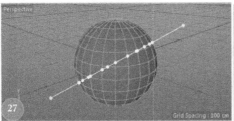
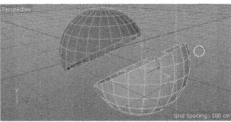

If you create a cut and switch to another view, cut points will be turned into the control points. The colored cut points can be grabbed and moved. The white cut points are automatically created when you cut the edges. You can adjust the colored points any time. The following scheme is used for colors:

- **Yellow:** Control points lie freely in space
- **Blue:** Control points lie on a polygon
- **Red:** Control points lie on an edge
- **Green:** Control points lie on a vertex
- **White:** Points of the cut line with edges

You can use the following hotkeys with this tool:

- **Shift+Click** on a newly created point to move a control point along the a straight section.
- **Ctrl+Click** on a point to delete it.
- **Shift+Drag** the start or end point to take the **Angle Constrain** setting into effect. The rotation will be quantized.
- **Shift+Ctrl** drag a point; the neighboring cut points will not move.
- You can also cut an object using a spline that partially overlaps the object that you want to cut. Pressing **Ctrl** and then clicking on the spline with project the line onto the object and cut it.

## Plane Cut
**Hotkeys: K~J, M~J**

This tool is particularly useful in architectural modeling. You can use it to cut along the surfaces of the planes even with when multiple objects are selected. Once a plane is cut, you can freely transform it. The line can snap to polygons, edges, or points. If you change the view, the plane will be replaced by a manipulator [see Fig. 28]. You can use this manipulator to freely transform the plane.

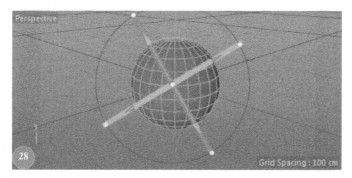

## Loop/Path Cut
**Hotkeys: K~L, M~L**

 This tool is primarily used to subdivide the edge loops interactively. It supports two modes: automatic loop selection [**Mode=Loop**] and manually created loop selection [**Mode=Path**]. Whenever you click on an edge, the HUD element will be activated in the viewport. The slider in HUD represents the length of the edge that you have clicked. It is represented by a green line in the viewport.

**Ctrl+click** on the slider to create a new loop cut. If you drag a handle with **Ctrl** held down, the corresponding loop cut will be duplicated. If you move the slider with **Shift** held down, the **Quantize Step** settings will be considered and handle will be snapped to fixed locations on the slider. The following hotkeys work in the viewport:

- **Ctrl:** Duplicates the cut.
- **Shift:** Uses the **Quantize Step** settings.
- **MMB:** Changes the cut count.
- **Ctrl+Shift+LMB:** Drag to left or right to control the bidirectional cut length.

## Bevel
**Hotkey: M~S**

The **Bevel** tool is a power tool in Cinema 4D. You can use this tool to change harsh edges and corners into flattened, rounded, and soft elements, see Fig. 29. This tool behaves differently in each mode.

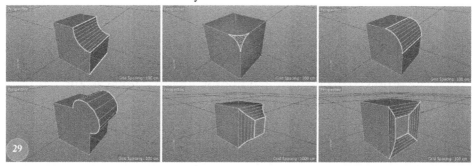

## Bridge
**Hotkeys: M~B, B**

This tool works in all three modes and allows you to create connections between the unconnected surfaces, see Fig. 30.

 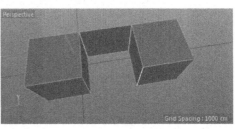

*Caution: Bridging Polygons*
*In the **Polygons** mode, first you need to select the polygons you want to connect.*

## Weld
**Hotkey: M~Q**

You can use this tool to weld several points on a polygon object or spline points to a single point. To weld points, select them and then using the **Weld** tool click on a point where the welded point will be placed.

## Stitch and Sew
**Hotkey: M~P**

You can use this tool to join edges with same number of points. It works in all three modes. However, it has some limitations in the **Polygons** mode. In this mode, most of the times, a polygon selection is required.

## Close Polygon Hole
**Hotkey: M~D**

This tool is used to fill a hole in a polygon mesh.

## Extrude
**Hotkeys: M~T, D**

This tool is used to extrude the selected points, edges, or polygons. If no elements are selected, it extrude the whole object. You can also interactively extrude in the viewport by dragging the mouse pointer to the left or right, see Fig. 31.

## Extrude Inner
**Hotkeys: M~W, I**

The functioning of this tool is similar to that of the **Extrude** tool, however, you can extrude polygons inwards or outwards. The object shown in Fig. 32 is created using a combination of the **Extrude** and **Extrude Inner** tools.

## Matrix Extrude
**Hotkey: M~X**

The functioning of the **Matrix Extrude** tool is similar to that of the **Extrude** tool, but with one difference; you can make as many extrusion steps as you want in one step, see Fig. 33. You can define the values for move, rotation, and size from the **Options** tab. You can also use **Shift, Ctrl**, and **Alt** to interactively set size, rotation, and directions values, respectively.

## Smooth Shift
**Hotkey: M~Y**

The **Smooth Shift** tool works similar to the **Extrude** tool. However, the value specified for the **Maximum Angle** value will be used to determine if new connecting surface should be created between polygons. Fig. 34 shows the initial selection of polygons and extruded polygons using **Maximum Angle** value of **71**.

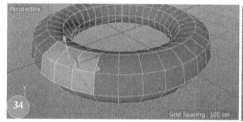 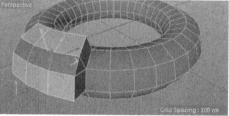

## Transform Tools Sub-menu

The following commands are available in the **Transform Tools** sub-menu:

## Brush
**Hotkey: M~C**

This tool works in all three modes. This tool allows you to deform polygon mesh and paint/edit vertex maps. When you select this tool a sphere of influence appears in the editor view. All points inside the sphere will be affected by the tool. You can interactively change the size of the sphere by MMB dragging in the editor view to the left or to the right. To change strength, MMB drag vertically.

## Iron
**Hotkey: M~G**

This tool behaves like a virtual iron and lets you smooth the uneven surfaces. The strength of the iron is controlled using the **Percent** value in the **Options** tab.

## Magnet
**Hotkey: M~I**

You can use this tool to pull sections out of polygons or spline objects.

## Mirror
**Hotkey: M~H**

You can use this tool to mirror points and polygons. It can also be applied on the splines. It works only in the **Points** and **Polygons** modes. You can also define mirroring axis interactively. To define the axis, click and drag in the editor view.

## Slide
**Hotkey: M~O**

This tool is used to move selected edges, and edge loops vertically outwards or inwards. To offset the edges, activate this tool and slide the selected edges. You can use the **Ctrl** key to create copy of selected edges. The **Shift** key is used to push edges inwards or outwards.

## Normal Move
**Hotkey: M~Z**

This interactive tool allows you to move the selected polygons in the direction of their normals. It works only in the **Polygons** mode.

## Normal Scale
**Hotkey: M~#**

This interactive tool allows you to scale the selected polygons in the direction of their normals. It works only in the **Polygons** mode.

## Normal Rotate
**Hotkey: M~,**

This interactive tool allows you to rotate the selected polygons in the direction of their normals. It works only in the **Polygons** mode.

## Weight Subdivision Surface
**Hotkey: M~R**

This tool is used with the **Subdivision Surface** objects. You can use it to weight subdivision surfaces.

## N-Gons Sub-menu

The following commands are available in the **N-Gons** sub-menu:

### N-gon Triangulation

**Hotkey: U~T**

While rendering and animating n-gons, Cinema 4D triangulates them internally. If you want to preview them in the viewport, select the **N-gon Lines** check box from the **Viewport Settings > Filter** tab. The **N-gon Triangulation** command is a toggle switch. When on, an n-gon will be internally re-triangulated each time you move any n-gon's points. When off, you can triangulate the n-gons manually by using command available in the **Mesh > N-gons** sub-menu.

### Retriangulate N-gons

**Hotkey: U~G**

See the **N-gon Triangulation** description.

### Remove N-gons

**Hotkey: U~E**

This command can be used to convert the selected objects' n-gons to triangles and quadrangles.

## Normals Sub-menu

The following commands are available in the **Normals** sub-menu:

### Align Normals

**Hotkey: U~A**

You can use this command to adjust and re-align the incorrect surface normals to the correct direction. The normals are used by Cinema 4D to recognize an object's inner and outer surfaces.

### Reverse Normals

**Hotkey: U~R**

You can use this command to reverse the normals of the object.

### Break Phong Shading

Use this command to break the phong shading.

### Unbreak Phong Shading

You can use this command to restore the phong shading.

### Select Broken Phong Edges

 This command selects all broken phong edges.

### Axis Center Sub-menu

The following commands are available in the **Axis Center** sub-menu:

### Axis Center

 This tool is used to quickly specify the object axis of a polygonal object. Choose this tool to open the **Axis Center** dialog box. Set options in this dialog box and then click **Execute** to set the object axis.

### Center Axis to

 The object axis will be moved but no geometry.

### Center Object to

 The object geometry will be moved along the axis.

### Center Parent to

 The object axis of the parent object of the object selected in **Object Manager** and its corresponding geometry will be moved onto the selected object.

### Center to Parent

The selected object's axis and its corresponding geometry will be placed onto the parent object.

### View Center

The object axis and the corresponding geometry will be moved to the center of the view.

## Working with Modeling Objects

Cinema 4D offers several modeling functions that provide some special modeling features. You can access them from the **Modeling** sub-menu of the **Create** menu. You can also access them from the **Modeling** command group of the **Standard** palette, see Fig. 35. The tools available in the **Modeling** command group and other related tools are discussed next:

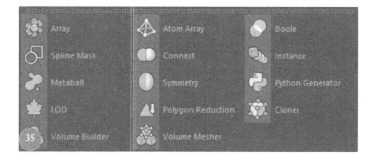

## Array

 This function is used to create copies of an object. The copied objects can be arranged in a spherical or wave form and are placed around the origin of the array object, see Fig. 36. The amplitude of the wave can be animated. The object you want to copy must be child of the array.

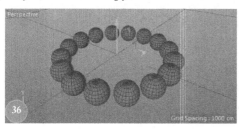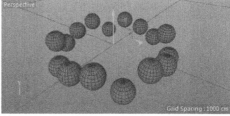

## Atom Array

You can use the **Atom Array** function to create atomic lattice structure from the child objects. When you apply this function, all edges are replaced with the cylinders and points are replaced with the spheres, see Fig. 37.

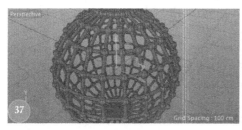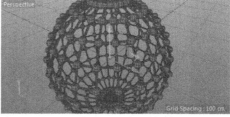

## Boole

This function is used to apply boolean operations on the primitives or polygons, see Fig. 38. You can also use this function on hierarchies. The two objects on which you want to apply this function should be children of the **Boole** object. The default operation for this function is A subtract B. Therefore, the order of the child objects is important.

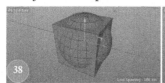

*Note: Boolean operations*
*You need to make sure the objects to which you want to apply this function should have closed volume and cleanly structured otherwise unwanted results may occur. Also, note that the higher the subdivisions of the objects, the cleaner the cut will be.*

## Spline Mask

This function is used to apply boolean operations on the splines. It produces best results when splines are smooth and all are in the same plane, see first two images in Fig. 39.

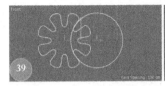

*Tip: Spline in polygons mode*
*You can display a closed booled spline shape in the **Polygons** mode, see the right-most image in Figure F39, by making it editable. To this to work, you need to select the **Create Cap** check box from the **Spline Mask's Object** tab.*

## Connect

This function combines separate objects using a defined tolerance. It also gives you ability to weld them together, see Fig. 40. To use this function, select all the objects that you want to connect and then press **Alt+G** to group them under a **Null** object and then make **Null** child of the **Connect** object. To smooth the connections, you can use a **Subdivision Surface** object.

## Instance

You can use this function to create instances of an object. An instance does not have its own geometry and it takes far less memory than the copied geometries. However, **MoGraph's Cloner** object is much more powerful than the **Instance** Object.

## Metaball

This function creates an elastic skin over the spline and objects points. You can use parametric objects, splines, and polygon objects with this function, see Figs. 41 and 42.

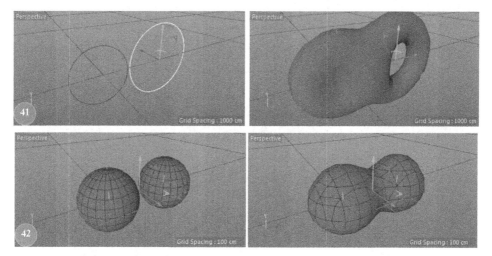

## Symmetry Object

If you are creating a model that is symmetric in nature, you only have to model half the model. The other half you can generate using this function. Only the part on which you applied this function will have the points. If you manipulate these points, the action will be reflected in the other part as well. This object works with geometry only, not with lights, camera, and so on.

## Python Generator

This function is used to enter **Python** code which can be used to generate the geometry.

## LOD

Some scenes can be very complex when they contain many objects with details. It is very rare that a camera would be able to depict all details of the scene either because the objects are not in the field of view of the camera or they are far away in the scene that the details can't be seen. In such cases, the LOD object helps in speeding the workflow in the viewport or for rendering.

If you want an object to be affected by an LOD object, you should make it child of the LOD object. Fig. 43 shows a **Cloner** object which is child of the **LOD** object. Notice in the **Attribute Manager > LOD > Object > Level -0- Cloner** area, the display mode is set to **Lines** and it is only affecting the **Cloner** object in the scene.

## Polygon Reduction

This tool is very useful in optimizing the models with the large number of polygons such as 3D scanned objects. It is often difficult to edit such models. This tool allows you to reduce polygon count of such objects by maintaining the original shape of the object to the highest degree. The object should be the child of the **Polygon Reduction** tool.

Fig. 44 shows a model before [Total polygons=11320] and after [Resulting polygons=4541] applying the **Polygon Reduction** tool. A value of **80%** used for the **Reduction Strength** parameter.

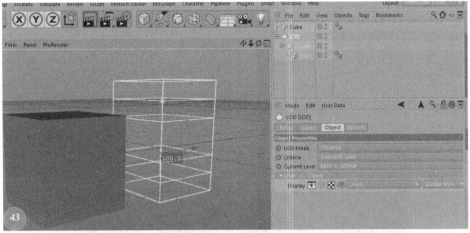

## Cloner

The **Cloner** object is a powerful MoGraph tool and used to create clones of an object(s). You can then arrange these clones in 3D space, onto vertices of other objects, onto splines, and so on. In order for the **Cloner** object to work, the object(s) that you want to clone must be a child of the **Cloner** object. Almost any element can be combined within MoGraph, which offers you endless creative possibilities.

## Volume Builder/Volume Mesher

These generators are discussed in detail in **Unit CM5**.

## Exploring Deformers

The deformer objects in Cinema 4D are used primarily to deform the shape of the primitive objects, Generator objects, polygon objects and splines, see Fig. 45. Unlike the objects that belong to the **Generators** and **Modeling** command groups, deformers act as children of their parents. A deformer will have no effect on the geometry if it is at the top of the hierarchy. It will affect its parent object as well as the hierarchy below that parent.

To add a deformer, select the parent object in **Object Manager**, hold **Shift** and then choose the desired deformer from the **Standard** palette > **Deformer** command group, see Fig. 46. You can apply multiple deformers on the same object.

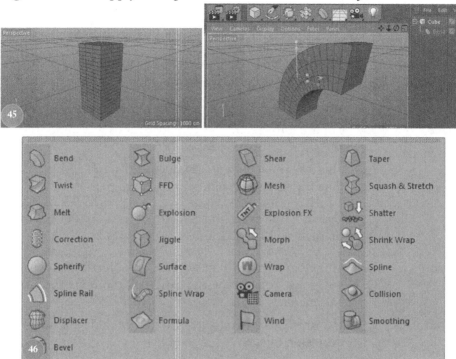

*Caution: Deformer Object*
*The* **Deformer** *object does not work in conjunction with the following functions in Cinema 4D:* **Explosion Object, ExplosionFX, Polygon Reduction, Spline Deformer,** *and* **Shatter Object**.

The following table summarizes the deformer objects available in Cinema 4D.

| Table 1: The deformer objects available in the Cinema 4D | | |
|---|---|---|
| **Function** | **Icon** | **Description** |
| Bend | | This deformer bends an object. You can drag the orange handle on the deformer surface to interactively control the amount of bend. |
| Bulge | | Use this deformer to make an object bulge or contract. You can drag the orange handle on the deformer surface to interactively control the amount of bulge. |
| Shear | | It shears an object. |
| Taper | | It tapers [narrows or widens towards on end] an object. |

| Table 1: The deformer objects available in the Cinema 4D | | |
|---|---|---|
| **Function** | **Icon** | **Description** |
| Twist | | It twists an object around its Y-axis. For smooth twist, ensure there are sufficient number of subdivisions along the twist axis. |
| FFD | | This deformer deforms objects using grid points. This deformer works in the **Points** mode only. |
| Mesh Deformer | | This deformer somewhat works like the **FFD** deformer. You can use it to create a custom low-res cage around the model and then deform freely. |
| Squash and Stretch | | This deformer allows to produce the squash and stretch effect that you see in the bouncing ball animation. |
| Melt | | Use this deformer to melt the object radially from origin [Y plane] of the deformer. |
| Explosion | | This deformer lets you explode an object to its constituent polygons. To animate the explosion, animate the **Strength** parameter. |
| ExplosionFX | | Use this deformer to quickly create and animate realistic explosion effects. |
| Shatter | | Use this deformer to shatter objects into individual polygons which then fall to the ground plane. |
| Correction | | This deformer allows you to access the points in their deformed state and then allows you to change the position of these points. |
| Jiggle | | You can use this deformer to create secondary motion for a character's motion. |
| Morph | | This deformer lets you blend in morph targets within the region of influence of the deformer. |
| Shrink Wrap | | This deformer allows you to shrink wrap the source object onto the target object. |
| Spherify | | You can use this deformer to deform an object into a spherical shape. |
| Surface | | Use this deformer to make an object follow the surface deformations of another object. You can use this tag, for example to quickly attach stitches to a cloth that is being deformed by a **Cloth** tag. |

| Table 1: The deformer objects available in the Cinema 4D | | |
|---|---|---|
| **Function** | **Icon** | **Description** |
| Wrap | | You can use this deformer to wrap flat surface onto a curved surface. |
| Spline Deformer | | This deformer takes two splines: original spline and modifying spline. It considers the difference in the position and shape of the two splines and then deforms the object accordingly. |
| Spline Rail | | It deforms the polygon objects using upto four splines. These splines define the target shape. |
| Spline Wrap | | This deformer allows you to deform an object along a spline. |
| Camera Deformer | | You can use this deformer to deform an object based on the grid overplayed on the camera view. |
| Collision Deformer | | This deformer deforms the objects using the collision interaction. You can think it as if a soft surface being pulled or pushed when it collides with another surface. |
| Displacer | | This deformer allows you to create effects like created by the displacement mapping. This deformer can handle RGB (XYZ Tangents). |
| Formula | | You can use this deformer and a mathematical formula to deform objects. |
| Wind Deform | | Use this deformer to create waves on an object. The effect of this deformer will be along the deformer's positive X direction. |
| Smoothing | | You can use this deformer to smooth a surface. It can make a surface behave almost like a cloth. It adds lots of flexibility to the modeling workflow when trying to model cloth objects. |
| Bevel | | The functioning of this deformer is almost similar to the **Bevel** tool. |

# Hands-on Exercises

## Exercise 1: Creating a Circular Hole in the Geometry
In this exercise, we will create a circular hole in the geometry [Fig. E1].

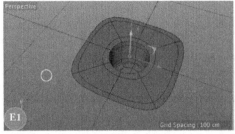 

The following table summarizes the exercise:

| Table E1 | |
|---|---|
| Difficulty level | Beginner |
| Estimated time to complete | 10 Minutes |
| Topics | • Getting Started<br>• Creating the Hole |
| Resources folder | **unit-cm4** |
| Units | **Centimeters** |
| Final file | **circular-hole-finish.c4d** |

### Getting Started
Start a new scene in Cinema 4D and set units to **Centimeters**.

### Creating the Hole
Follow these steps:

1. Click **Polygon** from the **Standard** palette > **Object** command group to create a polygon in the editor view. In the **Attribute Manager** > **Polygon Object** > **Object** tab, change **Segments** to **2**. Press **C** to make object editable. Press **NB** to enable the **Gouraud Shading (Lines)** mode.

2. Activate the **Points** mode. Select the four corner points and the center point. Press **MM** to connect the points and create edges [Fig. E2].

   ⊙→ *What Next?*
   *Now, we will bevel the center vertex to create a polygon. Then, we will delete the center polygon to create the hole.*

3. Select the center point. Press **MS** to invoke the **Bevel** tool and then bevel the selected edges. In the **Attribute Manager** > **Bevel** > **Tool Option** tab, change

**Offset** to **22** [Fig. E3]. Activate the **Polygons** mode and then select the center polygon. Delete the polygon [Fig. E4].

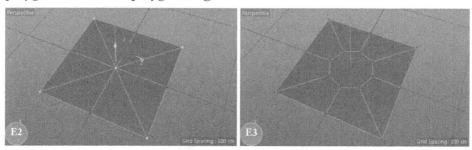

4.  Activate the **Edges** mode and then select the boundary loop [Fig. E5] and then extrude it down by using the **Ctrl** key and **Move** tool [Fig. E6].

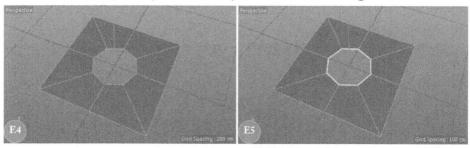

5.  Using the **Ctrl** key and **Scale** tool, create two inner extrusions [Fig. E7]. Activate the **Points** mode and then select point loop using the **Loop Selection** tool [Fig. E8]. Press **MQ** to activate the **Weld** tool and then weld the vertices at the center [Fig. E9].

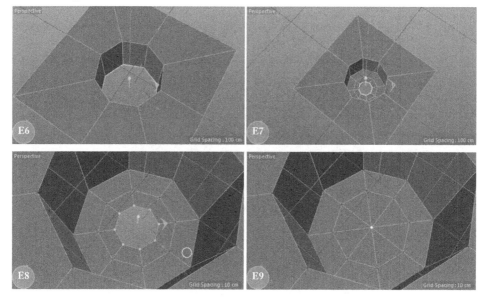

→ *What Next?*
*Now, we will select the edge loops and then we will bevel and chamfer them.*

6. Activate the **Edges** mode, press **UL** to invoke the **Loop Selection** tool and then select the loops [Fig. E10]. Press **MS** to invoke the **Bevel** tool and then bevel the selected edges. In the **Attribute Manager** > **Bevel** > **Tool Option** tab, change **Offset** to 1 and **Subdivision** to 1 [Fig. E11].

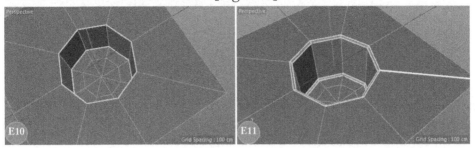

7. Activate the **Edges** mode and then select edges [Fig. E12]. Press **UZ** to melt the edges [Fig. E13].

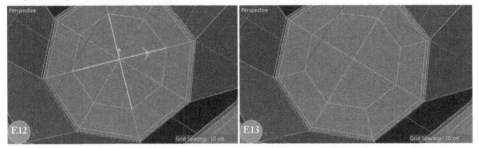

8. Choose **Subdivision Surface** 🔲 from the **Standard** palette > **Generators** command group with **Alt** held down to smooth the object [see Fig. E14].

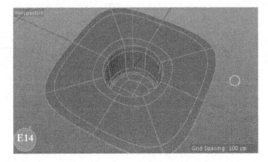

## Exercise 2: Creating a Cylinder with Holes

In this exercise, we will create a cylinder with holes [Fig. E1].

The following table summarizes the exercise:

| Table E2 | |
|---|---|
| Difficulty level | Beginner |
| Estimated time to complete | 20 Minutes |
| Topics | • Getting Started<br>• Creating the Model |
| Resources folder | **unit-cm4** |
| Units | **Centimeters** |
| Final file | **cylinder-holes-finish.c4d** |

### Getting Started
Start a new scene in Cinema 4D and set units to **Centimeters**.

### Creating the Model
Follow these steps:

1. Follow the steps 1 through 4 of the **Creating the Hole** section of the **Exercise 1**.

2. Activate the **Edges** mode and then press **UL** to invoke the **Loop Selection** tool and then select the edge loop [Fig. E2].

3. Press **MT** to invoke the **Extrude** tool and then extrude the loop inward [Fig. E3].

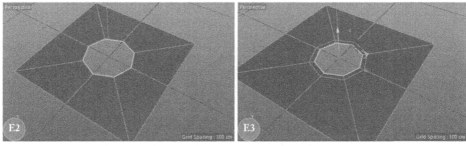

4. Activate the **Model** mode and make sure **Polygon** is selected in **Object Manager**. Choose **Arrange Objects > Duplicate** from the **Tools** menu. In the **Attribute Manager > Options** tab, change **Mode** to **Linear**. On the **Position** area, clear the Y and Z check boxes and then enter **100** in the **Move X** field. This action creates **8** copies of the **Polygon** object [Fig. E4].

5. Select everything in **Object Manager** and then right-click and choose **Connect Objects + Delete** from the popup menu. Activate the **Points** mode, select all points, and then press **UO** to optimize the object.

**What just happened?**

*Here, we have executed the **Connect Objects + Delete** command. This command connects the selected objects, create a new surface, and delete the selected objects.*

6. Activate the **Model** mode and invoke the **Move** tool. Press **L** to enable the axis. Press **Shift+S** to enable snap and make sure **Vertex Snap** is on from the **Snap** menu. Snap the axis, as shown in Fig. E4. Press **L** to disable the axis.

**What next?**

*Now, we will create few more strips and then we will use the **Bend** deformer to create the shape of the cylinder.*

7. Create a duplicate of the object, change its axis [refer to Fig. E5], as discussed in the previous step, and then align it [refer to Fig. E5]. Similarly, create few more strips [Fig. E6].

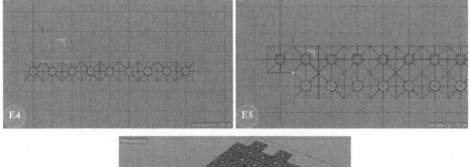

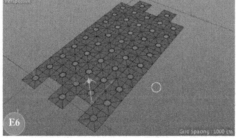

8. Select everything in **Object Manager** and then right-click and choose **Connect Objects + Delete** from the popup menu. Activate the **Points** mode, select all points, and then press **UO** to optimize the object.

9. Activate the **Model** mode and then rotate the object by **90** degrees [Fig. E7].

10. Choose **Bend** from the **Standard** palette > **Deformer** command group with **Shift** held down to attach a bend deformer to the object. In the **Attribute Manager** > **Bend Object** > **Coord** tab, change **R.B** to **90**. In the **Object** tab, change **Size** fields to **5, 1000,** and **500,** respectively. Change **Strength** to **400** [see Fig. E8].

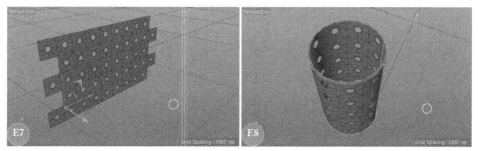

11. Select everything in **Object Manager** and then right-click and choose **Connect Objects + Delete** from the popup menu. Activate the **Points** mode, select all points, and then press **U** and then **Shift+O** to open the 1 dialog box. In this dialog box, set **Tolerance** to **0.03** and click **OK** to optimize the object.

12. Activate the **Polygons** mode and then select all polygons. Press **MT** to enable the **Extrude** tool and then extrude them outward by **8** units [Fig. E9].

13. Select the top and bottom edge loops of the cylinder [Fig. E10]. Press **MS** to invoke the **Bevel** tool and then bevel the selected edges. In the **Attribute Manager**, > **Bevel** > **Tool Option** tab, change **Offset** to **1** and **Subdivision** to **1**. In the **Topology** tab, change **Mitering** to **Uniform** [Fig. E11].

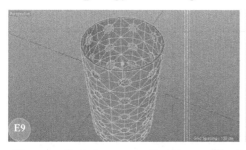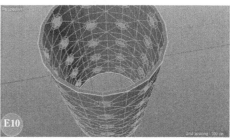

14. Choose **Subdivision Surface** 📦 from the **Standard** palette > **Generators** command group with **Alt** held down to smooth the object [see Fig. E12].

15. If you want to close the holes, activate the **Edges** mode and then invoke the **Close Polygon Hole** tool by pressing **MD**. Now, click on the border loops to close the holes [see Figs. E13 and E14].

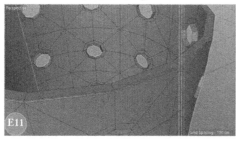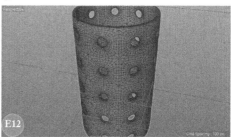

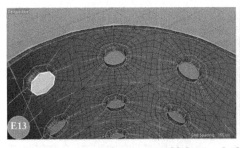

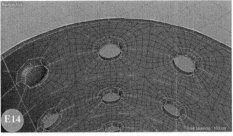

## Exercise 3: Creating a Solid Model

In this exercise, we will create a solid model [Fig. E1].

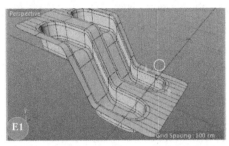

The following table summarizes the exercise:

| Table E3 | |
|---|---|
| Difficulty level | Beginner |
| Estimated time to complete | 20 Minutes |
| Topics | • Getting Started<br>• Creating the Model |
| Resources folder | **unit-cm4** |
| Units | **Centimeters** |
| Final file | **solid-model-finish.c4d** |

### Getting Started

Start a new scene in Cinema 4D and set units to **Centimeters**.

### Creating the Model

Follow these steps:

1. Click **Plane** from the **Standard** palette > **Object** command group to create a plane in the editor view. In **Attribute Manager** > **Plane** > **Object** tab, change **Width** to 150, **Height** to 200, **Width Segments** to 1, and **Height Segments** to 1. Press **NB** to enable the **Gouraud Shading (Lines)** mode.

2. Press **C** to make the plane editable.

3. Activate the **Edges** mode and then select the edge [Fig. E2]. Press **Ctrl** and drag the edge to extrude it [Fig. E3]. Extrude again [Fig. E4].

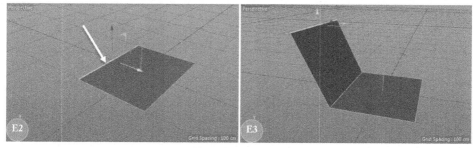

4. Press **UB** to invoke the **Ring Selection** tool and then select the edge ring [Fig. E5]. Press **MF** to invoke the **Edge Cut** tool. In the **Attribute Manager > Edge Cut > Options** tab, clear the **Create N-gons** check box and then change **Subdivision** to 4 [Fig. E6.].

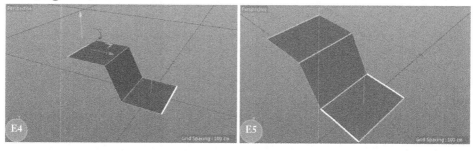

5. Select the edges [Fig. E7] using the **Move** tool and then scale them in using the **Scale** tool [Fig. E8]. Make a selection using the **Ring Selection** tool [see Fig. E9]. Now, press **MM** to connect the edges [Fig. E10].

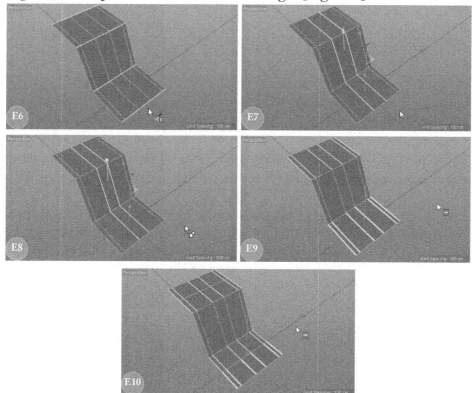

⊕ *What next?*

*Now, we will use the **Polygon Pen** tool to create arc from the edges. These arc will form the rounder corners.*

6. Press **ME** to invoke the **Polygon Pen** tool and then in **Attribute Manager**, select the **Create Semi Circle** check box. Now, press **Ctrl+Shift** and hover the mouse of the edge [Fig. E11]. When you see a semi circle, click to create the semi circle. Don't release the mouse button and then drag until tooltip shows **Sub:4** [Fig. E12].

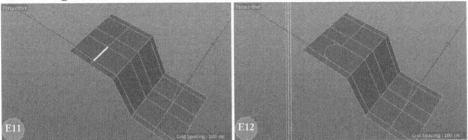

7. Similarly, create other semi circles [Fig. E13]. Notice that by creating the semi-circles, we have created n-gons. Let's convert them to quads.

8. Make sure the **Polygon Pen** tool is active. Click on a point on the circle and then click on the outer edge of the model to create an edge [Fig. E14]. Similarly, connect all four semi-circles.

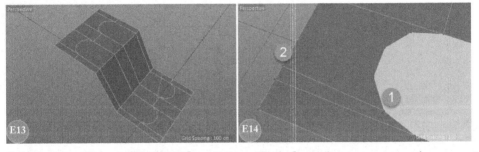

9. Select the polygons [Fig. E15] and then **Ctrl-drag** them to create the extrusion along the -Y axis [Fig. E16].

10. Press **UL** to invoke the **Loop Selection** tool and then select loops [Fig. E17]. Press **MS** to invoke the **Bevel** tool and then bevel the selected edges. In the **Attribute Manager > Bevel > Tool Option** tab, change **Offset** to **1.5** and **Subdivision** to **1**. On the **Topology** tab, change **Mitering** to **Uniform** [Fig. E18].

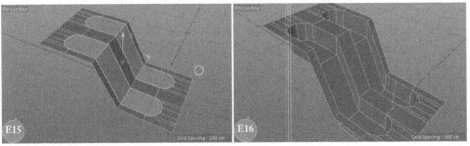

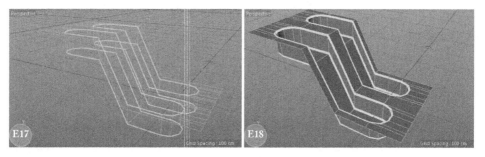

11. Press **KL** to invoke the **Loop/Path Cut** tool and ensure that **Mode** is set to **Loop** in **Attribute Manager**. Now, create two cuts [Fig. E19].

12. Choose **Subdivision Surface** 🔲 from **Standard** palette > **Generator** command group with **Alt** held down to smooth the object [see Fig. E20].

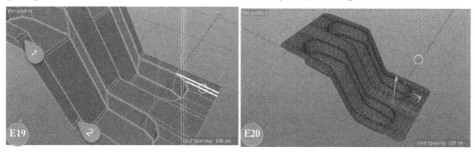

## Exercise 4: Creating a Solid Model
In this exercise, we will create a solid model [Fig. E1].

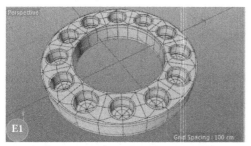

The following table summarizes the exercise:

| Table E4 | |
|---|---|
| Difficulty level | Beginner |
| Estimated time to complete | 20 Minutes |
| Topics | • Getting Started<br>• Creating the Model |
| Resources folder | **unit-cm4** |
| Units | **Centimeters** |
| Final file | **solid-model-2-finish.c4d** |

## Getting Started
Start a new scene in Cinema 4D and set units to **Centimeters**.

## Creating the Model
Follow these steps:

1.  Click **Tube** from **Standard** palette > **Object** command group to create a tube in the editor view. In the **Attribute Manager** > **Tube Object** > **Object** tab, change **Inner Radius** to **120**, **Outer Radius** to **200**, **Cap Segments** to **2**, **Rotation Segments** to **24**, and **Height** to **50**.

2.  Press **C** to make object editable. Press **NB** to enable the **Gouraud Shading (Lines)** mode.

3.  Activate the **Points** mode, select all points, and then press **UO** to optimize the object [Fig. E2].

    ⊖  *What next?*
       *We will first extract a part of the **Tube** object and then create a hole in the extracted part. Next, we will use the **Array** tool to create the complete circular geometry.*

4.  Activate the **Polygons** mode and then select the polygons [Fig. E3]. Press **UI** to invert the selection. Press **Delete** to delete the selected polygons [Fig. E4] and then press **UO** to optimize the object.

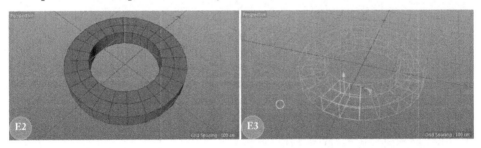

5.  Activate the **Points** mode and then select the middle point [Fig. E5]. Press **MS** to invoke the **Bevel** tool and then bevel the selected point. In the **Attribute Manager** > **Bevel** > **Tool Option** tab, change **Offset** to **29** [Fig. E6].

6. Activate the **Edges** mode and then select edges [Fig. E7]. Now, press **MM** to connect the edges [Fig. E8]. Similarly, connect other edges [Fig. E9].

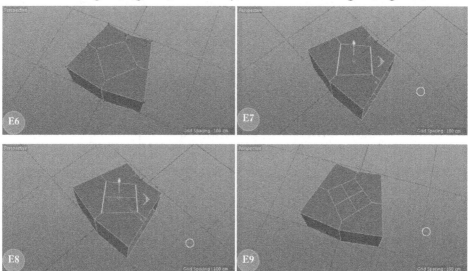

7. Activate the **Points** mode and then select the points [Fig. E10]. Using the **Scale** tool, uniformly scale the points to create a circular shape [Fig. E11].

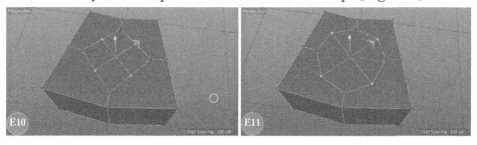

8. Press **ME** to invoke the **Polygon Pen** tool and then connect the points to get rid of the nGons and create quads [Fig. E12]. Activate the **Polygons** mode and then select and delete the polygons created using the **Bevel** operation [Fig. E13].

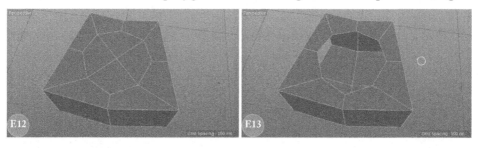

9. Activate the **Edges** mode and then press **UL** to invoke the **Loop Selection** tool. Select the loop [Fig. E14]. Using the **Move** tool and **Ctrl**, extrude the loop downward [Fig. E15].

10. Using the **Scale** tool and **Ctrl**, extrude the loop inwards twice [Fig. E16]. Activate the **Points** mode and then select the points [Fig. E17]. Press **MQ** to activate the **Weld** tool and then weld the vertices at the center [Fig. E18].

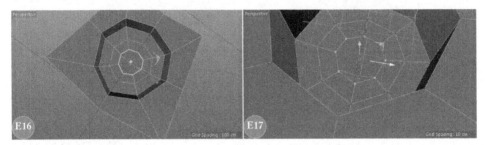

11. Press **UL** to invoke the **Loop Selection** tool and then select the loops [Fig. 19]. Press **MS** to invoke the **Bevel** tool and then bevel the selected edges. In the **Attribute Manager** > **Bevel** > **Tool Option** tab, change **Offset** to 1 and **Subdivision** to 1 [Fig. 20].

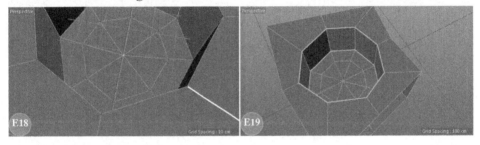

12. Choose **Array** from the **Standard** palette > **Modeling** command group with **Alt** held down. In the **Attribute Manager** > **Array Object** > **Object** tab, change **Radius** to **0** and **Copies** to 11 [Fig. E21].

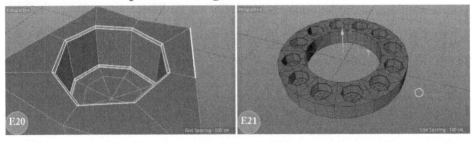

13. In **Object Manager**, select **Array** and then press **C**. This action will create **12** copies of the tube object and also group then under a **Null** object. In **Object Manager**, expand **Null** and select all objects. Now, right-click and then choose **Connect Objects + Delete** from the popup menu and create single object. Drag combined object out of **Null** and then delete **Null**.

14. Activate the **Points** mode and then select all points. Press **UO** to optimize the model. Activate the **Edges** mode and then select the boundary loops [Fig. E22].

15. Press **MS** to invoke the **Bevel** tool and then bevel the selected edges. In the **Attribute Manager** > **Bevel** > **Tool Option** tab, change **Offset** to **1** and **Subdivision** to **1**. In the **Topology** tab, change **Mitering** to **Uniform** [Fig. E23].

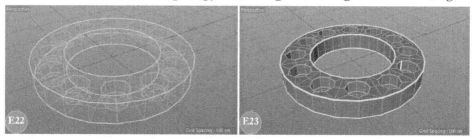

16. Switch to the **Model** mode. Choose **Subdivision Surface** 🔲 from the **Standard** palette > **Generators** command group with **Alt** held down to smooth the object [see Fig. E24].

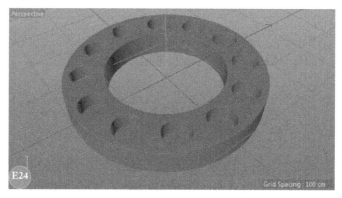

## Exercise 5: Creating a Solid Model
In this exercise, we will create a solid model [Fig. E1].

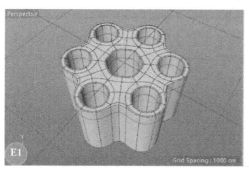

The following table summarizes the exercise:

| Table E5 | |
|---|---|
| Difficulty level | Beginner |
| Estimated time to complete | 20 Minutes |
| Topics | • Getting Started<br>• Creating the Model |
| Resources folder | **unit-cm4** |
| Units | **Centimeters** |
| Final file | **solid-model-3-finish.c4d** |

## Getting Started

Start a new scene in Cinema 4D and set units to **Centimeters**.

## Creating the Model

Follow these steps:

1. Click **Tube** from **Standard** palette > **Object** command group to create a tube in the editor view. In the **Attribute Manager** > **Tube** > **Object** tab, change **Inner Radius** to 140, **Outer Radius** to 200, **Rotation Segments** to 8, **Height** to 0, and **Cap Segments** to 1. Press **NB** to enable the **Gouraud Shading (Lines)** mode.

   ⊖→ *What next?*
   *Now, we will use the **Array** tool to create **5** more copies of the **Tube** object. Then, we will use different tools to connect these shapes.*

2. Choose **Array** from **Standard** palette > **Modeling** command group with **Alt** held down. In the **Attribute Manager** > **Array Object** > **Object** tab, change **Radius** to **460** and **Copies** to **5** [Fig. E2].

3. Press **Ctrl+A** to select all objects in **Object Manager**. Press C. Select all objects under **Array** null and then right-click, choose **Connect Objects + Delete** from the popup menu.

4. Drag **Tube** out of the **Array** and delete the **Array** object.

5. Activate the **Edges** mode and then press **ME** to invoke the **Polygon Pen** tool. Extrude the edges and then snap them to opposites edges using Ctrl-drag operation [Figs. E3 and E4]. Similarly, make all connections [Fig. E5]. Activate the **Points** mode, select all points, and then press **UO** to optimize the object.

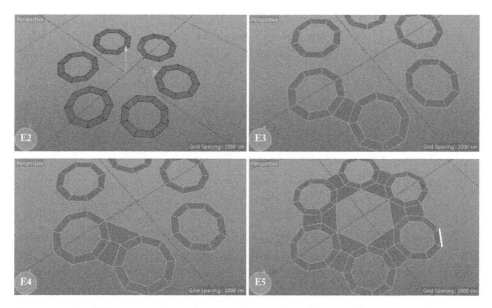

6. Activate the **Edges** mode and then select edges [Fig. E6]. Press **MM** to connect the edges [Fig. E7]. Similarly, make other connections [Fig. E8]. Activate the **Points** mode, select all points, and then press **UO** to optimize the object.

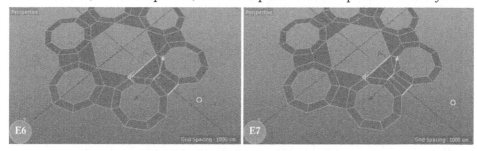

7. Select the points [Fig. 9] and then scale them in using the **Scale** tool [Fig. 10].

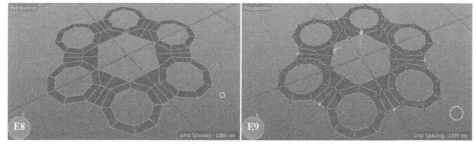

8. Activate the **Edges** mode and then select the edge loop [Fig. 11] and using the **Scale** tool and **Ctrl**, extrude the loop inwards [Fig. 12].

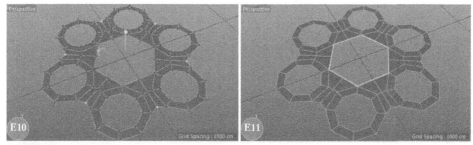

9. Select the edge loops [Fig. 13] and then extrude them down using the **Move** tool and **Ctrl** [Fig. 14]. Select the **Select Boundary Loop** check box in the **Attribute Manager** > **Loop Selection** > **Options** area for easy selection of the boundary loops.

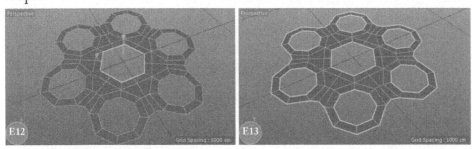

10. Select the edge loops [Fig. 15]. Press **MS** to invoke the **Bevel** tool and then bevel the selected edges. In the **Attribute Manager** > **Bevel** > **Tool Option** tab, change **Offset** to **5** and **Subdivision** to **1**. On the **Topology** tab, change **Mitering** to **Uniform** [Fig. 16].

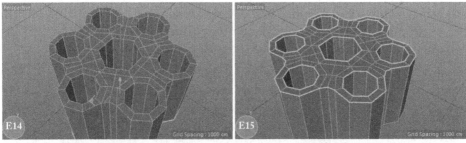

11. Choose **Subdivision Surface** 📦 from **Standard** palette > **Generators** command group with **Alt** held down to smooth the object [see Fig. E17].

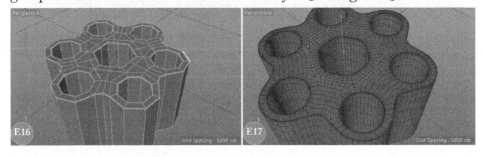

## Exercise 6: Creating a Serving Bowl
In this exercise, we will create model of a bowl [Fig. E1].

The following table summarizes the exercise:

| Table E6 | |
|---|---|
| Difficulty level | Beginner |
| Estimated time to complete | 20 Minutes |
| Topics | • Getting Started<br>• Creating the Bowl |
| Resources folder | **unit-cm4** |
| Units | **Centimeters** |
| Final file | **bowl-finish.c4d** |

### Getting Started
Start a new scene in Cinema 4D and set units to **Centimeters.**

### Creating the Bowl
Follow these steps:

1. Click **Cylinder** 🗇 from the **Standard** palette > **Object** command group to create a cylinder in the editor view. Rename **Cylinder** as **bowlGeo** in **Object Manager**. In the **Attribute Manager** > **bowlGeo** > **Object** tab, set **Radius** to **25.591, Height** to **13**, and **Height Segments** to **1**. Press **O** to frame the object in the editor view.

2. Press **NB** to enable the **Gouraud Shading (Lines)** mode, Fig. E2. Press **C** to make **bowlGeo** editable and then activate the **Points** mode. Select the top point, Fig. E3, and then press **Delete** to remove top part of **bowlGeo**.

3. Select the bottom point, Fig. E4, and then press **UZ** to melt the point to get a plane surface, Fig. E5.

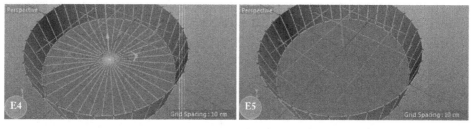

⊕ *What next?*
*If you move any of the bottom points using the **Move** ⊕ tool, you would notice that these cap points are not connected with the rest of the geometry. Now, we will fix it.*

4.  Undo the move operation, if any, and then click **Connect** ⬭ from the **Generator** tab with **Alt** held down to add make the **Connect** object parent of **bowlGeo**. In the **Attribute Manager** > **Connect** > **Object** tab, select **Manual** from the **Phong Mode** drop-down list. Ensure **Connect** is selected in **Object Manager** and then press **C** to convert it to a polygonal object.

❓ *What just happened?*
*The **Connect** generator connects the points of the cap area to the rest of the geometry. Notice in **Attribute Manager**, the **Weld** check box is selected by default. When selected, Cinema 4D welds the points using a tolerance value specified using the **Tolerance** parameter. Then, we converted the **Connect** object to an editable polygon object for farther changing the shape of the bowl.*

5.  Now, activate the **Polygons** 🔷 mode. Select the bottom polygon, Fig. E6, and then **Ctrl+click** on **Tools** palette > **Points** 🎯 to select the bottom points, refer to Fig. E7. In **Coordinate Manager**, enter **40** in the **Size X** and **Size Z** fields to scale the points, Fig. E8.

✏️ *Note: Live Selection tool*
*Press and hold the **9** key to temporarily enable the **Live Selection** tool.*

6.  Activate the **Polygons** mode and then select the bottom polygon. Press **MT** to enable the **Extrude** 🔷 tool and then in the **Attribute Manager** > **Extrude** > **Options** tab, enter **1** in the **Offset** field to extrude the polygon, Fig. E9. You can also extrude polygon interactively in the editor view by dragging the mouse pointer to the left or right.

7.  Press **MW** to enable the **Extrude Inner** 🔷 tool and then enter **1** in the **Attribute Manager** > **Extrude Inner** > **Options** tab > **Offset** field to extrude the polygon, Fig. E10. **Ctrl+click** on **Tools** palette > **Points** to select the points associated

with the previously selected polygon. Press **UC** to collapse the points, Fig. E11. Activate the **Polygons** ⬡ mode and then press **Ctrl+A** to select all polygons.

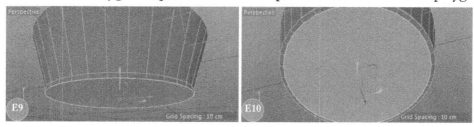

8.  Press **MT** to enable the **Extrude** ⬡ tool and then in the **Attribute Manager** > **Extrude** > **Options** tab, enter 1 [type 1 and then press **Enter**] in the **Offset** field to give thickness to the bowl, Fig. E12. In **Object Manager**, rename **Connect** as **bowlGeo**.

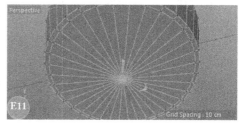

9.  Press **UL** to select the **Loop Selection** tool 🔲 and then select the loops, in the **Edges** mode, as shown in Fig. E13. Press **MS** to activate the **Bevel** tool 🔵 and then in the **Attribute Manager** > **Bevel** > **Tool Option** tab, set **Offset** to **0.1** and **Subdivision** to **1** to chamfer the edges, Fig. E14. Similarly, chamfer the bottom and inner edges, Fig. E15.

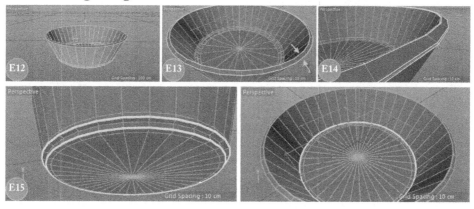

⚠️(?) *What just happened?*
*I have added some edge loops at the top and bottom of the bowl. It will help us to retain the shape of the bowl when we will apply smoothing to it.*

10. Activate the **Model** mode form the **Tools** palette. Now, choose **Taper** 🔵 from the **Deformer** tab with **Shift** held down to make the **Taper** object child of **bowlGeo**. In **Attribute Manager** > **Taper** > **Object** tab, set **Size X** to **25**, **Mode** to **Within Box**, and **Strength** to **-15%**, Fig. E16.

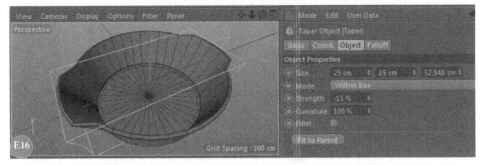

11. In **Object Manager**, create a copy of **Taper** object, Fig. E17 and then enter **90** in **Coordinate Manager** > **Rotation H** field, Fig. E18.

12. Ensure **Taper.1** is selected in **Object Manager** and then in the **Attribute Manager** > **Taper** > **Object** tab, set **Size Z** to **70**, Fig. E19.

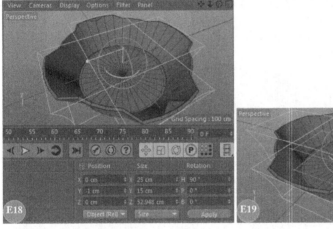
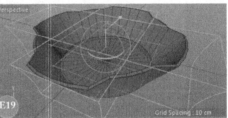

13. Ensure **bowlGeo** is selected in **Object Manager** and then choose **Subdivision Surface** 🔲 from the **Standard** palette > **Generators** command group with **Alt** held down to smooth the object.

## Exercise 7: Creating a Kitchen Cabinet
In this exercise, we will create model of a kitchen cabinet [Fig. E1].

The following table summarizes the exercise:

| Table E7 | |
|---|---|
| Difficulty level | Beginner |
| Estimated time to complete | 20 Minutes |
| Topics | • Getting Started<br>• Creating the Cabinet |
| Resources folder | **unit-cm4** |
| Units | **Centimeters** |
| Final file | **kitchen-cabinet-finish.c4d** |

## Getting Started

Start a new scene in Cinema 4D and set units to **Centimeters**.

## Creating the Cabinet

Follow these steps:

1.  Choose **Cube**  from the **Standard** palette > **Object** tab to create a cube in the editor view. Rename **Cube** as **cabinetGeo** in **Object Manager**. In the **Attribute Manager** > **cabinetGeo** > **Object** tab, set **Size X** to 38, **Size Y** to 76, and **Size Z** to **45**. Press **O** to frame the object in the editor view.

2.  Press **NB** to enable the **Gouraud Shading (Lines)** mode, Fig. E2. Press **C** to make **cabinetGeo** editable. Select the top and bottom polygons of the **cabinetGeo** and then press **UP** to split the polygons.

    (?) *What just happened?*
    *Here, I've applied the **Split** function on the selected polygons. As a result, Cinema 4D creates a new object from the selected polygons leaving the original geometry unchanged, Fig. E3.*

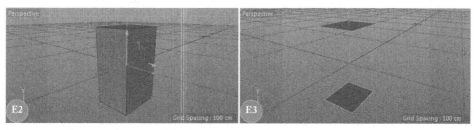

3.  Rename the newly created object as **topbotGeo**. Select the two polygons of the **topbotGeo** and then press **MT** to enable the **Extrude** tool and then in the **Attribute Manager** > **Extrude** > **Options** tab, enter **3** in the **Offset** field to extrude the polygons, Fig. E4. Now, select the polygon, Fig. E5, and then move it by **3** units in the negative Z direction using the **Move** ✛ tool, Fig. E6.

4. Select the top polygon and then extrude the polygon by 5 units using the **Extrude** tool, Fig. E7. Now, select the polygon shown in Fig. E8 and extrude it by 5 units along the positive Z direction, Fig. E9.

5. Select the edges of **cabinetGeo**, refer Fig. E10 and then press **MM** to connect the edges, Fig. E10. Select the polygons, Fig. E11, and then press **MW** to activate the **Extrude Inner** 🔷 tool. In **Attribute Manager** > **Extrude Inner** > **Options** tab, clear the **Preserve Groups** check box and then set **Offset** to 2, see Fig. E12.

6. Select the newly created polygons and then extrude them by **2.5** units, Fig. E13. Select all objects in **Object Manager** and then right-click, choose **Connect Objects + Delete** from the popup menu.

7. Press **Ctrl+A** to select all edges. Press **MS** to invoke the **Bevel** tool and then bevel the selected edges. In the **Attribute Manager** > **Bevel** > **Tool Option** tab, change **Offset** to **0.1** and **Subdivision** to **1**. In the **Topology** tab, change **Mitering** to **Uniform** [Fig. E14].

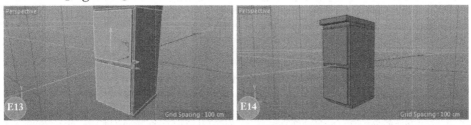

## Exercise 8: Creating a Book
In this exercise, we will create model of a book [Figs. E1 and E2].

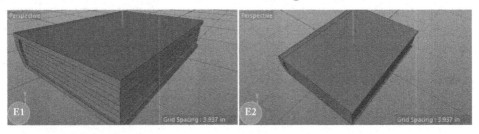

The following table summarizes the exercise:

| Table E8 | |
|---|---|
| Difficulty level | Beginner |
| Estimated time to complete | 20 Minutes |
| Topics | • Getting Started<br>• Creating the Book |
| Resources folder | **unit-cm4** |
| Units | **Inches** |
| Final file | **book-finish.c4d** |

### Getting Started
Start a new scene in Cinema 4D and set units to **Inches**.

### Creating the Book
Follow these steps:

1.  Choose **Cube** from the **Standard** palette > **Object** command group to create a cube in the editor view. Rename **Cube** as **bookGeo** in **Object Manager**. In the **Attribute Manager** > **bookGeo** > **Object** tab, set **Size X** to **7.44**, **Size Y** to **2**, and **Size Z** to **9.69**. Press **O** to frame the object in the editor view. Press **NB** to enable the **Gouraud Shading (Lines)** mode, Fig. E3.

2.  Press **C** to make **cabinetGeo** editable. Press **UB** to activate the **Ring Selection** tool and then select the edge ring, refer Fig. E4. Press **MM** to connect the edges. Select the newly created edge loop by double-clicking on it using the **Move** tool and then slide it towards the negative X axis, Fig. E5.

3.  Select the edge ring using the **Ring Selection** tool, Fig. E6. Press **MM** thrice to create new edge loops, Fig. E7. Select the polygons that will make pages of the book, Fig. E8.

4.  Press **MT** to enable the **Extrude** tool and then in the **Attribute Manager** > **Extrude** > **Options** tab, enter **-0.1** in the **Offset** field and **180** in the **Maximum Angle** field to extrude the polygons inwards, Fig. E9. In the **Front** view, select the

points shown in Fig. E10. Make sure the **Only Select Visible Elements** check box is cleared in **Attribute Manager**. Move the points, as shown in Fig. E11.

5. Similarly, move other points to make shape of the book, Fig. E12. Select the outer edges of the book, Fig. E13.

6. Press **MS** to activate the **Bevel** tool and then in **Attribute Manager > Bevel > Tool Option** tab, set **Offset** to **0.01** and **Subdivision** to 1 to bevel the edges, Fig. E14.

## Exercise 9: Creating a Waste Bin

In this exercise, we will create model of a waste bin [Fig. E1].

The following table summarizes the exercise:

| Table E9 | |
|---|---|
| Difficulty level | Beginner |
| Estimated time to complete | 30 Minutes |
| Topics | • Getting Started<br>• Creating the Bin |
| Resources folder | **unit-cm4** |
| Units | **Inches** |
| Final file | **bin-finish.c4d** |

## Getting Started

Start a new scene in Cinema 4D and set units to **Inches**.

## Creating the Bin
Follow these steps:

1. Choose **Cylinder** from the **Standard** palette > **Object** command group. In the **Attribute Manager** > **Cylinder** > **Object** tab, set **Radius** to 15, **Height** to 45, **Height Segments** to 30, and **Rotation Segments** to 50. Press **NB** to enable **Gouroud Shading (Lines)** display mode. Press **C** to make **Cylinder** editable.

2. Switch to **Polygons** mode. Press **UB** to activate the **Ring Selection** tool and click at the top of the cylinder to select polygons. Press **Delete** to remove the top polygons, Fig. E2. Press **UL** to activate the **Loop Selection** tool and then select top and bottom rows of polygons using **Shift**, Fig. E3.

3. Press **MT** to enable the **Extrude** tool and then in the **Attribute Manager** > **Extrude** > **Options** tab, set **Offset** to 1.2, Fig. E4. Ensure the newly extruded polygons are selected and then press **MS** to activate the **Bevel** tool. In **Attribute Manager** > **Bevel** > **Tool Option** tab, set **Offset** to 0.6. In the **Attribute Manager** > **Bevel** > **Polygon Extrusion** tab, set **Extrusion** to 0.6 Fig. E5.

4. Press **UB** to activate the **Ring Selection** tool and then select every alternate column of polygons using **Shift**, Fig. E6. Activate the **Rectangle Selection** ☐ tool from the **Selection** command group and then in **Attribute Manager**, clear the **Only Select Visible Elements** check box. In the **Front** view, remove two top and bottom loops of polygons using **Ctrl**, Fig. E7.

5. Press **MT** to enable the **Extrude** tool and then in **Attribute Manager** > **Extrude** > **Options** tab, set **Offset** to **-0.5**, Fig. E8. Press **NA** to enable the **Gouroud Shading** display mode. Hold **Alt** and then choose **Subdivision Surface** from the **Generators** command group to make the cylinder smooth, Fig. E9. In **Object Manager**, rename **Subdivision Surface** as **Waste Bin**.

→ *What next?*
*Next, we will create a lid for the cylinder.*

6. Choose **Cylinder** from the **Standard** palette > **Object** tab. In **Attribute Manager** > **Cylinder** > **Object** tab, set **Radius** to **17**, **Height** to **2**, **Height Segments** to **1**, and **Rotation Segments** to **50**. Press **NB** to enable **Gouroud Shading (Lines)** display mode. Rename **Cylinder** as **Lid** in **Object Manager** and then press **C** to make it editable.

7. Press **UB** to activate the **Ring Selection** tool and click at the bottom of the **Lid** to select bottom polygons. Press **MW** to select the **Extrude Inner** tool and then in the **Attribute Manager** > **Extrude Inner** > **Options** tab, set **Offset** to **1**, Fig. E10. Now, using **Extrude** tool extrude the polygons by setting **Offset** to **-1** in **Attribute Manager**, Fig. E11.

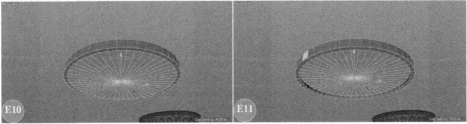

8. Select all points of the **Lid** in the **Points** mode and then press **UO** to optimize the **Lid**.

? *What just happened?*
*I have welded the points of the cap of the **Lid** with rest of geometry using the* ***Optimize*** *function. Now, when I will apply the **Bevel** tool in the next step, the whole geometry will remain intact.*

9. Select the edges loops shown in Fig. E12 and then press **MS** to activate the **Bevel** tool. In **Attribute Manager** > **Bevel** > **Tool Option** tab, set **Offset** to **0.2** and **Subdivision** to **2**, Fig. E13.

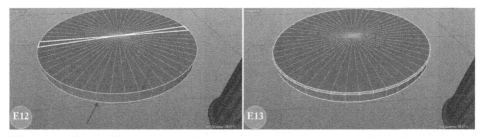

10. Using the **Ring Selection** tool, select the top polygons of the **Lid** and then press **MW** to select the **Extrude Inner** tool and then **in Attribute Manager > Extrude Inner > Options** tab, set **Offset** to **9.5**, Fig. E14.

11. Activate the **Move** tool and then move the selected polygon in the positive Y direction by **1** unit, Fig. E15. Press **NA** to enable the **Gouroud Shading** display mode and then align the **Lid** on top of the **Waste Bin**, Fig. E16. Now, we will create handle for the **Lid**.

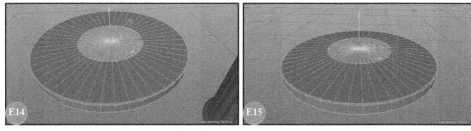

12. Choose **Torus** ⊚ from the **Standard** palette > **Object** command group. In the **Attribute Manager > Torus > Object** tab, set **Ring Radius** to **4.64**, **Ring Segments** to **50**, **Pipe Radius** to **0.84**, and **Pipe Segments** to **36** and then align it with the **Lid**, Fig. E17. Rename **Torus** as **Handle** in **Object Manager**. You can also use the options available in the **Slice** tab to create half torus and then align it with the lid.

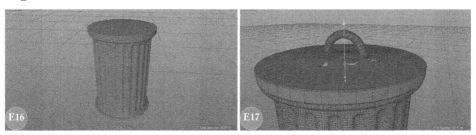

## Exercise 10: Creating a Desk

In this exercise, we will create model of a desk [Fig. E1].

The following table summarizes the exercise:

| Table E10 | |
| --- | --- |
| Difficulty level | Intermediate |
| Estimated time to complete | 30 Minutes |
| Topics | • Getting Started<br>• Creating the Desk |
| Resources folder | **unit-cm4** |
| Units | **Inches** |
| Final file | **desk-finish.c4d** |

### Getting Started

Start a new scene in Cinema 4D and set units to **Centimeters**.

### Creating the Desk

Follow these steps:

1.  Choose **Cube** from the **Standard** palette > **Object** command group to create a cube in the editor view. In the **Attribute Manager** > **Cube** > **Object** tab, set **Size X** to **60**, **Size Y** to **2.5**, and **Size Z** to **150**. Press **O** to frame the object in the editor view. Press **NB** to enable the **Gouraud Shading (Lines)** mode. Create another cube and then in the **Attribute Manager** > **Cube.1** > **Object** tab, set **Size X** to **60**, **Size Y** to **62**, and **Size Z** to **40**, Fig. E2.

2.  Select **Cube** and **Cube.1** in **Object Manager** and then choose **Arrange Objects** > **Center** from the **Tools** menu. In the **Attribute Manager** > **Center** > **Options** tab, select **Negative** from the **Y Axis** and **Z Axis** drop-downs. Click **Apply** from the **Tool** tab. Click **New Transform** from the **Tool** tab and then in the **Options** tab, select **Positive** from the **Y Axis** drop-down list to align the cubes, Fig. E3. Now, using the **Move** tool align the two cubes as shown in Fig. E4.

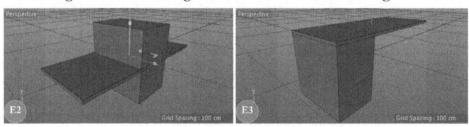

3.  Ensure **Cube.1** selected in **Object Manager** and then choose **Arrange Objects** > **Duplicate** from the **Tools** menu. In the **Attribute Manager** > **Duplicate** > **Duplicate** tab, set **Copies** to **1**. In the **Options** tab, select **Linear** from the **Mode** drop-down list. In the **Position** area, set **Move X**, **Move Y**, and **Move Z** to **0**, **0**, and **110**, respectively to align the duplicate to the other end of the table top, Fig. E5.

> **What just happened?**
> *Here, I've created a duplicate of the **Cube.1** using the **Duplicate** command and then offset it by **110** [150-40=110] units along the positive Z axis.*

4.  Press **Ctrl+A** to select all cubes and then press **C** to make them editable. Now, choose **Conversion** > **Connect Objects + Delete** from the **Mesh** menu. Rename the unified geometry as **deskGeo** in **Object Manager**.

> **What just happened?**
> *I've made all three cube primitives editable and then combined the result in a single unified polygon object.*

5.  Press **UB** to activate the **Ring Selection** tool and then select the edges [in the **Edges** mode] of the bases of the table using **Shift**, Fig. E6. Press **MM** to connect the edges, Fig. E7. Now, select the top rings of the bases, Fig. E8, and then press **MM** to connect the edges, Fig. E9.

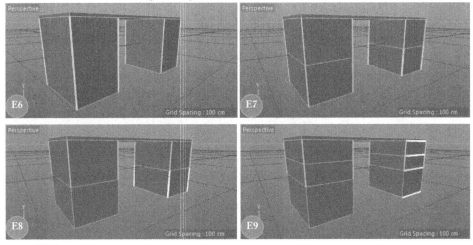

6.  Select the polygons shown in Fig. E10. Press **MW** to select the **Extrude Inner** tool and then in the **Attribute Manager** > **Extrude Inner** > **Options** tab, clear the **Preserve Groups** check box and then set **Offset** to 1.5, Fig. E11. Press **MT** to enable the **Extrude** tool and then in the **Attribute Manager** > **Extrude** > **Options** tab, set **Offset** to 1.5, Fig. E12.

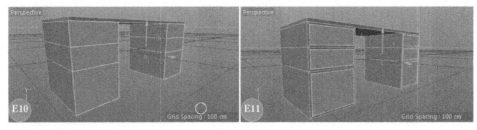

→ **What next?**
*Now, we'll create the keyboard support. To do so, we will place some edges using the **Plane Cut** tool.*

7. Activate the **Right** viewport and then press **MJ** to activate the **Plane Cut** tool. Now, click and drag to create two edge loops using **Shift**, Fig. E13. Now, select the polygons shown in Fig. E14 and press **UP** to split the polygons.

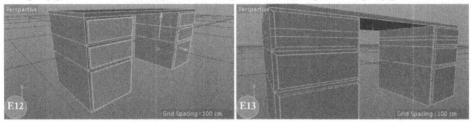

8. Rename the new geometry is **keyboardGeo** in **Object Manager**. Select the newly created polygons and press **MB** to activate the **Bridge** tool. In the **Attribute Manager > Bridge > Options** area, clear the **Delete Original Polygons** check box and then click and drag on one of the polygons to make a bridge between them, Fig. E15. Now, switch to the **Model** mode and pull out the keyboard little bit using the **Move** tool, Fig. E16.

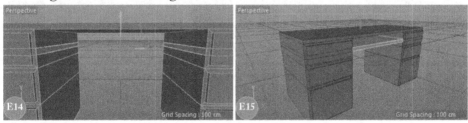

9. Press **Ctrl+A** to select all objects in **Object Manager** and then choose **Conversion > Connect Objects + Delete** from the **Mesh** menu. Rename the unified geometry as **deskGeo** in **Object Manager**.

> ✎ *Note: Cleaning the model*
> *You can remove the edges that we added for creating the keyboard support by first selecting them and then using the **Dissolve** [Hotkey: **M~N**] command.*

10. Select the polygon shown in Fig. E17 and then press **MT** to enable the **Extrude** tool and then in the **Attribute Manager > Extrude > Options** tab, set **Offset** to **2.5**, Fig. E18. In the **Edges** mode, press **Ctrl+A** to select all edges and then

press MS to activate the **Bevel** tool. In the **Attribute Manager** > **Bevel** > **Tool Option** tab, set **Offset** to **0.1** and **Subdivision** to **2**, Fig. E19.

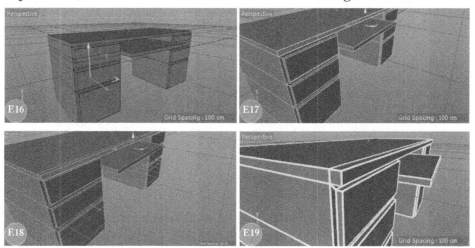

⊙→ *What next?*
*Now, we'll create knobs for the drawers using a cylinder.*

11. Choose **Cylinder** from the **Standard** palette > **Object** tab. In the **Attribute Manager** > **Cylinder** > **Object** tab, set **Radius** to **1.5**, **Height** to **6**, and **Rotation Segments** to **18**. In the **Caps** tab, select the **Fillet** check box and then set **Segments** to **3** and **Radius** to **0.074**. Press **C** to make the cylinder editable. Select the edge ring, shown in Fig. E20 and then press **MM** to connect the edges, Fig. E21.

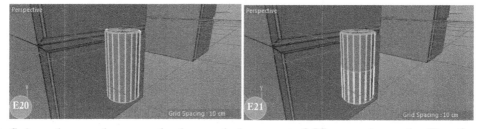

12. Select the newly created edge and then press **MS** to activate the **Bevel** tool. In the **Attribute Manager** > **Bevel** > **Tool Option** tab, set **Offset** to **0.05** and **Subdivisions** to **0**, Fig. E22. **Ctrl+click** on **Polygons** in **Tools** palette to select the newly created polygons. Now, interactively inset and extrude the polygons using the **Extrude Inner** and **Extrude** tools, respectively, Fig. E23. Make sure the **Preserve Group** check box is selected when you use the **Extrude Inner** and **Extrude** tools.

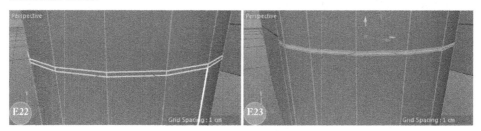

13. Ensure **Cylinder** is selected in **Object Manager** and then choose **Subdivision Surface** from the **Generator** command group with **Alt** held down to smooth the cylinder. Now, create copies of the cylinder and align them with drawers of the desk, Fig. E24. Similarly, create legs of the desk, Fig. E25.

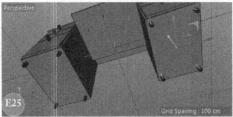

## Exercise 11: Creating an Exterior Scene

In this exercise, we will model an exterior scene using various modeling techniques [Fig. E1].

The following table summarizes the exercise:

| Table E11 | |
|---|---|
| Difficulty level | Beginner |
| Estimated time to complete | 90 Minutes |
| Topics | • Getting Started<br>• Creating the Scene |
| Resources folder | **unit-cm4** |
| Units | **Meters** |
| Final file | **ext-finish.c4d** |

### Getting Started

Start a new scene in Cinema 4D and set units to **Meters**.

### Creating the Scene

Follow these steps:

1. Choose **Cube** from the **Standard** palette > **Object tab** to create a cube in the editor view. In the **Attribute Manager** > **Cube** > **Object** tab, set **Size** X to **20**, **Size** Y to **8**, and **Size** Z to **60**. Press **NB** to enable the **Gouraud Shading (Lines)** mode.

2. Create another **Cube** object and then in the **Attribute Manager** > **Cube** > **Object** tab, set **Size X** to **14**, **Size Y** to **8**, and **Size Z** to **52**. Also, set **Segments X**, **Segments Y**, and **Segments Z** to **4**, **1**, and **14**, respectively. Now, align the **Cube.1** to the bottom of **Cube** [Fig. E2].

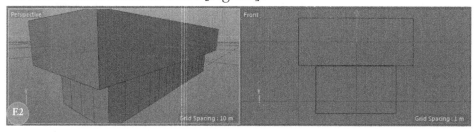

3. Choose **Filter** > **Grid** from the **MEV** menu to turn off the grid. Select **Cube** in **Object Manager** and then press **C** to make it editable. Similarly, make **Cube.1** editable. Select **Cube** in **Object Manager** and activate the **Edges** mode from the **Tools** palette.

4. Press **ML** to enable the **Loop/Path Cut** tool. Create an edge loop. In the **Attribute Manager** > **Options** tab, set **Offset** to **25**, Fig. E3. Now, select the front polygons, Fig. E4, and then press **MW** to select the **Extrude Inner** tool and then in the **Attribute Manager** > **Extrude Inner** > **Options** tab, clear the **Preserve Groups** check box and then set **Offset** to **0.6**, Fig. E4.

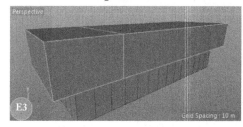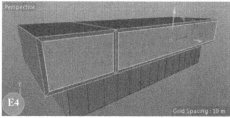

5. Press **MT** to enable the **Extrude** tool and then in the **Attribute Manager** > **Cube** > **Extrude** > **Options** tab, set **Offset** to **-5**, Fig. E5.

6. Choose **Cube** from the **Standard** palette > **Object** command group to create a cube in the editor view. In the **Attribute Manager** > **Cube** > **Object** tab, set **Size X** to **4.61**, **Size Y** to **6.827**, and **Size Z** to **0.602**. Align the cube, Fig. E6.

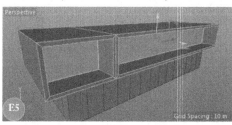

7. Make sure **Cube.2** is selected in **Object Manager** and then choose **Arrange Objects** > **Duplicate** from the **Tools** menu. In the **Attribute Manager** > **Duplicate** > **Duplicate** tab, set **Copies** to **39**, and **Clone Mode** to **Instances**. From the **Options** tab, set **Mode** to **Linear** and then in the **Options** tab > **Position** area, set **Move XYZ** to **0**, **0**, and **1.1**, respectively, Fig. E7.

8. Select **Cube.1** in **Object Manager** and then select the polygon shown in Fig. E8. Press **MW** to select the **Extrude Inner** tool and then in the **Attribute Manager > Extrude Inner > Options** tab, clear the **Preserve Groups** check box and then set **Offset** to **0.22**.

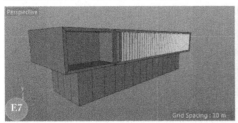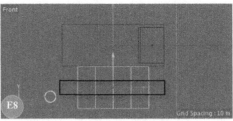

9. Press **MT** to enable the **Extrude** tool and then in the **Attribute Manager > Extrude > Options** tab, set **Offset** to **-0.25**, Fig. E9. Ensure polygons are still selected and then choose **Set Selection** from the **Select** menu to create a selection set. In the **Attribute Manager > Basic Properties** area, **glassSelection** in the **Name** field to name the selection.

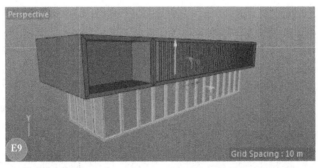

*What just happened?*

*Here, I've frozen the polygon selection. You can also create selection set for the point and edge selections. When you create a selection set, you can recall that selection later. For example, while texturing, if you want to apply glass material to these polygons, you can easily recall the selection by double-clicking on the selection tag in **Object Manager**. You can freeze more than **10** selections per object. However, many of the commands operate on the first **10** sets only.*

10. Choose **Plane** from the **Standard** palette **> Object** command group to create a plane in the editor view that will act as ground. In the **Attribute Manager > Plane > Object** tab, set **Width** to **600** and **Height** to **800**, and then align it as shown in Fig. E10.

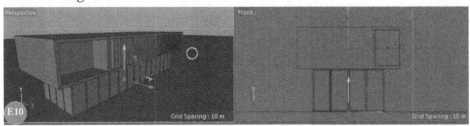

11. Choose **Cube** from **Standard** palette > **Object** command group to create a cube in the editor view. In the **Attribute Manager** > **Cube.3** > **Object** tab, set **Size X** to **36**, **Size Y** to **0.2**, and **Size Z** to **71**. Now, align it with plane, Fig. E11.

12. Choose **Rectangle** from the **Standard** palette > **Spline** command group to create a rectangle in the editor view. In the **Attribute Manager** > **Rectangle** > **Object** tab, set **Width** and **Height** to **12** and **48**, respectively. Select the **Rounding** check box and then set **Radius** to **4** and **Plane** to **XZ**.

13. Ensure **Rectangle** is selected in **Object Manager** and then choose **Extrude** from the **Standard** palette > **Generators** command group with **Alt** held down. In the **Attribute Manager** > **Extrude** > **Object** tab, set **Movement XYZ** to **0, 0.4**, and **0**, respectively. Now, align object with the ground plane, Fig. E12.

$\longrightarrow$ *What next?*
*Now, we will create the light pole.*

14. Choose **Circle** from the **Standard** palette > **Spline** command group to create a circle in the editor view. In the **Attribute Manager** > **Object** tab, set **Radius** to **0.5** and **Plane** to **XZ**. Now, align it, as shown in Fig. E13. Create three more copies of the **Circle** and set **Radius** to **0.4, 0.3**, and **0.2**, respectively. Align the circles, as shown in Fig. E14.

 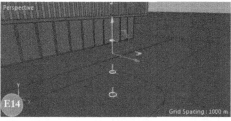

15. Choose **Loft** from the **Generators** command group. In **Object Manager**, drag all circle objects onto it to make them children of the **Loft** object, the pole geometry is created in the viewport, Fig. E15.

16. Choose **Cylinder** from the **Standard** palette > **Object** command group. In the **Attribute Manager** > **Cylinder** > **Object** tab, set **Radius** to **0.1**, **Height** to **3.168**, **Height Segments** to **1**, and then align it with the pole, Fig. E16.

$\longrightarrow$ *What next?*
*Now, we will create lights.*

17. Choose **Cube** from the **Standard** palette > **Object** command group to create a cube in the editor view. In the **Attribute Manager** > **Cube.4** > **Object** tab, set **Size** X to **1.39**, **Size** Y to **0.71**, and **Size** Z to **0.931**. Press **C** to make **Cube.4** editable. Select the points, as shown in Fig. E17 and then move them down, Fig. E18.

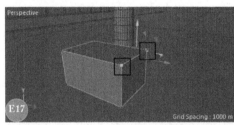

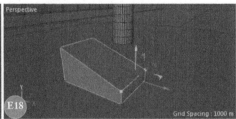

18. Select all polygons of the **Cube.4** and then press **MW** to select the **Extrude Inner** tool and then in the **Attribute Manager** > **Extrude Inner** > **Options** tab, clear the **Preserve Groups** check box and then set **Offset** to **0.04**. Press **UI** to invert the selection and then press **MT** to enable the **Extrude** tool. In the **Attribute Manager** > **Extrude** > **Options** tab, select the **Preserve Groups** check box. Set **Offset** to **0.018** and **Maximum Angle** to **180**, Fig. E19.

19. Ensure polygons are still selected and then choose **Set Selection** from the **Select** menu to create a selection set. In the **Attribute Manager** > **Basic Properties** area, type **lightCover** in the **Name** field to name the selection. Align **Cube.4** with the pole, refer Fig. E20. Create a copy of **Cube.4** and align it with the other side of the pole, Fig. E20.

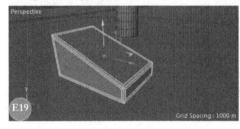

20. Select the **Loft, Cylinder, Cube.4,** and **Cube.5** objects in **Object Manager** and press **Alt+G** to group the objects. Rename **Null** as **Pole.1** in **Object Manager**. Make a duplicate of **Pole.1** and then rename it as **Pole.2**. Align **Pole.2**, as shown in Fig. E21.

21. Create main door of the building using **Box** and **Torus** primitives, Fig. E22.

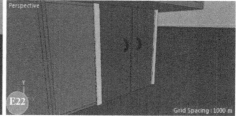

→ **What next?**
   *Now, let's create the logo of the company.*

22. Choose **Text** from the **Standard** palette > **Spline** command group to create a **Text** object in the editor view. In the **Attribute Manager** > **Text** > **Object** tab, set **Text** to **My Inc.** Choose a font of your choice from the **Font** drop-down list. Set **Height** to **3**. You might have to adjust the height as per the font you have chosen. Align text, as shown in Fig. E23.

23. Ensure **Text** is selected in **Object Manager** and then choose **Extrude** from the **Standard** palette > **Generators** command group with **Alt** held down. In the **Attribute Manager** > **Extrude** > **Object** tab, set **Movement XYZ** to **0, 0,** and **0.3**, respectively. In the **Caps** tab, select **Fillet Cap** from the **Start** and **End** drop-down lists. Set **Start Steps/Radius** to **3** and **0.05** and **End Steps/Radius** to **2** and **0.02**. Set **Fillet Type** to **Engraved**, Fig. E24.

## Exercise 12: Creating a Volleyball Model
In this exercise, we will create a volleyball model using the polygon modeling techniques [Fig. E1].

The following table summarizes the exercise:

| Table E12 | |
|---|---|
| Difficulty level | Intermediate |
| Estimated time to complete | 30 Minutes |
| Topics | • Getting Started<br>• Creating the Volleyball Model |
| Resources folder | **unit-cm4** |
| Units | **Centimeters** |
| Final file | **volleyball-finish.c4d** |

## Getting Started

Start a new scene in Cinema 4D and set units to **Centimeters**.

## Creating the Volleyball Model

Follow these steps:

1.  Choose **Sphere** from the **Standard** palette > **Object** command group to create a sphere in the editor view. Press **NB** to enable the **Gouraud Shading (Lines)** mode. In the **Attribute Manager** > **Sphere** > **Object** tab, set **Segments** to **27** and **Type** to **Hexahedron**. Press **C** to make object editable.

2.  Activate the **Edges** mode and then press **UL** to invoke the **Loop Selection** tool. Now, select the loop, as shown in Fig. E2. Press **UF** to invoke the **Fill Selection** tool and then select the polygons [Fig. E3]. Now, press **Delete** to remove the selected polygons [Fig. E4].

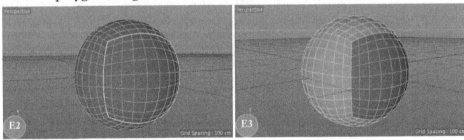

> **What just happened?**
> Here, I have first created a closed edge boundary selection using the **Loop Selection** tool and then applied the **Fill Selection** tool to the other side of the boundary. This tool allows you to create a polygon selection from an existing edge selection [**preferably closed**].

3.  Activate the **Model** mode and then choose **Mesh > Commands > Optimize** from the menubar.

*What just happened?*
When I selected the polygons and deleted them, Cinema 4D did not delete the points from the 3D space [Fig. E5]. The **Optimize** command allows to remove such left-over points and gives you clean geometry. You can also optimize edges and polygons as well. This command also works on the spline points.

 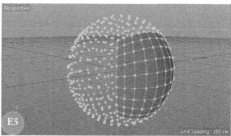

4. Activate the **Polygons** mode and then make a selection [Fig. E6]. Press **UD** to execute the **Disconnect** command.

*Why did we disconnect polygons?*
If you observe a real-world volleyball, you would notice that the volleyball is made up of 18 different patches. Disconnecting the patches will help us in selecting them easily when we will apply textures to them.

5. Press **MT** to invoke the **Extrude** tool. Now, on the **Attribute Manager > Extrude > Tool** tab, click **Apply** to apply a default 5 units extrusion to the selected polygons [Fig. E7].

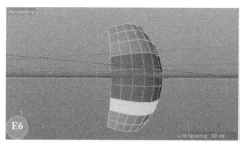 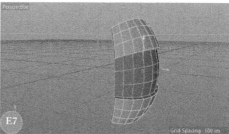

6. Make a polygon selection, as shown in Fig. E8 and then extrude by 5 units [Fig. E9]. Press **Ctrl+A** to select all polygons and then press **MY** to invoke the **Smooth Shift** tool. In the **Attribute Manager > Smooth Shift > Tool** tab, click **Apply**. In the **Options** tab, set **Maximum Angle** to 25 and **Offset** to 0.1.

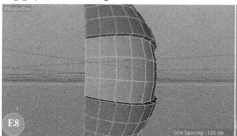 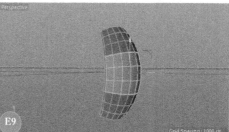

**What just happened?**

*Here, I have used the Smooth Shift tool which is similar to the Extrude tool. However, when you use Smooth Shift, the selected surfaces will be moved in the direction of the normals. The value of the Maximum Angle parameter controls if a new connection surface would be created between the polygons.*

7. Activate the **Model** mode and ensure that **Sphere** is selected in **Object Manager**. Now, choose **Subdivision Surface** from the **Standard** palette > **Generators** command group with **Alt** down to make sphere child of the **Subdivision Surface** object [Fig. E10].

8. Ensure that the **Subdivision Surface** object is selected in **Object Manager** and then choose **Mesh > Conversion > Current State to Object** from the menubar to bake the subdivisions into the sphere. Now, delete the **Subdivision Surface** object from **Object Manager**.

9. Press **NA** to enable the **Gouraud Shading** mode. Choose **Enable Quantizing** from the **Snap** menu or press **Shift+Q**.

**What just happened?**

*The Enable Quantizing option allows you to restrict the stepless motion to a defined grid. We will be creating copies of the existing geometry and then aligning them using the Rotate tool. The quantizing settings will allow us to rotate the geometry in fix increments. The default value for the rotation is 10 degrees. You can change this value from the Modeling mode page in Attribute Manager.*

10. Active the **Rotate** tool and then create and align copies using **Ctrl** [Fig. E11]. Now, select all objects in **Object Manager** and then choose **Mesh > Conversion > Connect Objects + Delete** to create a single object. Rename the object as **Volleyball**.

## Exercise 13: Creating a Shattered Abstract Sphere

In this exercise, we will create a shattered abstract sphere model using the **Explosion FX** deformer [Fig. E1].

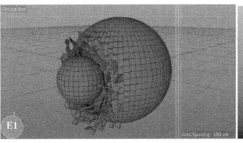

The following table summarizes the exercise:

| Table E13 | |
|---|---|
| Difficulty level | Intermediate |
| Estimated time to complete | 30 Minutes |
| Topics | • Getting Started<br>• Creating the Sphere |
| Resources folder | **unit-cm4** |
| Units | **Centimeters** |
| Final file | **abs-shape-finish.c4d** |

### Getting Started

Start a new scene in Cinema 4D and set units to **Centimeters**.

### Creating the Sphere

Follow these steps:

1.  Choose **Sphere** from the **Standard** palette > **Object** command group to create a sphere in the editor view. Press **NB** to enable the **Gouraud Shading (Lines)** mode. In the **Attribute Manager** > **Sphere** > **Object** tab, set **Segments** to **64**. Create another sphere and then in the **Attribute Manager** > **Sphere.1** > **Object** tab, set **Radius** to **50** and **Segments** to **32**. Place the spheres, as shown in Fig. E2.

2.  Select **Sphere** in **Object Manager** and then choose **Explosion FX** from the **Standard** palette > **Deformer** command group with **Shift** held down to make the **Explosion FX** object child of **Sphere**. Notice in the viewport the **Explosion FX** gizmo appears in the view and sphere is shattered into pieces [refer to Fig. E3]. Move the gizmo to see the effect.

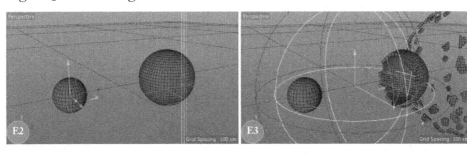

**?** *What are these elliptical concentric rings on gizmo control?*

*These concentric rings are controls that you can use to define various parameters interactively in the editor view. The innermost green rings control the **Time** parameters found in the **Attribute Manager > Object** tab. You can use this parameter to animate the explosion.*

*The red rings control the **Blast Range** parameter which is found in the **Attribute Manager > Explosion** tab. The objects that are outside the red rings [blast range] are not accelerated by the blast. The blue rings control the **Range** parameter which is found in the **Attribute Manager > Gravity** tab. These rings define an area in which the objects will be affected by the gravity. However, all objects inside the blast range defined by red rings will be affected by the gravity regardless.*

3. In the **Attribute Manager > Coord** tab, set P.Z to -245. In the **Attribute Manager > Object** tab, make sure **Time** is set to **10%**. In the **Explosion** tab, set **Strength** to **40**, **Decay** to **70**, **Variation** to **55**, **Direction** to **Except Z**, **Blast Speed** to **45**, **Decay** to **9**, and **Blast Range** to **180**.

**?** *What just happened?*

*Here, I've set the explosion parameters. The **Time** parameter can be used to animate the explosion. **Strength** controls the force used to accelerate the clusters. **Decay** sets a falloff for the Strength.*

*Variation controls vary the strength for each cluster. Here, **Direction** is set to **Except Z**. As a result, the acceleration of the clusters will be in all directions except the **Z** axis. The **Blast Speed** parameter controls the blast speed. A cluster remain in place until the blast reaches to it. The green rings in the editor view represent the blast. If you set this parameter to **0**, all clusters will be accelerated immediately. The blast speed is measured in meters per second. **Decay** is the falloff for the **Blast Speed**.*

4. In the **Cluster** tab, set **Thickness** to **2**, **Min Polys** to **1**, and **Max Polys** to **2**. In the **Rotation** tab, set **Speed** to **100**, **Decay** to **30**, and **Variation** to **10**. Also, set **Rotation Axis Variation** to **10** [see the effect of these values in Fig. E4]. Move

*What just happened?*
*Here, I've set the parameters for the clusters. **Thickness** extrudes the clusters in the direction of normals to give them thickness. If you want to reverse the direction of the extrude, enter a negative value for this parameter.*

*The **Min Polys** and **Max Polys** parameters define how cluster will be formed out of the object's polygons. If you want to create a cluster per polygon, select **Polygons** from the **Cluster Type** drop-down list. After setting the parameters for the clusters. I've changed values in the **Rotation** tab to give random rotation to the clusters.*

Now, you can texture the scene.

## Exercise 14: Creating a Chair

In this exercise, we will create model of a chair, as shown in Fig. E1.

The following table summarizes the exercise:

| Table E14 | |
| --- | --- |
| Difficulty level | Beginner |
| Estimated time to complete | 30 Minutes |
| Topics | • Getting Started<br>• Creating the Chair |
| Resources folder | **unit-cm4** |
| Units | **Inches** |
| Final file | **chair-finish.c4d** |

## Getting Started

Start a new scene in Cinema 4D and set units to **Inches**.

## Creating the Chair

Follow these steps:

1. Choose **Pen** from the **Standard** palette > **Spline** command group to create a shape in the **Front** view [Fig. E2]. Select the point, as shown in Fig. E3.

2. In **Coordinate Manager**, enter **9.886**, **0.086**, and **-10.75** in the X, Y, and Z fields of the **Position** parameter, respectively. Similarly, set the other points using the values shown in Table E2.1. After entering the values, the spline is shown in Fig. E4.

| Table E1.1 - Coordinates for creating points | | | |
|---|---|---|---|
| Point | X | Y | Z |
| 1st | 9.886 | 0.086 | -10.75 |
| 2nd | -9.886 | 0.086 | -10.75 |
| 3rd | -9.886 | 14.834 | -10.75 |
| 4th | 6.285 | 14.834 | -10.75 |
| 5th | 9.886 | 27.011 | -10.75 |

3. Choose **Circle** from the **Standard** palette > **Spline** command group to create a circle in the editor view. In the **Attribute Manager** > **Circle** > **Object** tab, set **Radius** to **0.4**. Make sure **Spline** is selected in **Object Manager** and then create a copy of it by **Ctrl** dragging it in the editor view about **21** units along the Z axis [Fig. E5].

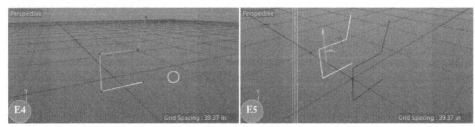

4. Choose **Pen** from the **Standard** palette > **Spline** command group and then connect the two splines [Fig. E6]. Press **UO** to optimize the spline. Select the points shown in Fig. E7.

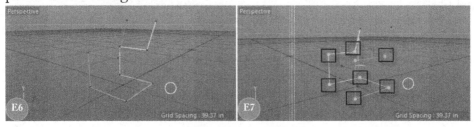

5. RMB click and choose **Chamfer** from the popup menu. Chamfer the points

[Fig. E8]. Now, using the **Circle** and **Sweep** generators, create the frame of the chair [Fig. E9]. Rename **Sweep** as **Frame** in **Object Manager**.

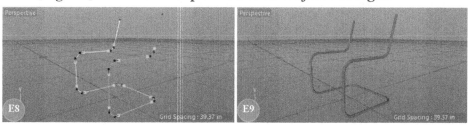

6.  Create caps for frame using the **Tube** primitive [Fig. E10]. Select all objects in **Object Manager** and then press **Alt+G** to group them. Rename the group as **frameGrp**. Now, we'll create seat for the chair.

7.  Choose **Cube** from the **Standard** palette > **Object** command group to create a cube in the editor view. In the **Attribute Manager** > **Cube** > **Object** tab, set **Size** X to **14.152**, **Size** Y to **2.5**, and **Size** Z to **24.283**, respectively. Also, set the **Segment** X, **Segment** Y, and **Segment** Z to **4**, **3**, and **4**, respectively. Align the **Cube** with the frame [Fig. E11].

8.  Add a **Subdivision Surface** generator to the **Cube** to smooth it. Now, press **C** to make the **Subdivision Surface** generator editable. Rename the object as **Seat** in **Object Manager**. Now, we'll create piping on the seat. Using the **Loop Selection** tool, select two edges as shown in Fig. E12.

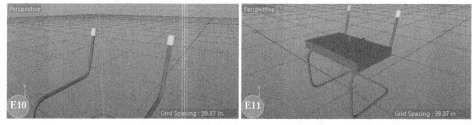

9.  Choose **Commands** > **Edge to Spline** from the **Mesh** menu to create spline from the selected edges. Select **Seat.Spline** in **Object Manager** and drag it out of the **Seat** group to the top level [Fig. E13].

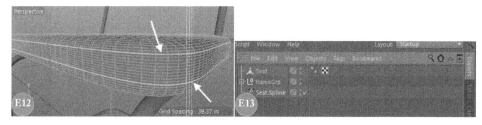

10. Create a copy of the **Circle** that you we created earlier and then set its **Radius** to **0.1**. Create piping geometry by using the **Sweep** generator [Fig. E14]. Use the commands available in the **Mesh** > **Conversion** menu to connect the elements and to make a single editable object for the seat and piping. Rename the object as **Seat** in **Object Manager** [Fig. E15]. Make sure **seat** is selected in **Object**

**Manager** and then center the axis on the seat using the **L** key, if not already at the center. Press **L** again.

11. Add a **FFD** deformer to the seat. Select the middle points of **FFD** and then move them along the negative **Y** axis to create a bend in the seat [Fig. E16]. Convert seat to a single object using the **Current State to Object** command. Delete the **Seat** object connected to the **FFD** deformer.

12. Create the back support of the chair, create a copy of the seat, and then align it with the frame. If required, scale down the height of the back support [Fig. E17]. Select everything in **Object Manager** and then group the object as **Chair**.

## Exercise 15: Creating a Chair

In this exercise, we will create a chair using the spline and polygon modeling techniques [Fig. E1].

The following table summarizes the exercise:

| Table E15 | |
| --- | --- |
| Difficulty level | Beginner |
| Estimated time to complete | 45 Minutes |

| Table E15 | |
|---|---|
| Topics | • Getting Started<br>• Creating the Chair |
| Resources folder | **unit-cm4** |
| Units | **Inches** |
| Final file | **chair-2-finish.c4d** |

## Getting Started

Start a new scene in Cinema 4D and set units to **Inches**.

## Creating the Chair

We'll first create a cube that will work like a template that will help us in the modeling process. Follow these steps:

1. Choose **Cube** from the **Standard** palette > **Object** command group to create a cube in the editor view. In the **Attribute Manager** > **Cube** > **Object** tab, set **Size X** to **20**, **Size Y** to **30**, and **Size Z** to **20**.

2. Set **Segment X**, **Segment Y**, and **Segment Z** to **4**, **2**, and **4**, respectively. Press **O** to frame the object in the editor view. Press **NB** to enable the **Gouraud Shading (Lines)** mode, Fig. E2.

3. Press **Shift+S** to enable snapping and then choose **Pen** from the **Standard** palette. Now, create a rectangular spline by clicking on the four corners of the lower half of the cube [Fig. E3].

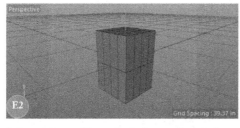
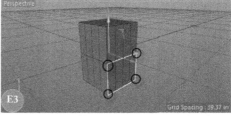

4. Move the spline slightly to the right of the cube so that it is visible clearly. Select the two top points and then chamfer them using the **Chamfer** tool [Fig. E4]. Also, chamfer the bottom points [Fig. E5].

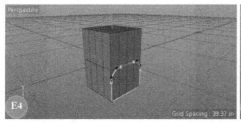
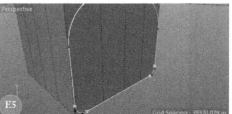

5. Create a circle of radius **0.3** and then create the frame of the chair using the **Sweep** generator [Fig. E6]. Create a cube and then set its **Size X** to **2.6**, **Size Y** to **1**, and **Size Z** to **1.5**. Also, select the **Fillet** check box and then set **Fillet Radius** to 0.3. Align, it with the bottom of the frame [Fig. E7]. Create copy of the cube and then align it as shown in Fig. E7.

6. Select everything in **Object Manager** except **Cube** and then press **Alt+G** to group the objects. Rename the group as **Frame.1**. Create a copy of the **Frame.1** and align it with the other side of the **Cube** [Fig. E8]. Hide **Cube**.

⊙ *What next?*
*Now, we will create the seat and back support.*

7. Create a plane and then in **Attribute Manager**, set **Width, Height, Width Segments**, and **Height Segments** to **23, 20, 1**, and **1**, respectively. Align the plane with the frame [Fig. E9].

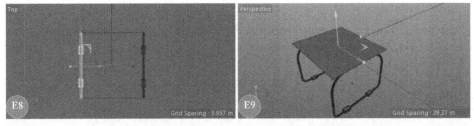

8. Make the plane editable by pressing **C**. Select the edge [Fig. E10] and then drag it upward about **15** units with the **Ctrl** held down to create the back support [Fig. E10]. Similarly, extrude the front edge using **Ctrl** [Fig. E11].

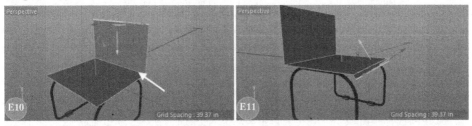

9. Select the edge [Fig. E12] and then bevel it using the **Bevel** tool [Fig. E13].

10. Use the value **1** for **Offset** and **3** for **Subdivision** in the **Attribute Manager > Bevel > Tool Option** tab. Create edge loops using the **Loop/Path Cut** tool [Fig. E14].

11. Select the edge ring, as shown in Fig. E15 and then press **MM** three times to connect the edges [Fig. E16]. Select all polygons of the **Plane** and then extrude them by **0.169** units using the **Extrude** tool [Fig. E17].

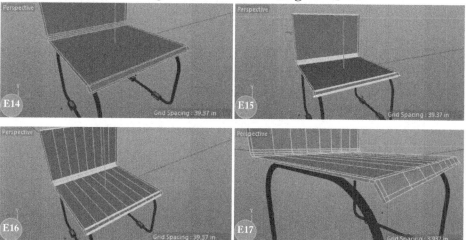

12. Now, you need to create a bend in the seat and back support using the **FFD** deformer. Finally, add a **Subdivision Surface** generator to smooth the chair [Fig. E18].

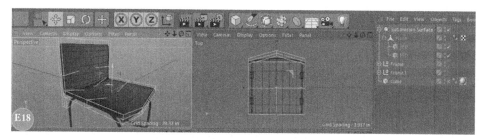

13. Delete **Cube** from the scene. In **Object Manager**, select all objects and press **Alt+G** to group them. Rename the group as **Chair**. Connect an **Array** object with **Chair**. In the **Attribute Manager > Array Object > Object** tab, set **Radius** and **Copies** parameters as required.

## Exercise 16: Creating an Abstract Shape Using the Metaball Object

In this exercise, we will create an abstract shape using the **Metaball** object and **Metaball** tag [Fig. E1].

The following table summarizes the exercise:

| Table E16 | |
|---|---|
| Difficulty level | Beginner |
| Estimated time to complete | 15 Minutes |
| Topics | • Getting Started<br>• Creating the Shape |
| Resources folder | **unit-cm4** |
| Units | **Centimeters** |
| Final file | **abs-meta-finish.c4d** |

## Getting Started
Start a new scene in Cinema 4D and change units to **Centimeters**.

## Creating the Shape
Follow these steps:

1. Choose **Sphere** from the **Standard** palette > **Object** tab to create a sphere in the editor view. In the **Attribute Manager** > **Sphere** > **Object** tab, change **Radius** to **1000** and **Segments** to **4**. Also, change **Type** to **Icosahedron**. Press **O** to frame the object [see Fig. E2].

2. Press **C** to make **Sphere** editable. Activate the **Edges** mode and then press **Ctrl+A** to select all edges. Now, choose **Commands** > **Edge to Spline** from **Mesh** menu to create spline. In **Object Manager**, drag the spline out of the **Sphere** group and rename it as **Spline**. Also, delete or hide the **Sphere** object [see Fig. E3].

3. Choose **Metaball** from **Standard** palette > **Modeling** command group with **Alt** held down to connect it with **Spline**.

4. In the **Attribute Manager > Object** tab, change **Hull Value** to **500, Editor Subdivision** to **15**, and **Render Subdivisions** to **15** [see Fig. E4]. Now, select the **Exponential Falloff** check box [see Fig. E5].

> **What just happened?**
> The **Metaball** object allows you to create an elastic skin that you can stretch over splines or object points. You can create the skin also referred to as hull by making the object child of metaball object. The **Hull Value** parameter defines how highly the hull or skin is applied. The **Editor Subdivision** and **Render Subdivision** parameters define the number of subdivisions that are displayed in the viewport and that are rendered, respectively. These settings are defined as distance units. The lower the value you specify, the higher the subdivisions will be.
>
> The default force of attraction between the spheres is like gravity and you can change this behavior by selecting the **Exponential Falloff** check box. On doing so, the attraction occurs at shorter distances and more abruptly. Compare Figs. E4 and E5. Fig. E5 shows the result when the **Exponential Falloff** check box is selected.

5. Select **Spline** in **Object Manager** and then RMB click. Now, choose **Cinema 4D Tags > Metaball** from the popup menu to apply the tag to **Spline**.

6. In the **Attribute Manager > Tag** tag, change **Strength** to **110%** and **Radius** to **50** [see Fig. E6].

7. Select **Metaball** object and then on the **Attribute Manager > Object** tab, change **Hull Value** to **900** [see Fig. E7].

 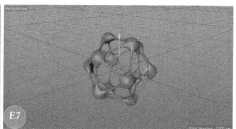

8. In the **Attribute Manager** > **Object** tab, select the **Accurate Normals** check box. See the result in the render or editor view [see Fig. E8].

> **What just happened?**
> The **Accurate Normals** check box produces internally calculated correct vertex normals. As a result, more even shading is produced.

## Quiz

Evaluate your skills to see how many questions you can answer correctly.

**Multiple Choice**
Answer the following questions:

1. Which of the following key combinations is used to invert the current selection?

   [A] UI            [B] UX
   [C] UJ            [D] UK

2. Which of the following key combinations is used to select all points, edges, or polygons connected to the selected element?

   [A] UX            [B] UW
   [C] UJ            [D] UK

3. Which of the following tools allows you to create connections between the unconnected surfaces?

   [A] Connect       [B] Bridge
   [C] Loft          [D] Sweep
4. Which of the following keys is associated with the **Extrude** tool?

   [A] D             [B] E
   [C] I             [D] H

**Fill in the Blanks**
Fill in the blanks in each of the following statements:

1. Cinema 4D provides three modes for polygonal modeling: _____, _____, and _____.

2. To make a polygon object editable, press _____.

3. You can use the _____ command to store selection sets and then recall them later.

**True or False**

State whether each of the following is true or false:

1. The tools and commands available in the **Select** menu are also available in the U hidden menu.

2. The **Path Selection** tool works only in the **Polygons** mode.

**Summary**

This unit covered the following topics:

- Polygons components
- Polygon modeling techniques
- Selection tools
- Polygons structure tools
- Modeling Objects
- Deformers

This page is intentionally left blank

# Unit CMP: Practice Activities [Modeling]

## Practice Activities

### Activity 1

Create a model of a road side sign [see Fig. A1].

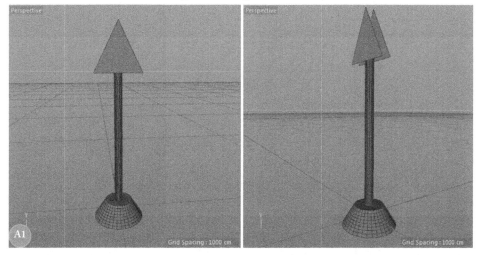

*Hint*
*Create the model using the* **Cone**, **Cylinder**, *and* **Polygon** *primitive objects.*

### Activity 2

Create a robo model [see Fig. A2].

*Hint*
*Create the model using the* **Cube**, **Sphere**, **Cylinder**, **Pyramid**, **Cone**, **Torus**, *and* **Tube** *primitive objects.*

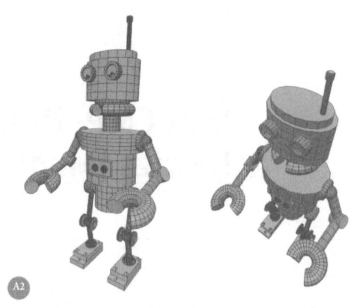

## Activity 3

Create the coffee table model [see Fig. A3] using the **Cube** primitive.

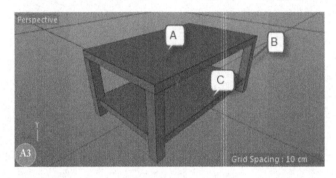

*Dimensions:*
**A:** *Length=35.433", Width=21.654", Height=1.5"*
**B:** *Length=34.037", Width=20.8", Height=1.5"*
**C:** *Length=2", Width=2", Height=13.78"*

## Activity 4

Create the 8-Drawer Dresser model [see Fig. A4] using the **Cube** primitive.

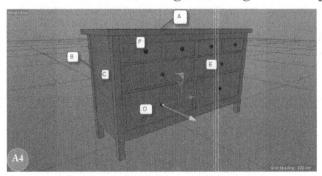

*Dimensions:*
*A: Length=65", Width=21", Height=1.5"*
*B: Length=2", Width=2", Height=35"*
*C: Length=60.76", Width=18.251", Height=30"*
*D: Length=27.225", Width=19.15", Height=11"*
*E: Length=27.225", Width=19.15", Height=7"*
*F: Length=12.871", Width=19.15", Height=5"*

## Activity 5

Create the foot stool model [see Fig. A5] using the **Cylinder** and **Cube** primitives.

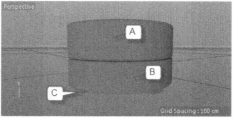

*Dimensions:*
*A: Radius=14", Height=5.91", and Fillet Radius=0.32"*
*B: Radius=14", Height=7.5", and Fillet Radius=0.74"*
*C: Length=1.651", Width=3.455", Height=1.496", and Fillet Radius=0.087"*

*Also, use the Slice feature for cylinders [From=-180 degrees and To 0 degrees].*

## Activity 6

Create shape of the word "Love" using splines and then use the **Cube** primitive, and the **Arrange** and **Duplicate** functions to create text, as shown in Fig. A6.

*Hint*
*Create a spline using the **Sketch** tool along which the cubes will be duplicated. Create another spline using the **Pen** tool that will be used to rotate the cubes, see Fig. A7. Use the **Duplicate** function to create **100** copies of the cube and then use the **Arrange** function to arrange duplicate cubes on the spline.*

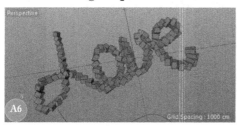

## Activity 7

Create a model of bowl using the **Lathe** generator [see Fig. A8]. Use **bowl.jpg** as reference.

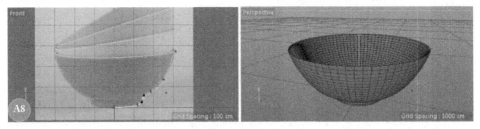

## Activity 8

Create the candle stand model [see Fig. A9] using the **Lathe** generator.

## Activity 9

Create model of a glass rack using the **Rectangle** spline, **Cylinder** primitive, and **Extrude** generator [see Fig. A10].

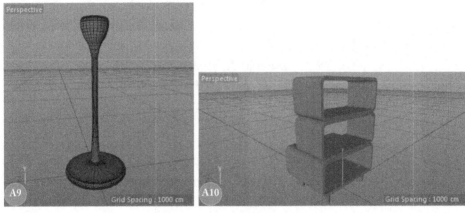

## Activity 10

Create model of a corkscrew using the **Helix** spline and the **Sweep** generator object [see Fig. A11].

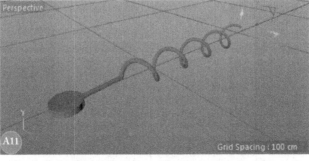

# Activity 11

Create the model shown in the first image of Fig. A12. Rest of the images in Fig. A12 show hints for creating the model.

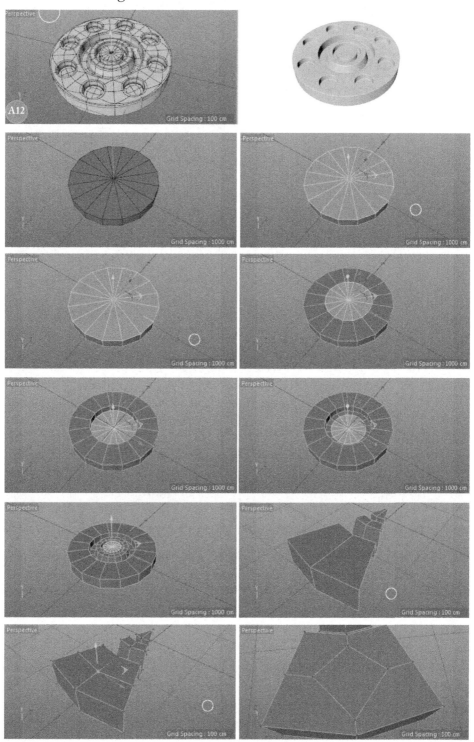

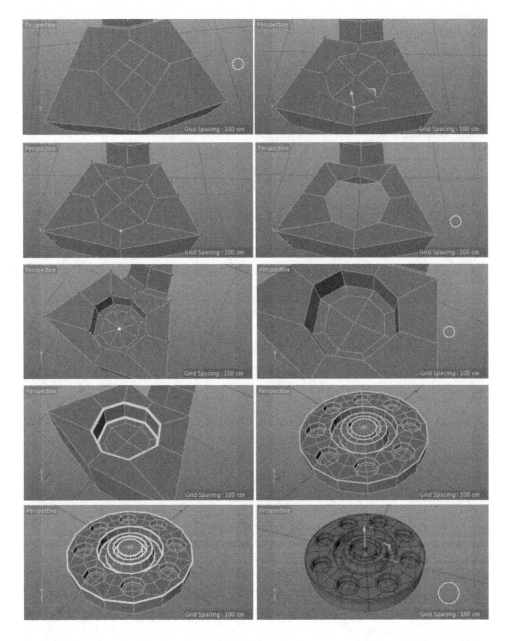

## Activity 12

Create a model of flash drive using polygon modeling techniques [see Fig. A13].

*Hint*

*Set **Units** to **Millimeters**. Create a **Cylinder** primitive and then set its **Radius** to 7.5, **Height** to 7, **Height Segments** to 1, and **Rotation Segments** to 36. Make it editable and then dissolve the top and bottom points using the **Dissolve** command, see Fig. A14. Weld the points using the **Connect** object. Select the one half of the points in the **Top** view and then move them about 25 units to the right see Fig. A15. Now, use various modeling tools and functions to create the flash drive model.*

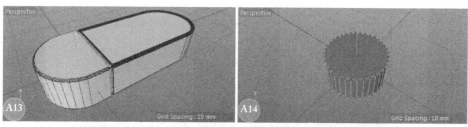

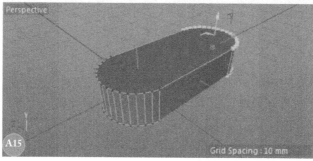

## Activity 13

Create a model of the USB connector using polygon modeling techniques [see Fig. A16].

### Hint

*Set **Units** to **Millimeters**. Create a **Box** and then set its **Size X**, **Size Y**, and **Size Z** to **15**, **5**, and **30**, respectively. Now, use various modeling tools and functions to create the USB connector model.*

## Activity 14

Create the kitchen cabinet model [see Fig. A17] using the **Cube** primitive. Use dimensions of your choice.

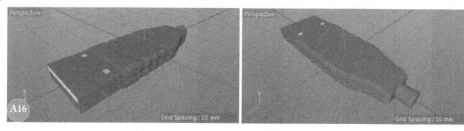

## Activity 15

Create the clutch model [see Fig. A18].

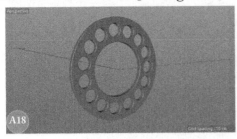

*Hint*

*Create a **Cogwheel** primitive. Use **Teeth Type** as **Flat**, set **Inlay Type** to **Holes**, and then set **Holes**, **Radius**, and **Ring Radius** parameters, as per you need. Next, extrude the primitive.*

## Activity 16

Create the clutch model [see Fig. A19].

*Hint*

*Refer to **Activity 15**. This time create three holes and then use the **Arc** setting to make holes elliptical.*

Using variations of **Cogwheel** settings and create models as shown in Figs. A20 through A31.

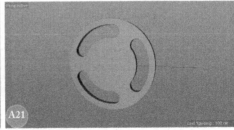

## Activity 17

The **Cogwheel** primitive is a powerful parametric object. Experiment with it and create different clutch, gear, and ratchet models [refer to Figs. A22 through A30].

## Activity 18

Create a model of a medical strip and capsules [see Fig. 32].

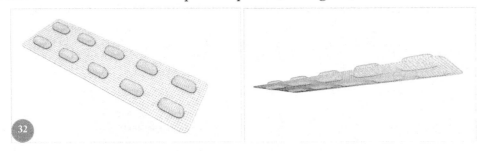

*Hint*

*Create a plane and then in the **Attribute Manager** > **Plane** > **Object** tab, change **Width**, **Height**, **Width Segments**, and **Height Segments** to **10**, **10**, **4**, and **4**, respectively. Now, modify plane to create the model. Also, refer to Fig. 33 through Fig. 36.*

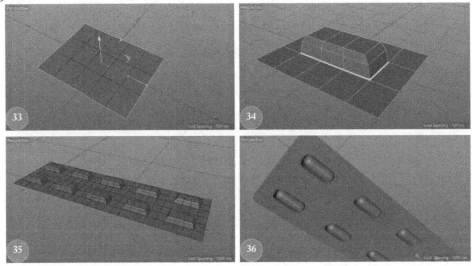

- Volume Builder
- Volume Mesher

# Unit CV1: Volumes - I

Cinema 4D's OpenVDB-based **Volume Builder** and **Volume Mesher** allow you to create complex models by adding and subtracting basic shapes in boolean-type operations. You can use volumes with MoGraph, turning noises and MoGraph fields into actual geometry. You can now build organic and hard-surface models in a very procedural way using the boolean operations such as **Union**, **Subtract**, and **Intersect**. With **Volume Mesher**, you can quickly re-topologize meshes to more effectively add details using Cinema 4D's powerful sculpting toolset.

The volumetric effects in Cinema 4D are created using Voxels, which are essentially three-dimensional pixels. Fig. 1 shows a torus defined by polygons, Fig. 2 shows a torus completely filled with voxels [**Fog**], and Fig. 3 shows the voxels layer distributed near the surface of the torus [**SDF - Signed Distance Field**]. Also, refer to **voxels.c4d**.

The Oscar Award-winning open source library **OpenVDB** is integrated into Cinema 4D. Voxels can be converted to polygon objects or polygon objects to Voxels at any time. While working with volumes, keep the following in mind:

- The **Volume Mesh** command can be used only to modify the polygon topology [remeshing].
- Some tasks such as boolean operations can be executed more effectively using voxels than with polygon objects. This is why the conversion works smoothly in both directions.
- Very precise modeling is very difficult with volumes.
- To render voxels, they must be converted to polygon surfaces.

# Volume Builder

The **Volume Builder** object can be used to create voxel objects from all sorts of Cinema 4D objects. You can create voxel objects in Cinema 4D in the following way:

- Choosing **Volume Builder** from the **Volume** menu.
- Choosing **Volume Builder** from the **Standard** palette > **Modeling** command group.
- By loading a **.VDB** file [**OpenVDB**].

Open **volume-builder.c4d** [see Fig. 4]. Select **Torus** and **Cube** in **Object Manager** in then choose **Volume Builder** from the **Standard** palette > **Modeling** command group with **Ctrl+Alt** held down to make **Volume Builder** parent of the selected objects. Fig. 5 shows the voxels displayed in the viewport.

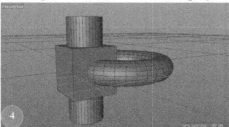
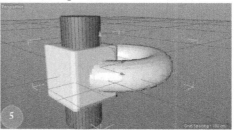

Notice that the selected objects also appear in the **Objects** list in the **Attribute Manager** > **Volume Builder** > **Object** tab [see Fig. 6]. There are two volume types available that you can select from the **Volume Type** drop-down list: **Signed Distance Field** [ref to Fig. 5] and **Fog**. Fig. 7 shows the output when **Volume Type** is set to **Fog**.

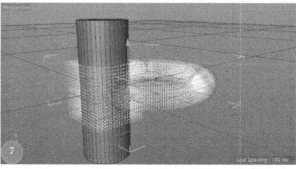

**What does Signed Distance Field [SDF] type do?**
*Polygons, points, and particles themselves have no volume. In order to generate volume, layers of voxels are placed around these elements i.e. over and under the polygon surface. These voxels are then arranged in a voxel grid.*

*Note: The Fog volume type*
*The **Fog** volume type is best suited for rendering fluids, fire, fog, and smoke. You can create these simulations using third-party applications.*

Now, change **Voxel Size** to 1 [see Fig. 8]. The **Voxel Size** parameter defines the voxel size [resolution of the voxel grid] in centimeters. The smaller the value you specify, the more precise the result will be, and the longer the render time. If you expand the **Voxel Size** parameter, four parameters will be revealed [see Fig. 9] namely, **Interior Voxel Range**, **Exterior Voxel Range**, **Spline Voxel Range**, and **Particle Voxel Range**.

Use these settings to define the number of voxel layers should be generated on the inner and outer areas. These settings are used in conjunction with the **Voxel Range Threshold** setting of the **Volume Mesher** object. The interior range is applied to the interior of the object. If you want to affect interior of an object using **Reshape Filer**, you must increase the value of the **Interior Voxel Range** parameter.

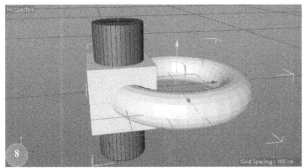

The **Objects** list is the heart of **Volume Builder**. Whenever you make any object child of the **Volume Builder** object, the object automatically appears in the **Objects** list. You can also drag objects into this list; a link will be established between the objects and the **Volume Builder** object.

Drag **Cylinder** from **Object Manager** to the top of the **Objects** list. Notice in the **Objects** list, the **Input Type** column displays **Link**. Now, hide **Cylinder** in **Object Manager** [see Figs. 10 and 11].

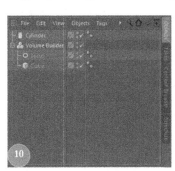
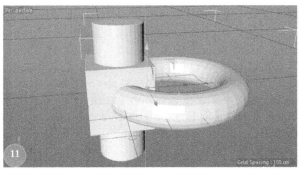

The objects in the **Objects** list are evaluated from the bottom to the top of the list. You can rearrange objects using the drag and drop operations. You can also create folder in the **Objects** list by clicking the folder icon ⬚. You can use a folder to restrict a **Volume Filter's** effect to specific objects or object groups. Elements will also be evaluated from bottom to top within a folder.

The following types of objects can be added to the **Objects** list:

- Polygon objects or their generators
- Spline objects or their generators
- Matrix objects and particles [use the particle group for Thinking Particles]
- Fields and Falloff objects
- Other volume objects [whose voxel values have to be combined for the voxel Builder's voxel values, which can result in longer calculation times]

*Caution: Deleting objects*
*If you delete child objects from the **Objects** list, these objects will be deleted from **Object Manager** as well. However, it will not happen with the linked objects.*

Now, change **Mode** to **Subtract** for both objects in the **Objects** list. Fig. 12 shows the result. Change **Mode** to **Union** for the **Torus** object [see Fig. 13]. Make sure **Cylinder** is selected in the **Objects** list and then click on **Smooth Layer** [see Fig. 14].

The **Smooth Layer** and **Reshape Layer** settings are used to create smooth and reshape filters, respectively. These objects will not be created as objects, and only exists in the **Objects** list.

A grid made up of cube-shaped grid cels is used to generate voxels. By default, this grid lies at the object's origin with no rotation. You can drag another object into the **Override Grid Matrix** field to define the origin and orientation of the voxel grid. This setting is good for removing artifacts.

By default, the **Auto Update Settings** check box is selected. As a result, the changes are reflected as you make them. If you want to quickly make several changes you should clear this check box before doing so. After the changes have been made, you can click on the **Update** button to recalculate the **Objects** list.

# Hands-on Exercises

### Exercise 1: Creating the Soap Dish Model

In this exercise, we will create the soap dish model using volumes [see Fig. E1].

The following table summarizes the exercise:

| Table E1 | |
| --- | --- |
| Difficulty level | Intermediate |
| Estimated time to complete | 20 Minutes |
| Topics | • Getting Started<br>• Creating the Model |
| Resources folder | **unit-cv1** |
| Units | **Centimeters** |
| Final file | **solid-model-01-finish.c4d** |

### Getting Started

Start a new scene in Cinema 4D and change units to **Centimeters**.

### Creating the Model

Follow these steps:

1. Choose **Cube** from the **Standard** palette > **Object** tab to create a cube in the editor view. In the **Attribute Manager** > **Object** tab, change **Size X** to **500**, **Size Y** to **144**, and **Size Z** to **330**. Next, select the **Fillet** check box and then change **Fillet Radius** and **Fillet Subdivision** to **5** and **3**, respectively.

2. Choose **Capsule** from the **Standard** palette > **Object** tab to create a cube in the editor view. In the **Attribute Manager** > **Object** tab, change **Radius** to **88** and **Height** to **415**. Next, change **Cap Segments** to **32** and **Rotation Segments** to **64**. Also, change **Orientation** to **-X**. In the **Coord** tab, change **P.Y** to **100** [see Fig. E2].

3. Make sure **Capsule** is selected in **Object Manager** then choose **Bulge** from the **Deformer** command group with **Shift** held down to make deformer child of the **Capsule** object.

4. Select **Bulge** in **Object Manager** and then in the **Attribute Manager** > **Coord** tab, change **R.B** to **90**. In the **Object** tab, click the **Fit to Parent** button and then set **Size X, Y, Z** to **216**, **415**, and **216**, respectively. Next, change **Strength** to **54** [see Fig. E3].

5. Select **Capsule** and **Cube** in **Object Manager** in then choose **Volume Builder** from the **Standard** palette > **Modeling** command group with **Ctrl+Alt** held down to make **Volume Builder** parent of the selected objects.

6. In the **Attribute Manager** > **Volume Builder** > **Object** tab, make sure the **Cube** object is at the bottom of the stack in the **Objects** list. Change **Mode** to **Subtract** for the **Capsule** object. Also, change **Voxel Size** to **1** [see Fig. E4]. Click the **Smooth Layer** button and select the **Smooth Layer** entry in the **Objects** list. Now, change **Strength** to **70**.

7. Select **Volume Builder** in **Object Manager** and then choose **Volume Mesher** from **Standard** palette > **Modeling** command group with **Alt** held down.

→ *What next?*
  *Next, we will create the soap using the **Cube** primitive and **FFD** deformer.*

8. Choose **Cube** from the **Standard** palette > **Object** tab to create a cube in the editor view. In the **Attribute Manager** > **Object** tab, change **Size X** to **300**, **Size Y** to **77**, and **Size Z** to **165**. Next, select the **Fillet** check box and then change **Fillet Radius** and **Fillet Subdivision** to **17.5** and **8**, respectively. Also, change **Segment X**, **Segment Y**, and **Segment Z** to **10** each. Align the objects, as shown in Fig. E5.

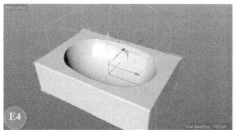

9. Make sure **Cube** is selected in **Object Manager** then choose **FFD** from the **Deformer** command group with **Shift** held down to make deformer child of the **Cube** object.

10. Select **FFD** in **Object Manager** and then in the **Attribute Manager** > **Object** tab, set **Grid Size X, Y, Z** to **250, 80**, and **170**, respectively. Activate the **Points** mode and then adjust the shape, as shown in Fig. E6.

11. Select **Cube** in **Object Manager** in then choose **Volume Builder** from the **Standard** palette > **Modeling** command group with **Ctrl+Alt** held down to make **Volume Builder** parent of the selected object.

12. In the **Attribute Manager** > **Volume Builder** > **Object** tab, change **Voxel Size** to **1**. Click the **Smooth Layer** button and then select the **Smooth Layer** entry in the **Objects** list. Now, change **Strength** to **70** [see Fig. E7].

 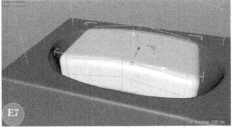

13. Select **Volume Builder** in **Object Manager** and then choose **Volume Mesher** from **Standard** palette > **Modeling** command group with **Alt** held down.

## Exercise 2: Creating a Solid Model

In this exercise, we will create a solid model using volumes [see Fig. E1].

The following table summarizes the hands-on exercise:

| Table E2 | |
|---|---|
| Difficulty level | Intermediate |
| Estimated time to complete | 20 Minutes |
| Topics | • Getting Started<br>• Creating the Model |
| Resources folder | **unit-cv1** |
| Units | **Centimeters** |
| Final exercise file | **solid-model-02-finish.c4d** |

## Getting Started

Start a new scene in Cinema 4D and change units to **Centimeters**.

## Creating the Model

Follow these steps:

1. Choose **Torus** from the **Standard** palette > **Object** tab to create a torus in the editor view. In the **Attribute Manager** > **Object** tab, change **Ring Segments** to **150, Pipe Segments** to **50**, and **Orientation** to **-Z**.

2. Choose **Cube** from the **Standard** palette > **Object** tab to create a cube in the editor view. In the **Attribute Manager** > **Object** tab, change **Size X** to **150**, **Size Y** to **120**, and **Size Z** to **150**. Next, select the **Fillet** check box and then change **Fillet Radius** and **Fillet Subdivision** to **7** and **6**, respectively [see Fig. E2].

3. Make sure **Cube** is selected in **Object Manager** and then choose **Array** from **Standard** palette > **Modeling** command group with **Alt** held down. Make sure **Array** is selected in **Object Manager** and then in **Coordinate Manager**, change **Rotation XYZ** to **0, -90**, and **0**, respectively [see Fig. E3].

 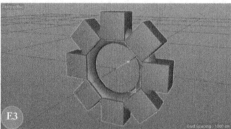

4. In the **Attribute Manager** > **Array** > **Object** tab, change **Radius** to **150** and **Copies** to **3**. Rename **Array** as **cut-array**.

5. Select **cut-array** and **Torus** in **Object Manager** in then choose **Volume Builder** from the **Standard** palette > **Modeling** command group with **Ctrl+Alt** held down to make **Volume Builder** parent of the selected objects.

6. In the **Attribute Manager** > **Volume Builder** > **Object** tab, make sure the **cut-array** object is at the first entry in the **Objects** list. Change **Mode** to **Subtract** for the **cut-array** object. Also, change **Voxel Size** to **1** [see Fig. E4]. Select **cut-array** in **Object Manager** and then in **Coordinate Manager**, change **Position XYZ** to **0, 0**, and **-100**, respectively.

7. Choose **Cylinder** from the **Standard** palette > **Object** command group to create a cylinder in the editor view. In the **Attribute Manager** > **Cylinder** > **Object** tab, change **Radius** to **50** and **Height** to **60**. Also, change **Orientation** to **+Y** [see Fig. E5].

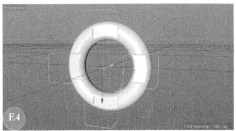

8. Make sure **Cylinder** is selected in **Object Manager** and then choose **Array** from **Standard** palette > **Modeling** command group with **Alt** held down. In **Coordinate Manager**, change **Rotation XYZ** to **0**, **-90**, and **0**, respectively.

9. In the **Attribute Manager** > **Array** > **Object** tab, change **Radius** to **149** and **Copies** to 3. Rename **Array** as **int-array**.

10. Make **int-array** child of **Volume Builder** and place it at the top in the **Objects** list. Make sure **Mode** is set to **Union** [see Fig. E6].

 *What next?*
*Next, we will increase the subdivisions on **Torus** and **Cylinder** to get smooth results.*

11. In the **Attribute Manager** > **Torus** > **Object** tab, change **Ring Segments** to **256** and **Pipe Segments** to **156**. In the **Attribute Manager** > **Cylinder** > **Object** tab, change **Rotation Segments** to **128** [see Fig. E7].

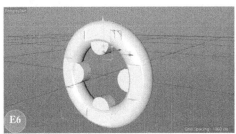
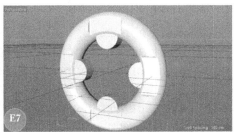

12. Select **int-array** in the **Objects** list and then click **Smooth Layer** to apply the smooth filter on all objects [see Fig. E8].

13. Choose **Circle** from the **Standard** palette > **Spline** tab to create a circle in the editor view. In the **Attribute Manager** > **Circle** > **Object** tab, change **Radius** to **251**.

14. Make **circle** child of **Volume Builder** and place it below **Smooth Layer** in the **Objects** list. Change **Mode** to **Subtract**. Make sure **Circle** is selected in the **Objects** list and then change **Radius** to **4.4** and **Density** to **1** [see Fig. E9].

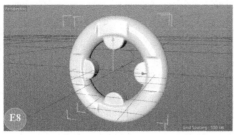
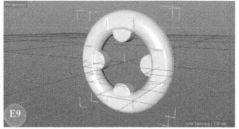

**What next?**
Next, we will use the **Volume Mesher** object to convert voxels back to polygons.

15. Select **Volume Builder** in **Object Manager** and then choose **Volume Mesher** from **Standard** palette > **Modeling** command group with **Alt** held down. Fig. E10 shows the objects in **Object Manager** and Fig. E11 shows the parameters of the **Volume Builder** object.

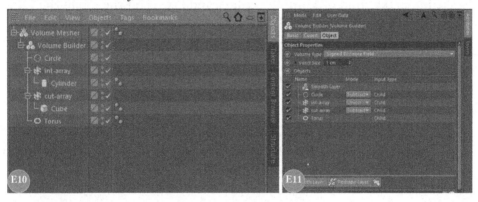

**What just happened?**
Here, we have converted voxels to polygon objects. The following objects can be made child of the **Volume Mesher** object:

- *Volume Builder*
- *Volume Group*
- *Volume Object*
- *Volume Loader*

The **Voxel Range Threshold** parameter can be used to span the generated polygon surface only between the existing inside and outside voxel layers [**SDF**] or the Minimum and Maximum Voxel values [**Fog**]. If you select the **Use Absolute Value (ISO)** check box, you can use absolute ISO values to create polygons. The **Surface Threshold** parameter allows you generate a polygon surface through voxels. The **Adaptive** parameter can be used to reduce the polygon count. If set to **0**, no reduction will take place.

# Quiz

## Fill in the Blanks

Fill in the blanks in each of the following statements:

1. Cinema 4D's OpenVDB-based _____ and _____ objects allow you to create complex models by adding and subtracting basic shapes in boolean-type operations.

2. Using volumes You can build organic and hard-surface models in a very procedural way using the boolean operations such as _____, _____, and _____.

3. The volumetric effects in Cinema 4D are created using _____, which are essentially three-dimensional pixels.

4. SDF stands for _____.

5. The _____ object can be used to create voxel objects from all sorts of Cinema 4D objects.

6. The _____ parameter defines the voxel size [resolution of the voxel grid] in centimeters.

## True or False

State whether each of the following is true or false:

1. You can use volumes with MoGraph, turning noises and MoGraph fields into actual geometry.

2. Voxels can be converted to polygon objects or polygon objects to voxels at any time.

3. You can precisely model with volumes.

4. To render voxels, they must be converted to polygon surfaces.

5. There are two volume types available that you can select from the Volume Type drop-down list: **Signed Distance Field** and **Fog**.

6. A grid made up of cube-shaped grid cels is used to generate voxels.

**Summary**

In this unit, the following topics are covered:

- Volume Builder
- Volume Mesher

# Unit CV2: Volumes - II

In **Unit CV1**, we learned about voxels, how to create them, and then how to convert them to polygons for rendering. In this unit, we will work on volume filters, volume group, and the **Volume Loader** object.

## Volume Filters

Before we go deep into filters, let's first understand, what is a volume filter?

Imagine a bitmap made up of pixels with RGB values. In Photoshop, a filter is used to modify RGB values. Volume filters work analogous to this in Cinema 4D. If voxels are viewed as pixels arranged in 3D space, these filters do nothing more than modify the voxel values in 3D space. Both Photoshop and Cinema 4D have filters with a gaussian blur function. In Photoshop, the effect of a filter can be restricted using masks. It can be done in Cinema 4D as well. However, in Cinema 4D the effect is masked using fields instead of selections.

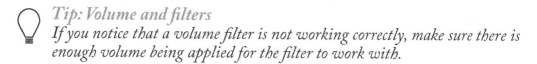

*Tip: Volume and filters*
*If you notice that a volume filter is not working correctly, make sure there is enough volume being applied for the filter to work with.*

*Tip: Filter as deformer*
*You can also use a filter as deformer in **Object Manager**. You can use it as a child object of the **OpenVDB** object. For this to work, select the **Use as Deformer** check box in the **Attribute Manager > Mode** tab.*

### Smooth Filter

The obvious effect of this filter is rounding of the sharp edges by blurring the voxel value transitions. For example, if a voxel has a value of **0** and neighboring voxel has a value of **1**, after filter is applied, these values will be modified to **0.4** or **0.6**, respectively. The **Strength** parameter defines the strength of the filter. Figs. 1, 2, and 3 show the result with **Strength** set to **0**, **50**, and **100**, respectively. Also, refer to **strength-smooth-filter.c4d**.

The options in the **Filter Type** drop-down list are used to select the type of the filter. The results generated by these options are often similar, the best you can do is experiment to see which result is the best for your scene. The default type is **Gaussian**.

The **Voxel Distance** parameter defines how many neighboring voxels [in a cubed-shaped area, in **6** directions total] should be used to calculate individual pixels. The larger the value you specify for this parameter, the better the quality will be, and the longer the render time.

Figs. 4, 5, and 6 show the result with **Voxel Distance** set to 2 [default value], 5, and 10, respectively. Also, refer to **voxel-distance-smooth-filter.c4d**. The **Iterations** parameter defines how often the filter should be applied. The render time will increase correspondingly as the value is increased.

## Reshape Filter

**Reshape Filter** allows you to offset surfaces in various ways along their surface normals. Internally, the voxel values will be increased or decreased with in the area affected by the filter. The **Strength** parameter defines the strength of the filter. Figs. 7, 8, and 9 show the result with **Strength** set to **0**, **50**, and **100**, respectively. Also, refer to **strength-reshape-filter.c4d**.

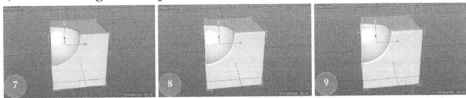

The **Filter Type** drop-down list provides the filter type. **SDF** offers two filter types:

- **Dilate/Erode:** Depending on whether a positive or negative **Offset** is used, the surfaces will be offset towards the inside or outside.
- **Open/Close:** Depending on whether a positive or negative **Offset** is used, the outside surfaces will first move towards the inside and then the same distance towards the outside [closes holes, for example, and smooths details] or vice-versa [connects objects that lie close to one another].

Fog offers three filter types:

- **Offset:** Depending on whether a positive or negative **Offset** is used, this value will be subtracted from or added to each voxel.
- **Range Map:** Works like the **Range Mapper** XPresso node. A voxel value range is converted linearly to another value range.
- **Curve:** Converts the value range using a spline - and not linearly.

The value you specify using the **Offset** parameter is added to each voxel value. You can also apply negative values. This will raise or lower the surface of most filter types.

## Volume Group

The **Volume Group** object is a combined object that can contain multiple volume objects. For example, if you load a **.VDB** file that contains three **OpenVDB** volumes, you can determine if these volumes should be imported as a volume group or as individual volume objects. You can separate volume groups by using the **C** key, each volume will be child object of a **Null** object. A **Volume Group** object can be made child of a **Volume Mesher** and subsequently be affected by volume filters.

## Volume Loader

The **Volume Loader** object is used to load volume sequences. To load a volume, choose **Volume Loader** from the **Volume** menu. Then, in the **Attribute Manager** > **Object** tab, click browse button corresponding to the **Filename** parameter to open the **Open File** dialog box. Select the single **.VDB** file or sequence in the dialog box and then click **Open**; the file will be loaded in the viewport [see Fig. 10]. If you load a sequentially numbers **.VDB** file, the **Volume Import** settings will open automatically.

The **Volume Loader** object can be made child of the **Volume Mesher** object in order to generate a polygon object. If the **Volume Loader** object is made editable, it will be converted to a single non-animated volume object in its current state.

*Caution: Scene size*
*When you load a .VDB file, the size of the Cinema 4D file barely increases. If you pass on the scene to other users, make sure that the individual files are also included.*

If you are using a volume file in the scene that is modified using an external application, clicking the **Reload** button will update the volumes in the scene. The **Volume Grids** list shows all volume grids in the scene.

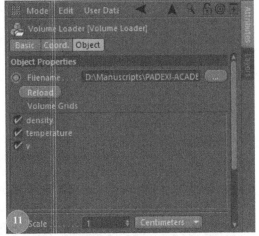

Fig. 11 shows the density, temperature, and velocity grids. Figs. 12, 13, and 14 show the density, temperature, and velocity grids in the viewport, respectively.

Also, refer to **volume-loader.c4d**.

## Volume Mesh

The **Volume Mesh** command is particularly useful removing artifacts while sculpting. For example, if an object is bent due to excessive use of sculpting, you can use this command to reshape the object. This command also produces good results in conjunctions with deformers. When you call this command with deformers, the deformation is taken into account. You can invoke this command by choosing **Volume Mesh** from the **Volume** menu or by pressing **UH**. To open its settings, press **U~Shift+H**.

To use this command, select the objects onto which you want to apply the **Volume Mesh** command or the object you want to combine. Press **UH** to execute the command. Fig. 15 shows the objects to be combined and Fig. 16 shows the combined mesh that now you can sculpt. See **volume-mesh.c4d**.

Press **U~Shift+H** to open the **Volume Mesh** dialog box. If you select the **Keep Objects** check box, new objects are created but the selected objects are placed in a hierarchy so that can be adjusted interactively. The **Voxel Size** parameter correspond to the **Voxel Size** parameter of the **Volume Builder**.

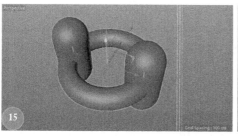 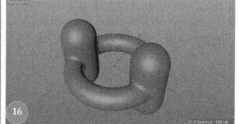

## Hands-on Exercises

### Exercise 1: Creating a Solid Model

In this exercise, we will create a solid model using volumes [see Fig. E1].

The following table summarizes the hands-on exercise:

| Table E1 | |
|---|---|
| Difficulty level | Beginner |
| Estimated time to complete | 30 Minutes |
| Topics | • Getting Started<br>• Creating the Model |
| Resources folder | **unit-cv2** |
| Units | **Centimeters** |
| Final file | **solid-model-01-finish.c4d** |

### Getting Started

Start a new scene in Cinema 4D and change units to **Centimeters**.

### Creating the Model

Follow these steps:

1. Choose **Cube** from the **Standard** palette > **Object** tab to create a cube in the editor view. In the **Attribute Manager** > **Object** tab, change **Size X** to **220**, **Size Y** to **170**, and **Size Z** to **400**. Next, select the **Fillet** check box and then change **Fillet Radius** and **Fillet Subdivision** to **4** and **5**, respectively. Rename **Cube** as **Cube-A**.

2. Create another cube. In the **Attribute Manager** > **Object** tab, change **Size X** to 220, **Size Y** to 360, and **Size Z** to 150. Next, select the **Fillet** check box and then change **Fillet Radius** and **Fillet Subdivision** to 4 and 5, respectively. Rename **Cube** as **Cube-B**. Align the cubes, as shown in Fig. E2.

3. Choose **Capsule** from the **Standard** palette > **Object** tab to create a cube in the editor view. In the **Attribute Manager** > **Object** tab, change **Radius** to 71 and **Height** to 415. Next, select the **Orientation** to -Z. Rename **Capsule** as **Cap-A** and align it with cubes, as shown in Fig. E3.

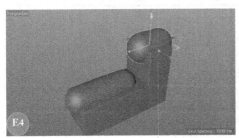

4. Create another capsule. In the **Attribute Manager** > **Object** tab, change **Radius** to 80 and **Height** to 280. Next, select the **Orientation** to -Z. Rename **Capsule** as **Cap-B** and align it with cubes, as shown in Fig. E4.

5. Choose **Cube** from the **Standard** palette > **Object** tab to create a cube in the editor view. In the **Attribute Manager** > **Object** tab, change **Size X** to 250, **Size Y** to 135, and **Size Z** to 300. Next, change **Rotation P** to 45. Rename **Cube** as **Cube-C** and then align it with cubes, as shown in Fig. E5.

6. Choose **Circle** from the **Standard** palette > **Spline** tab to create a circle in the editor view. In the **Attribute Manager** > **Circle** > **Object** tab, change **Radius** to 150. Align the circle, as shown in Fig. E6. Create three more copies of the and group all circles with the name **Circles** by pressing **Alt+G**. Align the group, as shown in Fig. E7.

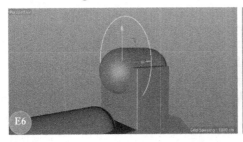

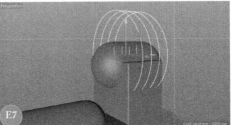

**What just happened?**

*Here, I have grouped the circles. It will help us when we will change properties of the volume object created using these circles. With the help of the group, we can change properties of all circles en masse.*

7. Select all objects in **Object Manager** in then choose **Volume Builder** from the **Standard** palette > **Modeling** command group with **Ctrl+Alt** held down to make **Volume Builder** parent of the selected objects.

8. Make sure the order of the objects in the **Objects** list from bottom to top is as follows: **Cube-A, Cube-B, Cap-A, Cap-B, Cube-C**, and **Circles**.

9. For **Cube-B**, change **Mode** to **Union**; for **Cap-A, Cap-B**, and **Cube-C** change **Mode** to **Subtract**; for **Circles**, change **Mode** to **Union** [see Fig. E8]. Next, change **Voxel Size** to **1**, see Fig. E9.

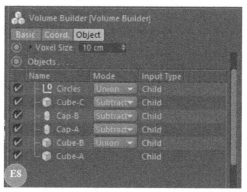

**What next?**

*Notice in Fig. E9, we need to increase subdivisions on capsules to get rid of faceting.*

10. Select **Cap-A** and then in the **Attribute Manager** > **Object** tab, change **Cap Segments** to **40** and **Rotation Segments** to **116**. Repeat the process for **Cap-B** [see Fig. E10].

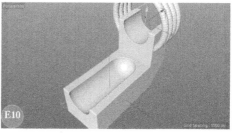

**What next?**

*Now, we will fix the circles.*

11. Select **Volume Builder** in **Object Manager** and then select **Circles** in the **Objects** list. Now, change **Radius** to **5** and **Density** to **1** [see Fig. E11].

12. Select **Circles** in **Objects** list and then click **Smooth Layer**. Select **Smooth Layer** in **Objects** list and then change **Strength** to **50**, **Filter Type** to **Mean**, **Voxel Distance** to **2**, and **Iteration** to **2** [see Fig. E12].

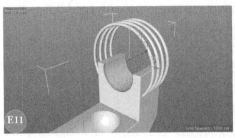 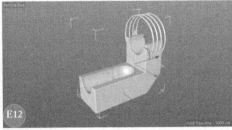

13. Select **Volume Builder** in **Object Manager** and then choose **Volume Mesher** from **Standard** palette > **Modeling** command group with **Alt** held down.

## Exercise 2: Creating a Solid Model

In this exercise, we will create a solid model using volumes [see Fig. E1]. Table E2 summarizes the exercise.

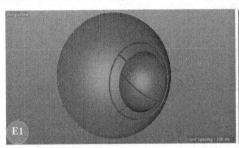 

| Table E2 | |
|---|---|
| Difficulty level | Intermediate |
| Estimated time to complete | 40 Minutes |
| Topics | • Getting Started<br>• Creating the Model |
| Resources folder | **unit-cv2** |
| Units | **Centimeters** |
| Final files | **solid-model-02-finish.c4d** |

## Getting Started

Start a new scene in Cinema 4D and change units to **Centimeters**.

## Creating the Model
Follow these steps:

1. Choose **Sphere** from the **Standard** palette > **Object** command group to create a sphere in the editor view. In the **Attribute Manager** > **Sphere** > **Object** tab, change **Radius** to **194** and **Segments** to **256**. Rename sphere as **A**.

2. Choose **Sphere** from the **Standard** palette > **Object** command group to create a sphere in the editor view. In the **Attribute Manager** > **Sphere** > **Object** tab, change **Radius** to **100** and **Segments** to **256**. Rename sphere as **B**. In **Coordinate Manager**, change **Position Z** to **-156**.

3. Choose **Sphere** from the **Standard** palette > **Object** command group to create a sphere in the editor view. In the **Attribute Manager** > **Sphere** > **Object** tab, change **Radius** to **80** and **Segments** to **256**. Rename sphere as **C**. In **Coordinate Manager**, change **Position Z** to **-156**. Refer to Fig. E2.

 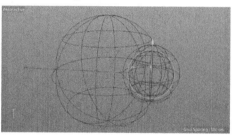

 *What next?*
*Next, we will subtract **B** from **A**.*

4. Select **A** and **B** in **Object Manager** in then choose **Volume Builder** from the **Standard** palette > **Modeling** command group with **Ctrl+Alt** held down to make **Volume Builder** parent of the selected objects.

5. Make sure **B** is at the top of the stack in the **Objects** list in **Attribute Manager**. Now, change **Mode** to **Subtract** and **Voxel Size** to **1** [see Fig. E3].

 *What next?*
*Now, we will perform the **B - Intersect - A** operation [refer to Fig. E4] followed by the **C - Subtract - A** operation to get the dent on **A**.*

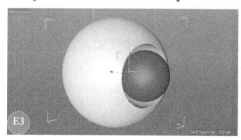 

6. Click on the **Create a Folder** button  to create a folder, rename it as **F1** by double-clicking on it and typing the new name. Move the folder at the top of the stack. Drag **A** and followed **B** to the **F1** in **Attribute Manager**. Next, change **Mode** to **Intersect** for **B** [see Figs. E5 and E6].

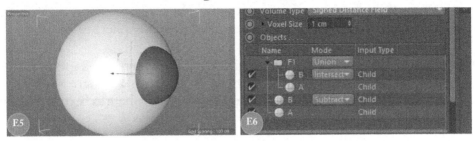

?  *What next?*
   *Notice in Fig. E5 that the groove we created is not clearly visible. Let's fix that using the smooth filter.*

7. Select the **B** object in **Objects** list which is outside the **F1** folder and then click **Smooth Layer** to add smooth filter. Make sure **Smooth Layer** is selected in the **Objects** list and then change **Strength** to 70 and **Voxel Distance** to 3 [see Fig. E7].

?  *What next?*
   *Now, we have results of **B - Subtract - A** [see Fig. E8] and **B - Intersect A** [see Fig. E9]. So the result we have is **Union** of [**B - Subtract - A**] and [**B - Intersect A**], see Fig. E10. Next, we will perform the **C - Subtract - Union***

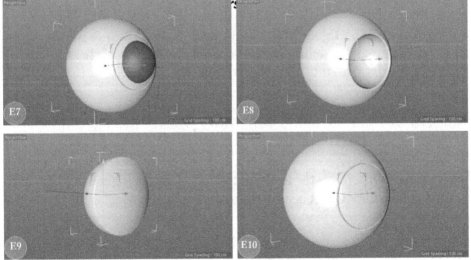

8. Make **C** child of **Volume Builder** and then make sure it is at the top of the stack in the **Objects** list. Next, change **Operation** to **Subtract** [see Fig. E11].

9. Choose **Cube** from the **Standard** palette > **Object** tab to create a cube in the editor view. In the **Attribute Manager** > **Object** tab, change **Size X** to 431, **Size Y** to 4, and **Size Z** to 419. In the **Coordinate Manager**, change **Rotation B** to 45. Rename **Cube** as **Cube-A**.

10. Choose **Cube** from the **Standard** palette > **Object** tab to create a cube in the editor view. In the **Attribute Manager** > **Object** tab, change **Size X** to 431, **Size Y** to 4, and **Size Z** to 419. In the **Coordinate Manager**, change **Rotation B** to -45. Rename **Cube** as **Cube-B** [see Fig. E12].

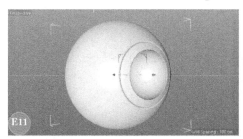 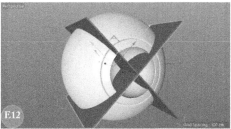

11. In **Object Manager**, make **Cube-A** and **Cube-B** child of **Volume Builder** and then change **Mode** to **Subtract** for both cubes [see Fig. E13].

 *What just happened?*
*Here, cubes are creating cuts through whole geometry. If we want to just affect the groove we made, we have to restrict the effect of the cubes using folders.*

12. Select **C** in **Objects** list and then click on the **Create a Folder** button 🗂 to create a folder, rename it as **F2** by double-clicking on it and typing the new name. Now, drag **C** and **F1** inside **F2** [refer to Fig. E14].

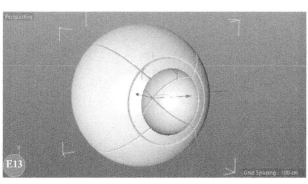 

13. Similarly, create a new folder, rename it as **F3** and move **F2**, **Cube-A**, and **Cube-B** inside **F3** [see Fig. E15]. Fig. E16 shows the folder structure.

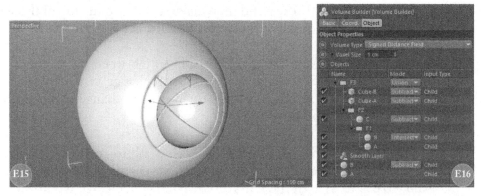

14. Select **F1 > B** in the **Objects** list and then click **Reshape Layer**. Select **Reshape Layer** in **Objects** list and then change **Offset** to -1 [see Fig. E17].

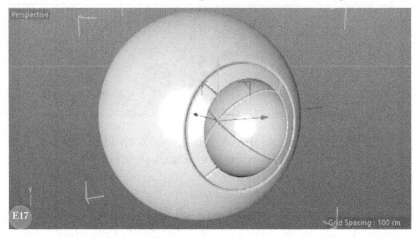

15. Select **Volume Builder** in **Object Manager** and then choose **Volume Mesher** from **Standard** palette > **Modeling** command group with **Alt** held down.

# Quiz

**Fill in the Blanks**

Fill in the blanks in each of the following statements:

1. If voxels are viewed as pixels arranged in 3D space, the volume filters do nothing more than modify the _____ values in 3D space.

2. The obvious effect of _____ layer is rounding of the sharp edges by blurring the voxel value transitions.

3. The _____ parameter defines the strength of the filter.

4. The _____ parameter defines how many neighboring voxels should be used to calculate individual pixels.

5. The _____ layer allows you to offset surfaces in various ways along their surface normals.

6. The _____ object is a combined object that can contain multiple volume objects.

7. The _____ object is used to load volume sequences.

**True or False**

State whether each of the following is true or false:

1. You can mask the volume effects in Cinema 4d using fields.

2. You can use a volume filter as deformer in **Object Manager**.

3. The default filter type is **Median** for the **SDF** objects.

4. You can not load a .**VDB** sequence into Cinema 4D.

**Summary**

In this unit, the following topics are covered:

- Volume Filters
- Volume Group
- Volume Loader
- Volume Mesh

# Unit CVP: Practice Activities [Volumes]

## Practice Activities

### Activity 1:
Create the solid model, as shown in Fig. A1.

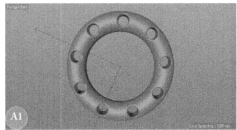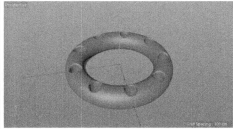

*Hint*

*Create a **Capsule** primitive and a **Torus** primitive. Now, create copies of the **Capsule** primitive using the **Duplicate** command. Arrange them on the **Torus** and then use the **Subtract** boolean operation with **Volume Builder** to create the model.*

### Activity 2:
Create the solid model, as shown in Fig. A2.

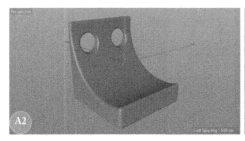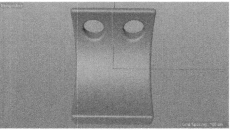

*Hint*

*Use three cylinders and a cube to create the model.*

## Activity 3:
Create the solid model, as shown in Fig. A3.

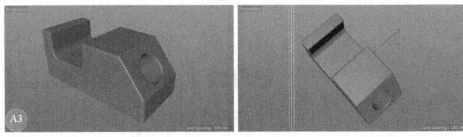

*Hint*
*Use three cubes and a cylinder to create the model.*

## Activity 4:
Create the solid model, as shown in Fig. A4.

*Hint*
*Create copies of the **Cogwheel** spline using the **Duplicate** command and then use a **Cube** object with them for boolean operations.*

## Activity 5:
Create the solid model, as shown in Fig. A5.

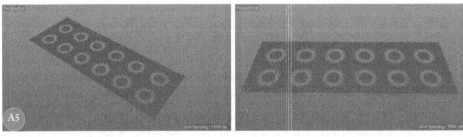

*Hint*
*Create copies of the **Cogwheel** spline using the **Duplicate** command. Then, extrude splines using the **Extrude** generator and then use a **Cube** object with them for boolean operations.*

## Activity 6:
Create the solid model, as shown in Fig. A6.

*Use a cylinder to create the base and a tube to create the top. Then, use a helix to create the thread. Use the **Union** operation for all three objects.*

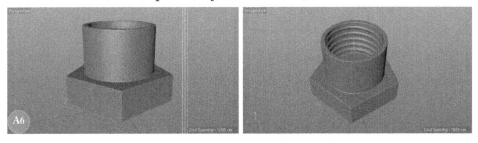

## Activity 7:

Create the solid model, as shown in Fig. A7.

*Hint*

*Create a cylinder as base geometry. For thread, use the helix, circle, and sweep objects and then use capsule for the top part.*

## Activity 8:

Create the solid model, as shown in Fig. A8.

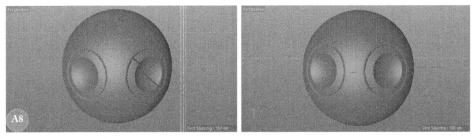

*Hint*

*Refer to **Unit CV2** > **Exercise 2**. Use the **Array** function to create multiple copies.*

This page is intentionally left blank

- Standard renderer
- Global Illumination
- Ambient Occlusion
- Render Settings
- Post Effects

# Unit CR1: Standard Renderer

The **Standard** renderer is the default renderer in Cinema 4D. In most cases, you can use this renderer as it is fast and stable. However, if you want to render special effects such as depth-off-field and motion blur, use the **Physical** renderer. This renderer and other built-in renderers available in Cinema 4D are discussed in later units.

## Exploring Render Settings Window

The settings for the **Standard** renderer can be accessed from the **Render Settings** window [see Fig. 1]. To open this window, choose **Edit Render Settings** from the **Render** menu or press **Ctrl+B**. Alternatively, you can click the **Edit Render Settings** button in the **Standard** palette > **Render** command group. You can also access these settings from the **Attribute Manager** [see Fig. 2]. To do so, select **Mode** > **Render Settings** from the **Attribute Manager's** menubar.

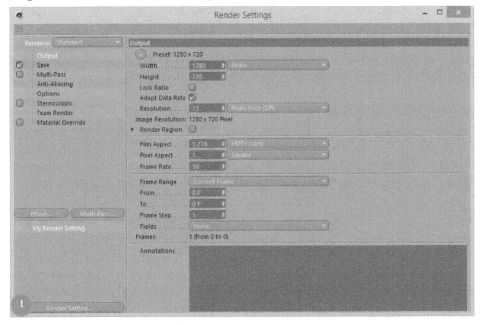

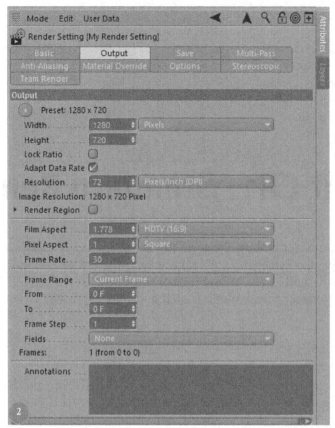

The **Render Settings** window is divided into two panes. The left pane contains a list of render options. When you select a render option from the left pane, the corresponding settings are displayed in the right pane. The post and multi-pass effects can be added by clicking on the **Effect** and **Multi-Pass** buttons, respectively. A check box is available on the left of most of the post effects and multi-pass effects options. You can use this check box to enable or disable the corresponding option. If the **Standard** renderer is not selected by default, you can select it from the **Renderer** drop-down list available on the top-left corner of the **Render Settings** window.

When you select an option from the left pane of the window, the corresponding options that you can modify will be displayed in the right pane. If you modify an option in the right pane, the corresponding label will be shown in black and in bold face because these values differ from default values. Let's explore the commonly used rendering options available in the left pane of the **Render Settings** window.

## Output

The **Output** settings only affect the rendering in the separate render window. These settings do not affect the rendering in the viewport. At the top-left corner, an **Arrow** button is available. Clicking on this button reveals the commonly used resolution settings for print, video, and films. For example, if you want to use the **HDV 1440x1080** resolution, click on the **Arrow** button and then choose **Film/Video** > **HDV 1080 25** or **HDV 1080 25** option.

The **Width** and **Height** parameters define the width and height of the image, respectively. The drop-down list on the right of the **Width** parameter is used to select the unit of measure. By default, the **Pixels** option is active. When you select a preset, it automatically sets the other settings such as resolution, aspect ratio, frame rate, and so on. The **Lock Ratio** check box allows you to adjust the width or height of the image automatically if one or the other is modified.

If you are rendering a video and want to define a bit rate for it, ensure the **Adapt Data Rate** check box is selected and then select the **Save** render option from the left pane. In the right pane, select a video format such as **MP4** from the **Format** drop-down list. Next, expand the **Format** area and then define a bit rate using the **Data Rate (kBit)** parameter [see Fig. 3]. You can expand the area by clicking the triangle located on the left of the **Format** label.

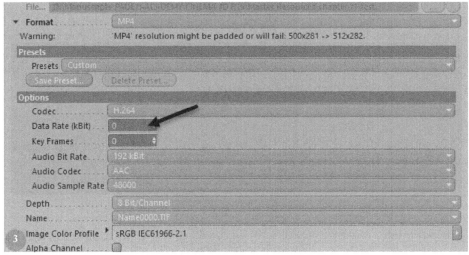

The **Resolution** setting does not apply to video but if you are rendering an image for the print, you can specify a DPI value using this setting.

If you have a made a minor modification in the scene that just affects a smaller area, you can render a small region instead of whole image. The **Render Region** function allows you to render a selected region of the scene. To define a region, expand the **Render Region** area and then define the region using the **Left Border, Top Border, Right Border**, and **Bottom Border** parameters [see Figs. 4 and 5]. In Fig. 5, I have specified values **50, 50, 100**, and **100** for the **Left Border, Top Border, Right Border**, and **Bottom Border** parameters, respectively.

The **Film Aspect** parameter reflects the **X:Y** ratio of the file to be rendered whereas the **Pixel Aspect** parameter defines the **on-screen-width:on-screen-height** ratio of a pixel. The pixel aspect ratio for most of the monitors is **1:1**. The **Frame Rate** parameter sets the frame rate for the render.

The options in the **Frame Range** drop-down list allow you select the frame or frame range to be rendered. Once you select an option form this drop-down list, the **From** and **To** parameters reflect the corresponding frame numbers. If you want to skip frames while rendering, you can use the **Frame Step** parameter. For example, if you setup this parameter to **5** for test renders, only every 5th frame will be rendered offering a rough estimation of the final output.

## Save

The **Save** settings allow you to save an image, a video, or sequence of images to the **Picture Viewer** window. There are two areas available in the right pane: **Regular Image** and **Compositing Project File**. These areas are discussed next:

### Regular Image

The **File** parameter is used to specify the path where you want to save the files. If you specify a file name without path, the image or image sequence will be saved in the active scene's folder. If you want to use relative paths, place periods at the beginning of the path name.

Create a folder with the name **path** and then create sub-folder with the name **x**. Now, save the scene with the name **test.c4d** inside the **x** folder. Create a folder with the name **y** inside the **x** folder. Now, specify path as **./y/diffuse** and then press **Shift+R** to render the scene; the rendered image with the name **diffuse** will be saved in the **path > y** folder. Because, when we use a single dot [.] in the path name, it refers to the absolute path. You can use two dots [..] to specify a relative path from the location at which the scene file is saved. Now, if you specify **../diffuse** as path, the control jumps one level up in the directory from the location [file is saved in the **x** folder] at which the scene file is saved. As a result, the file with the name **diffuse** will be saved in the parent folder **path**.

## Tokens

You can use variable path and file names known as **Tokens** in the **File** input field. Tokens are simple text variables, when they are rendered or displayed in the **Picture Viewer** window, they will be replaced by parameters such as name of the project, the current camera, take, and so on. The following tokens are available:

- **$prj:** Project file name
- **$camera:** Current camera name
- **$take:** Current take name
- **$pass:** Multi-pass or object channel name [the defined multi-pass names]. Primarily to be used as directory name.
- **$userpass:** Multi-pass or object channel name. Primarily to be used as a directory name.
- **$frame:** Current animation frame
- **$rs:** Current render setting name
- **$res:** Image resolution (e.g., 800*600: 800X600)
- **$range:** Animation range (e.g., from frame 23 to 76; 23_76)
- **$fps:** Frame rate

You can type these tokens or you can click on the arrow button corresponding to the **File** parameter to open a flyout and then select desired option from the flyout.

Create a folder with the name **tktest** in your system. Open the **tokens-start.c4d** file. Now, in the **Render Settings** window, specify path for the folder **tktest**. Now, append a \ at the end of the path and then choose **Current Camera** from the **Tokens** flyout; Cinema 4D shows the new path: .\tktest\$camera. Now, append a \ at the end of the path and then choose **Render Settings** from the **Tokens** flyout; the new path will be displayed as follows: **\tktest\$camera\$rs**. Add a \ at the end then type **tk-seq** as the file name. The complete path should now read like follows: **.\tktest\$camera\$rs\tk-seq**.

Notice in the **Object Manager, RN_CAM** is the name of the camera. Also, notice in the **Render Settings** window, the name of the active render settings is **Low Res**. Now, press **SHIFT+R** to render the sequence. Now, navigate to the **tktest** folder and then check the directory structure [see Fig. 6]. Also, see **tokens-finish.c4d**.

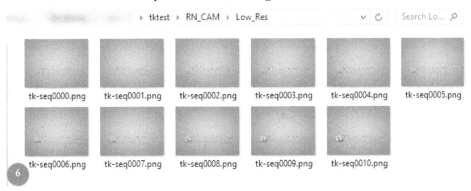

The options in the **Format** drop-down list are use to select the file format for the image or image sequence. If you expand the **Format** area, the **Presets** drop-down list will be revealed. It contains options [if available] for the format you selected from the **Format** drop-down list.

For example, if you select **WMV** from the **Format** drop-down list, you will notice that there are some presets available for the selected format. Below the **Presets** area is the **Options** area from where you can set various parameters for the selected parameters.

The **Depth** parameter defines the bit depth per channel of the image. You can select the **8 Bit/Channel, 16 Bit/Channel**, or **32 Bit/Channel** option from the **Depth** drop-down list. These options are used for **24-bit** color, **48-bit** color, and **98-bit** color, respectively.

The options in the **Name** drop-down list are used for sequential numbering of the image files. The letters **TIF** represent the extension of the selected file format such as **JPG**. For example, if you select **JPG** as file format and **beauty** as filename:

- **Name0000.TIF** will result in **beauty1234.JPG**
- **Name0000** will result in **beauty1234**
- **Name.0000** will result in **beauty.1234**
- **Name000.TIF** will result in **beauty123.JPG**
- **Name000** will result in **beauty123**
- **Name.000** will result in **beauty.123**

You can use the **Image Color Profile** setting to define which color profile should be embedded in the rendered image.

*Tip: Color profile*
*If you are using the **Linear** color profile [for example with the **HDR** format] with multi-pass feature, it is recommended that you render images with the **16-bit** color depth because multi-passes are saved with the **Linear** color profile. When the color profile management is disabled, no color profile will be embedded in the rendered images. Expand the **Image Color Profile** area; a big vertical arrow button will be revealed on the right. Click on this button to view options for selecting color profiles.*

*Caution: Color profile*
*Many of the programs can't read color profiles. For example, **Windows 7** partially reads profiles. Generally, the default **sRGB** profile will be the correct profile.*

Select the **Alpha Channel** check box to calculate a pre-multiplied alpha channel. The alpha channel is the grayscale image of the same resolution as the color image. The white pixels in the alpha channel indicate the presence of the object whereas the black pixels indicate there is no object. You can use the alpha channel to composite two images. The image at the top can be blended with the image underneath using the alpha channel. If the alpha value is white [opaque], the top color overwrites the destination color, if black [transparent], the color at the top is not visible. As a result, allowing the background to show through.

> *Note: Pre-multiplied alpha*
> *When you render an image with pre-multiplied alpha, the alpha channel picture is antialiased to ensure a soft transition in the composited picture.*

When the color channel and alpha are multiplied, the alpha channel causes a dark seam because both the color and alpha channels are rendered with antialiasing and black is multiplied twice. If you want to avoid the dark seam, select the **Straight Alpha** check box.

> *Caution: Straight alpha*
> *Straight alphas are only suitable for compositing images only, they are not useful for the conventional images.*

Usually, the alpha channels are integrated into those image formats which are alpha channel capable. In other words, they are saved with the color image. If you want to save the alpha channel as a separate image, select the **Separate Alpha** check box. The alpha channel files are saved in the same format as the color files.

The **8 Bit Dithering** check box is used to add a random patterns to the colors to prevent color banding. Enabling dithering enhances image quality but also increases the file size. Therefore, it is not recommended to be used if you are rendering web graphics.

If you select one of the video formats from the **Format** drop-down list, select the **Include Sound** check box to integrate a sound file into the video.

> *Note: Bitrate for videos*
> *The term **bitrate** refers to the number of bits that are processed in a unit of time. Remember that **1** byte consists of **8** bits. Video data rates are given in bits/second. The data rate for a video file is the bitrate. In Cinema 4D, you can define bitrate for both audio and video. To do so, expand the **Format** area and then in the **Options** area you can define bitrate for video and audio by using the **Data Rate (kBit)** and **Audio Bitrate (kBit)** options, respectively.*

## Multi-Pass Image

If you enable the **Multi-Pass** render option, you will have access to the **Multi-Pass Image** area [see Fig. 7]. By default, the **Multi-Layer File** check box is selected. As a result, all layers are saved in a multi-layer file such as a Photoshop [**PSD**], BodyPaint [**B3D**], or **TIFF** file. Also, Cinema 4D creates a separate file for each pass and suffix is added to each of the filenames to differentiate them.

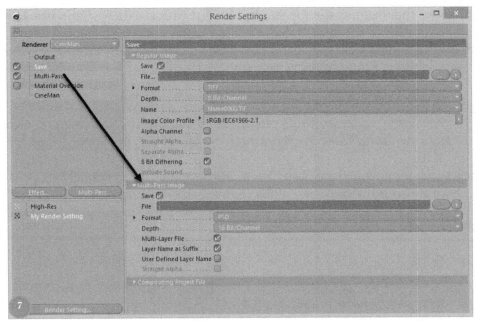

If you have chosen a format from the **Format** drop-down list that does not support multi-layers, each layer will be saved as separate file. If the **Layer Name as Suffix** check box is selected, the name of the layer [for example, _**diffuse**, _**reflection**, and so on] will be added after the filenames.

Each multi-pass has its default name such as **Ambient, Diffuse,** and so on. If you want to use your own names, double-click on the pass name in the left pane of the **Render Settings** window and then type a new name. Next, select the **User Defined Layer Name** check box. Now, the user defined names will be used for passes instead of the default ones.

### Compositing Project File

The options in this area [see Fig. 8] are used to create a compositing file made up of multiple layers. Each layer can be edited separately. You can select the application for the project from the **Target Application** drop-down list. The available options are: **After Effects, Nuke, Motion,** and **Digital Fusion.**

### Anti-Aliasing

The settings corresponding to the **Anti-Aliasing** option allow you to remove jagged edges from your images. The process works by first breaking down each pixel into sub-pixels and then calculating and averaging several color values to produce the final color for the pixel. The commonly used options are discussed next.

The default method is **Geometry** which smooths all object edges using a **16x16** sub-pixels. Figs. 9 and 10 show the render with **Anti-Aliasing** set to **None** and **Geometry**, respectively.

The **Best** method uses additional sub-pixels and Cinema 4D's adaptive antialiasing. The adaptive antialiasing is enabled for those pixels whose value substantially differs from the its neighboring pixels. It also affects the color edges as well as the objects behind transparencies.

The **Min Level** parameter defines the minimum number of sub-pixels that will always be rendered. The default value **1x1** is suffice in most of the cases. However, if you see some artifacts such as swelling of the shadows, a higher value should be used.

The **Max Level** parameter defines the sub-pixel dispersion that will be applied to the critical region such as the high contrast region, for example, color edges and object edges behind the transparencies. The default value **2x2** is suffice in most of the cases. The higher the value you specify, the more the render time will be.

The **Threshold** value can be used to specify the degree of color divergence at which the **Max Level** value should be applied for a given pixel. Figs. 11 and 12 show the render output when **Anti-Aliasing** set to **Best** and the **Max Level** set to **2x2** and **8x8**, respectively. Also, refer to **anti-aliasing.c4d**.

## Options

The **Options** settings are to used to define various parameters that affect the rendering. These settings are discussed next:

## Transparency

Use the **Transparency** check box to define whether or not **Transparency** or **Alpha** channel should be included in the render calculations. By default, this check box is selected. Fig. 13 show the rendered output when **Transparency, Refraction, Reflection,** and **Shadow** are enabled. Fig. 14 shows the output when **Transparency** is disabled. See the **rays.c4d** file for reference.

## Refraction

Use the **Refraction** check box to define whether or not the refraction index should be included in the render calculations for the transparent materials. By default, this check box is selected. Compare Figs. 13 and 15. Fig. 15 shows the output when **Refraction** is disabled.

 *Note: Refraction index*
*Materials such as glass and water look realistic when they are rendered with refraction index but they increase the render time as well. However, note that if the scene does not contain materials that reflect light, no additional render time will be added if the **Refraction** check box is selected.*

 *Tip: Rendering transparency*
*If the transparent objects that lie behind other transparent objects are rendered black, increase the value of the **Ray Depth** parameter. The default value for the **Ray Depth** parameter is **15**.*

## Reflection

Use the **Reflection** check box to define whether or not reflection should be included in the render calculations. By default, this check box is selected. Compare Figs. 13 and 16. Fig. 16 shows the output when **Reflection** is disabled.

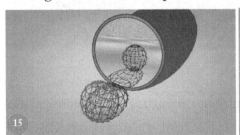 

## Shadow

Use the **Shadow** check box to define whether or not shadows should be included in the render calculations. If you select the **Limit Shadows to Soft** check box, Cinema 4D will render soft shadows that render fast. Note that the rendering area or hard shadows is much more computationally intensive than the soft shadows. The soft shadows appear more realistic than the hard shadows. Compare Figs. 13 and 17. Fig. 17 shows the output when **Shadow** is disabled.

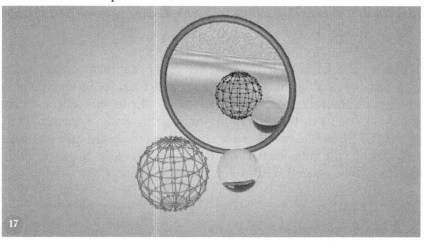

## Limit Reflections to Floor/Sky

Use this check box to cause the raytracer to calculate the reflection of the floor and sky onto the reflective surfaces in the scene and not onto other objects. This option when selected takes less time to render. Therefore, you can use it in test rendering or when you have to meet a deadline.

## Blurriness

Use the **Blurriness** check box to define whether or not the blur effect for the **Roughness** and **Transparency** material channels [blurriness resulting due to **Roughness** value] should be included in the render calculations.

## Cache Shadow Maps

Cinema 4D calculates shadow map for each light in the scene that casts a soft shadow. A shadow map is used to define where shadows will be rendered. In a complex scene, the render time go up considerably if shadow maps are rendered. When the **Cache Shadow Maps** check box is selected, the shadow map will be saved when you first time render the scene. The shadow map will be saved in the scene's **Illum** folder with the name **\*\*.c4d.smap**. This folder will be created automatically, if there is not one already.

## Active Object Only

When this check box is selected, only the selected objects will be included in the render calculations.

## Default Light

If you do not have a defined light source in the scene, a default light is used to render the scene. As soon as a light source is added, Cinema 4D automatically disables the default light.

 *Caution: Default light*
*When you use a **Sky** object with the **HDR** texture, the auto light is not disabled. If you add GI to scene, the auto light will be disabled when you render.*

## Textures

Use the **Textures** check box to define whether or not enable or disable textures when you render. You can disable this check box for a test render or when you are using the **Cel** renderer. When this check box is not selected, bitmaps will be replaced with the black color. When a texture is missing during rendering, Cinema 4D displays a dialog box. If the **Show Texture Errors** check box is selected and you confirm the alert, the rendering will continue without the missing texture. If you select this check box, rendering will be cancelled after you confirm the alert.

## Volumetric Lighting

If this check box is selected, shadows will be cast in the visible light. This option is render intensive therefore you can disable this check box for test render.

## Use Display Tag LOD

If this check box is selected, the renderer will use the level of detail specified in **Display** tags.

## Render HUD

Select this check box, if you want to include HUD in the rendered image or image sequence. The left image in Fig. 18 show the HUD elements in the editor view whereas the right image in Fig. 18 shows the elements in the render view.

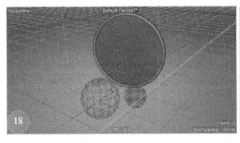

## Render Doodle

Use this check box to define whether or not the **Doodle** function should be included in the rendered output.

## Sub Polygon Displacement

This option is only available with the **Visualize** and **Studio** modules of Cinema 4D. You can use this check box to globally deactivate the sub-polygon displacement without having to do it separately for each sub-polygon displacement material. You can disable this check box for test renders.

### Post Effects
Use this check box to enable or disable post effects globally.

### Identical Noise Distribution
If you use low settings with many of the Cinema 4D effects, they produce grainy results. These results are often referred to as "**Noise**". Some of these effects are given next:

- Area shadows
- Subsurface Scattering (in the **Direct** mode)
- Depth-of-field
- Motion blur
- General sampling in the **Physical** renderer
- Post effects like **Global Illumination, Ambient Occlusion,** etc

If you select the **Identical Noise Distribution** check box, the noise distribution [even if no parameters are animated] will be random for each rendered frame which means that each successive frame will have random noise distribution.

*Caution: Noise distribution*
*Disable this option for animations as it will produce unexpected results. However, if you want to produce stills that look identical to each other as much as possible, select this check box.*

*Caution: Noise distribution*
*The settings such as multi-threading can still produce randomness. This can be seen in the GI rendering in which slightly different results will be produced even if you select the **Identical Noise Distribution** check box.*

### Subsurface Scattering
Use this check box to define whether or not to enable or disable **Subsurface Scattering** for the entire project.

### Bucket Sequence
Buckets are the square render regions [see Fig. 19], each calculated using a single processor or a processor core. This results in the optimized rendering in particular when rendering render instances.

You can choose an option from the **Bucket Sequence** drop-down list to define how buckets should process. You can choose any option from the drop-down list, no sequence bears a particular advantage over the others.

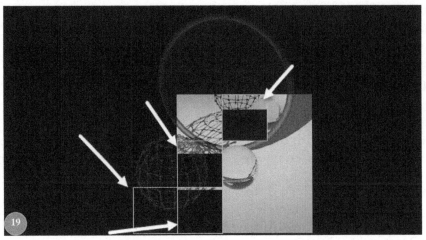

By default, the **Automatic Size** check box is selected. As a result, a bucket size between a range **8x8** to **64x64** is automatically chosen depending on the number of CPUs and image size. Smaller buckets require less memory than the larger buckets but this will have no effect on the render speed.

If you expand the **Automatic Size** area, the **Bucket Width** and **Bucket Height** parameters will be revealed. They are only available if you clear the **Automatic Size** check box. You can use these parameters to define a custom bucket region.

## Ray Threshold

The **Ray Threshold** parameter is used to control the movement of the rays in the scene. Rays stop their movement from the camera to the scene as soon as their brightness falls below the value you specify for the **Ray Threshold** parameter. You can use this value to optimize the render time because in a scene that contains many reflective and transparent surfaces **90%** of the processed rays contribute less than **10%** to the general brightness and color of the image. Higher the value you specify for the **Ray Threshold** parameter, the greater the degree to which very small reflections and transparencies will be taken into consideration - with correspondingly longer render times.

## Ray Depth

The **Ray Depth** parameter controls how many transparent objects will be penetrated by the renderer. The lower the value you specify for this parameter, the fewer the number of objects can be seen through. A value of **1** means that calculations are finished for a pixel as soon as ray hits something in the scene. The areas that the renderer cannot penetrate are rendered in black.

A value of **2** means that after a ray hits a surface, a second ray shot to calculate the transparency. Fig. 20 shows the rendered output with the **Ray Depth** parameter value set to **1** and **2**, respectively. Fig. 21 shows the rendered output with the **Ray Depth** parameter value set to **3** and **8**, respectively. See the **rays.c4d** file for reference.

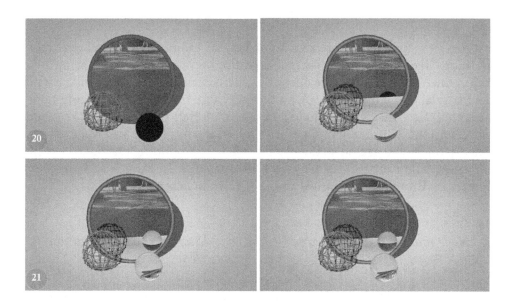

## Reflection Depth

When a ray is shot into the scene, it is reflected by the reflective surfaces. You can use the **Reflection Depth** parameter to limit the number of reflective rays [maximum number of rays] sent into the scene. Fig. 22 shows the rendered output with **Reflection Depth** parameter set to **2, 4**, and **8**, respectively.

 *Caution: Reflection depth*
*Usually, only the first set of reflections are important. If you add more rays, they tend to add little to the image quality but increase the render time.*

## Shadow Depth

The **Shadow Depth** parameter behaves analogous to the **Reflection Depth** parameter. If a surface lies in the shadow of another object, this parameter can be used to send additional shadow rays to check which shadow should be sent to the light source. Fig. 23 shows the rendered output with **Shadow Depth** parameter set to **1, 3**, and **5**, respectively.

## Material Override

Sometimes, it is necessary to render an object, for example, in neural gray color, to check things like shadows and light balance also known as "**clay rendering**". When you select the **Material Override** check box, all materials in the scene will be replaced by the material defined here. If you want to exclude materials from being replaced, in the scene, select the desired mode and drag materials that you want to include or exclude, from the **Material Manager** into the **Materials** list. If you want to preserve specific channels, you can do so by selecting the corresponding checkboxes from the **Preserve** area. The available channels are: **Diffuse Color**, **Luminance**, **Transparency**, **Reflectance**, **Bump**, **Normal**, **Alpha**, and **Displacement**.

 *Caution: Node materials*
*Node materials are not supported by the* **Material Override** *option.*

## Render Settings Contextual Menu

If you click on the **Render Settings** button located at the bottom-left corner [see Fig. 24] of the **Render Settings** window, a flyout will be displayed. The options in this flyout allow you to save presets for the render settings. You can also open this flyout by RMB clicking in this area. For example, you can make a preset for low-res settings and one for high-res settings. By default, the **My Render Setting** preset is used for saving the current settings. You can double-click on its name to rename it.

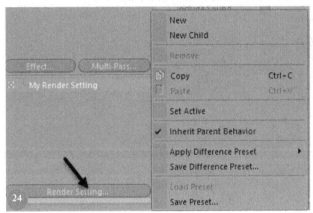

To add a new preset, click on the **Render Settings** button and then choose **New**. You can also copy and paste the presets using the **Ctrl+C** and **Ctrl+V** key combinations. Alternatively, you can also duplicate a preset by **Ctrl** dragging. You can create a child preset by choosing **New child** from the flyout. To make a preset active, either choose **Set Active** from the flyout or click on the icon to the left of the preset. If you want to create a preset that contains only the modified [bold] parameters, choose **Apply/ Save Difference Preset** from the flyout.

Note: Attribute Manager compatibility

*When you select an option from the left pane of the* **Render Settings** *window, the corresponding options that you can modify will be displayed in the right pane. These settings are compatible with the* **Attribute Manager** *which gives you access to all relevant* **Attribute Manager** *commands as well as two additional commands, namely* **Inherit Parent Setting** *and* **Override Parent Setting** *[see Fig. 25].*

If you select the **Inherit Parent Setting** option, parameters that have no values to be inherited [bold text] will reset. Selecting the **Override Parent Setting** option will prevent any parent values from being assumed. Also, the parameter name will be made black and in bold face.

Let's see this in action, follow these steps:

1. Open the **Render Settings** window and then rename the default **My Render Setting** preset to **High-Res**.

2. Select **Options** from the left pane and then in the right pane, change **Ray Depth** and **Shadow Depth** parameters to **20** each. Notice that parameters names are shown in bold face [see Fig. 26].

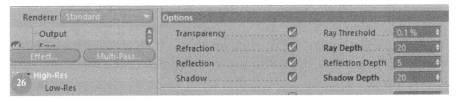

3. RMB click on **High-Res** and then choose **New Child** from the context menu. Rename it as **Low-Res**. Notice that the **Ray Depth** and **Shadow Depth** parameters inherited values from the parent settings **High-Res** [see Fig. 27] and their labels are not in bold face.

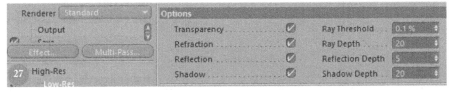

4. Change the **Ray Depth** and **Shadow Depth** parameters to **10** each. These parameters name turn black [see Fig. 28]. Now, switch to **Low-Res** and change **Ray Threshold** to **0.2**. Its label tuns black, switch to **High-Res**; its label is still in the default state. Change **Reflection Depth** to **6** and switch to **Low-Res**; notice the value has changed but label is still in the normal state.

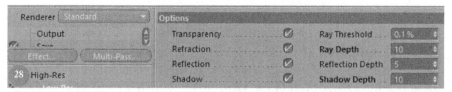

5. RMB click on **Ray Depth** and choose **Inherit Parent Setting** from the menu. Notice that value has been changed to **20** and also the color of the label is now changed to normal state [see Fig. 29]. RMB click on **Ray Depth** and choose **Override Parent Setting** to change the color of the label black [see Fig. 30].

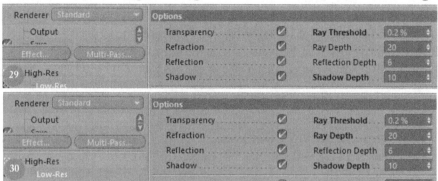

6. Delete **Low-Res**, select **High-Res**, and then change **Ray Depth**, **Reflection Depth**, and **Shadow Depth** to **6** each. Now, RMB click on **High-Res** and choose **Save Difference Preset** from the context menu to open the **Name** dialog box. In this dialog box, type **Name** as **Difference** and then click **OK**.

7. Now, create a new preset, RMB click on it, and then choose **Apply Difference Preset > Difference** to change the render settings that contain only the bold values.

As you can see, you can use these presets in variety of scenarios such as:

- Rendering images without antialiasing, shadows, and so on for test renderings.
- Rendering a specific range of animation.
- Creating presets for final rendering.
- Creating presets for multi-pass rendering and so on.

## Working with Effects

When you click the **Effect** button in the left pane of the **Render Settings** window, a popup will be displayed. Now, you can choose any effect from this popup to add to the scene. The chosen effect appears as an entry in the list of render effects on the left pane of the **Render Settings** window. To change the corresponding options, select the effect; the options appear on the right pane of the window.

The post effects are generated after the image has been rendered. Therefore, you will not see the effects until the image is fully rendered. To remove an effect, RMB click on it and then select **Remove** from the context menu. You can enable or disable an effect without removing it from the list. To do so, select or clear the check box to the left of a given effect.

*Tip: Order of the effects*
*The order of the effects is important. To move an effect up or down in the list, click-drag the desired effect at the new location.*

You can also copy and paste the effects including their parameters using **Copy** and **Paste** options. These option are available in the **Effect** popup. You can also save and load effect presets using the **Load Preset** and **Save Preset** options from the popup. These presets can be saved and loaded from the **Presets/User** directory of the **Content Browser**. The effects can be deleted from the **Content Browser**. Many of the post effects' parameters can be animated just like you animate parameters using the **Attribute Manager**.

Let's explore some of the most commonly used effects available in the **Effect** popup.

## Global Illumination

In real-world situations, when light hits an object's surface, some of the light is absorbed and some of it is reflected back. GI controls how light interacts between the objects. It allows you to render realistic evenly lit scenes. Follow these steps to understand global illumination:

1.  Open the **gi-start.c4d** file. This file contains several objects. A self-illuminating material is applied to **Sphere** in the scene. This scene has no lights.

2.  Press **Ctrl+B** to open the **Render Settings** window. Click on the **Effect** button and then choose **Global Illumination** from the popup menu to enable GI in the scene. Similarly, add the **Ambient Occlusion** effect. Render the scene [see Fig. 31].

*What just happened?*
*Here, I've added the **Global Illumination** and **Ambient Occlusion** effects. **Ambient Occlusion** or **AO** allows you to control the degree to which each surface point is exposed and then darkens it accordingly. When AO is turned on, areas such as corners, holes, or areas where objects are close to each other appear darker.*

*Note: Effects*
***GI** and **AO** are post effects meaning they are generated after the image is rendered. You won't be able to see them until the whole image is rendered. Also remember, the order of the effects in the **Render Settings** window is important. You can drag and drop the effects to change their order.*

*What next?*
*Notice in Fig. 31, there is very less illumination in the render. Let's increase that.*

3. In the **Material Manager**, double-click on the self-illumination material to open the **Material Editor** and then select **Illumination** from the left pane. In the right pane, change the **Generate GI** option's **Strength** to **1000**. Render the scene [see Fig. 32].

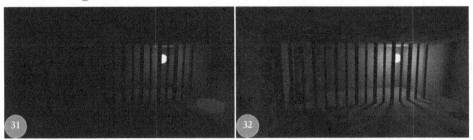

*What just happened?*
*By default, in the **Material Editor**, the **Generate GI** check box is selected. As a result, the given material affects other objects in the scene. The **Strength** setting controls how strong light this material will emit. Here, we have set **Strength** to **1000** which is **10** times more than its default value **100**. The maximum value you can specify is **10000**. Notice in Fig. 32, we have now lot more brightness but the shadows are not correct.*

4. In the **Material Editor**, select the **Polygon Light** check box and then render the scene [see Fig. 33]. Notice that we have much better render now.

*Note: Polygon Light*
*When the **Polygon Light** check box is selected, the object serves an area light. Such objects contain a material with an active **Luminance** channel.*

*Note: Uber and Node materials*
*If a **Uber** or **Node** material has an active **Emission** channel, enabling this option will produce a targeted sampling during GI calculation. As a result, the GI artefacting can be prevented. It is also beneficial to select the **Polygon Light** check box when displaying this material in rough reflections. Rendering the material reflection will take a little longer but the quality will be better.*

5. Open the **Render Settings** window by pressing **Ctrl+B**. Select **Global Illumination** from the left pane.

Notice in the **General** tab of the right pane, at the top we have the **Preset** drop-down list. The options in this drop-down list allow you to select a GI preset. These presets are the starting point. You can then fine tune these presets to optimize render time and quality. There are two main types of presets available: interior and exterior. Given below is a quick overview of the presets available:

- **Interior:** Interior spaces are more difficult to calculate GI. Therefore, use interior presets in those scenes which have fewer or smaller light sources.
- **Exterior:** Use exterior options in those open scenes which are setup under the open sky or space.
- **Custom:** As soon as you modify the GI settings, the **Custom** preset is activated.
- **Default:** The Default preset activates the **Irradiance Cache** method with **Diffuse Depth** set to **1**. This is the fastest GI method.
- **Object Visualization:** These presets are used in the scenarios where the objects are well lit and are at the center of the scene. As a result, they require fewer light reflections.
- **Progressive:** These presets are used with the **Physical** renderer's **Progressive Sampler** setting.

The following table summarizes the methods used with the presets:

| Table 1 | | |
|---|---|---|
| **Preset** | **Primary Method** | **Secondary Method** |
| Interior - Preview | Irradiance Cache | Radiosity Maps |
| Interior - Preview (High Diffuse Depth) | Irradiance Cache | Light Mapping |
| Interior - Preview (Small Illuminants) | Irradiance Cache | Light Mapping |
| Interior - High | Irradiance Cache | Irradiance Cache |

| Table 1 | | |
|---|---|---|
| Preset | Primary Method | Secondary Method |
| Interior - High (High Diffuse Depth) | Irradiance Cache | Light Mapping |
| Interior - High (Small Illuminants) | Irradiance Cache | Light Mapping |
| Exterior - Preview | Irradiance Cache | Radiosity Maps |
| Exterior - Physical Sky | Irradiance Cache | QMC |
| Exterior - HDR Image | Irradiance Cache | QMC |
| Object Visualization Preview | Irradiance Cache | Light Mapping |
| Object Visualization High | Irradiance Cache | Irradiance Cache |
| Progressive No Prepass | QMC | QMC |
| Progressive Fast Complete Diffuse | QMC | Light Mapping |

Notice in Table 1, **Irradiance Cache** is the dominant primary method whereas the **Light Mapping** is the dominant secondary method. The **Radiosity Maps** method is used with the preview settings because this method is well suited for fast rendering previews. This method uses less reflected light. The term **High Diffuse Depth** refers to the effects of many rays (light) reflections which produces much more realistic effect. The term **Small Illuminants** refers to the scene illumination mainly created using smaller lights. These lights are defined using GI portals or polygon lights.

The difference between the **Exterior - Physical Sky** preset and the **Exterior - HDR Image** preset is that the **Force Per-Pixel** check box is selected when you use the **Exterior - HDR Image** preset. This check box is displayed when you expand the **Discrete Sky Sampling** area in the **General** tab. When you select the **Force Per-Pixel** check box, the calculation of the light emitted by the sky will split from the cache and calculated separately for each pixel. This check box is relevant when you use **Irradiance Cache** as the primary method.

**Irradiance Cache+QMC** is the best combination for the exterior scenes. **Irradiance Cache** as secondary method works best with the interior spaces with small lights defined as the polygon or GI portals lights.

Notice in the **Render Settings** window the **Primary Method** is set to **Irradiance Cache**. In this method, several pre-passes are calculated in which scene is analyzed in order to determine the indirect lighting regions also referred to as shading points.

The brightness and color values of these points will be saved in the irradiance cache referred to as **entries**. You can save and reuse the cache data using the settings available in the **Cache Files** tab.

*Note: Cache files*
*The cache files are only used when you render the scene using the **Picture Viewer** window not when you render in the viewport.*

The other mode called **Quasi-Monte Carlo (QMC)**, offers best GI quality in comparison to the **Irradiance Cache** mode. **QMC** is most precise method but slowest. It works very well with **Light Mapping** used as secondary method.

*Caution: Flickering*
*The **Irradiance Cache** mode tends to flicker when you use it with animations. It flickers more when you use bright and small polygon lights in the scene.*

*Tip: Flickering*
*The **QMC+QMC** combination produces flicker free results with animations. **Irradiance Cache+QMC** is also prone to flickering. **QMC** works well with **Light Mapping** as secondary method.*

If you expand the **Primary Method** area, you would see two settings: **Intensity** and **Saturation**. These settings are used to adjust the GI brightness and color saturation.

6. In the **Render Settings** window, change **Secondary Method** to **Light Mapping**. Render the scene [see Fig. 34].

The **Secondary Method** options allow you to specify the mode for calculating secondary bounces. The **Light Mapping** as secondary method works well when there are lots of lights in the scene. **Light Mapping** offers very fast GI calculations.

*Caution: Light Leaks*
*Light leaks can occur when **Light Mapping** is used. Reduce the **Sample Size** value in the **Light Mapping** tab to fix it. Also, ensure that you are using thicker objects instead of single polygon surfaces.*

In **Light Mapping**, samples are emitted from the angle of view of the camera. These samples are reflected back and then colors are calculated when geometry is struck. If you get brighter results, you can always reduce the **Intensity** value.

7. In the **General** tab, change **Maximum Depth** to **32** and then render the scene [see Fig. 35].

**What just happened?**

You are already aware that when **Light Mapping** is used as GI method, samples are emitted from the angle of view of the camera. These samples are often reflected in the scene depending on the **Maximum Depth** value. The colors are calculated when the light mapping rays hits the geometry. The colors are then saved in a cell pattern [that you can save in a file and then reuse it later] and made available to the primary method algorithm, **Irrandiance Cache** in this case. The **Maximum Depth** value produces more dispersion of light without increasing the render time.

**Caution: Gamma**

The **Gamma** value in the **General** tab only affects the indirect GI lighting. It can be used to brighten the relatively darker renders. Be careful with the gamma value, high values tend to kill contrast in the image and flatten it.

**Note: Light reflection**

If you use **Irradiance Cache** or **QMC** as secondary method, you will get access to the **Diffuse Depth** parameter which allows you to define that how often the light should be reflected from a surface. High values will increase the render time.

The **Path Count (x1000)** setting in the **Light Mapping** tab is one of the important settings to control the quality of the light map. The value you specify is internally multiplied by **1000**. This setting defines the number of samples that should be calculated for the entire scene. The higher the value you specify, the more homogeneous the light dispersion will be, and the longer will be the corresponding render time.

You are already aware that in light mapping, colors are saved in a cell pattern. You can use the **Sample Size** setting in the **Light Mapping** tab to control the size of the cells. If you want to see the progress of cell sampling during the render process, select the **Show Preview Paths** check box [see Fig. 36].

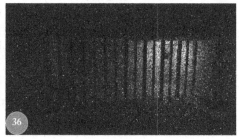

8.  Switch to the **General** tab. Change **Maximum Depth** back to **16**, the default value.

In the **General** tab, notice that the **Medium** option is selected from the **Samples** drop-down list. The options in this drop-down list control the **Accuracy** and **Sample Count** settings. You can view these settings by expanding the **Samples** area. The **Low**, **Medium**, and **High** options in the **Samples** drop-down list let you set the **Accuracy** setting to **50%**, **75%**, and **90%**, respectively. The **Accuracy** setting automatically defines the optimized sample count. If you want to specify your own accuracy or custom sample settings, select the **Custom Sample Count** or **Custom Accuracy** option from the **Samples** drop-down list.

The number of samples you specify here will also be used by the **Discrete Area Sampling** and **Discrete Sky Sampling** settings if you haven't defined a specific number of samples for them.

*Tip: Higher sample value*
*A higher **Custom Sample Count** value produces a corresponding better render quality. If you are using the **QMC** method, it will remove graininess and if you are using the **Irrandiance Cache** method, it will remove spots from the render.*

*What is a sample?*
*A sampler samples the scene's cache [**colors+brightness**] from the camera's angle of view. In other words, a sample is the combination of a **color** and **brightness** of a shading point. The higher number of samples that are calculated, the more precise the GI calculation will be.*

9.  In the **General** tab, change **Samples** to **Custom Sample Count** and **Sample Count** to **8**. Render the scene [see Fig. 37]. Notice there are lots of spots in the render. Change **Sample Count** to **64** and notice the change in the render quality [see Fig. 38].

10. Switch to the **Irrandiance Cache** tab.

In this tab, we have the **Record Density** drop-down list at the top. Expand the **Record Density** area to see the corresponding options. The options available in the **Record Density** drop-down list are: **Preview**, **Low**, **Medium**, and **High**. If you change any of the default options in the **Record Density** area, the **Custom** option will be made available.

These settings are used to fine tune the results. The **Preview** mode offers a quick preview of the final result. The **Record Density > Density** parameter adjusts the general dispersion of the shading points. The higher the value you set for this parameter, the higher the shading point density will be.

GI methods calculate shading points and their position point-by-point. The point-by-point dispersion of brightness must be converted to a planar dispersion during rendering. The **Smoothing** option does it for you. It interpolates the brightness of the neighboring points to render a given pixel. The higher the value you specify for the **Smoothing** parameter, the more samples will be used for rendering at a given point. Smaller values produce a spotty result.

*Note: Smoothing value*
**Smoothing** *is a setting whose value you will rarely have to modify.*

11. In the **General** tab, change **Secondary Method** to **None**. Render the scene [see Fig. 39]. In the **Irradiance Cache** tab, change **Color Refinement** to **100**. Render the scene [see Fig. 40].

*What just happened?*
*Compare Figs. 39 and 40. Fig. 40 has more defined shadows. The* **Color Refinement** *setting improves the render quality in the regions in which the GI lighting changes abruptly such as areas with GI shadows and bright polygon lights. When you use the* **Color Refinement** *setting, additional shading points will be calculated thus increasing the render time.*

*Caution: Spotty regions*
*It is important that you increase the value of* **Record Density** *enough so that the light distribution is homogenous otherwise these will be spotty regions in the render.*

💡 *Tip: GI caustics*
*GI caustics also benefits from the higher values.*

12. In the **General** tab, change **Primary Method** > **Intensity** to **200**, **Secondary Method** to **Light Mapping**, **Secondary Method** > **Maximum Depth** to **32**, and **Samples** > **Sample Count** to **256**. Render the scene. Notice in Fig. 41, we have a better looking result now. Also, see **gi-finish.c4d**. You can also increase the **Radius** of the **Sphere** to get more illumination in the scene.

## Ambient Occlusion

**Ambient Occlusion** allows you to control the degree to which each surface point is exposed and then darkens it accordingly. When **Ambient Occlusion** is turned on, areas such as corners, holes, or areas where objects are close to each other appear darker. **Ambient Occlusion** can be defined at two locations in Cinema 4D:

- Using the **Effect** button in the **Render Settings** window. You can also output ambient occlusion as a multi-pass channel.
- As a channel shader for a material. You can access it by choosing **Texture** > **Arrow** button > **Effects** > **Ambient Occlusion** [see Fig. 42]. You should use this effect in the **Diffusion** channel. You can also use channels for special effects such as applying dirt textures in the corners.

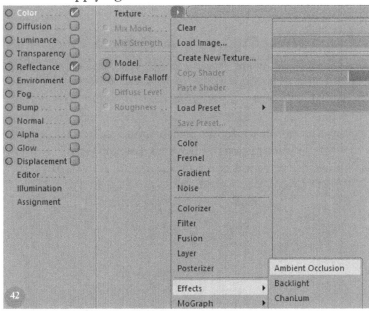

When you select **Ambient Occlusion** in the left pane of the **Render Settings** window, the corresponding options are displayed in the right pane [see Fig. 43]. The first option at the top is **Apply to Project** check box which is selected by default. As a result, you don't have to worry about creating/modifying individual materials. Fig. 44 shows the render with and without the **Ambient Occlusion** effect, respectively. Refer to the **ao.c4d** file.

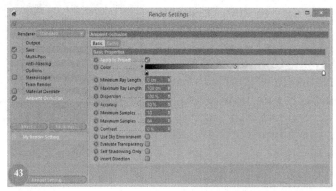

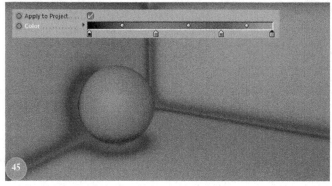

 *Tip: Compositing tag*
*You can remove ambient occlusion from individual objects using the* **Compositing** *tag.*

 *Caution: Amplified effect*
*If you define* **Ambient Occlusion** *in the* **Render Settings** *window, it will be applied to all objects globally. The objects that have the* **Ambient Occlusion** *shader applied, ambient occlusion calculations will be done twice. As a result, the* **Ambient Occlusion** *effect will be amplified for these objects.*

The **Color** option allows you to define a color gradient for the effect. Generally, a simple black to white gradient is used. However, you can define any color for special effects. Fig. 45 shows the render when a gradient is used as **Color**.

The **Minimum Ray Length** parameter controls how the defined gradient will be rendered between the exposed and non-exposed areas. It is recommended that you do not modify this parameter and leave it at its default value **0**. The **Maximum Ray Length** parameter defines the distance to which surfaces see each other. Fig. 46 shows the rendered output with the **Maximum Ray Length** value set to **10, 30, 60,** and **200**, respectively. In general, you should use lower values for the **Maximum Ray Length** parameter.

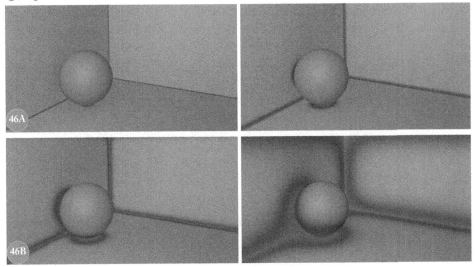

The **Dispersion** parameter controls the samples to be used for the **Ambient Occlusion** calculations. During the calculations, several samples or rays are emitted for each point within a virtual hemisphere. These rays check whether geometries lie within the **Maximum Ray Length** value. A **Dispersion** value of **100** takes whole hemisphere in account whereas a value of **0** only takes the zenith [the areas that are perpendicular to each point] of the hemisphere into account. Fig. 47 shows the rendered output with the **Dispersion** value set to **0, 50,** and **100**, respectively.

The **Accuracy, Minimum Samples,** and **Maximum Samples** parameters control the quality of the **Ambient Occlusion** effect. The more samples you will use, the more homogeneous the output will be, and more render time will be required for calculations. The **Minimum Samples** and **Maximum Samples** parameters are used to control the critical and less critical areas in the scene. The **Accuracy** setting determines how the samples must be distributed to get the best possible results.

The **Contrast** parameter defines the contrast of the **Ambient Occlusion** effect. Fig. 48 shows the rendered output with the **Contrast** value set to **0, 50,** and **100**, respectively.

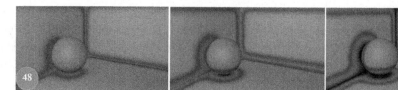

When the **Self Shadowing Only** check box is selected, separate objects will not see each other, they will only see themselves [see Fig. 49]. The **Invert Direction** switch allows you to invert the **Ambient Occlusion** effect. As a result, outward pointing edges and corners/peaks will be ascertained for the **Ambient Occlusion** effect [see Fig. 50]. Also, refer to **ao-2.c4d**.

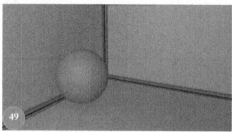
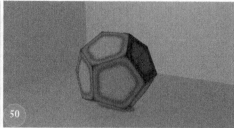

*Tip: Alpha channel*
*You can place the **Ambient Occlusion** shader into the alpha channel of a material; the respective material will only have an effect on the outward pointing edges and corners/peaks.*

## Points to Remember - Render Settings

- **Tokens** are simple text variables, you can use them in a path string in the **File** input field.
- Select the **Alpha Channel** check box to calculate a pre-multiplied alpha channel. The alpha channel is the grayscale image of the same resolution as the color image. The white pixels in the alpha channel indicate the presence of the object whereas the black pixels indicate there is no object. If you want to avoid the dark seam in the composition, select the **Straight Alpha** check box. The straight alphas are only suitable for compositing images only, they are not useful for the conventional images.
- The default anti-aliasing method is **Geometry** which smooths all object edges using **16x16** sub-pixels. The **Best** method uses additional sub-pixels and Cinema 4D's adaptive antialiasing. The default value of **2x2** of the **Max Level** parameter is suffice in most of the cases.
- If a scene does not contain materials that reflect light, no additional render time will be added if the **Refraction** check box is selected.
- If the transparent objects that lie behind other transparent objects are rendered black, increase the value of the **Ray Depth** parameter.
- Rendering the area or hard shadows is much more computationally intensive than the soft shadows. Soft shadows appear more realistic than the hard shadows.
- When you select the **Active Object Only** check box, only the selected objects will be included in the render calculations.

- The **Textures** check box is used to define whether or not enable or disable textures when you render. You can disable this check box for a test render or when you are using the **Cel** renderer. When this check box is not selected, bitmaps will be replaced with black color.
- When the **Volumetric Lighting** check box is selected, the shadows will be cast in the visible light. This option is render intensive therefore you can disable this check box for test renders.
- The **Ray Threshold** parameter is used to control the movement of the rays in the scene. Rays stop their movement from the camera to the scene as soon as their brightness fall below the value you specify for the **Ray Threshold** parameter. You can use this value to optimize the render time because in a scene that contains many reflective and transparent surfaces, **90%** of the processed rays contribute less than **10%** to the general brightness and color of the image.
- The **Ray Depth** parameter controls how many transparent objects will be penetrated by the renderer.
- You can use the **Reflection Depth** parameter to limit the number of reflective rays [maximum number of rays] sent into the scene. If you add more rays, they tend to add little to the image quality but increase the render time.
- When you select the **Material Override** check box, all materials in the scene will be replaced by the defined material. You can use this check box to check things like shadows and light balance also known as "clay rendering".

## Points to Remember - Global Illumination

- Post effects are generated after the image is rendered. You won't be able to see them until the whole image is rendered. Also remember, the order of the effects in the **Render Settings** window is important.
- When you use a **Sky** object with the **HDR** texture, the auto light is not disabled. If you add GI to the scene, the auto light will be disabled.
- When the **Generate GI** check box is selected for the material, the given material affects other objects in the scene. The **Strength** setting controls how strong light this material will emit.
- **Primary Method** only brightens surfaces that are directly lit and the **Secondary Method** is responsible for additional reflected light. The primary method calculates the effect of diffuse depth which means it calculates the light emitted by polygon lights and by the surfaces illuminated via real lights or **Physical Sky**. In typical settings, a blue sphere illuminated by a white light reflects blue light. The **Secondary Method** calculates the brightness of the surface that do not have to lie in the field-of-view of the camera. The left image in Fig. 51 shows the surfaces lit by the primary method and the primary + secondary methods, respectively.

- The **Diffuse Depth** parameter is only available if the **Irradiance Cache** or **QMC** method is used as a secondary method. It controls how often light should be reflected from a surface. Fig. 52 shows the rendered output with **Diffuse Depth** set to **2** and **3**, respectively. Note that it brightens the image but adds to the render time. A value greater than **3** in a normal scene is less and less noticeable; the render scene simply becomes brighter.

- The **Maximum Depth** parameter is available when **Light Mapping** is used as **Secondary Method**. Higher values create homogeneous dispersion of light with no increase in render time. The increase in brightness is less noticeable in interior scenes. No other GI method calculates high **Diffuse Depth** values as fast as **Light Mapping**. Fig 53 shows the render with **Maximum Depth** set to **8** and **32**, respectively. Notice that there is very slight difference between the two images.

- The **Samples** settings lets you set the number of samples and **Accuracy** setting. You can use the **Sample Count** setting to optimize the scene.
- The **Discrete Area Sampling** settings only work if **Polygon Light** is active for the polygon lights (or for GI Portals). These settings send additional samples to polygon lights. Check the **summary-1.c4d** for reference. Left image in the Fig. 54 shows the render when the **Force Per-Pixel** option is disabled and enabled, respectively.

- The **Discrete Sky Sampling** settings are only advantageous when **Irradiance Cache** is used as primary method. For bright region such as Sun, the **Irradiance Cache** method has some limitations which results in the spotty rendering. To fix this, you can use the **Discrete Sky Sampling** setting. The images in the Fig. 55 shows the render when the **Force Per-Pixel** option is disabled and enabled, respectively. Also, see **summary-2.c4d** for reference.

- The **Radiosity Maps** method is used with the preview settings because this method is well suited for fast rendering previews.
- A sampler samples the scene's cache [colors+brightness] from the camera's angle of view.
- The difference between the **Exterior - Physical Sky** preset and the **Exterior - HDR Image** preset is that the **Force Per-Pixel** check box is selected when you use the **Exterior - HDR Image** preset. When you select the **Force Per-Pixel** check box, the calculation of the light emitted by the sky will split from the cache and calculated separately for each pixel. This check box is relevant when you use **Irradiance Cache** as the primary method.
- **Irradiance Cache+QMC** is the best combination for the exterior scenes. **Irradiance Cache** as secondary method works best with the interior spaces with small lights defined as polygon lights or GI portals lights.
- A higher **Custom Sample Count** value produces a corresponding better render quality. If you are using the **QMC** method, this parameter will remove graininess from the render and if you are using the **Irrandiance Cache** method, it will remove spots from the render.
- The cache files are only used when you render the scene using the **Picture Viewer** window not when you render in the viewport.
- The **QMC** method offers best GI quality in comparison to the **Irradiance Cache** method. **QMC** is most precise method but slowest. It works very well with **Light Mapping** used as secondary method.
- The **Irradiance Cache** mode tends to flicker when you use it with animations. It flickers more when you use bright and small polygon lights in the scene.
- The **QMC+QMC** combination produces flicker free results with animations. **Irradiance Cache+QMC** is also prone to flickering. **QMC** works well with **Light Mapping** as secondary method.
- Light leaks can occur when **Light Mapping** is used. Reduce the **Sample Size** value in the **Light Mapping** tab to fix it. Also, ensure that you are using thicker objects instead of single polygon surfaces.
- The **Maximum Depth** value produces more dispersion of light without increasing the render time.

- The **Gamma** value in the **General** tab only affects the indirect GI lighting. It can be used to brighten the relatively darker renders. Be careful with the gamma value, high values tend to kill contrast in the image and flatten it.
- If you use **Irradiance Cache** or **QMC** as secondary method, you will get access to the **Diffuse Depth** parameter which allows you to define that how often the light should be reflected from a surface. High values will cost you in render time.
- It is important that you increase the value of **Record Density** enough so that the light distribution is homogenous otherwise there will be spotty regions in the render. GI caustics also benefits from the higher values.
- When you use the **QMC** method, a lot of CPU power is needed to render the animation.

## Points to Remember - Ambient Occlusion
- **Ambient Occlusion** allows you to control the degree to which each surface point is exposed and then darkens it accordingly. When **Ambient Occlusion** is turned on, areas such as corners, holes, or areas where objects are close to each other appear darker.
- The **Ambient Occlusion** effect can be used with a material.
- You can remove ambient occlusion from individual objects using the **Compositing** tag.
- If you have applied the **Ambient Occlusion** shader to an object and also enabled global **Ambient Occlusion** effect in the **Render Settings** window, the **Ambient Occlusion** calculations will be done twice. As a result, the **Ambient Occlusion** effect will be amplified for the object.
- The **Accuracy, Minimum Samples,** and **Maximum Samples** parameters control the quality of the **Ambient Occlusion** effect.
- When the **Self Shadowing Only** check box is selected, separate objects will not see each other, they will only see themselves.
- You can place the **Ambient Occlusion** shader into the alpha channel of a material; the respective material will only have an effect on the outward pointing edges and corners/peaks.

## Cel Renderer
The **Cel Renderer** post-effect allows you to render pictures and animations in a cartoon style. When you use this effect, the render time increases linearly with the number of polygons in the scene. Open the **cell-renderer.c4d** file [see Fig. 56] and then press **Ctrl+B** to open the **Render Settings** window. In this window, click the **Effect** button to open the **Effect** popup and then choose **Cel Renderer** from the popup to add the effect to the left pane of the **Render Settings** window. Select it in the left pane; the corresponding parameters will be displayed in the right pane [see Fig. 57].

By default, the **Outline** check box is selected. As a result, an outline will be drawn around the silhouette of objects [see Fig. 58]. If you clear both the **Color** and **Outline** checkboxes, only background color will be displayed. The background color is controlled by the **Background Color** swatch. Fig. 59 shows the render with both the **Color** and **Outline** checkboxes selected.

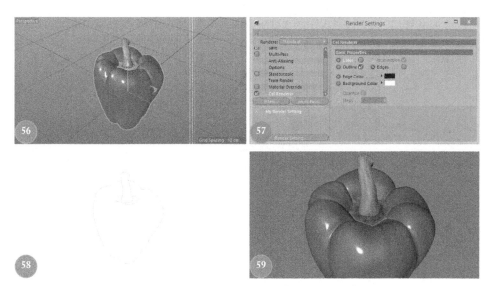

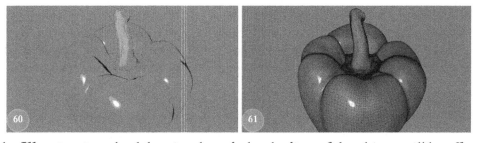

The **Quantize** check box and the **Steps** parameter can be used to render the cartoon effect with color steps. Fig. 60 shows the render with **Steps** set to **6**. If you select the **Edges** check box, all polygon edges will be outlined in black creating shaded wireframe feel [see Fig. 61]. The color of the edges can be changed using the **Edge Color** swatch.

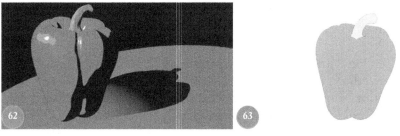

If the **Illumination** check box is selected, the shading of the objects will be affected by illumination in the scene. The cartoon effect will also affect the shadows, refer to Fig. 62 and the **cell-renderer-finish.c4d** file. If the **Illumination** check box is cleared, each color will be displayed in a monotone color. The color will be defined using the right-most texture tag in the **Object Manager**. Also, shadows will not be rendered [see Fig. 63].

## Color Correction

The **Color Correction** post-effect allows you to make common color corrections in Cinema 4D without having to switch to a post-application such as **Photoshop** or **After Effects**. I recommend that instead of using color correction as post effect, you can use it as a filter in the **Picture Viewer** window for greater control [see Fig. 64]. When you use it as post effect, it affects the internal rendering process in 32-bit full color width.

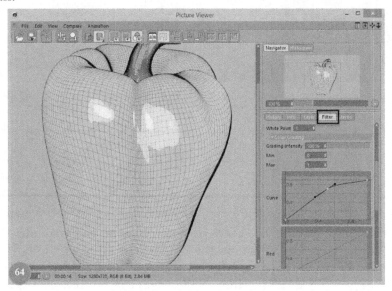

## Color Mapping

When you render a scene using GI with low ray depth, the rendered output appears very bright in some areas and very dark in others. **Color Mapping** allows you to create a nice balanced allocation between the color and brightness to achieve consistent lighting. Fig. 65 shows the options corresponding to the **Color Mapping** effect.

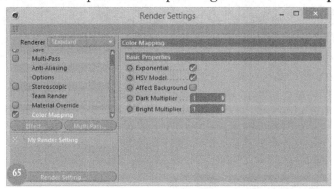

You can achieve this in one of two ways:

- Save the rendered image in **32-bit** depth and then use the appropriate external compositor/editor.
- Use the **Color Mapping** effect and let it calculate the internal interpolation. This post effect kicks in before Cinema 4D applies the sub-pixel anti-aliasing and produces better results than the external application workflow.

By default, the color dispersion is controlled linearly. The **Exponential** check box allows you to control dispersion exponentially. The exponential dispersion results in an even and harmonious color progression.

Open the **color-mapping.c4d** file. In this file, we have a blue backdrop and a **Disc** object is serving as a light source in the scene. A bright white material is applied on the disc with very high brightness in the **Luminance** channel. Also, the **Polygon Light** check box is enabled for the material.

Render the scene [see Fig. 66]. Notice in Fig. 66 that the blue backdrop is lit strongly [also referred to as burnout] in the vicinity of the disc. Press **Ctrl+B** to open the **Render Settings** window. In this window, click the **Effect** button to open the **Effect** popup and then choose **Color Mapping** from the popup to add the effect to the left pane of the **Render Settings** window. Select it in the left pane; the corresponding parameters will be displayed in the right pane. In the right pane, clear the **HSV Model** check box and then select the **Affect Background** check box. Render the scene [see Fig. 67].

Notice in Fig. 67 the color progression on the blue backdrop is harmonious. The **HSV Model** check box allows you to convert colors to HSV model and only the **V** component [**brightness**] component will be affected; the colors will remain identical. If there is any background present in the scene such as a **Sky** or a **Background** object, you can use the **Affect Background** check box to define whether or not **Color Mapping** should affect the background.

The **Dark Multiplier** and **Bright Multiplier** settings allow you to strengthen or weaken the dark and light colors. The left image in Fig. 68 shows the render with no **Color Mapping** applied. In the right image, the **Exponential** and **Affect Background** checkboxes are selected. The **HSV Model** check box is cleared, the **Dark Multiplier** and **Bright Multiplier** parameters are set to **3** and **1**, respectively.

*What is the HSV model?*

*The **HSV** model defines the color using three components: **Hue**, **Saturation**, and **Value [Brightness]**. No prior knowledge of primary colors [red, green, and blue] is required to define a HSV color. As a result, this model allows you to intuitively define the color palettes and this is the reason Cinema 4D uses HSV model for the color wheels. This model comes close to representing perception of color of the human's eye.*

*The **H** value defines the hue and it is displayed as angle on the color wheel. The **S** value defines the saturation of hue. The **V** value defines brightness of the color. A value of **0** produces a black color.*

## Cylindrical Lens

The **Cylindrical Lens** post effect allows you to create **360** degree rendering. This effect is particularly useful if you are a matte painter. Get a rough scene from the modeling department and then render it using the **Cylindrical Lens** effect. Now, you can paint your scenery with help of the rendered output.

Open the **cylindrical-lens.c4d** file. It contains a **Sphere** object that is cloned using the **Cloner** object [see Fig. 69]. Create a **Camera** in the scene and then make it the current camera. Press **Shift+C** to open the **Commander** window and then execute the command **Reset PSR**. This command zero outs all position and rotation coordinates.

*Note: Angle of view*

*Ensure that the angle of view should be parallel to the floor which essentially means that the **R.P** and **R.B** values for the camera should be zero.*

Press **Ctrl+B** to open the **Render Settings** window. In this window, select **Output** from the left pane and then in the right pane, set **Width** and **Height** to **1500** and **200**, respectively. Note that the **Width** value should be larger in relation to the **Height** value.

Click the **Effect** button to open the **Effect** popup and then choose **Cylindrical Lens** from the popup to add the effect to the left pane of the **Render Settings** window. Select it in the left pane; the corresponding parameters will be displayed in the right pane. Now, change **Horizontal Field of View** to **360** and **Vertical Size** to **300**. You have to tweak the value of **Vertical Size** to get rid of any distortion. Render the scene, refer to Fig. 70 and the **cylindrical-lens-finsh.c4d** file.

## Depth of Field

The **Depth of Field** effect is a post effect, it calculates fast but with some restrictions. For example, artifacts may occur in the areas when blurred objects are seen in the reflections or behind the transparent surfaces. You can achieve higher quality depth of field effect using the **Physical** renderer. The process of creating depth-of-field effect using the **Physical** renderer is discussed in next unit.

## Glow

The **Glow** post effect allows you to create glow effects. You can use it to simulate glow of LEDs, neon lights, incandescent lights, and so on. This effect also allows you to:

- Control the transparency of glow.
- Restrict glow to edges or specific colors.
- Apply fractal noise to glow.
- Use additive or non-additive glow to surfaces.
- Prevent unwanted overexposures.
- Change glow according to the surface normals.

Refer to the **glow-start.c4d** and **glow-finish.c4d** files. Also, refer to Figs. 71 and 72.

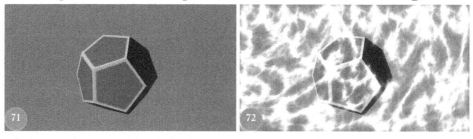

> *Note: Glow effect*
> *This effect can be calculated to a maximum width and height of **4096** pixels.*

> *Note: Glowing materials*
> *The **Glow** channel of the materials is different from the **Glow** effect. Glowing materials always create glow whereas the **Glow** effect generates glow according to the brightness of the rendered pixels. Note that if you have no lights in the scene, the glow materials will always generate glow whereas the **Glow** effect would not.*

# Render Menu

The options in the **Render** menu are used to render an image or an image sequence. Let's explore these options.

### Render View

You can use the **Render View** option to render the active viewport. An active viewport in Cinema 4D has a thick gray border. If you are working in a four-panel view, you can render each view in succession. To do, make a view active and then choose **Render > Render View** from the menubar. You can also click the **Render View** icon in the **Standard** palette > **Render** command group. Now, you can use the **Tab** key to cycle through the views and render them one by one. You can stop the rendering anytime by pressing **Esc** or by clicking in the view. The hotkey to run the **Render View** command is **Ctrl+R**.

 *Caution: Rendering support*
*When you render the active viewport, all types of rendering [e.g. multi-passes] is not supported. Furthermore, certain post processing effects such as motion blur will not be displayed. The rendering progress is displayed in the form of a blue bar at the lower left area of the Cinema 4D interface.*

### Render Region

The **Render Region** tool allows you to render a specific area of the view. This tool is useful when you want to tweak an specific area of the view. You can also press and hold the LMB on the **Render to Picture Viewer** icon in the **Standard** palette > **Render** command group and then choose **Render Region** from the popup menu. You can stop the rendering anytime by pressing **Esc** or by clicking in the view.

### Render Active Objects

The **Render Active Objects** commands renders the selected objects and their children in the active viewport. Select the objects that you want to render and then choose **Render > Render Active Objects** from the menubar. You can also press and hold the LMB on the **Render to Picture Viewer** icon in the **Standard** palette > **Render** command group and then choose **Render Active Objects** from the popup menu.

### Render to Picture Viewer

The **Render to Picture Viewer** command [Hotkey: **Shift+R**] renders the scene in the **Picture Viewer** window. You can also invoke this command by clicking the **Render to Picture Viewer** icon in the **Standard palette** > **Render** command group. Once rendering starts, a progress bar appears in the status bar. This bar shows the time lapsed since the rendering started. If you are rendering an animation, the bar also shows the current frame number and total number of frames. To cancel the rendering, press **Esc**. Fig. 73 shows the **Picture Viewer** window.

The **Picture Viewer** is the output window of Cinema 4D. The rendered image and animations are displayed in this window. Render images of a session are saved in the **History** tab and images rendered for a given session can be called up any time from this tab. A ram player is integrated in the **Picture Viewer** that you can use to play the animation without having to save it in advance as a video. You can also load the sound in the **Picture Viewer**. Let's explore the **Picture Viewer**.

At the top right corner of the viewer are these icons: ▉ ⊞ ✦ ✦. The first icon is used to maximize the display area. It toggles the visibility of the **Navigator** and **Histogram** tabs. The next icon is used to open a new **Picture Viewer**. The next icon is used to move the **Picture Viewer's** clipping region. The right-most icon is used to scale the **Picture Viewer's** clipping region.

Following options are available for the display view:

1. Click-drag in a clipping region to move it.
2. If you press **2** and then click drag, you can scale the image. The mouse wheel scroll will do the same thing.
3. Double-click on the display to scale it to **100%**; double-click again to fit to full screen.
4. If you RMB click, a context menu will open. You can use the options in this menu to select an alternate background color.

### Ram Player

The ram player [see Fig. 74] is used to load and play the image sequence. It loads the sequence temporarily into the dynamic memory of the system so that it can be played back in real-time - even HD quality.

*Caution: Memory*

*The images in the ram player are stored uncompressed. As a result, lots of memory is consumed.*

*Tip: Timeline*

*You can scale the timeline by pressing the **2** key and then dragging the mouse pointer in the timeline. Similarly, you can use the **1** key to move.*

## Navigator

The **Navigator** tab displays the rendered image in the preview size. Depending on the zoom level, the visible region with a moveable square will be displayed. You can double-click in the navigator to set **Zoom** to **100%**. Click and drag to freely move the square. By **Shift**+clicking, the square can be moved horizontally or vertically. You can define a different square region using **Ctrl** dragging.

## Histogram

The **Histogram** tab displays a static dispersion of brightness, color, and luminance information for an image. Peaks in the **Histogram** represent values that occur more often. The drop-down list below histogram defines which color channel will be used. Fig. 75 shows different values. The **Display Filer** check box is only enabled, if you have turned on **Enable Filter** in the **Filter** tab. On selecting this check box, histogram will take the effect of the filter into account.

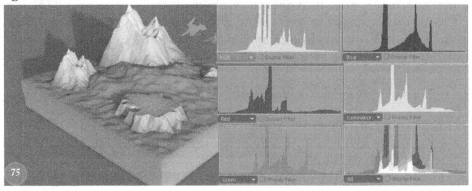

*Note: Human eye*

*The green value carries more weight than red and blue. The human eye sees green as brighter than red/blue.*

## History

The **History** tab [see Fig. 76] displays a list that shows the all the rendered or loaded images for the current session. The list remains empty until a rendering or render session takes place. Click on one of the entries to display it in the **Picture Viewer**. Image names with a * next to them represent images that have not been saved.

The **History** tab contains the following columns:

1. **Name:** The name of the image or directory.
2. **Resolution:** The image resolution in pixels.
3. **R:** Displays image state. **Green:** Cached, **Gray:** Not Cached, **Orange:** Currently being rendered, **A/B:** Images currently being compared.
4. **F:** Frame number
5. **Render Time:** Displays the time system took to render the image.

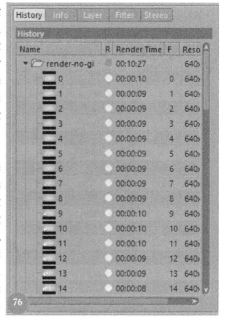

You can select frames in the list using the **Shift** and **Ctrl** keys. You can drag and drop individual images or complete directories to a different location in the hierarchy. Also, you can copy individual images by simultaneously pressing the **Ctrl** key. The arrow keys can be used to navigate up or down through the hierarchy or open [right arrow] or close [left arrow] directories.

You can also compare images in the **Picture Viewer** window. You can only compare images with same resolution. To compare images, select the first image and then choose **Compare > Set As A** from the viewer's menu bar or press **A**. Now, select the second image and then choose **Compare > Set As B** from the viewer's menu bar or press **B**; a dividing line appears in the display. Now, you can drag the line to compare the two images. You can toggle the display of the line by choosing **Compare > AB Compare** from the viewer's menu bar. To swap the AB images choose **Compare > Swap AB** from the viewer's menu bar or press **S**. To toggle the orientation of the line choose **Compare > Swap Vert./Horiz.** from the viewer's menu bar.

Press the RMB to open a context menu whose commands can all be found in the **Picture Viewer** menu with the exception of the following:

Show File in Explorer/Finder
This command opens the corresponding application on your system and displays the file, if the file was loaded via the **Picture Viewer**.

Create Render Setting from Render
If you have made several test renderings using different render settings and want to select the settings that fit best, you can use this command to creates a new, separate render presets for rendered images or image sequences for the current Cinema 4D session.

## Info

The **Info** panel displays several self-explanatory pieces of information regarding the selected image. For newly rendered scene, this tab also displays render time per image and the total render time. The **Title Safe** and **Action Safe** parameters are used control the size of the title safe and action safe frames, respectively. The title safe and action safe settings can be enabled from the viewer's **View** menu. The **Pixel Aspect** parameter can be used to distort the aspect ratio in the **Picture Viewer**.

## Layer

The **Layer** tab displays the images selected in the history tab, including all passes and alpha channel. There are three radio buttons in the **Layer** area: **Image**, **Single-Pass**, and **Multi-Pass**. On selecting the **Image** radio button, only the layer defined as "**background**" will be shown [see Fig. 77].

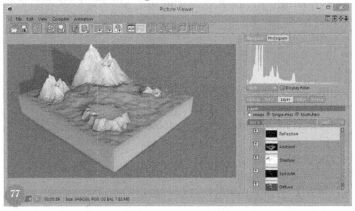

If you select the **Single-Pass** radio button, you can display an individual pass by selecting it. Fig. 78 shows the **Shadow** pass. When you select the Multi-Pass radio button, the image mode is switched to **Multi-Pass** mode, you can now select blending mode from the drop-down list in this tab. Also, you can adjust the mix strength using the float slider available on the left of the drop-down list. Fig. 79 shows the mix strength and blending mode set to **34** and **Multiply**, respectively, for the **Shadow** pass.

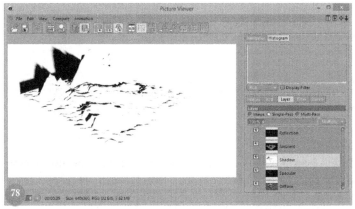

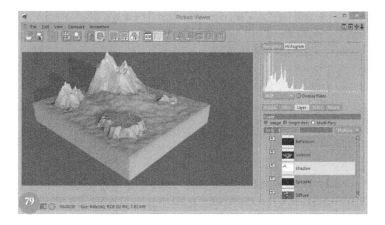

### Filter

The options in the **Filter** tab are used to adjust the properties of the image. The effect are temporarily applied to the loaded or rendered sequence. Only when the images are saved with the **Enable Filter** option enabled, the **Filter** actually be applied to the images.

### Render To Picture Viewer

This command renders the scene to the **Picture Viewer**. Once rendering starts, a progress bar appears in the status bar.

### Render to Picture Viewer (Team Render)

The functionality of this command is same to that of the **Render to Picture Viewer** command, only that rendering will be done using **Team Render**.

### Takes

The **Render All Takes to PV** and **Render Marked Takes to PV** options are used to render all or marked **Takes** in succession to the **Picture Viewer (PV)**. The **Team Render All Takes to PV** and **Team Render Marked Takes to PV** options are used to render all or marked takes in succession to the **Picture Viewer (PV)** using **Team Render**. These options are also available in the **Render to Picture Viewer** popup.

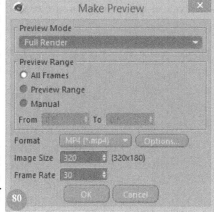

### Make Preview

On executing the **Make Preview** command [Hotkey: **Alt+B**], the **Make Preview** dialog box will be displayed [see Fig. 80]. You can use the options in this dialog box to create a preview of the animation.

The preview will be played in the **Picture Viewer.** The OpenGL options offer excellent render quality. Make sure the **Enhanced OpenGL** option is activated in the **Display** menu of the **Menu in editor view**.

## Add to Render Queue

You can use the **Add to Render Queue** command to add currently opened scene to the list of **Render Queue** window.

## Render Queue

The options in the **Render Queue** window [see Fig. 81] allow you to batch render any number of files without supervision.

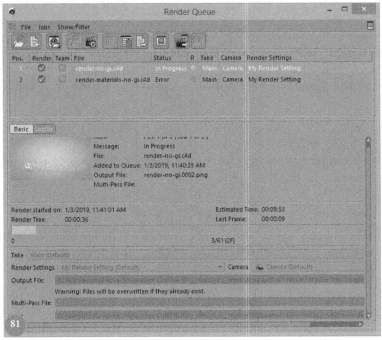

The following functions are available in this window:

- Render any number of files consecutively without any supervision.
- Redirect save paths, select cameras, select takes, and render settings without opening the files itself.
- Extensive **Render Queue** configurations can be saved as presets.
- Log files can be saved and viewed.
- Rendered images are displayed in a preview window during rendering.
- The rendering of animations can be interrupted and later continued automatically at the same location. Note that you cannot interrupt and continue videos, only individual frames can be continued.
- Simultaneous rendering in the **Picture Viewer** and the **Render Queue**.
- Scenes can be rendered without opening them in the view, which saves memory.

The job list in the **Render Queue** contains the following information:

- **Pos.:** The sequence no of the jobs. You can change the position of the jobs by using drag-drop operations.
- **Render:** You can enable or disable a job using the check box available in this column.
- **Team:** Select the check box in this column to define which jobs should be rendered using **Team Render**.
- **Status/R:** Displays the current status of the job. *In Queue/R* - ready to render, *In Progress* - is being rendered, *Take* - the Take selected for rendering, *Finished* - render completed successfully, *Stopped* - render was halted before being completed, and *Error* - error occurred during rendering
- **Camera:** The camera from which the scene is rendered.
- **Render Settings: Render Settings** with which the file is rendered.
- **Message:** Pertinent messages are displayed here, for example, if a file is missing, information for saving, etc.

When you select a job in the job list, the related information such as render progress, estimated render time, take name, render settings, camera, output file name path, and so on is displayed at the bottom half of the **Render Queue** window. You can change these options, as per your requirement. An existing job list will be maintained even if you close Cinema 4D. The list will reappear when Cinema 4D is restarted and the **Queue Manager** is opened.

## Interactive Render Region

The **Interactive Render Region** or **IRR** tool is used for test renderings. The **IRR** can be placed and scaled freely in a scene [see Fig. 82]. It is saved along with the scene. The region defined by **IRR** is re-rendered as soon as a new region is selected, or an object is edited, or any other change is made that affects the rendering state such as repositioning the lights in the scene.

Click-drag the handles of the region to scale the box. To move, hover the mouse pointer on one of region edges and drag when mouse pointer icon changes to a hand.

At the right edge of the **IRR** you will find a triangular slider with which the render resolution can be adjusted. If you want the best render quality, move the triangle all the way to the top. However, as always, the better the render quality, the longer the preview will take to render. RMB click on the edges to open a context menu. Using the options available in the context menu, you can define the behavior of **IRR**.

### Edit Render Settings

This command opens the **Render Settings** window. The options in this window have already been discussed. Below the **Edit Render Settings** option in the **Render** menu, the render preset are listed. You can select the preset to make it active. As discussed earlier in the unit, you can create these presets in the **Render Settings** window.

### Team Render Machines

With **Team Render,** you can quickly and easily render on multiple computers [on which the same version of Cinema 4D must be installed] across a local network with the click of a button. On choosing the **Team Render Machines** option, the **Team Render Machines** window will open. You can manage the network rendering from this window.

### Share Machine Over Network

The **Share Machine Over Network** command is used to remove or add the current computer to **Team Render**. You can use this command to temporarily free up memory on the computer on which you're currently working. If you remove the current computer during rendering, the process will continue when the computer is added again using this command.

### Flush Illumination Caches

If you enable cache on the **Render Settings** window > **Global Illumination** or **Caustics** tabs, files will be saved in the **Illum** folder of the scene so that subsequent renders can reuse the data. Choose the **Flush Illumination Caches** option to delete these files. If you have selected the **Cache Shadow Maps** check box in the **Render Settings** window > **Options** > **Options** area, this command will also flush cached shadow maps.

 *Caution: Missing textures*
*If Cinema 4D is unable to find textures when you render, it will display an alert. If you choose to continue rendering, materials will be used without the missing texture.*

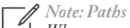 *Note: Paths*
*When you render, Cinema 4D searches for texture in the following locations:*

1. *The same folder as the scene file.*
2. *In the **Tex** sub-folder of the scene's folder.*
3. *In the **Text** sub-folder of the Cinema 4D installation folder.*
4. *If you have specified an absolute path, Cinema 4D will search only in that path.*
5. *If you are using assets from the Cinema 4D libraries, the corresponding path can be specified in texture's file name parameter.*
6. *And finally, Cinema 4D also searches in the paths specified in the **Preferences** window. To define the path, open the **Preferences** window and then select **Files** > **Paths** in the left pane of the window. Now, in the right pane, add paths in the **File Assets** area.*

## Compositing Tag

The **Compositing** tag contains several options that affect rendering. You can add compositing tag by choosing **Tags** > **Cinema 4D Tags** > **Compositing** from the **Object Manager** menu or RMB clicking on an object and then choosing **Cinema 4D Tags** > **Compositing** from the context menu. Select the tag's icon in the **Object Manager**, the corresponding parameters will be displayed in the **Attribute Manager** [see Fig. 83].

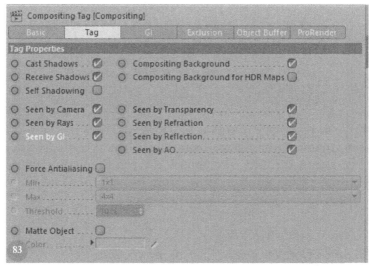

You can use the **Cast Shadows** and **Receive Shadows** checkboxes to enable/prevent objects from casting or receiving shadows. If you want an object to cast shadows onto other objects but not on itself, clear the **Self Shadowing** check box.

 *Caution: Soft shadows*
*If you are using soft shadows in the scene, you cannot disable self shadowing.*

If **Seen by Camera** check box is selected, all first generation rays; the visual rays from the camera from which the scene is being viewed will see a given object. If you clear the **Seen by Camera** check box, Cinema 4D will not hide the respective object from view entirely because it will, depending on the settings used, still be visible in transparent or reflective surfaces.

If the **Seen by Rays** check box is selected, subsequent [higher] generations of rays [those of a reflection or refraction] will also be calculated. These rays can in turn be applied separately in conjunction with the checkboxes [**Seen by Transparency**, **Seen by Refraction**, and **Seen by Reflection**] described below.

If you want the object to generate global illumination, select the **Seen by GI** check box. If you clear this check box, the object will not generate global illumination. You can use the **Global Illumination** effect in the **Render Settings** window to globally enable or disable GI.

When you select the **Compositing Background** check box, the object will be self-illuminated and will receive shadows. The object in question must have its own material. In the example shown in Fig. 84, the floor has its own material.

Select the **Compositing Background for HDR Maps** check box to integrate rendered objects in a scene that was illuminated using the GI and HDRI textures. The HDRI textures must be assigned to the **Sky** object. You can then apply the **Compositing** tag to the **Floor** object; light and shadows from GI will then be combined with the background image.

*Tip: Shadow Catcher shader*
*The **Shadow Catcher** shader can do pretty much the same. However, the shader works more flexibly with the **Alpha** channel.*

The **Seen by GI** check box can be used to exclude individual objects from the GI calculations. This can be useful, for example, when you are using multiple **Sky** objects: one for direct visibility, one for reflected/refracted rays and one for generating GI.

When the **Seen by Transparency** check box is clear, an object with this **Compositing** tag setting will not be visible when behind transparent objects. The **Seen by Refraction** setting only applies when **Refraction** in the material's **Transparency** channel menu is not equal to **1**. Otherwise, the **Seen by Transparency** setting will apply. When this check box is clear, the object with this **Compositing** tag setting will no longer be visible behind transparent objects that have a refraction index. If **Seen by Reflection** check box is clear, the object with this **Compositing** tag setting will no longer be visible in reflective objects. You can use the **Seen by AO** check box to define whether or not an object should be included in **Ambient Occlusion**.

The global antialiasing settings are defined in the **Render Settings** window. To override the global settings, select the **Force Antialiasing** check box and then you can use the **Min**, **Max**, and **Threshold** parameters to define new antialiasing settings.

When you select the **Matte Object** check box, the **Color** parameter will be activated. The object to which the **Compositing** tag is assigned will be colored with only the color defined using the **Color** parameter. No shading or lighting will be applied. Compare Figs. 85 and 86. The **Compositing** tag is assigned to red spheres and pink color is assigned to the **Color** parameter. The object in question will not appear in the **Alpha** channel.

# Hands-on Exercises

## Exercise 1: Rendering a Flicker Free Animation

One of the challenges that you generally face while rendering an image sequence from a GI enabled scene is to remove flicker from the rendered output. In this exercise, we will look at the different scenarios. The following table summarizes the exercise:

| Table E1 | |
|---|---|
| Difficulty level | Intermediate |
| Estimated time to complete | 2 Hours |
| Topics | • Getting Started<br>• Rendering the Animation |
| Resources folder | **unit-cr1** |
| Units | **Centimeters** |
| Start file | **flicker-free-start.c4d** |
| Final file | **flicker-free-finish.c4d** |

### Getting Started

Open the **flicker-free-start.c4d** file. In this file, we have an animated MoGraph setup. Scrub the timeline to see the animation. Before you start rendering a scene, you need to make sure that the lighting and shadows are correct in the scene. If you properly illuminate the scene, you don't need the global illumination in the scene. Also, make sure the quality of shadows is correct in the scene.

If you are using area shadows in the scene, to check the quality of the shadows, apply a neutral-gray material to all objects in the scene. Solo each light and then check the shadows it is casting in the scene. Select the light and then go to the **Shadow** tab in the **Attribute Manager**. The **Density, Color, Accuracy, Minimum Samples**, and **Maximum Samples** parameters in this tab control the quality of the area shadows. Follow the steps given next to use optimal settings for shadows:

1. Find out the grainy areas in the scene.

2. Set the **Minimum Samples** and **Maximum Samples** parameters to the same value and then render the grainy areas using the **Render Region** feature.

3. Raise the values of the **Minimum Samples** and **Maximum Samples** parameters to same value until you get good results.

4. Lower the value of the **Minimum Samples** parameter to **25%** of the **Maximum Samples** parameter's value and set **Accuracy** to **50%**. Now, raise the **Accuracy** value until you see the good result.

Once you are satisfied with the results, you can apply the materials to the objects and proceed with rendering. The **flicker-free-start.c4d** file is already optimized for the shadows. Let's first check how the render looks with no **Global Illumination** effect applied and default render settings.

### Rendering the Animation

Follow these steps:

1. Press **Ctrl+B** to open the **Render Settings** window. Make sure **Standard** from the **Renderer** drop-down list.

2. Select **Output** from the left pane of the window, if not already selected. In the right pane, select the **Lock Ratio** check box and then change **Width** to **320**; the **Height** automatically changes to **180**. You can set a higher resolution as per the configuration of your computer.

3. Select **All Frames** from the **Frame Range** drop-down list. The **From** and **To** parameters reflect the frame range.

4. Select **Save** from the left pane. In the **Regular Image** area of the right pane, click the browse button corresponding to the **File** parameter to open the **Save File** dialog box. In this dialog box, navigate to the location where you want to save the file and then create a new folder with the name **flicker-free**. Now, create a sub-folder with the name **no-gi** and then open this folder. Now, type **render-no-gi** in the **File name** field and then click **Save**. Change **Format** to **PNG** and then change **Name** to **Name.0000.TIF**.

*What just happened?*
*Here, we have set the **Name** parameter to **Name.0000.TIF**. As a result, the rendered **PNG** files will be named as **render-no-gi.0000.png**, **render-no-gi.0001.png**, **render-no-gi.0002.png**, and so on.*

5. Save the file as **render-no-gi.c4d**. Now, press **Shift+R** to render animation in the **Picture Viewer** window. Fig. E1 shows the render at frames **10** and **42**, respectively.

Once the render is complete, you can choose the **Play Forwards** button from the **Picture Viewer** window. The playback controls are located at the bottom-right corner of the **Picture Viewer** window [see Fig. E2]. This render without GI took **3.03** minutes on my system.

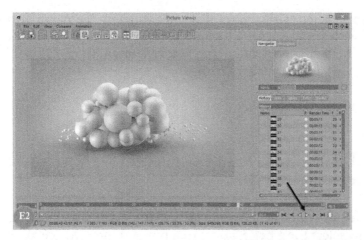

If you want to skip rendering, you can open the render sequence available with the resources of this book. To do so, choose **File > Open** from the **Picture Viewer** window's menubar to open the **Open File** dialog box and then navigate to the location where you have downloaded the sequence. Select the file and then click **Open**. In the **Open** dialog box that is displayed [see Fig. E3], click **OK** to load the sequence in the window.

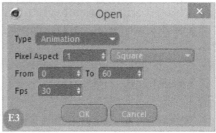

Notice during the playback, we have got almost flicker/noise free render. Whenever possible, avoid using GI with animation and try to illuminate the scene using the various lights available in Cinema 4D.

*What next?*
*Now, we already have the scene with optimized shadows. Before we apply the **Global Illumination** settings, we need to make sure that our materials are looking right. If there is any issue, you need to fix it before you proceed. In next steps, you will apply materials and also specify the optimized render settings.*

6.  Save the file with the name **render-materials-no-gi.c4d**. Apply the **Green, Violet, Red**, and **Yellow** materials to **Sphere, Sphere.1, Sphere.2**, and **Sphere.3**, respectively.

7.  Press **Ctrl+B** to open the **Render Settings** window. Select **Save** from the left pane. In the **Regular Image** area of the right pane, click the browse button corresponding to the **File** parameter to open the **Save File** dialog box. In this dialog box, navigate to **flicker-free** folder and then create a new sub-folder with the name **materials-no-gi**. Open this folder and then type **render-materials-no-gi** in the **File** name field and then click **Save**.

8. Select **Anti-Aliasing** from the left pane. In the **Anti-Aliasing** area, change **Anti-Aliasing** to **Best**, **Max Level** to **2x2**, and **Threshold** to **20**.

9. Select **Options** from the left pane. In the **Options** area, change **Ray Depth** to **6**, **Reflection Depth** to **3**, and **Shadow Depth** to **3**. Clear the **Automatic Size** check box and then expand the **Automatic Size** area. Now, change **Bucket Width** and **Bucket Height** to **32** each.

10. Choose the **Effect** button from left pane and then choose **Ambient Occlusion** to add the **Ambient Occlusion** effect. Ensure it is selected in the left pane and then in the **Basic** tab, change **Maximum Ray Length** to **30**.

11. Press **Ctrl+S** to save the file. Press **Shift+R** to render the animation in the **Picture Viewer** window.

If you now play the rendered sequence, you will notice that we have now acceptable render quality and there is no flicker in the scene. This render took **4.59** minutes on my system.

 *What next?*
*Now, we have seen the rendered output without any GI in the scene. Let's now enable the GI and see how the rendered output looks. We already know that* **Irradiance Cache** *produces flickering results but let's see how flicker looks in this case.*

12. Save the scene as **render-ic-low.c4d**. Press **Ctrl+B** to open the **Render Settings** window.

13. Select **Save** from the left pane. In the **Regular Image** area of the right pane, click the browse button corresponding to the **File** parameter to open the **Save File** dialog box. In this dialog box, navigate to **flicker-free** folder and then create a new sub-folder with the name **ic-low**. Open this folder and then type **render-ic-low** in the **File** name field and then click **Save**.

14. Choose the **Effect** button from left pane and then choose **Global Illumination** to add the **Global Illumination** effect. Ensure it is selected in the left pane and then in the **General** tab, change **Preset** to **Interior - Preview**. Notice that **Irradiance Cache** and **Radiosity Maps** are selected as **Primary Method** and **Secondary Method**, respectively.

15. Press **Ctrl+S** to save the file. Now, press **Shift+R** to render the animation in the **Picture Viewer** window. This render took **7.16** minutes on my system. Notice that the render time increased as we introduced GI in the scene.

*What next?*
*Check the image sequence, you will notice that there are lots of artifacts in the rendered sequence. The preview settings are well-suited for test renderings. Let's now see what happens when we use high GI settings.*

16. Save as the file with the name **render-ic-high.c4d**. Press **Ctrl+B** to open the **Render Settings** window.

17. Select **Save** from the left pane. In the **Regular Image** area of the right pane, click the browse button corresponding to the **File** parameter to open the **Save File** dialog box. In this dialog box, navigate to **flicker-free** folder and then create a new sub-folder with the name **ic-high**. Open this folder and then type **render-ic-high** in the **File** name field and then click **Save**.

18. Select **Global Illumination** from the left pane. In the **General** tab, change the **Primary Method** and the **Secondary Method** to **Irradiance Cache** and **Light Mapping**, respectively. Change **Samples** to **Custom Sample Count** and **Sample Count** to **1000**.

19. Expand the **Discrete Sky Sampling** area and then select the **Custom Count** check box. Also, change **Sample Count** to **3000**.

20. In the **Irradiance Cache** tab, change **Record Density** to **Medium**. In the **Light Mapping** tab, change **Path Count (x1000)** to **6000**.

21. Press **Ctrl+S** to save the file. Now, press **Shift+R** to render animation in the **Picture Viewer** window. This render took **44.29** minutes on my system.

*What next?*
*Notice that we still have flickering in the rendered sequence even when we are using a high **Sample Count** value.*

22. Save the file with the name **render-ic-rm-high.c4d**.

23. In the **Render Settings** window, select **Save** from the left pane. In the **Regular Image** area of the right pane, click the browse button corresponding to the **File** parameter to open the **Save File** dialog box. In this dialog box, navigate to **flicker-free** folder and then create a new sub-folder with the name **ic-rm-high**. Open this folder and then type **render-ic-rm-high** in the **File** name field and then click **Save**.

24. Select **Global Illumination** from the left pane and then in the **General** tab of the right pane, change **Secondary Method** to **Radiosity Maps**. In the **Radiosity Maps** tab, change **Sampling Subdivisions** to **2** and then save the file.

25. Press **Shift+R** to render animation in the **Picture Viewer** window. Play the animation, still notice that we have flickering in the rendered output. This render took **36.22** minutes on my system.

→ *What next?*
  *We already know that the **QMC+QMC** algorithm produces flicker free output but if you use **QMC** both for the primary as well as for the secondary GI method, the rendering process will be very slow. Let's see if we can get away with using any other method for secondary bounces.*

26. Save the file with the name **render-qmc.c4d**.

27. Press **Ctrl+B** to open the **Render Settings** window. Select **Save** from the left pane. In the **Regular Image** area of the right pane, click the browse button corresponding to the **File** parameter to open the **Save File** dialog box. In this dialog box, navigate to **flicker-free** folder and then create a new sub-folder with the name **qmc**. Open this folder and then type **render-qmc** in the **File** name field and then click **Save**.

28. In the **Global Illumination > General** tab, change the **Primary Method** and the **Secondary Method** to **Quasi-Monte Carlo** and **Light Mapping**, respectively. Change **Samples** to **Medium**. In the **Light Mapping** tab, change **Path Count (x1000)** to **1000**.

29. Save the file. Now, press **Shift+R** to render animation in the **Picture Viewer** window.

After completing the render, play the animation. You will notice that now we have flicker free and noise free rendered output. After all the experiments with different render settings, it is evident that **QMC + Light Mapping** is the best combination for rendering scenes with GI. On my machine, it took **83** minutes to render **60** frames at the **320x180** resolution.

## Exercise 2: Rendering a Specific Region of the Scene

Suppose, you have found a mistake in a specific region of the render; you can use the **Interactive Render Region** tool to render just that part of the scene and then fix the wrong image in post. This will save you lot of time as you don't have to render the whole image again. In this exercise, we will work on the **Interactive Render Region** feature to render a specific region of the scene [see Fig. E1]. Table E2 summarizes the exercise.

| Table E2 | |
|---|---|
| Difficulty level | Beginner |
| Estimated time to complete | Depends on the scene complexity |
| Topics | • Getting Started<br>• Using the Interactive Render Region Tool |
| Resources folder | **unit-cr1** |
| Units | **Centimeters** |
| Start file | **render-region-start.c4d** |
| Final file | **render-region-finish.c4d** |

### Getting Started

Open **render-region-start.c4d**.

### Using The Interactive Render Region Tool

Follow these steps:

1. Make sure the **Camera** view is active and then render the scene in the **Picture Viewer** window [see Fig. E1A]. Notice in Fig. E1A that the front landscape is not rendered as low poly. Save the image using the image format of your choice.

*What next?*
*Now, instead of rendering the whole image, we will just render the problematic region.*

2. Choose **Render > Interactive Render Region** from the menubar. Now, place the render region, as shown in Fig. E2.

3. Place the quality triangle all the way to the top [see Fig. E3] and then in the **Object Manager**, delete the **Phong Tag** corresponding to the **L5** object.

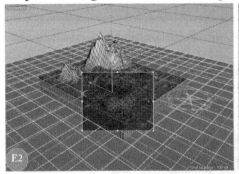
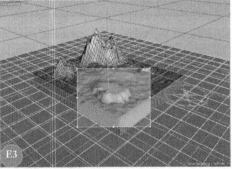

*What just happened?*
*Here, I have deleted the **Phong Tag** so that the corresponding object appears low poly in the render. By anchoring the quality triangle at the top, we have ensured that the **IRR** tool will use the render settings defined in the **Render Settings** window.*

4. Open the **Render Settings** window and then select **Output** from the left pane of the window. In the right pane, select the **Render Region** check box and then expand the **Render Region** area. Now, click on the **Copy from IRR** button.

5. Select **Save** from the left pane and then in the right pane, select the **Alpha Channel** check box. Render the scene in the **Picture Viewer** [refer to Fig. E1B]. Save the image using the image format of your choice. Now, you can composite the two saved images in a post-production application such as Nuke, Photoshop, or After Effects.

### Exercise 3: Dynamically Controlling the Depth-of-Field Effect

In this exercise, we will create the dynamic depth-of-field effect using the **Standard** renderer and the **Depth** pass [see Fig. E1]. We will use the **Lens Blur** filter in **Photoshop** to create and control the blur effect. Table E3 summarizes the exercise.

| Table E3 | |
|---|---|
| Difficulty level | Intermediate |
| Estimated time to complete | 20 Minutes |
| Topics | • Getting Started<br>• Create the Effect |
| Resources folder | **unit-cr1** |
| Units | **Centimeters** |
| Start file | **dof-depth-start.c4d** |
| Final file | **dof-depth-finish.c4d** |

### Getting Started
Open **dof-depth-start.c4d**.

### Creating the Effect
Follow these steps:

1. Open the **Render Settings** window and then make sure that **Renderer** is set to **Standard**.

2. Select the check box corresponding to the **Multi-Pass** option and then click on the **Multi-Pass** button to open a flyout. Choose **Depth** from the flyout to add the **Depth** pass.

3. Select the check box corresponding to the **Save** option and then click on the **Save** option. In the **Regular Image** area, make sure the **Save** check box is selected and then type **beauty-pass** in the **File** field.

4. In the **Multi-Pass Image** area, make sure the **Save** check box is selected and then type **depth-pass** in the **File** field. Also, change **Format** to **PNG** and clear the **Layer Name as Suffix** check box.

5. Select the **Ant-Aliasing** option from the left pane and then in the right pane, select **Best** from the **Ant-Aliasing** drop-down list. Close the **Render Settings** window.

6. Select **Camera** in the **Object Manager** and then in the **Attribute Manager > Object** tab, change **Focus Distance** to **856.566**. In the **Attribute Manager > Details** tab, select the **DOF Map Front Blur** and **DOF Map Rear Blur** checkboxes.

7. Change **DOF Map Front Blur > End** to **306.428** and **DOF Map Rear Blur > End** to **564.673** [see Figs. E2 and E3]. Leave the **Start** values at **0**. Now, make sure **Camera** view is active and then render the scene. Figs. E4 and E5 show the beauty and render passes, respectively.

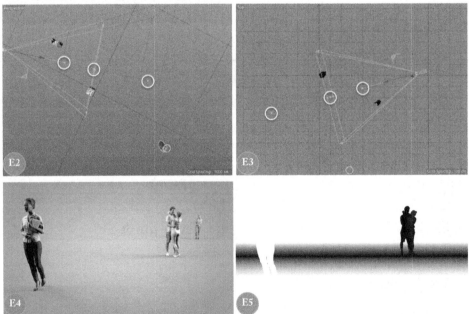

*What just happened?*
*The **DOF Map Front Blur** and **DOF Map Rear Blur** parameters allow you to define which part of an images should be in focus and which out of focus.*

8. Start **Photoshop** and then open the **diffuse-pass.png** and then place the **depth-pass.png** file in another layer [see Fig. E6].

9. Press **Ctrl+A** to select all pixels, press **Ctrl+C**, and then switch to the **Channels** panel. In this panel, click the **Create new channel** icon and then press **Ctrl+V**. Switch to the **RGB** channel.

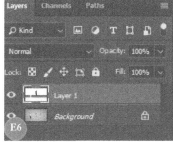

10. Switch to the **Layers** panel and then press **Ctr+D** to clear the selection. Hide the top layer. Select the **Background** layer and then choose **Filter > Blur > Lens Blur** from the menubar to open the **Lens Blur** window. In the **Depth Map** area of this window, change **Source** to **Alpha1** and **Blur Focal Distance** to **0**.

11. In the **Iris** area, change **Shape** to **Octagon (6)**, **Radius** to **8**, and **Blade Curvature** to **87**. Click **OK**. Save the file as **dynamic-dof.psd**.

 *Tip: Changing focus*
*In the **Lens Blur** window, use the **Blur Focal Distance** parameter to dynamically change the focus. The strength of the effect can controlled using the **Radius** parameter.*

## Quiz

**Multiple Choice**
Answer the following questions:

1. Which of the following key combinations is used to open the **Render Settings** window?

   [A] Ctrl+R          [B] Ctrl+B
   [C] Ctrl+S          [D] Ctrl+A

2. Which of the following parameters is used to control the movement of the rays in the scene?

   [A] Ray Depth Threshold          [B] Ray Threshold
   [C] Depth Threshold          [D] None of these

3. Which of the following key combinations is used to render images in the **Picture Viewer**?

[A] Shift+P          [B] Ctrl+P
[C] Shift+R          [D] Ctrl+R

4. Which of the following keys is used to swap AB images?

[A] A                [B] S
[C] B                [D] W

**Fill in the Blanks**
Fill in the blanks in each of the following statements:

1. The _____ function allows you to render a selected region of the scene.

2. If you have defined an interactive render region in the viewport, you can quickly define the **Left Border, Top Border, Right Border,** and **Bottom Border** parameters by clicking on the _____ button.

3. In Cinema 4D, you can use variable path and file names known as _____ in the **File** input field.

4. The settings corresponding to the _____ option allow you to remove jagged edges from your images.

5. You can remove ambient occlusion from individual objects using the _____ tag.

6. The _____ check box is used to define whether or not enable or disable textures when you render.

7. The _____ post-effect allows you to render pictures and animations in a cartoon style.

8. The _____ post-effect allows you to make common color corrections in Cinema 4D without having to switch to a post-application such as Photoshop or After Effects.

9. The _____ post effect allows you to create 360 degree rendering.

10. To toggle the orientation of the AB line choose _____ from the viewer's menu bar.

**True or False**

State whether each of the following is true or false:

1. You can open render settings from the **Attribute Manger**.

2. When you render a video, you cannot specify video and audio bitrate for the video.

3. Selected objects cannot be rendered using the **Standard** renderer.

4. If you do not have a defined light source in the scene, a default light is used to render the scene.

5. Node materials are not supported by the **Material Override** option.

6. If a scene does not contain materials that reflect light, additional render time will be added if the **Refraction** check box is selected.

7. When you use a **Sky** object with the HDR texture, the auto light is not disabled. If you add GI to the scene, the auto light will disabled.

8. The **Primary Method** only brightens surfaces that are directly lit and the **Secondary Method** is responsible for additional reflected light.

9. The **Diffuse Depth** parameter is only available if the **Irradiance Cache** or **QMC** method is not used as a secondary method.

10. The **Irradiance Cache** method offers best GI quality in comparison to the **QMC** method.

**Summary**
This unit covered the following topics:

- Standard renderer
- Global Illumination
- Ambient Occlusion
- Render Settings
- Post Effects

- Physical Renderer
- Hardware OpenGL Renderer
- Software OpenGL Renderer
- Depth-of-field
- Motion Blur

# Unit CR2: Other Renderers

You can use the **Physical** renderer if you want to render special effects such as depth-of-field, motion blur, and so on. In most cases, you can use the stable and fast **Standard** renderer. However, if you want to achieve the following photographic effects, you should use the **Physical** renderer.

- Depth-of-field and corresponding blur effects
- Motion blur
- Vignetting
- Chromatic aberration

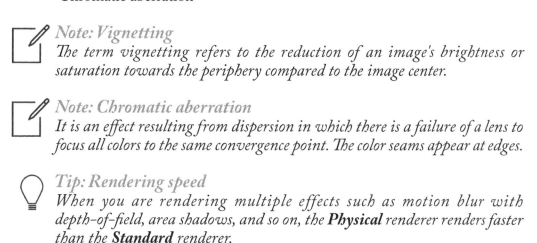

*Note: Vignetting*
*The term vignetting refers to the reduction of an image's brightness or saturation towards the periphery compared to the image center.*

*Note: Chromatic aberration*
*It is an effect resulting from dispersion in which there is a failure of a lens to focus all colors to the same convergence point. The color seams appear at edges.*

*Tip: Rendering speed*
*When you are rendering multiple effects such as motion blur with depth-of-field, area shadows, and so on, the **Physical** renderer renders faster than the **Standard** renderer.*

There some drawbacks with the **Physical** renderer:

- To calculate special effects such as depth-of-field and motion blur, it requires more calculations and more time. However, it provides some settings that you can use to optimize the render time.
- It does not work in conjunction with the **Sketch and Toon** effect, the **Cel Renderer** post effect, specular lights, the **Cylindrical Lens** effect, and some other effects available in the **Effects** menu.

- Motion blur does not work in conjunction with several special elements such as PyroCluster, visible lights, and object glow.
- Hair is rendered much slower; hair multi-passes cannot be rendered.
- Area shadows are rendered; no hard shadows can be rendered.

## Exploring Physical Renderer

To make the **Physical** renderer active renderer, press **Ctrl+B** to open the **Render Settings** window. Select **Physical** from the **Renderer** drop-down list located at the upper-left corner of the window. A entry with the name **Physical** will be added in the left pane. Select it; the corresponding options will be displayed on the right pane under the **Basic** and **Advanced** tabs [see Fig. 1].

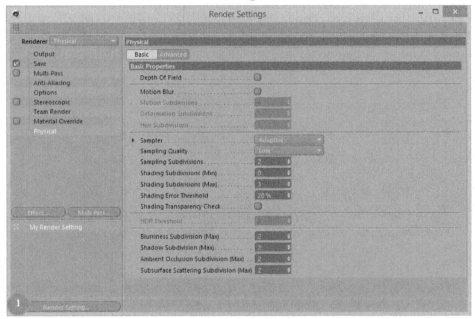

### Sampler

A sampler samples the scene's cache [colors] from the camera's angle of view. To achieve the render quality, it determines which regions of the scene has to be sampled again with regard to the anti-aliasing and blur effects such as depth-of-field and motion blur. The number of samples [colors/cache] gathered by the sampler exceeds the number of actual pixels. These samples in the end are turned into pixels color using an anti-aliasing filter. There are three methods available in Cinema 4D for sampling: **Adaptive, Fixed**, and **Progressive**. You can select these modes from the **Basic** tab > **Sampler** drop-down list. These modes are discussed next:

### Fixed

The **Fixed** method uses an unchangeable, fix per-pixel sample number. This is comparable to the default renderer's **Best** and **Min/Max** anti-aliasing settings. When you select this method, the **Sampling Subdivisions** parameter is made available. It defines the number of shading samples required per pixel.

## Progressive

In the **Progressive** method, the sampler can run indefinitely and will continuously pick [calculate] the samples. During this time, the result will continuously improve. The longer you run the render with the **Progressive** method, the better the quality of the anti-aliasing and blur effects will be. The improved quality will not be so obvious on the homogeneously colored surfaces but can be seen in regions of blur effects such as depth-of-field, motion blur, and area shadows.

 *Caution: Unbiased rendering*
*The **Physical** renderer does not offer unbiased rendering. In this type of rendering, GI among other things is biased which essentially means is that GI is unadulterated with regard to physical correctness and precision. As a result, the GI effect is continuously improved with time. The **Progressive** method does not offer this functionality.*

When the **Progressive** method is selected, all sampling parameters are disabled [see Fig. 2]. This method is primarily suitable for fast preview renderings because it allows you to assess the overall quality of the render. No other method offers such a fast rendition of the quality of the entire image.

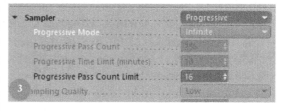

Click on the black triangle at left to **Sampler** to make numerous settings visible related to the **Progressive** method [see Fig. 3]. The default **Progressive Mode** is **Infinite**. As a result, the render will never end. If you want to end the render after a specified  number of passes, change **Progressive Mode** to **Pass Count** and then specify the count using the **Progressive Pass Count** parameter. You can also run render for a specified time by first changing **Progressive Mode** to **Time Limit** and then specify time in minutes using the **Progressive Time Limit (minutes)** parameter.

## Adaptive

The **Adaptive** method is the recommended method because it offers a good mix between the quality and render speed. It renders faster than the **Fixed** sampler. When you use this method, an increased number of samples are used for the critical and important regions. This is comparable to the default renderer's **Best** anti-aliasing setting.

*Caution: Detailed textures and sharp edges*
*The **Adaptive** sampler renders less sharp edges than the **Fixed** sampler. Therefore, if you want to render a detailed texture with sharp edges, use the **Fixed** sampler.*

The **Adaptive** sampler gives good results but it's hard to control as it uses four settings to sample pixels: **Sampling Subdivisions, Shading Subdivisions (Min), Shading Subdivisions (Max)**, and **Shading Error Threshold**. However, the options in the **Sampling Quality** drop-down list make your life easier by automatically defining the parameter combination. There are five combinations available: **Preview, Low, Medium, High**, and **Automatic**. When you change any parameter manually, the **Sample Quality** changes to **Custom**. The higher the settings you specify, the less the grain will be in the image, and the longer it will take to render.

*Tip: Alpha channel and transparency*
*If you are rendering an animated object with the alpha channel and motion blur, select the **Shading Transparency Check** check box to fix artifacts in the transparent motion blurred regions. When you select this check box, render time might increase drastically, if you are rendering a complex project.*

*Caution: Fixing anti-aliasing/blur*
*If you face problems in rendering antialiasing and/or blur effects due to extremely bright lights of HDR sources or bright light sources, use the **HDR Threshold** field. But be careful, if you use this field, the render output will loose some of its dynamic. It is recommended that you use a value between **2** and **8** to control the brightness. A value greater than **8** increases the brightness whereas lesser values reduce the brightness.*

## Subdivisions

The four subdivision settings: **Blurriness Subdivision (Max), Shadow Subdivision (Max), Ambient Occlusion Subdivision (Max)**, and **Subsurface Scattering Subdivision (Max)** are the quality settings for the respective effects such as blurriness, area shadows, and ambient occlusion. These settings have scene wide effect, they are not set at the material level or the object level.

*Tip: Progressive mode*
*If you are previewing the render and are in the **Progressive** mode, it is recommended that you set subdivision settings to **0** for faster calculations.*

The **Blurriness Subdivision (Max)** parameter allows you to define the quality [graininess] for the blurriness effects. These blur values are defined in the **Transparency** and **Reflectance** channels of the material. Larger values produce less grain but take longer to render.

*Caution: Render time*

*Whenever you increase the value by a factor of 1, the render time will double.*

The **Shadow Subdivision (Max)** parameter controls the quality of the shadows. Note that the **Physical** renderer simulates the shadows maps because it cannot calculate them. Use the **Ambient Occlusion Subdivision (Max)** parameter to control the quality of the ambient occlusion effect.

If the **Mode** is set to **Direct** for the **SSS** material, you can define the quality of SSS using the **Subsurface Scattering Subdivision (Max)** parameter. The larger the value you specify here, the better [high-quality] the result will be, and the longer it will take to render. If you want to specify SSS subdivisions for materials or object, in the **Multiple** tab of the **Subsurface Scattering** shader, select the **Custom Sampling** check box and then specify a value for the **Sampling Subdivision** parameter [see Fig. 4].

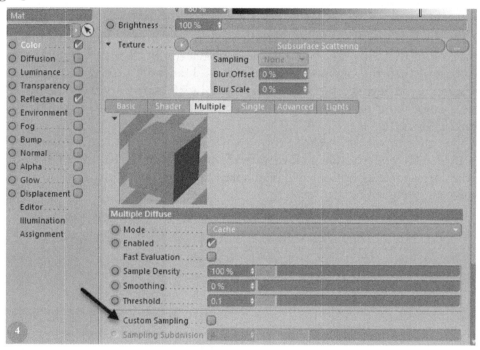

## Advanced Settings

The advanced settings for the **Physical** renderer are available under the **Advanced** tab. The **Raytracing Engine** drop-down list allows you to select **Embree** technology. This technology was developed by **Intel** and it works only with latest newgen processors that can handle **SSE3**. This technology is particularly useful if lots of polygons/objects, glass objects with lots of refraction, areas shadows, ambient occlusion, blur effects, and complex textures are in the scene. This technology renders much faster with visible loss of quality.

The **Physical** render engine requires least memory to render. The **Embree (Faster)** engine is the fastest embree engine and requires most amount of memory. The

**Embree (Smaller)** engine is slightly slower than the **Embree (Faster)** engine but it requires less memory.

The options in the **Quick Preview** drop-down list allow you to generate quick preview of the image. A rough preview is generated as soon as possible which is then immediately replaced by the bucket-by-bucket rendering. The **Preview Only** option renders a quick preview not the final render quality. Use the **Progressive Mode** option, if you are using the **Progressive** sampler mode. The **All Modes** option always enables the **Quick Preview** [for all modes]. Select **Never** to disable **Quick Preview**.

The options in the **Debug Information Level** drop-down list output the internal render details in the console. As a user of Cinema 4D, this information has no relevance for you but it can be used by support staff for troubleshooting.

## Hardware OpenGL Renderer

The **Hardware OpenGL** renderer renders the output in the Hardware OpenGL format. Note that this renderer produces better result [thanks to graphics card acceleration] then the viewport display because Hardware OpenGL can do more. For example, you have access to the **Super Sampling (Brute Force)** parameter which offers a smoothing function. Also, the shadows are optimized in the Hardware OpenGL format.

To activate this renderer, select **Hardware OpenGL** from the **Renderer** drop-down list; the corresponding options will be displayed in the right pane [see Fig. 5]. These options are discussed next:

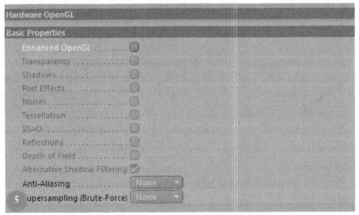

Use the **Enhanced OpenGL, Transparency, Shadows, Post Effects,** and **Noises** checkboxes to enable or disables these effects. Use the **Tessellation** check box to enable or disable tessellation for the respective objects. Use the **SSAO** check box to enable or disable a fast approximation of ambient occlusion. Use the **Reflections** check box to define whether or not reflections should be output. Use the **Depth of Field** check box to define whether or not depth-of-field should be rendered.

If banding appears when shadow casting light sources are rendered using Hardware OpenGL, select the **Alternative Shadow Filtering** check box. The anti-aliasing settings can be selected from the **Anti-Aliasing** drop-down list.

When **Transparency** is enabled, the OpenGL antialiasing will not work. In order to deliver acceptable results, you can use the options available in the **Super Sampling (Brute Force)** drop-down list to render the respective sub-pixels. The higher the value you specify, the slower the rendering speed will be. For example, if you set **Super Sampling (Brute Force)** to **4 x 4** at **100 x 100** pixels, the image will be rendered internally at a resolution **4** times larger [**400 x 400**] and will in the end be compressed to **100 x 100** via a filter.

## Software OpenGL Renderer

The **Software OpenGL** renderer renders the output in the Software OpenGL format. Note that this renderer produces modest quality compared to the normal render quality but is calculated very quickly. However, the speed is much slower than the Hardware OpenGL. With **Software OpenGL** renderer, no hardware acceleration is used. To activate this renderer, select **Software OpenGL** from the **Renderer** drop-down list; the corresponding options will be displayed in the right pane [see Fig. 6].

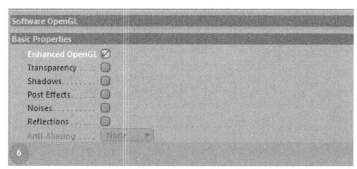

The **Enhanced OpenGL, Transparency, Shadows, Post Effects, Noises,** and **Reflections** checkboxes and the **Anti-Aliasing** drop-down list is used to enables or disables the respective effects.

# Hands-on Exercises

## Exercise 1: Creating a Studio Light Setup

In this exercise, we will create a simple studio light setup [see Fig. E1]. We will use **Area** lights to create the setup. Fig. E1 shows the rendered output.

The following table summarizes the exercise:

| Table E1 | |
|---|---|
| Difficulty level | Beginner |
| Estimated time to complete | 40 Minutes |
| Topics | • Getting Started<br>• Creating the Setup |
| Resources folder | **unit-cr2** |
| Units | **Centimeters** |
| Start file | **shader-ball-start.c4d** |
| Final file | **shader-ball-finish.c4d** |

### Getting Started
Open the **shader-ball-start.c4d** file in Cinema 4D.

### Creating the Setup
We will first define the render settings for the scene. We will be using the **Physical** renderer in this exercise. Follow these steps:

1. Click **Edit Render Settings** on the **Standard** palette to open the **Render Settings** window. Click the **Render Settings** button on the bottom-left corner of the **Render Settings** window and then choose **New** from the flyout. Double-click on the **My Render Setting.1** label and then rename it as **PhysicalTest**.

*What just happened?*
*Here, I have created a preset for test renderings. We will create one more preset for final renders. Presets make it easy to switch between different render settings.*

2. Make sure the **PhysicalTest** preset is selected and then RMB click on it. Choose **Set Active** from the popup. Change **Renderer** to **Physical** at the top-left corner of the window. Ensure **Output** is selected in the left pane of the window and then select the **Lock Ratio** check box. Now, change **Width** to **500**.

3. Click the **Effect** button and then choose **Global Illumination** from the popup. Repeat the process to choose **Ambient Occlusion**.

4. Close the **Render Settings** window and then click the **Camera Object [Camera]** icon in the **Object Manager** to make the camera active.

5. Open the **Render Settings** window and select **Physical** [available below **Material Override**] from the left pane. In the **Basic** tab of the right pane, set **Sampler** to **Progressive**. Expand the **Sampler** area by clicking on the small triangle and then set **Progressive Mode** to **Pass Count** and **Progressive Pass Count** to **10**. Close the window.

6. Render the scene.

*What just happened?*
*Notice that the shader ball is rendered completely dark because there is no light in the scene and no environment to reflect on the surfaces we have in the scene. Let's first add some light sources and then we will re-visit the render settings again.*

7. Choose **Area Light** from the **Standard palette > Light** command group to create an area light in the editor view.

*Note: Area lights?*
*In Cinema 4D, area lights are two or three dimensional lights that are used to create realistic lighting. If you enable **Area** shadows, you can create realistic shadows as well. However, **Area** shadows take longer to render. The following options are available in Cinema 4D for creating area light shapes: **Disc, Rectangle, Line, Sphere, Cylinder, Cylinder (Perpendicular), Cube, Hemisphere,** and **Object/Spline**. When you use 3D area light types such as cube or sphere, the objects within the volume of the light source require high sampling rates, especially when **Area** shadows are used. You can use the parameters given next to adjust the sampling quality:*

- *For diffuse lighting:* The **Samples** parameter in the **Details** tab.
- *For Area shadows:* The **Accuracy**, **Minimum Samples**, and **Maximum Samples** parameters in the **Shadow** tab.

*But, these options will not be available if you are using the **Physical** renderer. The scene-wide quality settings are controlled from the **Render Settings** window.*

8. In the **Attribute Manager** > **Light Object** > **Details** tab, change **Size X** and **Size Y** to **500** and **400**, respectively. In the **General** tab, change **Intensity** to **95**. Now, in the **Coord** tab, change **P.X**, **P.Y**, and **P.Z** to -**550, 385,** and -**546**, respectively. Also, change **R.H**, **R.P**, and **R.B** to -**50**, -**21**, and -**4**, respectively [see Fig. E2].

*What just happened?*
*Here, we are using the default **Rectangle** shape type for the area light. I've set size of the rectangle to **500x400**. If you want to cover larger area of the scene, you need to increase the size of the light. The larger the size of the light, the more the diffuse light it will emit.*

9. Ensure light is selected in the **Object Manager** and then on the in the **Attribute Manager** > **General** tab, change **Shadow** to **Area**. Render the scene, notice that now we have soft shadows in the scene [see Fig. E3] but the fall of the light is not correct.

*Note: Progressive passes*
*Note at the bottom of the **Picture Viewer** window, status of the progressive passes is displayed in the status line as Cinema 4D calculates them. Do not worry about the grain in the render, we will fix it later.*

10. In the **Details** tab, select **Inverse Square (Physically Accurate)** from the **Falloff** drop-down list. Also, select the **Z Direction Only** check box. Render the scene [see Fig. E4].

**Note: Light Decay**

*In real-world, the brightness of the light is strongest at its origin and it decreases or decays [luminosity absorbed] further away from the light source. To achieve this, Cinema 4D provides several options that you can access from the **Falloff** drop-down list. When you use the **Inverse Square (Physically Accurate)** or **Inverse Square Clamped** option, the light will reach to the distance defined by the **Radius/Decay** parameter and then will fade away proportionally opposite to the square of the original distance.*

11. In the **Details** tab, select the **Show in Reflection** check box.

**What just happened?**

*By selecting this check box, the light's shape [**500x400** rectangle in this case] will appear in the reflections on the objects. If you select the **Show in Render** check box, the area light shape will be visible in the render except for the **Line** shape type and splines. You can control brightness of the visible area light or its reflection using the **Visibility Multiplier** parameter.*

12. Change **Radius/Decay** to **950** and then in the **General** tab, change **Intensity** to **100**. Render the scene [see Fig. E5].

13. Choose **Null** from the **Standard** palette > **Object** command group to create a null in the editor view. Rename **Null** as **LeftLight** and then make **Light** its child.

**Why Light is grouped?**

*Placing light under a **Null** will help us placing the axis at the origin and then we can easily create and align copy of the light by **Ctrl** dragging. The new light will rotate around the origin [0, 0, 0].*

14. Activate the **Rotate** tool, hold **Ctrl** and then rotate **LeftLight** around the **Y** axis to create a copy of the **LeftLight** [see Fig. E6]. Rename the copied null as **RightLight**.

15. Apply the **Red - A** material to **Geo2** and **Geo3** and render the scene [see Fig. E7]. The **Geo2** and **Geo3** surfaces are under the **ShaderBall** null.

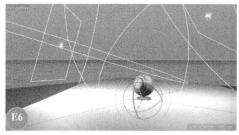

*What next?*

*Now, we will create a **Cloner** setup that we will use to create reflections on the shader ball.*

16. Choose **Plane** from the **Standard** palette > **Object** command group to create a plane in the editor view. In the **Attribute Manager** > **Object** tab, change **Width, Height, Width Segments, Height Segments** to **619, 174, 1**, and **1**, respectively [see Fig. E8].

17. Select **Plane** in the **Object Manager** and then choose **Cloner** from the **MoGraph** menu with **Alt** held down to create a **Cloner** object and to make **Plane** its child. Select **Cloner** and then in the **Attribute Manager** > **Object** tab, change **Count** to **4, P.X** to **0, P.Y** to **0**, and **P.Z** to **202**. Now, align **Cloner**, as shown in Fig. E9.

18. RMB click on **Cloner** and then choose **Cinema 4D Tags** > **Compositing** from the context menu. Select tag from the **Object Manager** and in the **Attribute Manager** > **Tag** tab, clear the **Cast Shadows, Receive Shadows**, and **Seen by Camera** checkboxes.

19. Create a new material, rename it as **RefMat** and then open it in the **Material Editor**. Enable the **Luminance** channel and then disable the **Color** channel. Apply this material to **Cloner**. Render the scene [see Fig. E10].

*What next?*

*Now, let's adjust the **Global Illumination** and **Ambient Occlusion** effects.*

20. Open the **Render Settings** window and select **Global Illumination** from the left pane, the settings are displayed in the right pane. Notice in the **General** tab, there is a **Preset** drop-down list. You can use one of these presets as quick starting point. Leave the **Primary Method** to **Irradiance Cache** and then change **Secondary Method** to **Light Mapping**.

21. In the **General** tab, change **Samples** to **Custom Sample Count**. Expand the **Samples** area and then set **Sample Count** to **100**.

22. In the **Light Mapping** tab, change **Path Count (x1000)** parameter to **1500**. Render the scene [see Fig. E11].

E11

> *?* **What Path Count (x1000) does?**
> *This setting defines the number of samples that are calculated for the entire scene. The value you specify for this parameter will be multiplied internally by **1000**. The higher the value you specify for this parameter, the more the dispersion of the light will be, and the longer the render time will be.*

23. Select **PhysicalTest** and press **Ctrl+C** and then press **Ctrl+V** to create a copy of the preset. Rename the pasted preset as **PhyscialFinal**. Ensure the **PhyscialFinal** preset is selected. RMB click on it and then choose **Set Active** from the popup, if not already active.

> *→* **What next?**
> *Now, let's specify the final settings for GI.*

24. In the **General** tab, set **Primary Method > Intensity** to **110** and **Samples** to **Custom Sample Count**. Now, change **Sample Count** to **600**. In the **Irradiance Cache** tab, change **Record Density** to **Medium** and **Smoothing** to **60%**. In the **Light Mapping** tab, set **Path Count (x1000)** to **3000**.

> *?* **What just happened?**
> *These settings in the **Record Density** area are used to fine tune the results. The **Preview** mode offers a quick preview of the final result. The **Density** parameter adjusts the general dispersion of the shading points. The higher the value you set for this parameter, the higher the shading point density will be.*

> *→* **What next?**
> *Let's now specify the settings for the **Physical** renderer for final rendering.*

25. Select **Physical** from the left pane of the **Render Settings** window. In the **Basic** tab, change **Sampler** to **Adaptive** and **Sampling Quality** to **Automatic**. Set **Shading Error Threshold** to **8**.

> *?* **What the Sampling Quality parameter does?**
> *You can set quality to **Low**, **Medium**, **High**, **Custom**, or **Automatic**. Higher settings reduce grain in the image but take longer to render. When **Automatic** is selected, only **Shading Error Threshold** will be made available. This value controls the number of samples that will be calculated.*

The *Shading Subdivisions (Max)* parameter defines the maximum number of shading samples, in correlation with the *Shading Error Threshold* parameter, that should be calculated. The *Shading Error Threshold* parameter controls the number of samples that will in fact be calculated. The lower the value, the more the number of samples will lean towards *Shading Subdivisions (Max)*, however, only in critical regions.

26. Change **Shadow Subdivision (Max)**, **Blurriness Subdivision (Max)**, and **Ambient Occlusion Subdivision (Max)** to **3** each.

*What are these settings?*
*The **Shadow Subdivision (Max)** setting controls the quality of the shadows. Larger values produce better results but at the cost of the render time. The **Ambient Occlusion Subdivision (Max)** setting controls the quality of the ambient occlusion effect.*

27. Select **Ambient Occlusion** from the left pane of the **Render Settings** window. In the right pane, change **Maximum Ray Length** to **20**. Render the scene [see Fig. E12].

28. Click on the **Effect** button in the **Render Settings** window and then choose **Color Mapping** to add the **Color Mapping** post-effect. Select it and then in the right pane, select the **Exponential** check box, clear the **HSV Model** check box, and then select the **Affect Background** check box. Now, change **Dark Multiplier** to **2**. Render the scene [see Fig. E13].

*Note: Rendering scenes with GI, things to remember*
*When you are using the **Global Illumination** effect, consider the following points:*

- *First render the scene at very low resolution such as **320x240**. It will allow you to quickly check the brightness of the scene.*
- *Use the **Progressive** sampler for fast previews.*
- *Use the **Interactive Render Region** tool at low resolutions to check the brightness and light dispersion.*
- *Check if you need additional light sources.*
- *Once you are satisfied, you can use high quality settings for GI.*
- *If you see spotty rendering, most of the time you can fix it by increasing **Samples** value in the **General** tab.*

*Why rendering is slow?*
*Well, there might be numerous reasons for slow rendering but here's is list that you can use to diagnose the problem:*

- *Have you specified high values for **Samples** and **Record Density**?*
- *Are you using **OMC+QMC** as primary and secondary methods? The **QMC+QMC** model produces best quality but this combination is the slowest.*
- *Have you turned on the **Force Per-Pixel** check box for polygon and portal lights?*
- *Are you using very high settings for the **Physical** renderer?*

## Exercise 2: Using Polygon Lights
In this exercise, we will use polygon lights to illuminate a scene [see Fig. E1].

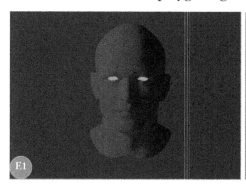

Table E2 summarizes the exercise.

| Table E2 | |
|---|---|
| Difficulty level | Intermediate |
| Estimated time to complete | 40 Minutes |
| Topics | • Getting Started<br>• Using Lights |
| Resources folder | **unit-cr2** |
| Units | **Centimeters** |
| Start file | **polygon-lights-start.c4d** |
| Final file | **polygon-lights-finish-1.c4d**<br>**polygon-lights-finish-2.c4d** |

## Getting Started
Open **polygon-lights-start.c4d**.

## Using Lights
Follow these steps:

1. Double-click in the **Material Manager** to create a new material and then rename the material as **matDiffuse**. Apply the material to **Head** and **Back Drop**.

2. Select **diffuseMat** in the **Material Manager** and then in the **Attribute Manager** > **Basic** tab, clear the **Color** check box. Make sure the **Reflectance** check box is selected.

3. In the **Reflectance** channel, change **Type** to **Lambertian (Diffuse)** and **Attenuation** to **Average**. Change **Reflection Strength** to **100** and **Specular Strength** to **0**. In the **Layer Color** area, change **Color** to **HSV [0, 0, 83]**.

4. Open the **Render Settings** window and then select **Physical** from the **Renderer** drop-down list. Close the window.

> *What next?*
> *Now, we will create a spherical polygon light to illuminate the head in the scene.*

5. Create a **Sphere** in the scene and then in the **Attribute Manager** > **Object** tab, change **Radius** to **20**. Now, align the sphere, as shown in Fig. E2.

6. Double-click on the **Material Manager** to create a new material and then rename the material as **matLight**. Assign this material to the sphere in the scene. In the **Attribute Manager** > **matLight** > **Basic** tab, clear the **Color** and **Reflectance** checkboxes and then select the **Luminance** check box.

7. Render the scene [see Fig. E3].

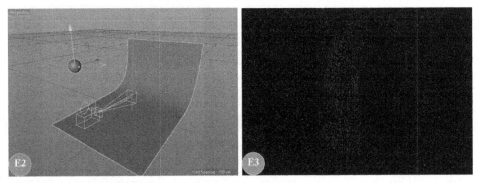

8. In the **Attribute Manager** > **matLight** > **Illumination** tab, select the **Polygon Light** check box. Render the scene [see Fig. E4].

9. Open the **Render Settings** window and then change **Sampler** to **Progressive**. Also, change the **Blurriness Subdivisions (Max)** to **4**.

10. In the **Attribute Manager > matLight > Luminance** tab, change **Brightness** to **500**. In the **Object Manager**, move the **Eyes** texture tag to the right and then render the scene [see Fig. E5].

11. Change **Radius** of the **Sphere** to **80** and then render the scene [see Fig. E6]. In the **Attribute Manager > matLight > Luminance** tab, change **Brightness** to **200**. Render the scene [see Fig. E7].

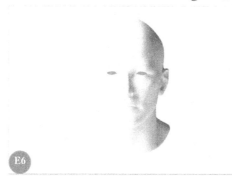
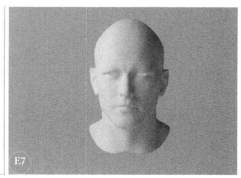

*What just happened?*
*Notice in Fig. E6, the render is too bright. We adjusted the luminance of the material to get the right illumination in the scene [see Fig. E7]. We can use the size of the light and the luminance strength of the material to create the desired lighting.*

12. Open the **Render Settings** window and then select **Physical** from the left pane. In the right pane, change **Sampler** to **Adaptive**. Change **Sampling Subdivisions** to **0**, **Sampling Subdivisions (Min)** to **1**, **Sampling Subdivisions (Max)** to **3**, and **Shading Error Threshold** to **10**. Render the scene [see Fig. E8]. Refer to **polygon-lights-finish-1.c4d**.

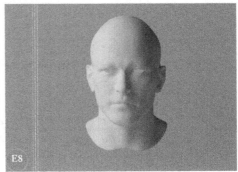

*Note: Things to remember-I*
*Keep the following in mind:*

1. *A small light relative to its distance from the object will cast hard shadows. Refer to Figs. E9, E10, and **polygon-lights-hard-shadows.c4d**.*
2. *A big light with the same intensity as the small light will cast soft shadows. In the real-world, photographers are producing the same effect using umbrellas and soft boxes. They change the position of the umbrella or soft box to cerate soft shadows. Simply put, they create a bigger light out of small one by positioning the umbrella or soft box in front of the light. The closer you move the diffuser to the light, the harder shadows light will produce. Refer to Figs. E11, E12, and **polygon-lights-soft-shadows.c4d**.*
3. *To eliminate the noise you can use higher values for the **Shading Subdivisions (Max)** and **Blurriness Subdivision (Max)** parameters. Keep in mind the higher values take longer to render.*
4. *If you are using the depth-of-field effect, you need to increase the value of the **Sampling Subdivisions** parameter. You can set it to **0** if you are not using the depth-of-field effect.*

 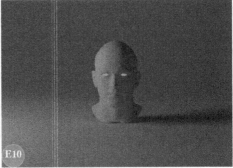

**What next?**

Notice in **Step 10**, we have reduced the intensity of the light by reducing the luminance strength of the polygon light. Let's now work on the camera's exposure controls to reduce the exposure without changing the intensity of the light. Also, refer to point **2** in the **Note** above.

13. In the **Attribute Manager > matLight > Luminance** tab, change **Brightness** back to **500**. If you render the scene, you will notice that scene is over exposed.

14. Select **Camera** and then in the **Attribute Manager > Physical** tab, select the **Exposure** check box. Now, change **ISO** to **100** and **Shutter Speed** to **0.01**. Render the scene [see Fig. E13].

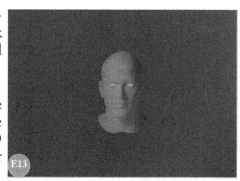

*Note: Things to remember-II*

*Since we are using a polygon light, we don't have access to the **Include/Exclude** function of the Cinema 4D light. Now, if you don't want the light from the polygon light to spill over in the back drop, you can use a plane with black material [black card] to block the light. Refer to Figs. E14, E15, and* **polygon-lights-blackcard.c4d**.

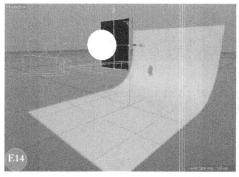

## Exercise 3: Working with the Depth-Of-Field Effect

In this exercise, we will create the depth-of-field effect using the **Physical** renderer [see Fig. E1].

Table E3 summarizes the exercise.

| Table E3 | |
|---|---|
| Difficulty level | Intermediate |
| Estimated time to complete | 30 Minutes |
| Topics | • Getting Started<br>• Creating the Effect |
| Resources folder | **unit-cr2** |
| Units | **Centimeters** |
| Start file | **dof-start.c4d** |
| Final file | **dof-finish.c4d** |

### Getting Started
Open **dof-start.c4d**.

### Creating the Effect
Follow these steps:

1. Open the **Render Settings** window. In this window, select **Physical** from the **Renderer** drop-down list. Select **Physical** from the left pane of the window and then in the right pane, select the **Depth Of Field** check box. Close the window.

2. Select **Camera** in the **Object Manager** and then in the **Attribute Manager > Physical** tab, change **F-Stop (f/#)** to **0.2**.

*What just happened?*
*Here, I have used the **F-Stop** value to adjust the focal aperture. The larger the focal aperture (i.e. the smaller the **F-Stop** value), the smaller the depth-of-field will be and vice-versa. The smaller the **F-Stop** value, the more pronounced the depth-of-field effect will be.*

3.  In the **Attribute Manager > Object** tab, click the arrow button corresponding to the **Focus Distance** parameter and then click on the middle character in the view. Make sure the camera view is active and then render the scene [see Fig. E2].

*What just happened?*
*Here, I have defined the focus distance which is the distance measured from the camera's origin out (=film or sensor plane). It defines the distance to a plane that lies perpendicular to the angle of view, on which all objects are displayed perfectly in focus. In front of and behind this plane, all objects are rendered progressively blurred. You can also interactively change the focus distance using camera's center front handle [see Fig. E3].*

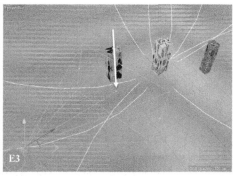

*What next?*
*Notice in Fig. E2, the quality of the blur is not good. Next, we will adjust the quality settings to get a better looking results.*

4.  In the **Render Settings** window, change **Sampler** to **Adaptive** and **Sampling Quality** to **High**. Also, change **Blurriness Subdivision (Max)** to **4**. Render the scene.

## Exercise 4: Working with the Motion Blur Effect

In this exercise, we will create the motion blur effect using the **Physical** renderer [see Fig. E1].

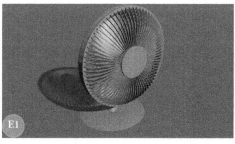

Table E4 summarizes the exercise.

| Table E4 | |
|---|---|
| Difficulty level | Intermediate |
| Estimated time to complete | 30 Minutes |
| Topics | • Getting Started<br>• Creating the Effect |
| Resources folder | **unit-cr2** |
| Units | **Centimeters** |
| Start file | **mb-start.c4d** |
| Final file | **mb-finish.c4d** |

## Getting Started
Open **mb-start.c4d**.

## Creating the Effect
Follow these steps:

1.  Open the **Render Settings** window. In this window, select **Physical** from the **Renderer** drop-down list. Select **Physical** from the left pane of the window and then in the right pane, select the **Motion Blur** check box. Close the window.

2.  Select **Camera** in the **Object Manager** and then in the **Attribute Manager > Physical** tab, change **Shutter Speed (s)** to **0.125**. Render the scene [see Fig. E2].

-o- **Parameter: Shutter Speed**
The **Shutter Speed** parameter is generally used with the **Exposure** settings. It controls the amount of light that reaches the film. In other words, it defines how long the shutter will remain open when a picture is taken. If **Motion Blur** is enabled, it controls the amount of motion blur. The slower the shutter speed is, the greater the motion blur will be.

3.  Open the **Render Settings** window. Select **Physical** from the left pane of the window and then in the right pane, change **Motion Subdivisions** to **6**. Render the scene [see Fig. E3].

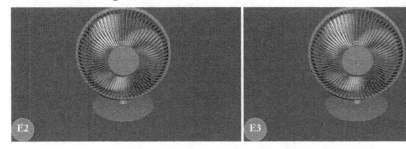

> ⊘ *What just happened?*
> *When calculating motion blur for the fast circular motion, it is important to calculate the position between animation frames. The **Motion Subdivisions** value defines the degree of subdivision between two sequential frames of animation. Higher values consume more memory. It is noticeable if motion blur is applied to many objects, in normal scenes it will not make much difference. For still images, you should apply a value greater than **4** to ensure the maximum quality.*

4. In the **Render Settings** window, change **Sampler** to **Adaptive** and **Sampling Quality** to **High**. Also, change **Blurriness Subdivision (Max)** to **4**. Render the scene.

## Quiz

**Multiple Choice**
Answer the following questions:

1. Which of the following sampling modes is not available in Cinema 4D for the **Physical** renderer?

   [A] Adaptive                          [B] Fixed
   [C] Preview                           [D] Progressive

2. Which of the following embree engines is not available in Cinema 4D?

   [A] Physical                          [B] Embree (Faster)
   [C] Embree (Smaller)                  [D] Embree (Standard)

3. Which of the following options is not available in Cinema 4D for controlling the quality of the blur effects?

   [A] Blurriness Subdivision (Max)      [B] Shadow Subdivision (Max)
   [C] Ambient Occlusion Subdivision (Max)
   [D] Subsurface Subdivision (Max)

**Fill in the Blanks**
Fill in the blanks in each of the following statements:

1. The term _____ refers to the reduction of an image's brightness or saturation toward the periphery compared to the image center.

2. The _____ renderer renders faster than the _____ renderer.

3. The _____ sampling method uses an unchangeable fix per-pixel sample number.

**True or False**
State whether each of the following is true or false:

1. The **Standard** renderer is a preferred renderer for rendering blur effects such as depth-of-field, motion blur, and so on.

2. The **Physical** renderer works with the **Sketch and Toon** post-effect.

3. The **Physical** renderer can render hard shadows.

4. In the **Progressive** method, the sampler can run indefinitely and cannot be stopped.

5. The **Physical** renderer does not offer unbiased rendering.

6. The **Adaptive** method is the recommended method because it offers a good mix between the quality and render speed.

7. The **Physical** renderer simulates the shadows maps because it cannot calculate them.

**Summary**
This unit covered the following topics:

- Physical Renderer
- Hardware OpenGL Renderer
- Software OpenGL Renderer
- Depth-of-field
- Motion Blur

- Cinema 4D Lights
- 3-Point Lighting
- Product Visualization
- Interior Rendering

# Unit CR3 - Lighting

To achieve professional-quality, realistic renders in CINEMA, you need to master the art of lighting. Lights play an important role in the visual process. They shape the world you see. The trick to simulate realistic looking light effects is to observe the world around us. The lights you create in a scene, illuminate other objects in the scene. The material applied to the objects simulates color and texture.

## Light Objects

When you build a new scene in Cinema 4D, a default light [called auto light] is used to illuminate the scene. When you add Cinema 4D's **Light** object to the scene, the auto light is turned off. Cinema 4D's auto light will switch on automatically when you switch off lights during an animation unless you disable the **Auto Light** option. This option is available in the **Render Settings window > Options** category.

*Tip: Default lighting*
*You can change the default lighting setup for the future new scenes. To do so, build a new scene that contains only the lights that you need for the default lighting and save this scene within the Cinema 4D folder under the name* **new.c4d** *in your Cinema 4D directory. This default light setup will be used each time you start a new Cinema 4D scene.*

*Tip: Default scene*
*Along with the light objects, you can also save the environment attributes such as* **Sky, Floor, Environment**, *and so on. To do so, build a scene and then choose* **Window > Customization > Save As Default Scene** *from the menubar.*

To create lights in Cinema 4D, click on the desired light object in the **Standard** palette > **Light** command group. You can also access these objects from the **Create > Light** menu. These light objects are discussed next.

*Tip: Displaying lights in the viewport*
*You can preview lights in the viewport by enabling the **Gouraud Shading** option from the **Display** menu of the **Menu in editor view**.*

To create the **Light** object, click **Light** on the **Standard** palette or choose **Create > Light > Light** from the menubar. Fig. 1 shows the **Light** object in the scene. When you select a light object, its parameters are displayed in the **Attribute Manager** in different tabs. These tabs are discussed next:

## General Tab

The **Color** parameter is used to adjust the color of the light. Fig. 2 shows the output when **Color** is set to **HSV [56, 65, 100]**. If you want to adjust color of the light using the color temperature, select the **Use Temperature** check box and then specify the color temperature using the **Color Temperature** parameter. The images in Fig. 3 show the render with **Color Temperature** set to **4000** and **7000**, respectively.

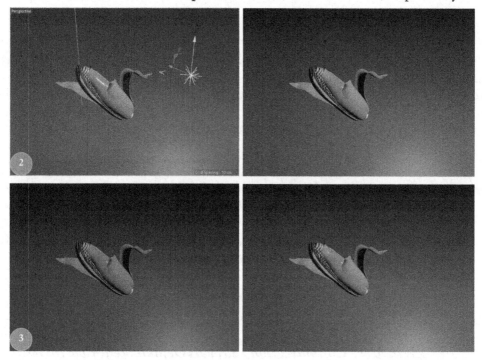

The **Intensity** parameter controls the overall brightness of the light source. You can not only use this parameter to brighten the scene but also in negative lighting by specifying a negative value. When you use a negative value, the color of the light plays an important role here.

That color will not be added to the scene where a negative light source is in effect. Using this feature, you can artificially darken and shade specific areas of your scene. In the **Intensity** field, you can enter values greater than **100%**. The images in Fig. 4 show the render with **Intensity** set to **25**, **50**, and **75**, respectively.

The options in the **Type** drop-down list allow you to select the type of the light:

- **Omni:** This type works like a real-world light bulb — casting light in all directions. If you place the **Omni** light at the center of the scene, it will illuminate the scene evenly in all directions [see Fig. 1].
- **Spot:** This type of lights cast their rays in just one direction, which is along the Z axis by default [see Fig. 5].
- **Infinite:** This light type simulates distant light sources such as Sun [see Fig. 6].
- **Area:** This type of light source expands light rays from all points on its surface outwards in all directions [see Fig. 7].
- **Square Spot:** See **Spot**. This type projects a square cone of light [see Fig. 8].
- **Parallel:** This type resembles the **Infinite** light. Unlike the **Infinite** light source however, the **Parallel** light has an origin and simulates a large, single axis wall of light.
- **Parallel Spot:** This light type resembles the regular spotlight but do not have light cone to define falloff or distance. Instead, light rays are cast along cylinders [see Fig. 9].
- **Square Parallel Spot:** See **Parallel** Spot. In this type, light rays are cast along bars [see Fig. 10].

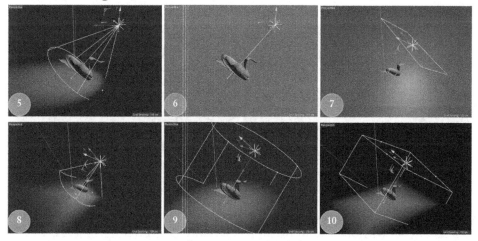

The options in the **Shadow** drop-down list are used to specify the type of shadow generated by a light source. Select **None** if the light is to cast no shadows. The clone of this drop-down list is also available in the **Shadow** tab. These options are discussed later in the **Shadow Tab** section.

The options in the **Visible Light** drop-down list allow you to define the visibility of the light in a scene. For example, you can use these options to simulate a light in the smoky room. This effect is comparable to fog, which does not diminish light, but rather adds to its brightness. With these options, you can create effects like headlights, shimmering lights, laser beams, and so on. In Cinema 4D, all light sources can be made visible.

If you set **Visible Light** to **Visible** [see Fig. 11] the light source will produce visible light that passes through all objects. For example, a visible light could be placed in the center of a planet's sphere to simulate an atmosphere. You can use the **Visible** light to create a range of effects such as nebula clouds, smoke, comet tails, fire, flames, and so on. Refer to **light-visible.c4d**.

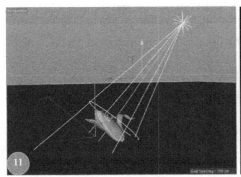

As discussed above, the **Visible** light penetrates objects unhindered, casting no shadow in the visible light's beam. If you want a **Visible** light source to cast shadows, you require to use the **Volumetric** option [see Fig. 12]. The **Inverse Volumetric** option inverts the effect [see Fig. 13]. You can use this option in logo design. You can place the light behind the logo, giving the impression that the light is radiating from the logo itself.

Select the **No Illumination** check box if you want to see just the visible light and/or its lens effects without the light source actually illuminating objects. The **Show Illumination** check box is selected by default. As a result, a wireframe approximation of the light's illumination is shown in the viewports, like the white wireframe of the spot light is shown in the left image of Fig. 11.

Normally, the brightness of a surface is controlled by the angle at which a ray of light hits the surface. The greater the angle between the ray and a tangent to the surface, the more the surface will be lit by the light. When the **Ambient Illumination** check box is selected, this law is not considered and the angle does not matter. All surfaces are lit with the same intensity by light rays. As a result, only the color of the material is considered in the lighting calculations. Therefore, creating a much flatter look. The images in Fig. 14 show the render with the **Ambient Illumination** check box disabled and enabled, respectively. Refer to **ambient-illumination.c4d**.

In the right image, **Ambient Illumination** check box was selected with **Falloff** enabled. You can use this technique to lighten specific areas of the scene in a similar way as you would do with negative lighting, discussed earlier.

If you want to see an approximation of the **Visible** light in the viewports, select the **Show Visible Light** check box. You can interactively adjust the approximation in the viewport using handles. The images in Fig. 15 show the render with the **Show Visible Light** check box disabled and enabled, respectively.

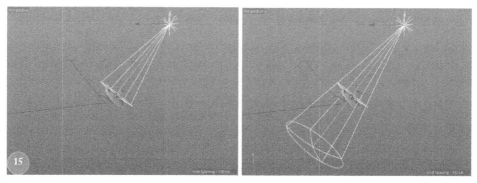

When the **Diffuse** check box is disabled, the color properties of the object are ignored by the light source. The images in Fig. 16 show the render with the **Diffuse** check box enabled and disabled, respectively. When the **Specular** check box is disabled, the light source does not produce specular highlights. The images in Fig. 17 show the render with the **Specular** check box disabled and enabled, respectively. Select the **Show Clipping** check box to show an approximation of the selected light's clipping range in the viewports that can be interactively adjusted with the wireframe's handles.

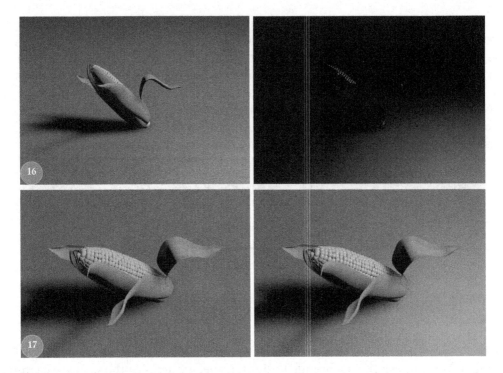

If you select the **Separate Pass** check box, Cinema 4D will create separate diffuse, specular, and shadow layers will be created for the light source when you render. If you clear the **GI Illumination** check box, no GI will be calculated for the light source. The light sources will affect the objects but these objects will not reflect light onto any other object(s). If you are exporting the scene to a external application for compositing, select the **Export to Compositing** check box to export the light source.

## Details Tab

The **Use Inner** check box allows you to enable a brightness falloff at a light's edge. This parameter works with in conjunction with the **Inner Angle** and **Inner Radius** parameters. Depending on the type of light you are using, these parameters will adjust either the **Inner Angle** for a standard **Spot** light or the **Inner Radius** for a **Parallel Spot** light. Within the area defined by the **Inner Angle** parameter, the intensity of the light will be **100%**. From the **Inner Angle** to the **Outer Angle** the luminosity value of the light falls from **100%** to **0%**. Fig. 18 shows the result when the **Inner Angle** and **Outer Angle** parameters are set to **50** and **80**, respectively.

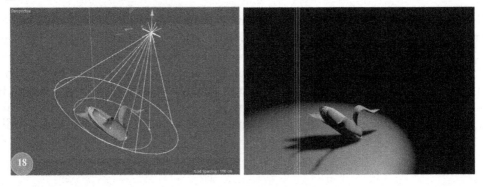

If the **Use Inner** check box is clear, the luminosity of the light in its cone will be **100%** resulting in the hard cone of the light [see Fig. 19]. If you specify a value of **0** for the **Inner Angle** parameter, the light source will have a soft transition spreading from the center of the light to the light's edge.

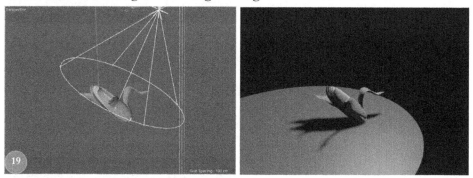

The **Aspect Ratio** parameter allows you to stretch and shear the cone of the light. For example, if you set this parameter's value to **2**, Cinema 4D will double the light cone's height relative to its width. Similarly, decreasing the value to **0.5** will make the light cone only half as high as it is wide. Fig. 20 shows the cone of the light with **Aspect Ratio** set to **1**, **0.5**, and **2**, respectively.

If you are not using falloff, the intensity of a light source on an object is not dependent on the distance of the light from the object. The intensity depends on the angle [called the angle of incidence] at which its rays hit that object. If a ray hits a surface at an angle of **90** degrees, the object is illuminated with the light's maximum intensity taking any falloff into account. As the angle of incidence decreases, the strength of the illumination decreases as well. As a result, a soft transition occurs between the lit and shadowed part of the surface. The **Contrast** parameter controls the transition of the lit surface to shadowed edge of the surface. Fig. 21 shows the render with **Contrast** set to **0, 50**, and **100**, respectively.

If you enable the **Shadow Caster** check box, the light cast shadows without adding illumination to the scene. You can use such lights to fix shadows in the scene. Fig. 22 shows the render when the scene is lit by four lights all casting shadows. Fig. 23 shows the render when shadows are disabled for all lights except the top light. And, for the top light, the **Shadow Caster** check box is selected. Refer to **shadow-caster.c4d**.

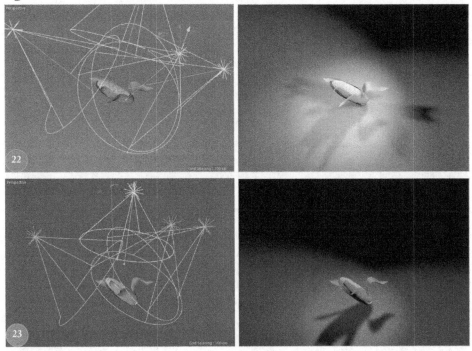

When falloff is not enabled for a light, it illuminates its surrounding environment with a continuous, linear brightness. However, in real-world, light is absorbed from the light sources and their luminosity reduced over any distance.

The **Falloff** drop-down list provides several falloff functions that you can use to simulate falloff in Cinema 4D. Figs. 24 [scene], 25 [**Falloff: Inverse Square (Physically Accurate), Radius/Decay: 70**], 26 [**Falloff: Linear, Inner Radius:35, Radius/Decay: 135**], and 27 [**Falloff: Inverse Square Clamped, Radius/Decay: 150**] show the effect of falloff functions. Refer to **falloff.c4d**.

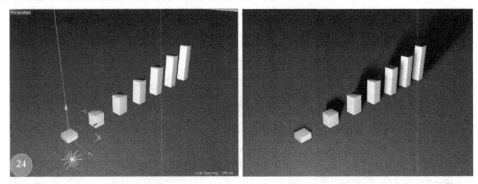

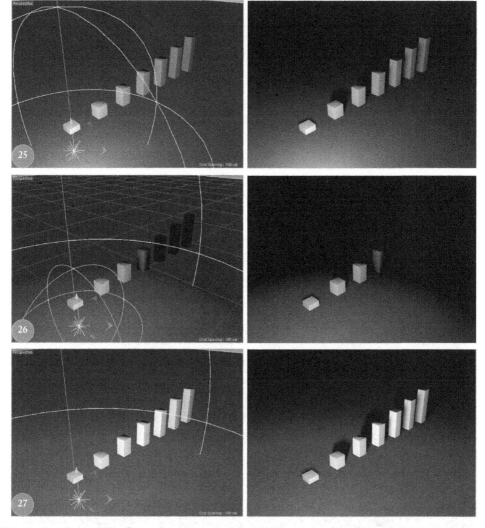

Within the **Inner Radius** there is no falloff. Upto the boundary defined by **Inner Radius**, the brightness of the light remains constant. Outside this boundary, the falloff begins. The **Colored Edge Falloff** check box works in conjunction with the **Use Gradient** check box, see Figs. 28 and 29. Also, refer to **falloff-2.c4d**.

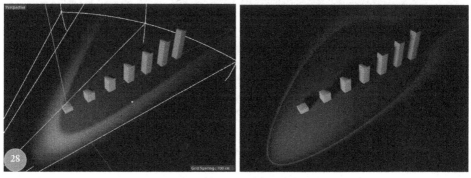

If you select the **Z Direction Only** check box, light will only be emitted in the light's positive Z-direction. Fig. 30 show the scene illuminated by an area light. In the right image, the **Z Direction Only** check box is selected. Refer to **z-direction-only.c4d**.

You can use the **Near Clip** and **Far Clip** checkboxes to restrict the illumination. The **Near Clip** check box is used to restrict the illumination radially with an **Omni** light and linearly with all other light types. You can use these checkboxes, for example, to cause the illumination start from a certain distance from the origin, see Fig. 31. The clipping range can be adjusted interactively in the viewport using wireframe handles. Also, refer to **clipping.c4d**.

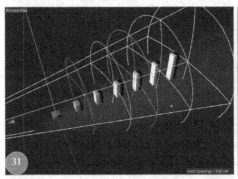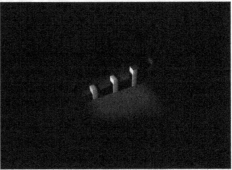

The options in the **Area Shape** drop-down list are used to define the shape of the area light. Area lights offer very realistic lighting and shadows in conjunction with the area shadows. However, the area lights with area shadows take longer to render. An area light can be given any shape and can be made visible in the viewport and in the rendering. Once you select a shape from the **Area Shape** drop-down list, Cinema 4D reveals corresponding parameters [**Size X, Size Y**, and **Size Z**] to define the size of the area.

The images in Fig. 32 show the **Disc, Rectangle,** and **Line** shapes, respectively. The images in Fig. 33 show the **Sphere, Cylinder,** and **Cylinder (Perpendicular)** shapes, respectively. The images in Fig. 34 show the **Cube** and **Hemisphere** shapes, respectively.

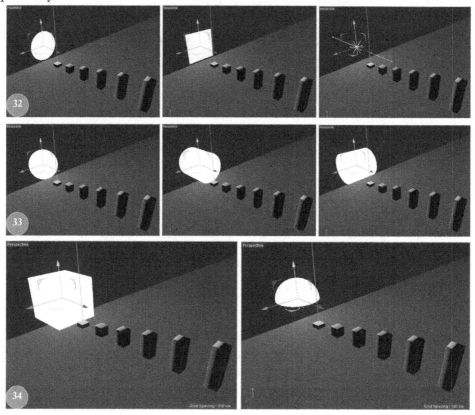

You can select the **Object/Spline** option if you want to use any polygonal object or spline for the shape of the light. Simply drag the object to **Object** field in the **Attribute Manager.**

The **Falloff Angle** parameter allows you to regulate the light emitted by a **Disc** or **Rectangle** area light. The smaller the value you specify, the more light will be removed from the edges. The images in Fig. 35 show the result with **Falloff Angle** set to **0** and **180,** respectively. The images in Fig. 36 show the result with **Falloff Angle** set to **150** and **120,** respectively. Refer to **falloff-angle.c4d.**

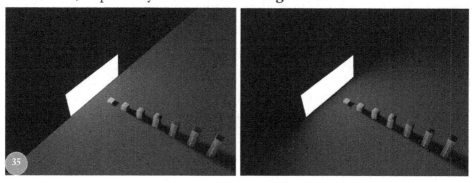

Sometimes, the sample structure of the area light becomes visible in specular highlights and the output appears as if the object is lit by several light sources. If you face such issues, raise the value of the **Samples** parameter. This value can be raised in case of the uneven light dispersion.

You can also remove the uneven light dispersion [discussed above] by selecting the **Add Grain (Slow)** check box. On selecting this check box, a grainy rendering will be used to eliminate any visible light source structures. The **Samples** value should be high enough to avoid an extremely grainy look. However, when you select the **Add Grain (Slow)** check box, the render time will increase considerably compared to normal render.

Select the **Show in Render** check box if you want to render the source of the light. Depending on the intensity of the light, the shape will be rendered in white. However, the **Line** and spline object shape types cannot be rendered. Select the **Show as Solid in Viewport** check box to display light shape as luminous surface in an un-rendered viewport.

The **Show in Specular** check box is used to specify if the light shape should be rendered as a specular highlight in a reflective material. Select the **Show in Reflection** check box to mirror an area light in another object. However, the **Line** and spline object shape types cannot be rendered. The only exception is if the roughness of the material is greater than **0**.

The **Visibility Multiplier** parameter is used to adjust the brightness of a visible area light or its reflection in another object. This parameter is only available if you select the **Show in Render** or **Show in Reflection** checkboxes.

## Visibility Tab

The **Use Falloff** check box is selected by default. As a result, you get access to the **Falloff** parameter which controls the percentage reduction in the light's density. The axial falloff of the visible light is set to a standard **100%** [default behavior]. The images Fig. 37 show the render with **Falloff** set to **0** and **100**, respectively.

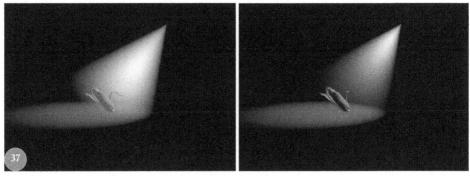

The **Use Edge Falloff** and **Edge Falloff** parameters are relevant with **Spot** lights. The **Edge Falloff** parameter controls how quickly the density of the light decreases towards the edge of the cone of the light. The images Fig. 38 show the render with **Edge Falloff** set to **0**, **50**, and **100**, respectively.

The **Colored Edge Falloff** check box is only available with **Spot** lights, and in addition, the **Use Edge Falloff** check box must be selected. The **Colored Edge Falloff** check box causes the inner color to also spread outwards radially from the inner angle to meet the outer color. The images in Fig. 39 show the render with **Use Edge Falloff** enabled and disabled, respectively. The **Edge Falloff** parameter was set to **50%**. Refer to **colored-edge-falloff.c4d**.

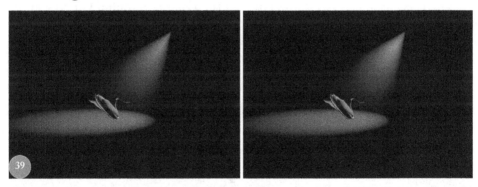

The **Inner Distance** parameter controls the density of the visible light. Beneath the value specified for this parameter, the density of the visible light is always a constant **100%**. The falloff begins only outside this distance. Between the **Inner Distance** value and the **Outer Distance** value, the density of the visible light changes from **100%** to **0%**.

Open **colored-edge-falloff.c4d** and experiment with these parameters. The **Relative Scale** parameter works in conjunction with **Omni** lights. You can use this parameter to scale the **Outer Distance** value.

The **Sample Distance** parameter controls how finely the visible light's volumetric shadow will be computed. Smaller values produce much finer results but take longer to render. This value is measured in world units and defines how finely the shadows within a visible light will be sampled.

The values for the **Sample Distance** parameter usually be from **1/10**th to **1/1000**th of the radius of the light source. If you increase the value, you will get faster renders but at the same time you will get some artifacts. The images in Fig. 40 show the render with **Sample Distance** set to **8** and **20**, respectively.

Refer to **sample-distance.c4d**.

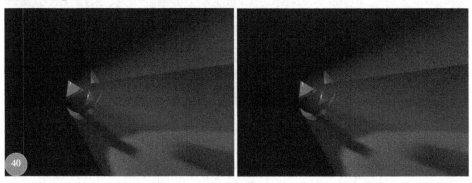

The **Brightness** parameter controls the brightness of the visible light source. The **Dust** parameter controls the darkness of the visible light source. Lower the value of the **Brightness** parameter to see full effect of the **Dust** parameter. When you specify a value greater than **0** for the **Dust** parameter, brightness is subtracted instead of added. The **Dithering** parameter produces irregularities in the visible light. You can use this parameter to remove unwanted banding or contouring in the visible light source.

You can use the **Color** parameter to create color and brightness gradients in the visible light. The images in Fig. 41 shows the color gradient generated using the **Omni** and **Spot** lights, respectively. Also, refer to the **color-gradient.c4d**.

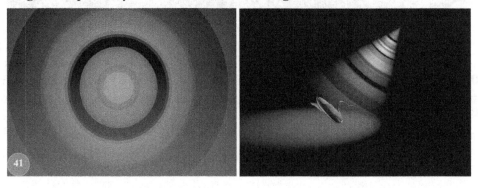

*Note: Intensity*

*The **Intensity** parameter in the **Details** tab also affects the gradient i.e. the brightness of the visible light.*

*Caution: Gradient*

*If the **Use Gradient** check box is not selected, the gradient defined in the **Details** tab may not be applied.*

On selecting the **Additive** check box, you can mix the light beam additively with other light sources. Select the **Adapt Brightness** check box to prevent a light beam from being over-exposed. The brightness of the light is reduced until the over-exposed effect disappears.

## Shadow Tab

You can select shadow types from this tab. You can select these types from the **Shadow** drop-down list and are discussed next:

## Shadow Maps (Soft)

In real-world, the objects are lit by several partial light sources. As a result, there is a gradual transition of light to shadow. You can simulate this soft edge [umbra] in Cinema 4D using the **Shadow Maps (Soft)** shadow type.

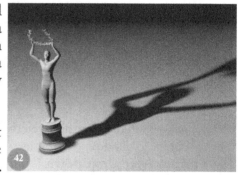

This shadow type is computed very fast and produces natural looking shadows [see Fig. 42]. Also, refer to **shadow-map-soft.c4d**.

*Note: Soft shadow map*

*A soft shadow map is a grayscale picture of the scene as viewed from the light source. This map contains all the objects lit by the light source. During the render calculations, the renderer decides which objects will fall into the shadow of the light source.*

*Caution: Memory consumption*

*Depending on the size of the map, for the **Shadow Maps (Soft)** shadow type, a great deal of additional memory may be needed. So be careful when selecting this type and specifying the map size.*

The **Density** parameter is used to adjust the intensity of the shadows. At **0%** the shadow is invisible, at **50%** the shadow will be half transparent, and at **100%** shadow will have full intensity. The images in Fig. 43 show the shadow when **Density** is set to **50** and **80**, respectively.

Since shadows in nature are not jet black, you can use the **Color** setting to change the color of the shadows thus creating contrast between the light and shade. If shadow maps should take the transparency and alpha channels into account, select the **Transparency** check box. The images in Fig. 44 show the result when the **Transparency** check box is disabled and enabled, respectively. Refer to **transparency.c4d**.

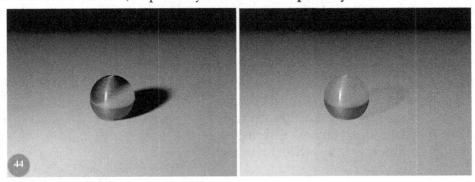

If you have enabled the clipping settings in the **Details** tab and you want to apply these settings to shadow casting as well, select the **Clipping Influence** check box. The **Shadow Map** drop-down is only available if you have selected the **Shadow Maps (Soft)** shadow type. By default, a standard size of **250x250** is used. However, you can increase it to a substantial size. If you want the shadows to be sharp and smoothly defined, you need to increase the size of the map. However, if you want the edges of the shadows smooth, you need to increase the value of the **Sample Radius** parameter. In both scenarios, the render time will increase.

*Tip: Map size*
*Rather than using a map with a doubled **Shadow Map** size, you can achieve an equivalent soft edge by doubling the **Sample Radius** value.*

You can specify the size of the map manually by using the **Resolution X** and **Resolution Y** parameters. The **Memory Usage** label displays the maximum memory used for the shadow map. You can use this information to estimate how much memory will be needed for the shadow maps. The **Sample Radius** parameter defines the shadow map accuracy. The higher the value you specify, the more accurate the shadows will be, and the longer it will take to render them.

*Tip: Render time vs memory*
*If you are using a small shadow map, you can trade off render time against memory usage by specifying high value for the **Sample Radius** parameter.*

During animations, it can happen that the shadow flickers and don't move properly due to the fact that shadows maps using fixed resolution. To fix this issue, you need to reduce the resolution of the map. This will result in sharper edges which in turn has to be compensated for the larger **Sample Radius** value.

The **Boost Sample Radius** parameter prevents the **Sample Radius** value from having to be set too high. It enables a function that increases the **Sample Radius** value and randomly disperses the samples. This replaces the stepping effect with noise, which is less noticeable in animations. The **Absolute Bias** parameter is available for compatibility reasons and you should leave this check box selected.

You can use the **Bias (Abs)** parameter to adjust the position of the shadow. When you zoom in close on small objects in the scene, the distance between object and shadow will become apparent. You can fix this by lowering the value for the **Bias (Abs)** parameter. On selecting the **Outline Shadow** check box, Cinema 4D displays a thin shadow outline instead of a full shadow [see Fig. 45].

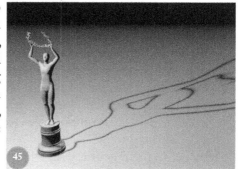

When an **Omni** light is used in a scene, six shadow maps must be computed in total. As a result, you might see some artifacts in shadows. On selecting the **Shadow Cone** check box, Cinema 4D generates a single shadow map and limits shadows to a cone. This results in speeding up render times. The **Angle** parameter is used to set the vertex angle of the shadow cone. Select the **Soft Cone** check box to give the shadow cone a softer edge.

### Raytraced (Hard)

The **Raytraced (Hard)** type is of particular interest for technical illustrations as it produces hard shadows [see Fig. 46]. This type required to compute many more additional rays therefor increasing the render time dramatically.

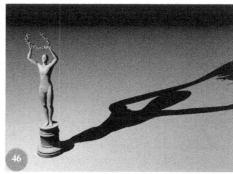

### Area

The **Area** shadow type takes longer to render. Therefore, use this type when you have luxury of time on your hands. Soft shadows [produced by the **Shadow Maps (Soft)** shadow type] are more natural than the hard shadows but still not perfectly natural because the soft edge always has the same width. In real-world, this does not happen. The closer an object is to a surface, the sharper the soft edge will be. Area shadows simulate this effect in Cinema 4D [see Fig. 47].

The area shadows are controlled by the **Accuracy**, **Minimum Samples**, and **Maximum Samples** parameters. The area shadows are calculated using samples, the more samples you use, the less grainy the rendering will be, and the longer they will take to render.

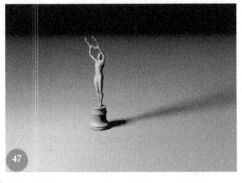

The **Minimum Samples** and **Maximum Samples** parameters allow you to specify samples for the area light. The **Accuracy** parameter controls how and how many samples will be allotted in order to achieve the best result. In the most critical areas, the value of the **Maximum Samples** parameter may be set to its highest value.

Follow the steps given next to optimize area lights:

1. Find out critical areas in your scene where you see grain.
2. Set the **Minimum Samples** and **Maximum Samples** parameters to the same value and render the critical regions using the **Render Region** tool.
3. Increase the value of the **Minimum Samples** and **Maximum Samples** parameters equally until you achieve a good result.
4. Lower **Minimum Samples** to **25%** of the **Maximum Samples** value and set **Accuracy** to **50%**.
5. Raise the **Accuracy** setting until you have a result you are happy with.

 *Caution: Area shadows*
*No matter which value **Accuracy**, **Minimum Samples**, or **Maximum Samples**] you increase, the render time will increase. If you set value of **Minimum Samples** equals to the **Maximum Samples**, the **Accuracy** will have no effect in the render. Generally quality can be improved, by increasing values of the **Maximum Samples** and **Accuracy** parameters but even **100%** **Accuracy** value will not improve the quality if you have specified a very low value for the **Maximum Samples** parameter.*

 *Caution: PyroCluster clouds*
*The area shadows do not work with the **PyroCluster** clouds. If you user area shadows with them, Cinema 4D will render them with hard shadows.*

 *Tip: Anti-aliasing*
*If you set **Anti-aliasing** to **Best** in the **Render Settings** window, you can reduce the graininess in the shadows. You can use the **Compositing** tag to override the global anti-aliasing settings on object-to-object basis.*

*Note: Render time*
*Given below are some points about render time:*

- *Soft shadows are calculated far more quickly than hard shadows, hard shadows being much faster to calculate than area shadows.*
- *If you make a light visible in the render, a negligible amount of render time is added.*
- *A volumetric light increases render time, sometimes substantially, according to the **Sample Distance** parameter.*
- *The **Noise** function adds to the render time. The hard and soft turbulence types need more time to render than the basic noise.*
- *The wavy turbulence takes roughly double time to render than the basic noise function.*
- *If you use a high value for the **Sample Radius** parameter, the render time will increase.*
- *Area lights add to the render time but not to the same extent as the processor intensive volumetric lights.*

## Photometric Tab

The parameters in the **Photometric** tab allow you to use the IES [Illuminating Engineering Society] format in a Cinema 4D scene. Using this format, the light sources can be made to behave as real lights do. A file with the **.ies** file extension is an IES Photometric file. They are plain text [ASCII] files that contain data on light for architectural programs that can simulate light and published by light manufacturers online.

To create an **IES** light, create a **Light** object and then in the **Attribute Manager > General** tab, change **Type** to **IES**. Now, you can align the light in the scene. The direction of the emitted light is defined by the z-axis. Next, load the **.ies** file using the **Filename** parameter. You can also drag **.ies** files from the **Content Browser** to the **Filename** field [see Fig. 48]. Also, refer to the **ies-light.c4d**.

*Tip: IES File*
*The **Filename** field displays the path of the IES file. However, the IES data is within the Cinema 4D's scene file. If you want to distribute the file, you don't have to include the IES file with it.*

The **Intensity** parameter is used to adjust the intensity of the light, it is the maximum intensity of the IES light. The options [**Candela**, **Lumen**, and **Lux**] in the **Units** drop-down list are used to specify units that can be applied to the light. The **Photometric Data** check box is selected by default. As a result, the IES data is evaluated by Cinema 4D. If you clear this check box, the light source will revert to being an **Omni** light source with adjustable **Lumen** or **Candela** intensity.

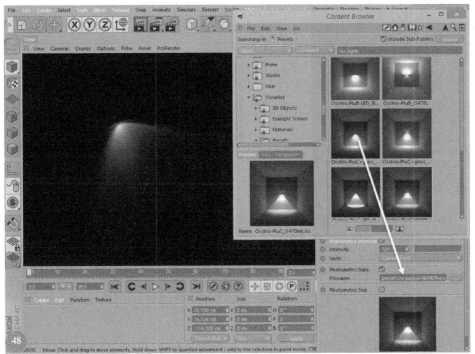

Very often IES files contain information regarding the size of the actual light. If you are using such file, on selecting the **Photometric Size** check box, you can turn the IES light into an **Area** light. Otherwise, the IES light will function as an **Omni** light. In the **Information** area, you will find details saved with the IES file such as name of the manufacture, catalog number, and so on. If there is no information saved with the file, these fields will remain empty.

## Noise Tab

The options in the **Noise** tab can be used to create effects such as animated fog and Sun flares without using the time consuming volume shaders. The **Noise** feature is slower to calculate. As a result, there will be longer render times.

In nature, the surface of an object is not illuminated evenly. If dust or small particles are present in the environment, there will be irregularities in the illumination.

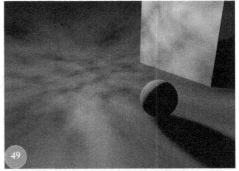

The **Illumination** option in the **Noise** drop-down list is used to add these irregularities to the light source [see Fig. 49]. Also, refer to the **noise.c4d**.

The **Type** drop-down list allows you to select the noise type. Fig. 49 shows the **Soft Turbulence** type. Other types are **Noise, Hard Turbulence**, and **Wavy Turbulence**. Fig. 50 shows these types.

The **Octaves** parameter works in conjunction with the turbulence types and controls the graininess of the noise. The higher the value you specify for this parameter, the grittier the appearance will be. The images in Fig. 51 show the result with **Octaves** set to **1** and **5**, respectively. The **Velocity** parameter sets the speed of the irregularities. The **Brightness** and **Contrast** parameters are used to raise the overall brightness of the irregularities and adjust the contrast of the noise, respectively. Higher **Contrast** values increase the contrast of the noise, lower values reduce it.

In nature, the dust and particles move due to forces of nature, they don't move when the source of the light moves. However, in Cinema 4D, you can move these irregularities when light moves. To do so, select the **Local** check box. However, leave this check box clear to make scene look natural.

The **Visibility Scale** parameter adjusts the size of the irregularities in the **X, Y** and **Z** directions in relation to the scene's coordinates. If the noise effect is too severe, try reducing these values. The **Illumination Scale** parameter defines the size of the noise on lit objects. Lower values will result in rough noise whereas the larger values will result in finer noise. The **Wind** parameter is used to add wind effect to the noise. It will appear as if wind is blowing it away. The strength of the wind is controlled by the **Wind Velocity** parameter. These two parameters add realism to the animation.

## Lens Tab

The options in the **Lens** tab are used to generate real-world camera effects in Cinema 4D. If you select the **No Illumination** check box in the **General** tab, the light source will not illuminate the object in the scene, you can then use the light for the lens effects. In real-world, the cameraman will try to avoid these as they can soon become distracting.

Experiment with the options in this tab to get hang of them. Note that lens effects cannot be displayed in **QuickTime VR** panoramas. Figs. 52 [**Wideangle, Artifact,** and **Sun 1**] and 53 [**Blue1, Candle,** and **Zoom**] show some of the lens effects available in Cinema 4D.

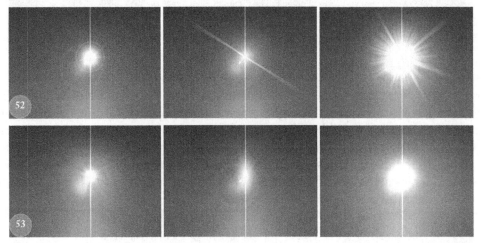

## Project Tab

The options in the **Project** tab are used to define which objects will be affected by the light. If a light should affect specific object(s), set **Mode** to **Include** and then drag object(s) from the **Object Manager** to the **Objects** list in the **Project** tab. If light should be switched off for an object(s), set **Mode** to **Exclude** and then drag object(s) from the **Object Manager** to the **Objects** list in the **Project** tab.

When you add objects to the **Objects** list, five icons appear next to the object's label [see Fig. 54]. Click the icons in the **Objects** list to enable or disable illumination, specularity, and shadows for that object. The names of the icons [from left to right] are: **Object, Illumination, Specularity, Shadows,** and **Include Entire Hierarchy.** When you click the **Include Entire Hierarchy** icon, the object's children should also be affected by the inclusion or exclusion.

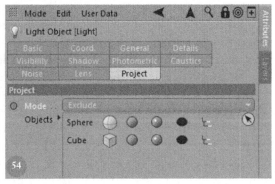

The **PyroCluster Illumination** and **PyroCluster Shadow Casting** checkboxes define whether or not a given light source should illuminate smoke/steam or whether or not the smoke/steam should cast shadows based on a given light source. These checkboxes will only appear if you are using the Studio version of Cinema 4D.

# Hands-on Exercises

### Exercise 1: Creating a 3-Point Lighting Setup

In this exercise, we will create the 3-point light setup using the **Area** lights then render the scene [see Fig. E1].

The following table summarizes the exercise:

| Table E1 | |
|---|---|
| Skill level | Intermediate |
| Time to complete | 30 Minutes |
| Topics | • Getting Started<br>• Creating Setup |
| Resources folder | **unit-cr3** |
| Units | **Centimeters** |
| Start file | **3point-start.c4d** |
| Final file | **3point-finish.c4d** |

### Getting Started

Open **3point-start.c4d**.

### Creating Setup

Let's first start by assigning a material to the **Floor** object. Follow the steps given next:

1.  Double-click on the **Material Manager** to create a new material and assign it the **Floor** object in the **Object Manager**. Rename material as **mat-floor**. In the **Color** channel of the material, change **Color V** value to **75**.

*What Floor object does?*
*The **Floor** object creates a floor that always lies in the XZ plane. When you render it, it is stretched to the infinity. Although, the name of the object is floor but you can use it to create skies as well. You can create as many floors as you want and transform them independently. This feature helps in creating different layers of clouds.*

2. Choose **Create > Light > Area Light** from the menubar to create an area light in the scene. This light will work as key light and will be the main source of light in the scene. Rename this light as **key-light** in the **Object Manager**. Now, enter the following coordinate values in the **Coord.** tab of the **Attribute Manager** to position the light:

   **Position [XYZ]:** -165, 818, -26          **Rotation [HPB]:** -82.8, -78.75, 0

3. In the **General** tab, change **Shadows** to **Shadow Maps (Soft)**. In the **Shadows** tab, change **Shadow Map** to **500x500**. Render the scene [see Fig. E2].

E2

4. Create another light in the scene and then rename it as **fill-light**. Now, enter the following coordinate values in the **Coord.** tab of the **Attribute Manager** to position the light:

**Position [XYZ]:** 409, 644, -281          **Rotation [HPB]:** 59.445, -46.431, 0

5. In the **General** tab, clear the **Specular** check box.

 *What just happened?*
*By disabling the **Specular** check box, we are making sure that the light will not affect the specular component of the material.*

6. Create another light in the scene and then rename it as **back-light**. Now, enter the following coordinate values in the **Coord.** tab of the **Attribute Manager** to position the light:

**Position [XYZ]:** 676, 799, 1035          **Rotation [HPB]:** 146.578, -34.814, 0

7. In the **General** tab, turn off the **Specular** check box. Drag **Floor** from the **Object Manager** to the **Objects** field of the **Project** tab. Render the scene [see Fig. E3].

 *What just happened?*
*Here, I don't want **back-light** to illuminate the floor. Therefore, I've excluded it from illuminating the **Floor** object. By default, the **Mode** is set to **Exclude**. If you want that the light should illuminate specific objects, change **Mode** to **Include** and drag objects from the **Object Manager** to **Objects** field of the **Project** tab. If an object has children and if they should be affected by inclusion or exclusion use the forth icon.*

8. Choose **Create > Environment > Sky** from the menubar to add a **Sky** object to the scene. RMB click on **Sky** in the **Object Manager** and then choose **Cinema 4D Tags > Compositing** from the context menu. Make sure the tag is selected in the **Object Manager** and then in the **Attribute Manager > Tag** tab, clear all checkboxes except the **Seen by Rays, Seen by GI, Seen by Reflection**, and **Seen by AO** checkboxes.

> **What is the Compositing tag used for?**
> The **Compositing** tag has numerous settings that affect the render. This tag allows you to prevent objects from certain operations such as casting and receiving shadows. Here, the **Sky** object will only be seen by rays, global illumination, reflection, and ambient occlusion.

9. Assign the **Sunny Marketplace 01** material to the **Sky** object.

> **Why this material is applied?**
> This material contains an HDR [High Definition Range Imagery] image. HDR images are well suited when you want realistic looking reflections in the scene. HDR images contains 32-bit color depth which is much higher than normal 8-bit images. By assigning this material to the **Sky** object, we have ensured that objects will have reflections from the HDR image. Cinema 4D provides many HDR images that you can use in your projects. These images are available at the following location: **Content Browser > Prime > Materials > HDRI**.

10. Open the **Render Settings** window and then add the **Global Illumination** effect. Render the scene. You will notice that scene is bright, we need to reduce the intensity of the lights to get the desired effect.

11. Change intensity of **key-light, fill-light**, and **back-light** to **70, 60**, and **60** respectively.

12. Select **mat-floor** in the **Material Manager** and then in the **Attribute Manager > Basic** tab, select the **Diffusion** check box. In the **Diffusion** tab, click **Texture > Triangle** button and then choose **Effects > Ambient Occlusion** from the popup. Click on the **Ambient Occlusion** button to open the shader settings.

> **What Ambient Occlusion effect does?**
> The **Ambient Occlusion** shader is a fast alternative to Global Illumination with some limitations. It determines upto which extent each individual surface point is exposed and then colors it accordingly. It darkens the areas such as corners, holes, and objects closer to each other. By applying it to the **Diffusion** channel, the areas where tires touch the floor will be darkened by this shader.

13. Change **Maximum Ray Length** to **200**, **Accuracy** to **100**, and **Maximum Samples** to **128**. Render the scene [see Fig. E4]. The images in Fig. E5 show the scene from the **key-light**, **fill-light**, and **back-light**, respectively. Fig. E6 shows the three lights in the scene.

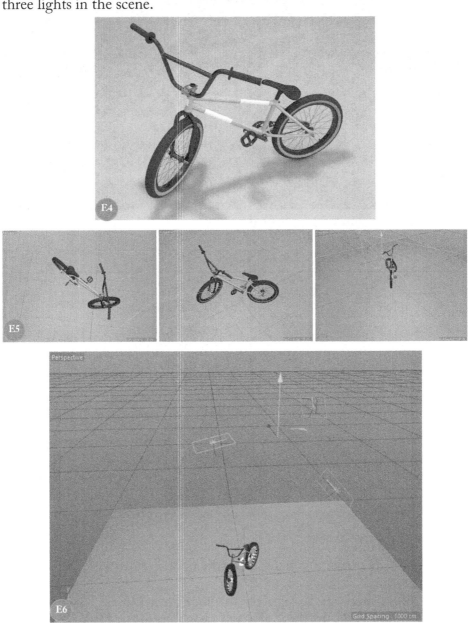

## Exercise 2: Creating a Product Visualization Render

In this exercise, we will render a bike on dark background using the **Area** and **Spot** lights [see Fig. E1].

The following table summarizes the exercise:

| Table E2 | |
|---|---|
| Skill level | Intermediate |
| Time to complete | 1 Hr 30 Minutes |
| Topics | • Getting Started<br>• Creating Render<br>• Post-Production |
| Resources folder | **unit-cr3** |
| Units | **Centimeters** |
| Start file | **bike-start.c4d** |
| Final file | **bike-finish.c4d** |

### Getting Started
Open **bike-start.c4d**.

### Creating Render
Let's first start by first creating material for the floor. Follow these steps:

1. Create a new material and assign it to the floor in the **Object Manager**. Rename material as **floor-mat**. In the **Color** tab, change color to **HSV [0, 0, 6]**. In the **Reflectance** tab, change **Type** to **GGX**, **Attenuation** to **Average**, **Roughness** to **10**, **Reflection Strength** to **100**, **Specular Strength** to **0**, and **Brightness** to **60**.

2. Create a new camera and adjust its angle of view. RMB click on **Camera** in the **Object Manager** and then choose **Cinema 4D Tags** > **Protection** from the popup.

3. Create a new spot light, rename it as **Main Light** and then in the **General** tab, change **Type** to **Square Spot**. Make sure **Main Light** is selected and then choose **Cameras > Set Active Object as Camera** from **Menu in editor view**. Now, using the navigation tools place the light as shown in Fig. E2 and also adjust outer angle of the light in the view interactively or using the **Outer Angle** parameter in the **Details** tab.

4. Switch back to **Camera** view and then in **Render Settings** make sure the **Physical Test** preset is active. Render the scene see Fig. E3.

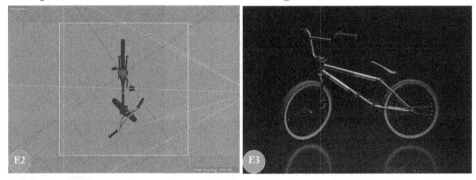

5. Create an area light and then position it, as shown in Fig. E4. Rename the light as **Fill Light**. In the **General** tab, change **Intensity** to 3 and on the **Details** tab, select the **Z Direction Only** check box. Switch to camera view and render the scene [see Fig. E5].

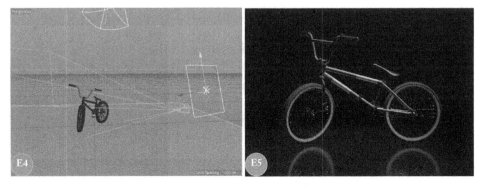

6. Create a new **Spot** light and aim it at the seat of the bike [see Fig. E6]. In the **Attribute Manager > General** tab, change **Intensity** to **500** and clear the **Diffuse** check box. Switch to the **Project** tab and then drag **Sport Bike > Saddle** from the **Object Manager** to **Objects** field. Also, change **Mode** to **Include**. Render the scene [see Fig. E7].

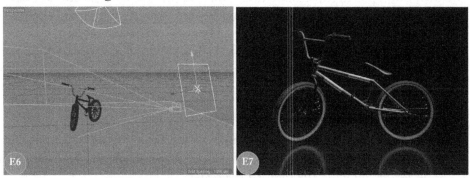

> *What just happened?*
> *Here, I have included the seat of the bike in the **Project** tab. Now, the **Spot** light will only illuminate the seat of the bike. Also, it will not affect the **Diffuse** component. By adding this light, you will get a nice rim highlight on the seat.*

7. Create another **Spot** light and this time focus it on the **Handle Bar** object [see Fig. E8]. Switch to the **Project** tab and then drag **Sport Bike > Handle Bar** from the **Object Manager** to **Object** field. Also, change **Mode** to **Include**. Change spot light's **Intensity** parameter to **250**. Render the scene [see Fig. E9].

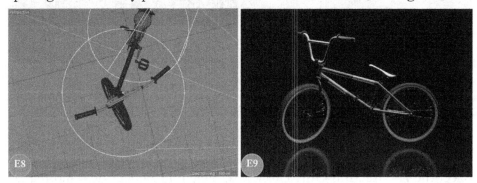

> *What next?*
> *Now, let's add a **Sky** object to the scene.*

8. Press **Shift+F8** to open the **Content Browser**. In the browser, choose **Presets > Prime > Presets > Light Setups > HDRI** and double-click on **Photo Studio** swatch to add it to the **Material Manager**.

9. Create a **Sky** object and then apply the **Photo Studio** material to the **Sky** object. Add a **Compositing** tag to the **Sky** object. Make sure tag is selected in the **Object Manager** and then in the **Attribute Manager > Tag** tab, clear all

checkboxes except **Seen by Rays**, **Seen by GI**, **Seen by Reflection**, and **Seen by AO** checkboxes. Add the **Ambient Occlusion** effect to the **floor-mat**, as done in **Exercise 1**.

10. Add a **Compositing** tag to the **Sport Bike** object and then in the **Attribute Manager > Object Buffer** tab, select the first **Enable** check box and make sure if **Buffer** is set to **1**.

11. Switch to the **Render Settings** window. Ensure that **PhysicalFinal** preset is active. RMB click on **Multi-Pass** in the left pane of the window. Choose **Object Buffer** from the popup. Also, select the **Multi-Pass** check box.

12. In the left pane, select the **Save** check box and select this option. In the **Regular Image** section of the right pane, choose a location and set file name to **bikeRender**. Change **Format** to **PNG** and **Depth** to **16 Bit/Channel**. Also, use the same settings in the **Multi-Pass Image** section. In the left pane, select the **Anti-Aliasing** and then on the right pane select the **Consider Multi-Passes** check box.

> ? *What Consider Multi-Passes check box does?*
> *When this check box is selected, Cinema 4D ensures that quality in multi passes and **Alpha** channels is not affected. Generally, quality issues arise when you render an object in front of a black background or render an object which is placed behind thin transparent surface.*

13. Render the scene [see Fig. E10]. Notice that the **Floor** object is getting affected by the HDR illumination. Next, we will fix it.

14. Select the **Compositing** tag of the **Sky** object and then switch to the **Exclusion** tab in the **Attribute Manager**. Drag **Floor** from the **Object Manager** to this tab. Make sure **Mode** is change to **Exclusion**. Render the scene. Notice that light is little bright therefore you need to reduce the intensity of the **Main Light**.

15. Change its **Intensity** to **50** and render the scene [see Fig. E11]. After completion of the rendering process, you will get two PNG files namely, **bikeRender.png** and **bikeRender_object_1.png**. These files contains the regular image and the multi-pass image, respectively.

## Post Production

Follow the steps given next:

1. Start **Photoshop** and then open two PNG files. In the **bikeRender_object_1.png** file, press **Ctrl+A** to select the whole image and then press **Ctrl+C**. Switch to the **bikeRender.png** file. Switch to the **Channels** panel, click the **Create new channel** icon at the bottom of the panel and then press **Ctrl+V** to paste the image from the clipboard [see Fig. E12]. Now, turn of the alpha channel and turn on the RGB channels.

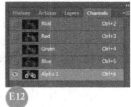

> *What next?*
> *Notice in the **bikeRender.png** file there is a horizon line. Next, we need to fix it.*
2. Switch to the **Layers** panel and then press **Ctrl+D** to clear the selection. Make sure the **Background** layer is selected and then press **Ctrl+J** to duplicate the layer. Switch to the **Channels** panel and **Ctrl** click on the **Alpha 1** layer swatch to load the selection. Press **Ctrl+Shift+I** to invert the selection.

3. Switch back to the **Layers** panel and click on the **Add layer mask** icon at the bottom of the panel to add a mask. Change blending mode to **Overlay** and **Opacity** to **60**. Notice that now the horizon line has disappeared [see Fig. E13]. Press **Ctrl+E** to merge the layers and rename it as **Base**. Save the file as **bikeRender.psd**.

4. Duplicate **Base** and rename it as **Clarity**. Choose **Filter > Camera Raw Filter** from the menubar and then change **Clarity** to **15** [see Fig. E14]. Click **OK**.

5. Duplicate the **Clarity** layer and rename it as **High Pass**. Choose **Filter > Other > High Pass** from the menubar to open the **High Pass** dialog box. In this dialog box, change **Radius** to **2** and click **OK** [see Fig. E15]. Change **Blending Mode** to **Overlay** and **Opacity** to **50** [see Fig. E16].

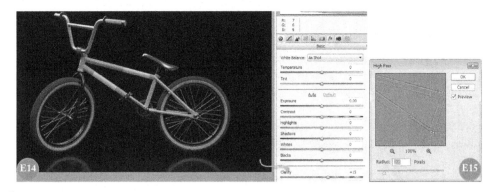

> **What Clarity and High Pass do?**
> **Clarity** adds midtones contrast to the image and makes it sharper without actually sharpening the image. The **High Pass** filter allows you to bring back the highlights and edges in the image. The **Radius** parameter controls how many pixels on either side of the edge would be used as part of the edge. For example, a value of **1** pixel means that Photoshop will include only a single pixel on either side of the edge.

6. Click **Create new fill or adjustment layer** and choose **Color Lookup** from the popup. In the **Properties** panel, change **3DLUT File** to **Fuji F125 Kodak 2393**. Change **Opacity** to **35** [see Fig. E17].

7. Now, apply a curve adjustment [see Fig. E18]. Save the PSD file.

# Exercise 3: Rendering an Interior Scene

In this exercise, we will render an interior scene[see Fig. E1].

The following table summarizes the exercise:

| Table E3 | |
| --- | --- |
| Skill level | Intermediate |
| Time to complete | 2 Hrs |
| Topics | • Getting Started<br>• Specifying Settings for Test Rendering<br>• Illuminating the Scene<br>• Specifying Settings for Final Rendering |
| Resources folder | **unit-cr3** |
| Units | **Centimeters** |
| Start file | **int-start.c4d** |
| Final file | **int-finish.c4d** |

## Getting Started

Open **int-start.c4d**. One of the key materials in the scene is the one applied on the curtains [the name of the material is **mat-curtain**]. Since the curtains will be illuminated from outside the room, we need a special material to create that effect.

Here, I have used the **Backlight** shader in the **Illumination** channel [see Fig. E2]. Also, applied the curtain texture to the **Transparency** channel and changed its **Brightness** to **54%** [see Fig. E3].

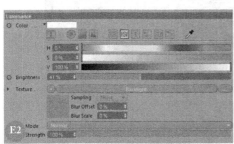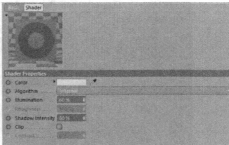

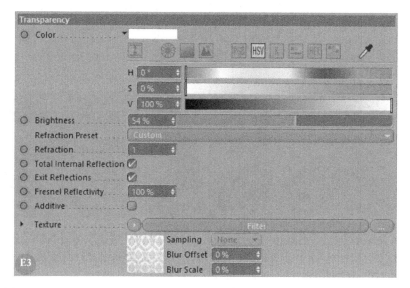

The **Backlight** shader allows you to gather illumination from the back face of an object. This shader works with real lights. For example, it will not work with the polygon lights. Generally, this shader is used with the **Luminance** channel.

## Specifying Settings for Test Rendering

Follow these steps:

1.  Press **Ctrl+B** to open the **Render Settings** window. Select **Physical** from the **Renderer** drop-down list. Select **Physical** from the left pane. In the right pane, make sure the **Sampler** is set to **Adaptive**. Change **Sampling Subdivisions** to **0**, **Blurriness Subdivision (Max)** to **0**, **Shadow Subdivision (Max)** to **1**, **Ambient Occlusion Subdivision (Max)** to **1**, and **Subsurface Scattering Subdivision (Max)** to **0**. Rename **My Render Settings** to **Test**.

2.  Click on the **Effect** button and then choose **Global Illumination** from the popup menu. Select **Global Illumination** from the left pane and then in the **General** tab of the right pane, change **Primary Method** to **Irradiance Cache**, **Secondary Method** to **None**, and **Samples** to **Low**.

3.  In the **Irradiance Cache** tab, change **Record Density** to **Low**. Save the scene as **int-start-01.c4d**.

## Illuminating the Scene

Let's first simulate the light coming from the Sun, using three **Infinite Light** objects: **Sun**, **Sun Diffuse**, and **Sun Beam**. The **Sun light** will the main light for the scene with warm color. We will use the **Infinite Angle** parameter to vary the angle of the shadow cast by the Sun. A value of **0** results in hard shadows. The **Sun Diffuse** light will be used for extending the soft illumination using a larger value for the **Infinite Angle** parameter. The **Sun Beam** light will be used for simulating only the Sun rays coming inside the window. Follow these steps:

1. Create an **Infinite Light** and then rename it as **Sun**. In the **Attribute Manager >
   Coord** tab, change **P.X, P.Y,** and **P.Z** to **420, 585,** and **1272,** respectively. Change
   **R.H, R.P,** and **R.B** to **180, -26,** and **0,** respectively [see Fig. E4]. Render the
   scene [see Fig. E5].

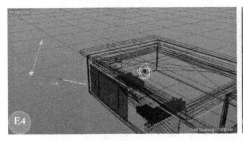 

2. In the **General** tab, change **Color** to HSV **[26, 24, 100]** and **Shadow** to **Area**.
   Render the scene [see Fig. E6]. In the **Details** tab, change **Infinite Angle** to **0.38**
   and then render the scene [see Fig. E7].

 *What just happened?*
*Notice the **AB** compare shown in Fig.
E8, the impact of the **Infinite Angle**
parameter; now we have more realistic
soft shadow edges.*

3. In the **Render Settings** window, disable
   **Global Illumination** for the time being
   so that we get faster test renders while we
   are placing the direct light sources. In the **Object Manager,** create a copy of **Sun**
   and rename the new object as **Sun Diffuse.** In the **Attribute Manager > General**
   tab, select the **Use Temperature** check box and then change **Color Temperature**
   to **5536.** In the **Details** tab, change **Infinite Angle** to **6.5** and then render the
   scene [see Fig. E9].

 *What just happened?*
*Here, we have used a larger value for the **Infinite Angle** parameter. As a result,
we are able to vary the angle of the shadow [see Fig. E9].*

4. In the **Object Manager**, create a copy of **Sun Diffuse** and rename the new object as **Sun Beam**. In the **Attribute Manager > General** tab, change **Color Temperature** to **5532** and **Type** to **Square Parallel Spot**. In the **Details** tab, change **Outer Radius** to **160**.

5. In the **General** tab, select the **No Illumination** check box and then change **Visible Light** to **Volumetric**. In the **Visibility** tab, change **Brightness** to **126**. Align the light, as shown in Fig. E10 and then render the scene [see Fig. E11].

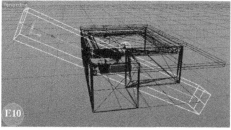

*What just happened?*
*The **Sun Beam** light has been used for simulating only the sun rays coming inside the window. Also, I have selected the **No Illumination** check box in the General tab. As a result, this light will only cast rays and will not illuminate the scene.*

*What next?*
*Next, we will simulate the day light using an **Area** light.*

6. Create an **Area** light and then rename it as **Day Light**. In the **Attribute Manager > Coord** tab, change **P.X**, **P.Y**, and **P.Z** to **407**, **213**, and **535**, respectively. Change **R.H**, **R.P**, and **R.B** to **0**, **180**, and **0**, respectively. In the **Details** tab, select the **Z Direction Only** check box. Also, change **Size X** and **Size Y** to **360** and **287**, respectively [see Fig. E12].

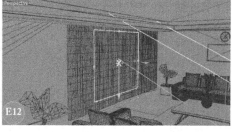

7. In the **General** tab, select the **Use Temperature** check box and then change **Color Temperature** to **6800**. Also, change **Shadow** to **Area**. Render the scene [see Fig. E13].

*What just happened?*
*Here, the **Day Light** is used for simulating the day light coming inside the room. The other lights are used for simulating the sky light and room light scattering in the scene.*

8. Create a **Light** object and then rename the light as **Bounce Light**. In the **Attribute Manager > Details** tab, change **Falloff** to **Inverse Square (Physically Accurate)** and **Radius/Decay** to **386**. Now, align the light, as shown in Fig. E14.

 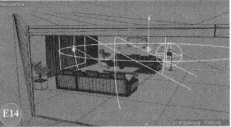

9. In the **General** tab, select the **Use Temperature** check box and then change **Color Temperature** to **4958**. Change **Intensity** to **65** and then render the scene [see Fig. E15]. Now, in the **Render Settings** window, enable **Global Illumination**

> ⚠ *What just happened?*
> *Here, the **Bounce Light** is used for simulating the bouncing of the light in the room. Although, we have used **Global Illumination** in the scene but this light will break the uniform **Global Illumination** pattern. Now, let's adjust some parameters to get even distribution of light.*

10. Select **Day Light** in the **Object Manager** and then in the **Attribute Manager > General** tab, change **Intensity** to **55**. Similarly, change **Intensity** to **20** for the **Bounce Light**. Render the scene [see Fig. E17].

11. In the **Render Settings** window, select **Global Illumination** from the left pane of the window and then in the right pane > **General** tab, change **Secondary Method** to **Light Mapping**. In the **Light Mapping** tab, change **Path Count (x1000)** to **2000** and **Sample Size** to **0.02**. Render the scene [see Fig. E18].

> ⚠ *How to fine tune render?*
> *To fine tune results, solo each light and then render to see the effect. This process allows you to observe and correct influence of each light. Fig. E19 through E23 show the individual output of the **Sun**, **Sun Diffuse**, **Sun Beam**, **Day Light**, and **Bounce Light**, respectively.*

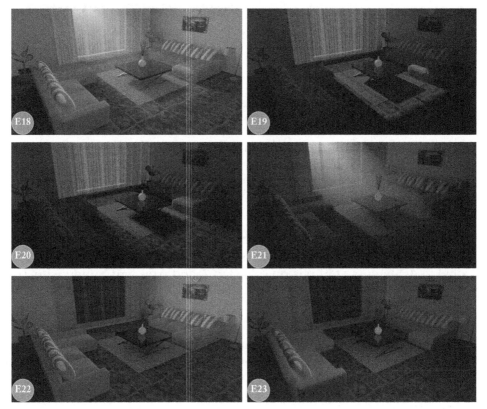

12. Disable all lights in the scene. Create an **Area** light and then rename it as **SkyLight-01**. In the **Attribute Manager > Coord** tab, change **P.X, P.Y**, and **P.Z** to **-761, 237**, and **577**, respectively. Change **R.H, R.P**, and **R.B** to **0, 180**, and **0**, respectively. In the **Details** tab, change **Size X** and **Size Y** to **469** and **341**, respectively, [see Fig. E24]. Also, select the **Z Direction Only** check box.

13. In the **General** tab, change **Intensity** to **40**. Select the **Use Temperature** check box and then change **Color Temperature** to **7516**. Next, change **Shadow** to **Area**. Render the scene [see Fig. E25].

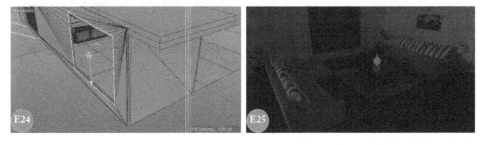

14. Create a copy of **SkyLight-01** and then rename it as **SkyLight-02**. In the **Attribute Manager > Coord** tab, change **P.X, P.Y**, and **P.Z** to **-574, 237**, and **-263**, respectively. Change **R.H, R.P**, and **R.B** to **90, 180**, and **0**, respectively. In the **Details** tab, change **Size X** and **Size Y** to **585** and **282**, respectively, [see Fig. E26]. In the **General** tab, change **Intensity** to **20**. Render the scene [see Fig. E27].

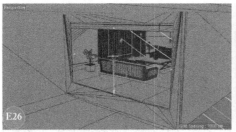

15. Enable all lights in the scene and then render it [see Fig. E28].

## Specifying Settings for Final Rendering
Follow these steps:

1. Open the **Render Settings** window. Select **Physical** from the left pane. In the right pane, change **Shading Subdivisions (Min)** to **1**, **Shading Subdivisions (Max)** to **4**, **Shadow Subdivision (Max)** to **2**, and **Ambient Subdivision (Max)** to **2**.

2. Select **Global Illumination** from the left pane and then in the **General** tab of the right pane, **Samples** to **Medium**. In the **Irradiance Cache** tab, change **Record Density** to **Medium** and **Smoothing** to **50**. In the **Light Mapping** tab, change **Path Count (x1000)** to **5000** and **Sample Size** to **0.01**. Select the **Show Preview Paths** check box and then select the **Prefilter** check box. Change **Prefilter Samples** to **8**.

3. Click the **Effect** button and then choose **Ambient Occlusion** from the flyout. Select the **Ambient Occlusion** option and then in the **Basic** tab of the right pane, change **Maximum Ray Length** to **150**. Render the scene [see Fig. E29].

# Quiz

Evaluate your skills to see how many questions you can answer correctly.

**Multiple Choice**
Answer the following questions:

1. Which of the following shadow types is available for the light object?

   [A] Soft Shadows        [B] Hard Shadows
   [C] Area        [D] Raytrace

2. Which of the following parameters are used to control the quality of the area shadows?

   [A] Minimum Samples        [B] Maximum Samples
   [C] Accuracy        [D] All of these

**Fill in the Blanks**
Fill in the blanks in each of the following statements:

1. The _____ parameter controls the overall brightness of the light source.

2. The _____ light type simulate distant light sources such as Sun.

3. The options in the _____ drop-down list allow you to define the visibility of the light in a scene.

4. Select the _____ check box if you want to see just the visible light and/or its lens effects without the light source actually illuminating objects.

5. If you select the _____ check box, Cinema 4D will create separate diffuse, specular, and shadow layers for the light source when you render.

6. You can select the _____ option from the **Area Shape** drop-down list if you want to use any polygonal object or spline for the shape of the light.

7. Select the _____ check box if you want to render the source of the light.

8. The _____ parameter is used to adjust the brightness of a visible area light or its reflection in another object.

9. The _____ parameter is used to adjust the intensity of the shadows.

10. If you have enabled clipping settings in the **Details** tab and you want to apply these settings to shadow casting as well, select the _____ check box.

**True or False**
State whether each of the following is true or false:

1. Cinema 4D's auto light will switch on automatically when you switch off lights during an animation unless you disable the **Auto Light** option.

2. Cinema 4D lights cannot be previewed in the viewport.

3. The color of the light can be adjusted using the color temperature values.

4. The options in the **Shape** drop-down list are used to define the shape of the area light.

5. Hard shadows are calculated far more quickly than soft shadows, soft shadows being much faster to calculate than area shadows.

6. The wavy turbulence function takes roughly double the time to render than the basic noise function.

7. Volumetric lights add to the render time but not to the same extent as the processor intensive area lights.

8. **IES** stands for Illuminating Engineering Society.

9. The **Illumination** option in the **Noise** drop-down list is used to add irregularities to the light source.

10. The options in the **Details** tab are used to define which objects will be affected by the light.

**Summary**
This unit covered the following topics:

- Cinema 4D Lights
- 3-Point Lighting
- Product Visualization
- Interior Rendering

- UV Manager
- UVs
- UV Projection

# Unit CT1: Introduction to UV Mapping

UV Mapping is a process in 3D modeling in which a 2D image is projected onto a 3D mesh's surface for texture mapping. The letters **U** and **V** denote the axes for the 2D texture in 2D texture space because X, Y, and Z are used by Cinema 4D to represent the position of the mesh in the model space. The UV axes are sufficient for projecting conventional 2D textures. The third dimension [W] is used for 3D shaders, it is automatically created when required.

## Hands-on Exercises

### Exercise 1: Texturing a Cardboard Box

Let's start by texturing a cardboard box [see Fig. E1] using the **BP-UV Edit** layout.

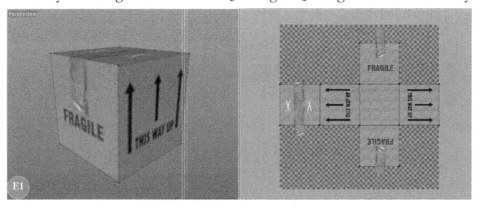

The following table summarizes the exercise:

| Table E1 | |
| --- | --- |
| Skill level | Beginner |
| Time to complete | 20 Minutes |
| Topics | • Getting Started<br>• Texturing the Cardboard Box |

| Table E1 | |
|---|---|
| Resources folder | **unit-ct1** |
| Units | **Centimeters** |
| Final file | **cardboard-finish.c4d** |

## Getting Started
Start a new scene in Cinema 4D and change units to **Centimeters**.

## Texturing the Cardboard Box
Follow these steps:

1. Choose **Cube** from the **Standard** palette > **Object** command group to create a cube in the editor view. Press **C** to make the cube editable. Double-click on the **Material Manager** to create a new material node. In the **Attribute Manager** > **Material [Mat]** > **Color** tab, click on the **Browse** button [see Fig. E2] to open the **cardboard_texture.png** file.

 *What just happened?*
*Here, I've created a new material and assigned the **cardboard_texture.png** file to it. We will use the UVs of the cube to fit on this pre-made texture.*

2. Drag the **Mat** material to the **Cube** in the viewport. The texture is displayed on each face of the cube [see Fig. E3]. Also, the **Texture Tag "Mat"** is added to the **Cube** in **Object Manager** [see Fig. E4].

 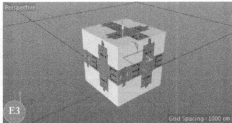

 *What just happened?*
*When we apply a material to an object, a texture tag is automatically assigned to the object. The texture tag controls how the texture is mapped or placed on the object. The settings appear in the **Attribute Manager**.*

3. In the **Attribute Manager** > **Texture Tag [Texture]** > **Tag** tab, change **Projection** to **Spherical**; notice in the 3D view that the texture is wrapped around the object

using the spherical projection. Click **Texture** on the **Tools** palette to view the projection sphere in the 3D view [see Fig. E5]. You can move the texture on the cube by transforming the projection sphere [displayed in wireframe], see Fig. E6. Experiment with other projection types available in the **Projection** drop-down list. Click **Model** on the **Tools** palette to switch to the **Model** mode.

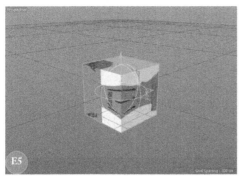
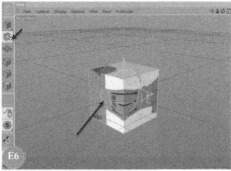

*Note: Projection Display*
*The options in the **Projection Display** drop-down list allows you to define how the projection assistance display can be adjusted in the viewport. There are three options available:*

- **Simple:** *Only the projection shape is displayed [see Fig. E7].*
- **Grid:** *The yellow grid known from Cinema 4D versions prior to R20 is displayed [see Fig. E8].*
- **Solid:** *A solid grid is displayed that allows you to gauge the orientation easily [see Fig. E9].*

4. Change **Projection** to **UVW Mapping** in the **Attribute Manager**.

*What just happened?*
*The **UVW Mapping** projection type is the default projection type in Cinema 4D. This projection type only works when an object has **UVW** coordinates. All primitive and generator objects have **UVW** coordinates by default. All polygon objects have a **UVW** tag in the **Object Manager** whereas primitive and generator objects have internal **UVW** coordinates. They do not have a **UVW** tag in the **Object Manager**. The tag appears when you convert them to editable polygon objects.*

> **?** *What are UVW coordinates?*
> *You might be wondering if a texture image is 2 dimensional, why we need a third dimension. Conventional textures have two dimensions: horizontal position **X** [U] and vertical position **Y** [V]. These two coordinates would be sufficient for conventional shaders but the third dimension is required for 3D shaders. These shaders require a third dimension [**W**] in order to appropriately place textures onto the objects.*

> **?** *What is the structure of the UVW coordinates?*
> *A **UV** grid is divided into a **U** direction and a **V** direction [see Fig. E10]. The range starts at **0,0** and ends at **0,1**. A texture is stretched between four coordinates. The grid represents a conventional 2D texture.*
>
> *You might be wondering where the third coordinate **W** is? It is only created when it is required and behaves in the same way as **UV** coordinates.*

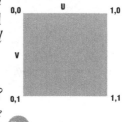

5. Choose **BP - UV Edit** from the **Layout** drop-down list to switch to the **BP-UV Edit** layout. The **BP-UV Edit** layout appears [see Fig. E11].

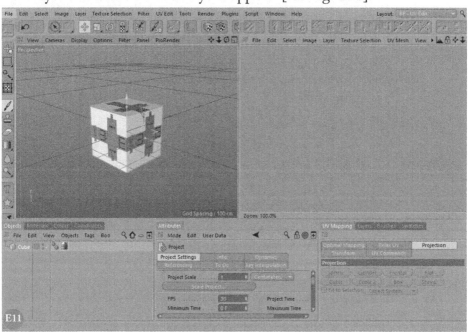

6. Choose **File > Open Texture** from the **Texture View** and then navigate to the **cardboard_texture.png** file and then click **Open**, the texture appears in the **Texture View** [see Fig. E12].

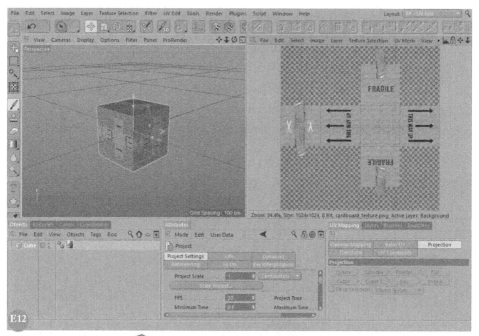

E12

7. Click **UV Polygons**  on the **Standard Palette** and then press **Ctrl+A** to select all UV polygons. In the **UV Manager > UV Mapping** tab > **Projection** command group, click **Cubic 2**, the selected polygons are unwrapped and displayed in the **Texture View** [see Fig. E13]. Notice in the viewport, the text **THIS WAY UP** is not oriented in the right direction [see Fig. E13]. Now, you will fix it.

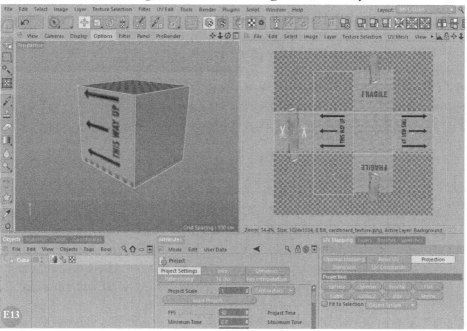

E13

> **What just happened?**
> When you click **UV Polygons**, Cinema 4D gives you ability to select and modify UVs using various tools. The **Cubic 2** mapping type projects textures onto all six sides of the cube and also relaxes them.

8. Switch back to the **Standard** Layout. Now, activate the **Points** mode and select the bottom four points of the cube [see Fig. E14].

> **?** *Why these points are selected?*
> *When you will relax UVs in the next steps of the exercise, these four points will be pinned [locked] to their current position and will not move. The idea here is to fix the bottom face in its place and unfold other faces around it.*

9. Activate the **Edges** mode and select the edges [see Fig. E15].

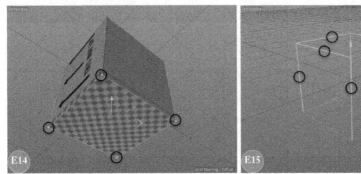

> **?** *Why these edges are selected?*
> *Cuts [seams] are applied on these edges of the cube to avoid UV-coordinate distortion.*

10. Switch back to the **BP-UV Edit** layout. Switch to the **Bottom** or **Top** viewport and then in the **UV Manager > UV Mapping** tab > **Projection** command group, click **Frontal**. In the **UV Mapping** tab > **Relax UV** command group, specify the settings as shown in Fig. E16 and click **Apply**. The polygons are unwrapped in **Texture View**.

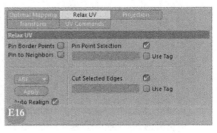

> **?** *What is relaxing?*
> *Relaxing UVs is a method for optimizing the UV mesh. When you relax a mesh, CINEMA attaches invisible springs to the UVs and then stretches them to avoid overlap. Click **Apply** repeatedly to get rid of the overlaps. If no UVs are selected, this command is applied to the whole mesh. There are two modes available for relaxing the UVs: **ABF** and **LSCM**. The **ABF** mode is better than **LSCM** but it is much slower. It is recommended to use **ABF** with organic shapes.*

11. Click **UV Polygons** in the **Standard** palette and then press **Ctrl+A** to select all polygons. In the **UV Manager > UV Maping** tab > **Transform** command group, enter **180** in the **Rotate** field and then click **Apply** to flip the polygons. Now, use the **Move** and **Scale** tools to roughly fit polygons on the texture [see Fig. E17].

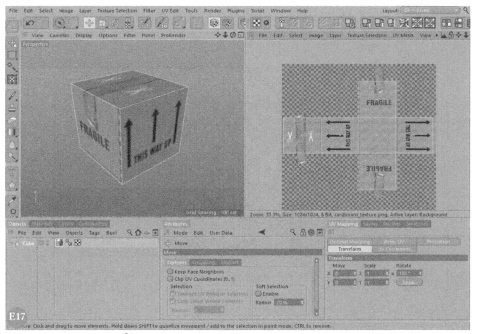

12. Click **UV Points** on the **Standard** palette and then adjust the points using the **Move** tool to perfectly align polygon edges with the texture [see Fig. E18]. Switch back to the **Standard** layout.

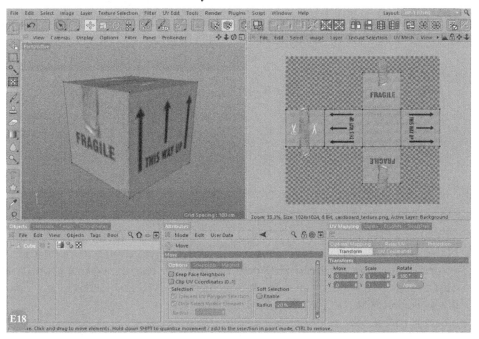

**What just happened?**

*When you click **UV Points**, the UV coordinates are displayed as points. You can select these points and modify them using various tools. When you select a point in the **Texture View**, the corresponding point is also selected in the 3D view and vice versa.*

## Exercise 2: Texturing a Dice

In this exercise, we will texture a dice [see Fig. E1] using the **BP-UV Edit** layout and Photoshop.

The following table summarizes the exercise:

| Table E2 | |
| --- | --- |
| Skill level | Beginner |
| Time to complete | 30 Minutes |
| Topics | • Getting Started<br>• Texturing the Dice |
| Resources folder | **unit-ct1** |
| Units | **Centimeters** |
| Start file | **dice-start.c4d** |
| Final file | **dice-finish.c4d** |

### Getting Started
Open open **dice-start.c4d** [see Fig. E2].

### Texturing the Dice
Follow these steps:

1.  Choose **File > New Texture** from the **Texture View** menu to open the **New Texture** dialog box. In this dialog box, rename the texture as **diceText**. Change **Color** to white and then click **OK**. Notice **diceText.tif** is selected in the **Texture View's Textures** menu [see Fig. E3].

   *Tip: Empty canvas*
   *If you want to show the empty canvas, choose **Empty Canvas** from the **Textures** menu.*

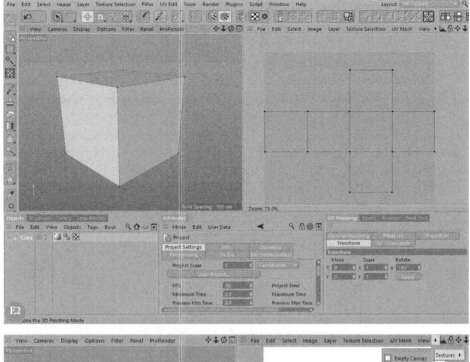

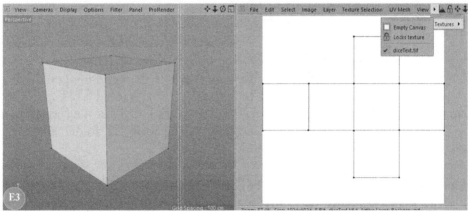

2. Choose **Layer > New Layer** from the **Texture View's** menu to create a new layer.
   Notice in the **UV Manager > Layers** tab, a new layer with the name **Layer** appears
   [see Fig. E4]. The **Background** layer is the layer created when you assigned the
   white color using the **New Texture** dialog box. Double-click on **Layer** label in
   the **Layers** tab and rename it as **Outlines**.

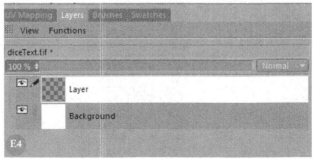

*Why new layer?*

*Initially, a texture has just one layer [canvas] with the name **Background**.
Layers allow you to perform non-destructive editing. You can paint on each
layer. Each layer can be edited independent of the canvas or other layers. Here,
I wanted to create outlines for the polygons so that when the **UV Template** is
opened in Photoshop, the outlines will appear in a separate layer.*

3. Select all UV polygons and ensure the **Outlines** layer is selected and then choose
**Layer > Outline Polygons** from the **Texture View's** menu. Now, if you click the
eye icon of the **Background** layer to turn it off, you will notice that the outlines
are created in white color [see Fig. E5]. Select the **Background** layer.

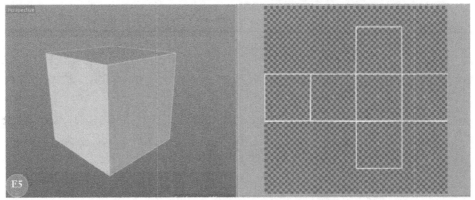

4. Choose **Save Texture As** from the **Texture View's File** menu to open the **Please
choose the file format** dialog box. In this dialog box, select **PSD (*.psd)** option
from the **Save File as** drop-down list and then click **OK**. In the **Save Channel
as *.psd** dialog box that appears, navigate to the **unit-ct1** folder and save the
texture with the name **diceTextPSD**.

5. Launch **Photoshop** and open **diceTextPSD.psd**. Notice in the **Layers** panel,
two layers **Background** and **Outlines** appear. These are the layers we created in
Cinema 4D. Fill the **Background** layer with **Black** color [see Fig. E6].

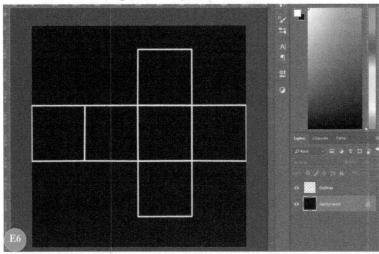

6. Create dots on the dice layout using white color [see Fig. E7]. Delete the **Outlines** layer and then merge all dots layers. Also, create an alpha channel for the dots [refer to Fig. E8]. Now, rename dots layer as **DiceDots** and alpha channel as **diceAlpha**. Save the Photoshop file.

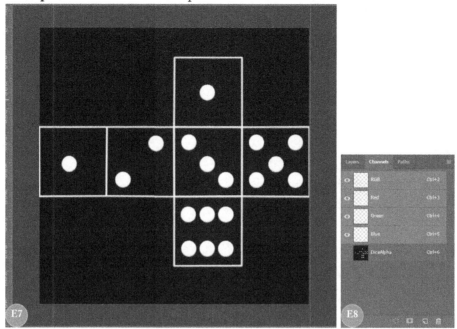

7. Switch back to the **Standard** layout in Cinema 4d and then select the **Mat** node in the **Material Manager**. In the **Attribute Manager** > **Mat** > **Color** tab, change **HSV** to **233, 90,** and **87,** respectively. In the **Reflectance** tab, click **Add** and then choose **Phong** from the popup to create a Phong reflectance layer with the name **Layer 1**. In the **Layer Color** section, change **Brightness** to **50**.

8. Create another material and then apply it to the **Cube**. In the **Attribute Manager** > **Color** tab, click the **Browse** button corresponding to the **Texture** parameter and then load the **diceTextPSD.psd**. In the **Basic** tab, select the **Alpha** check box to activate the **Alpha** channel. In the **Alpha** tab, click arrow next to the **Texture** label and then choose **Bitmaps** > **diceTextPSD.psd** from the popup menu. Make sure the order of the material should be same as shown in Fig. E9. Press **Ctrl+R** to render.

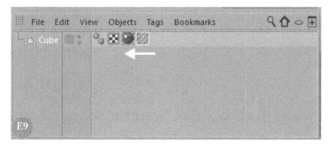

**What alpha is required?**
*The alpha channel allows you to mask out area of the material. The idea is to define the area of the material that become non-existent and the underlying material show through. Here, we have created a blue material and also we have alpha channel in the PSD. When we applied the **diceTextPSD.psd** to the alpha channel of the material, the dots obscured the blue material and rest of the blue shown through.*

## Exercise 3: Relaxing a Head Model

In this exercise, we will unwrap a head model by relaxing UVs [see Fig. E1].

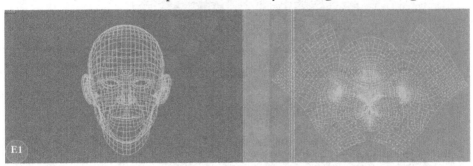

The following table summarizes the exercise:

| Table E3 | |
| --- | --- |
| Skill level | Beginner |
| Time to complete | 20 Minutes |
| Topics | • Getting Started<br>• Unwrapping the Head Model |
| Resources folder | **unit-ct1** |
| Units | **Centimeters** |
| Start file | **head-start.c4d** |
| Final file | **head-finish.c4d** |

### Getting Started
Open the **head-start.c4d** file.

### Unwrapping the Head Model
Follow these steps:

1. In order to relax the UVs, we will first define the lock points and cut edges. Activate the **Points** mode and then select the points shown in Fig. E2. Now, activate the **Edges** mode and select the edges as shown in Fig. E3.

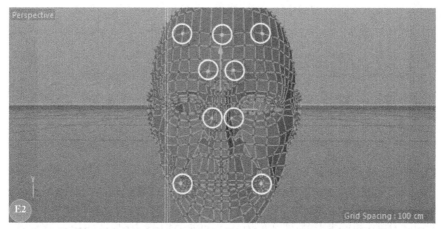

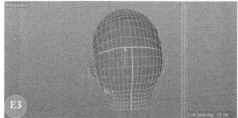

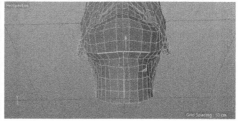

2. Switch to the **BP-UV Edit** layout and click **Paint Setup Wizard** 🖌 from the **Standard** palette to open the **BodyPaint 3D Setup Wizard** dialog box. Make sure **Objects** is selected and then click **Next**. Click **Next, Finish,** and then **Close.** Click **UV Polygons** on the **Standard** palette, the UVs appear in the **Texture View** [see Fig. E4]. Notice that the UVs are scattered all over.

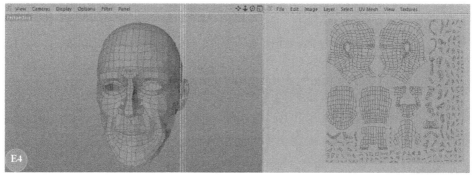

> **?** *Why to use Paint Setup Wizard?*
> *You might have noticed that the head model in the start file does not have the material or a texture tag applied to it. When we use the **Paint Setup Wizard**, it lets you add missing materials and textures, scale multiple textures [even to exact size], and you can also delete textures from specific channels. If you want separate textures to be created for each channel, clear the **Single Material** check box in this dialog box.*

3. Switch to the **Front** view and then press **Ctrl+A** to select all polygons. In the **UV Manager > UV Mapping** tab > **Projection** tab, click **Frontal,** the UVs are projected using the **Frontal** projection [see Fig. E5].

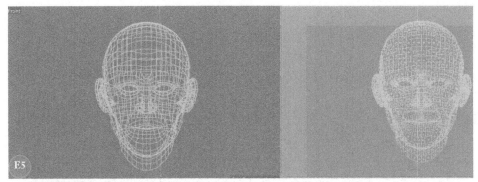

4. In the **UV Manager > Relax UV** tab, select the **Pin Point Selection** and **Cut Selected Edges** checkboxes. Select **ABF** as relaxing algorithm and ensure the **Auto Realign** check box is selected. Click **Apply** to relax the UVs. Align the UVs using the **Scale** and **Move** tools. Now, you can export the texture to the **Photoshop** and paint head.

 *What Auto Realign does?*
*This check box makes sure that the relaxed mesh fits the texture.*

# Quiz

Evaluate your skills to see how many questions you can answer correctly.

**Fill in the Blanks**
Fill in the blanks in each of the following statements:

1. The _____ layout is used to edit UVs.

2. _____ UVs is a method for optimizing the UV mesh.

3. When you apply a material to an object, a _____ tag is automatically assigned to the object.

**True or False**
State whether each of the following is true or false:

1. The **UVW Mapping** projection type is not the default projection type in Cinema 4D.

2. The letters **U** and **V** denote the axes for the 2D texture in 2D texture space.

3. 3D shaders require a third dimension [W] in order to appropriately place textures onto the object.

**Summary**
This unit covered the following topics:

- UVs
- UV Manager
- UV Projection

This page is intentionally left blank

- Material Manager
- Material Presets
- Channels
- Creating Different Materials
- Blending Modes

# Unit CT2: Material Presets

A material defines how light is reflected and transmitted by the objects in a scene. Materials are used to simulate surface qualities such as color, reflectivity, roughness, bumpiness, and so on. They help you in creating realistic looking renders.

You can use the **Material Editor** [see Fig. 1] to create and edit materials as well as to assign them to the objects in the scene. You can open the **Material Editor** by double-clicking on the material node in the **Material Manager**. The parameters of the material can be modified from the **Material Editor** as well as using the **Attribute Manager** [see Fig. 2]. In the **Material Editor**, the channels are displayed at the left whereas in the **Attribute Manager** they are in the **Basic** tab.

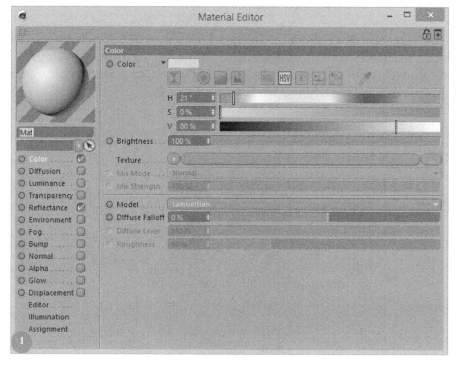

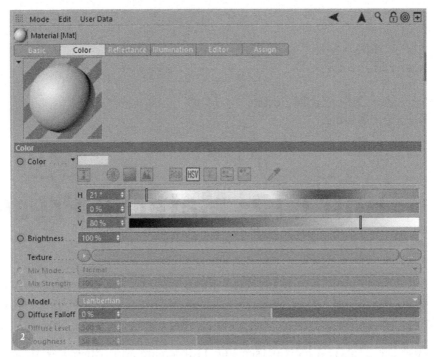

The **Material Editor** comprises of two panes. A preview of the material is shown at the top-left corner of the left pane. You can change the preview geometry by RMB clicking on the preview and then choosing an option from the context menu. For example, if you want to see preview using a torus knot, choose **Knot** from the popup. If you choose the **Open Window** option, a floating window appears with the preview. You can resize the window to get a larger preview.

Below preview, a list of channels is displayed. Enable the channels by selecting the checkboxes available next to each channel. Most of the time, you don't need all channels. The selection of channels depends on the type of material you are creating. Table 1 summarizes the channels name and what they control:

| Table 1: Channels in the Material Editor | |
|---|---|
| **Channel** | **Description** |
| Color | Controls the color of the surface. |
| Diffusion | Controls the irregularities in the color of the surface by darkening or brightening the color channel. |
| Luminance | Controls the luminescent color which is light independent color. |
| Transparency | Controls the transparency and refraction index. |
| Reflectance | Controls the reflection on the surface. |
| Environment | Controls the reflection from the environment. |
| Fog | Controls the fog effect. |

| Table 1: Channels in the Material Editor | |
| --- | --- |
| Bump | Creates bumps on the surface. |
| Normal | Creates bumps on the surface like the **Bump** channel but the bumps are lit realistically when you use the **Normal** channel. |
| Alpha | Controls the localized texture invisibility. |
| Glow | Creates a halo around the object. |
| Displacement | Creates realistic bumps on the surface. |
| Editor | Controls material display in the viewport. |
| Illumination | Controls the global illumination, caustics, and illuminations functions. |
| Assignment | It lists all object that use the material. |

When you select a material in the **Material Manager**, its preview is displayed in the **Attribute Manager** [see Fig. 3].

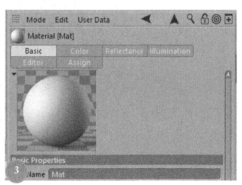

You can collapse or expand the preview area by clicking on the triangle next to the preview. To rotate the preview, **RMB+Drag** or **Shift+Drag** the preview.

 *Caution: Preview*
*Not all parameter changes will necessarily have an effect on the material preview but will nevertheless have an effect on the rendering.*

 *Tip: Color picker*
*This tip only works with the **Material Editor** but not in the **Attribute Manager**. Ctrl+clicking in the preview will turn the cursor into a color picker for the current channel color.*

 *Tip: Animation for the preview*
*If you want to switch on the animation for the preview, RMB click on the preview and then choose **Animate** from the context menu; the animation will be played automatically, without moving the **Timeslider**, according to the **Frame Rate (FPS)** settings in the **Preferences** window > **Material** category > **Material Preview** area.*

## Tip: Copying textures

*The bitmaps and shaders can be easily copied between materials and/or channels by dragging the preview image on the targets. For example, if you have connected a bitmap to the **Texture** parameter in the **Color** tab and now you want to copy it to the **Texture** parameter in the **Bump** tab, drag the **Texture**'s preview from the **Color** tab [see Fig. 4] and then hover the mouse over the **Bump** tab. When the content of the **Bump** tab appears, drop the preview onto the **Texture** parameter's arrow or button [see Fig. 5].*

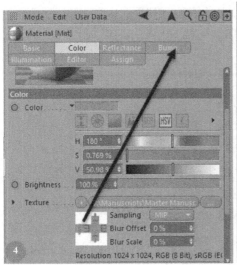 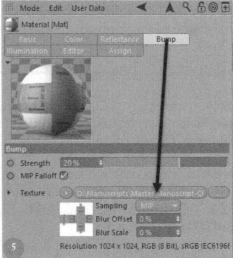

## Note: Material presets

*Cinema 4D comes with number of material presets that you can use to quickly apply the material onto the objects. You can access these presets from the **Create > Load Material Preset** menu of the **Material Manager** [see Fig. 6].*

*We will dissect some of the material presets in this unit. If you have installed render plugins such as **Arnold** or **V-Ray**, the presets for those plugins will also be available in the **Load Material Preset** sub-menu.*

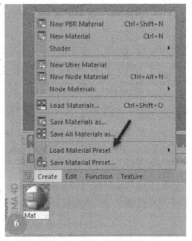

# Hands-on Exercises

## Exercise 1: Creating Plastic Materials

In this exercise, we will create different kind of plastic materials, refer to Figs. E11, E13, E15, E17, and E19. The following table summarizes the exercise:

| Table E1 | |
|---|---|
| Difficulty level | Intermediate |
| Estimated time to complete | 30 Minutes |
| Topics | • Getting Started<br>• Creating Plastic Materials |
| Resources folder | **unit-ct2** |
| Units | **Centimeters** |
| Start file | **shader-ball.c4d** |
| Final file | **plastic-finish.c4d** |

### Getting Started
Open the **shader-ball.c4d** file.

### Creating Plastic Materials

1. Double-click on the **Material Manager** to create a new material. Rename the material as **matShinyPlastic**. Apply the material to the **Geo2** and **Geo3** objects in the **Object Manager**.

 *What just happened?*
*Here, I've applied material to the objects. When you apply a material to an object, a texture tag is automatically assigned to the object [see Fig. E1]. This tag controls how the texture is mapped or placed on the object. The settings for the tag appear in the* ***Attribute Manager***.

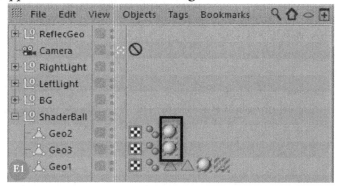

2. Select **matShinyPlastic** in the **Material Manager** and then in the **Attribute Manager > matShinyPlastic > Basic** tab, select the **Normal** check box.

*What just happened?*
Here, I've selected the **Normal** check box. This action enabled the **Normal** channel and also the **Normal** tab is displayed in the **Attribute Manager**. The settings on the **Normal** tab are used for normal mapping.

*What is Normal Mapping?*
The term normal mapping comes from the computer game development. In this technique, a detailed texture is applied to a low-poly object thus reducing the render time.

The normal mapping is different from the bump mapping. In the bump mapping, a grayscale image is used to generate height data whereas in the normal mapping, a RGB texture is used that contains the orientation of the normals. The orientation of the normals is used to generate height data.

3.  In the **Color** tab > **Color** area, change **H, S, V** to **0, 0, 9,** respectively. Render the scene [see Fig. E2].

*What just happened?*
Here, I've assigned a dark gray color to the surfaces using the **HSV** model. The **HSV** model defines the color by using **Hue, Saturation,** and **Value** or **Brightness** [HSV]. **H** defines the hue and it is displayed as an angle on the color wheel. **S** defines the amount of saturation of the hue and **V** defines brightness of the color. Notice that we have created a black surface but the surface is not looking shiny. Next, we will adjust the reflectivity of the surface.

4.  In the **Reflectance** tab, click **Remove** to remove the **Default Specular** layer. Click **Add** and then choose **GGX** from the flyout, a new reflectance layer with the name **Layer 1** appears in the **Attribute Manager**. Rename it as **Reflection** by double-clicking on the label and typing the new name.

*Note: Reflectance channel*

The **Color**, **Specular**, and **Reflection** channels are the most important aspect of creating a material. The other channels are essentially used for creating special or enhanced effects. Cinema 4D reflectance model now includes the **Color**, **Specular**, and **Reflection** channels in a single enhanced channel called **Reflectance**.

This model uses layers to create complex materials. Each layer has its own alpha, bump, and normal channels. You can now create a material by just using the **Reflectance** channel. You can ignore the **Color** channel, however, it should not be done across the board.

*Caution: Color channel*

The **Global Illumination** function takes values from the **Color** channel not from the **Reflectance** channel. Keep in mind that you would not be able to create **Global Illumination** solution if you ignore the **Color** channel.

**Parameter: Type**

The **Beckman**, **GGX**, **Phong**, and **Ward** are four most important reflection types available in **Type** drop-down list. They uniformly weaken the reflections from the ideal reflection angle or angle of incidence. For normal use, you should use **Backmann** as it produces physically accurate results and it is computed faster than other types. The **GGX** type is suitable for creating metallic surfaces as it produces greater dispersion. It produces bright specular highlights with diminishing brightness. The **Ward** type should be used for soft surfaces such as rubber or skin.

5. Change **Attenuation** to **Average**, **Roughness** and **Reflection Strength** to **100** each, and then change **Specular Strength** to **0**.

**Parameter: Attenuation**

The options in the **Attenuation** drop-down list control how the **Color** channel should be mixed with the value of the **Layer Color > Color** parameter with various **Reflection Strength** settings. If you have disabled the **Color** channel, the **Attenuation** parameter will have no effect. The following options are available for this parameter:

- **Average:** This mode produces most realistic looking results. In this mode, both colors are averaged. This does not differ from the **Maximum** mode, if no color is defined for the **Layer Color > Color** parameter.
- **Maximum:** This mode is used to generate colored reflections. The **Color** channel's effect will be reduced and the color defined using the **Layer Color > Color** parameter will dominate.
- **Additive and Metal:** These two modes are available for reasons of compatibility if an older project is loaded.

### Parameter: Roughness

A perfectly polished surface is made up of many microscopic reflective facets. Each facet has different orientation. The rougher surfaces have random distribution of those facets producing spread out highlights. The **Roughness** setting produces the spread out highlights on the objects. We will create a texture for the **Roughness** setting using the **Layer** shader in the next steps. You can apply a texture to the **Roughness** parameter, by first clicking on the triangle next to it and then assigning a shader or bitmap to the **Texture** parameter.

### Parameter: Reflection Strength

The **Reflection Strength** parameter defines the strength with which the material should reflect. As the reflection strength increases, the strength of the **Color** channel decreases as per the energy conservation laws. If you specify a value of **0** for this parameter, the material will not reflect at all. A value of **100** will produce maximum reflection. Click on the triangle next to the **Reflection** parameter to reveal the **Texture** and **Colored** parameters. If the **Colored** check box is selected, the **Color** defined in the material's **Color** channel will be used as the reflection color

*Note: Creating realistic materials*
*In nature, every material reflects to some degree, even if it is minor. Keep this in mind, if you want to create realistic materials in Cinema 4D.*

### Parameter: Specular Strength

The **Reflection** parameter defines the strength of the specular highlights. You can use the specular highlight as a trick to add reflection to the material without substantially affecting the render times. In nature, specular highlights are nothing more than light sources reflected in objects' surfaces. If you want to create a realistic scene, set this value to **0** and use the **Reflection Strength** setting instead.

*Tip: Combined reflective strength*
*The combined reflective and specular strength of multiple layers can be adjusted together using the **Global Reflection Brightness** and **Global Specular Brightness** parameters.*

6. In the **Reflectance** tab > **Reflection** > **Layer Fresnel** area, change **Fresnel** to **Dielectric** and **Preset** to **PET**.

### Parameter: Fresnel

The **Fresnel** setting defines the fresnel reflections. They depend on the angle of view and index of refraction. Fig. E3 shows the difference between the normal reflection and fresnel reflection. Cinema 4D provides two options for the fresnel model. The **Dielectric** option is used for materials such as glass and water whereas the **Conductor** option is used for opaque and reflective materials such as metals. The **PET** preset has an **IOR** of **1.575**.

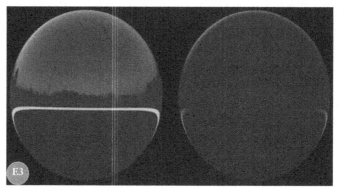

*Caution: Render time*

*The render time increases if you use a high value for the **Roughness** setting. Also, this value should be greater than **0** for the calculation of specular highlights and anisotropy.*

7. Click **Roughness > Texture > Triangle** button [you need to first expand the **Roughness** settings by clicking on the triangle] and then choose **Layer** from the popup [see Fig. E4]. Now, click the **Layer** button to open the **Layer Shader** settings [see Fig. E5].

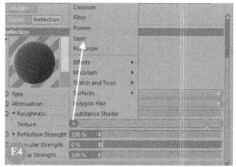
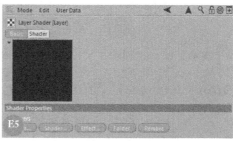

*Note: Layer Shader*

*The **Layer Shader** is a powerful shader that is used to combine other shaders and bitmaps. You can stack shaders and bitmaps in layers and folders. To change the order of the layers, you can drag and drop them to their new positions.*

8. Click **Folder** to create a new folder and then rename it as **Roughness** by double-clicking on its label. Now, click **Image** and load **dc.jpg**. Click **Effect** and then choose **Colorize** from the popup. Click below the gradient bar to create two knobs and position them, as shown in Fig. E6. Double-click on first knob to open the **Gradient Knot Settings** dialog box. Change **V** to **9%** and then click **OK**. Similarly, change **V** to **10%** for the other knob.

*What just happened?*
*You can apply various effects to a layer. The effect is applied to all layers below it in the list. Here, the **Colorize** effect takes a value from a channel [**Luminance** in this case] and then remaps it based on a gradient. The preview of the **Layer** shader appears at the top of the **Layer Shader** area but it will appear dark because we have used pretty dark gray values for the gradient. If you want to see it clearly, RMB click on the preview and then choose **Open Window** from the context menu.*

9. Click **Shader** and then choose **Gradient** from the popup. Rename it as **EdgeFalloff**. Make sure the gradient layer is at the top of the stack [see Fig. E7]. You can drag and drop layers to change their order.

10. Click on the gradient swatch to open the **Gradient Shader** settings. Change **Type** to **2D-V** and then change gradient as shown in Fig. E8. Click the **Up Arrow** button in the **Attribute Manager** menu to go back to the **Layer Shader** settings.

11. Change **Edge Falloff** drop-down list to **Multiply** [see Fig. E9]. Click the **Up Arrow** button in the **Attribute Manager** menu to go back to the **matShinyPlastic** settings. Render the scene [see Fig. E10].

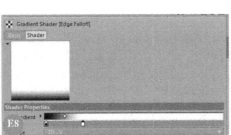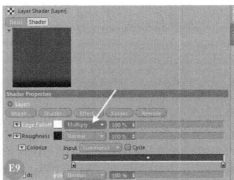

*What just happened?*
*Here, I have created a gradient layer at the top of the stack. It will produce roughness on the edges. Setting mix mode to **Multiply** will ensure that the white color of the gradient does not affect the edge roughness.*

*Note: Rough Plastic*
*If you want to create rough plastic material, change **Colorize's** gradient knobs to **25** and **30**, respectively and then render the scene, refer to Fig. E11.*

E10    E11

*What next?*
*Now, let's create a matte plastic material.*

12. Create a new material and rename it as **matMattePlastic** and apply it to **Geo2** and **Geo3**. Select the material in the **Material Manager** and then in the **Basic** tab, select the **Diffusion** check box.

*What just happened?*
*Here, I have selected the **Diffusion** check box to enable the **Diffusion** channel. The **Diffusion** channel is used to make the material look dirty. It darkens or lightens a material using a diffusion map. The darker the area in the diffusion map, the darker the corresponding region of the material will be.*

13. In the **Attribute Manager > matMattePlastic > Color** tab, change **V** to **100** to make the color white and then change **Brightness** to **90**. Click **Texture > Triangle** button and then choose **Fresnel** from the popup. Click the **Fresnel** button to open the **Fresnel Shader** settings. Specify the value **76** for the **V** parameter for the second knob.

14. In the **Attribute Manager > matMattePlastic > Color** tab, change **Mix Mode** to **Multiply**, **Model** to **Oren-Nayar**, **Diffuse Falloff** to -20, and **Roughness** to **30**. Render the scene.

*What just happened?*
*Here, I've change model to **Oren-Nayar**. This model is suitable for creating matte materials. The **Diffuse Falloff** setting controls the falloff of brightness between the specular highlights. The larger the value, the more uniform the brightness will be, up to the point of producing uniform colors [comic-like look].*

*If negative values are used, they produce correspondingly smaller regions from which light will be reflected. The **Roughness** setting applies only to the **Oren-Nayer** model and produces more diffuse light dispersion. As a result, the material will become correspondingly darker an more dull.*

15. In the **Attribute Manager > matMattePlastic > Diffusion** tab, click **Texture > Triangle** button and then choose **Noise** from it. Click the **Noise** button to open the **Noise Shader** settings. Change **Noise** to **Voronoi 1** and **Global Scale** to **5**. In the **Attribute Manager > matMattePlastic > Diffusion** tab, change **Mix Strength** to **8**.

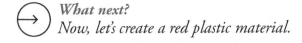

*What just happened?*
*Here, I've used the **Noise** shader as diffusion map. The **Noise** shader is a special type of shader that can produce **32** types of noise. The **Global Scale** setting scales the noise in the **UVW** directions. The **Relative Scale** setting allows you to individually scale the noise in the **UVW** directions. The **Mix Strength** setting controls the mixing between the **Color** channel and texture. The **Octave** parameter controls octaves of details in the noise.*

16. In the **Reflectance** tab, click **Remove** to remove the **Default Specular** layer. Click **Add** and then choose **Ward** from the flyout, a new reflectance layer with the name **Layer 1** appears in the **Attribute Manager**. Rename it as **Reflection** by double-clicking on the label and typing the new name.

17. Change **Attenuation** to **Average**, **Roughness** to **7**, **Reflection Strength** to **12**, **Specular Strength** to **0**. In the **Layer Fresnel** area, change **Fresnel** to **Dielectric** and **IOR** to **1.44**. Render the scene [see Fig. E12].

*What next?*
*Now, let's create a red plastic material.*

18. Double-click on the **Material Manager** to create a new material. Rename the material as **matRedPlastic**. Apply the material to the **Geo2** and **Geo3** objects in the **Object Manager**.

19. In the **Attribute Manager > matRedPlastic > Basic** tab, select the **Normal** check box. In the **Color** tab, change **HSV** to **0, 80, 94**, respectively. In the **Reflectance** tab, delete the **Default Specular** layer. Click **Add** and then choose **Beckman** from the popup. Change **Specular Strength** to **0**. In the **Layer Fresnel** area, change **Fresnel** to **Dielectric** and **IOR** to **1.5**. Render the scene [see Fig. E13].

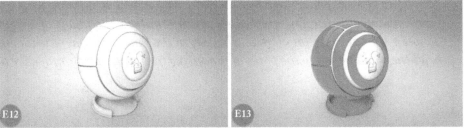

20. In the **Attribute Manager > matRedPlastic > Normal** tab, click **Texture > Triangle** button and then choose **Effects > Normalizer** from the popup menu. Click on the **Normalizer** button. In the **Normalizer Shader** properties area, click **Texture > Triangle** button and then choose **Load Image** from the popup to open the **Open File** dialog box. Select **noise.jpg** and click **Open**. Now, change **Strength** to **3** and **Filter** to **Sobel 4x**. Render the scene [see Fig. E14].

**?** *What just happened?*
*Here, I've used an image with the **Normalizer** shader to create grain on the surfaces. The **Strength** setting controls the overall strength of the shader. The **Filter** setting allows you to select a method of calculation for the normal texture. The **Condensed** method can be used for very fine surfaces and **Sobel** for rougher surfaces. However, the **Condensed** method is faster than the **Sobel** method. Fig. E15 shows the normal texture with **Strength** set to **50** and **100**, respectively.*

**→** *What next?*
*Now, let's create a plastic material with **Subsurface Scattering [SSS]**.*

**?** *What is SSS?*
***SSS** stands for **Subsurface Scattering**. This technique is used to simulate light's penetration in slightly transparent surfaces. In a SSS material, light travels through partially or fully and some of it is absorbed.*

21. Double-click in the **Material Manager** to create a new material. Rename the material as **matSSSPlastic**. Apply the material to the **Geo2** and **Geo3** objects in the **Object Manager**. In the **Attribute Manager > matSSSPlastic > Basic** tab, select the **Normal** and **Luminance** check boxes and clear the **Color** check box.

22. In the **Luminance** tab, change **HSV** to **222**, **25**, and **100**, respectively. Click **Texture > Triangle** button and then choose **Effects > Subsurface Scattering** from the popup. Click on the **Subsurface Scattering** button.

23. In the **Subsurface Scattering Shader > Shader** tab, change **HSV** to **224**, **83**, and **80**, respectively. Change **Path Length** to **1**. Expand the **Path Length** area and then change **Blue** to **200**.

*What just happened?*
*Here, I've assigned a color using the **Color** parameter that will represent the general color of the **SSS** effect. The **Path Length** parameter controls how far light travels beneath the surface. The lower the value for this parameter, longer will be the render time. The **Red**, **Blue**, and **Green** parameters in the **Path Length** area are multipliers for the **Path Length** parameter. You can use these parameters to define which color penetrates deeper beneath the surface.*

*Caution: Path Length parameters*
*You can use values less than **100%** for these parameters but on doing so render time will increase.*

24. In the **Subsurface Scattering Shader > Advanced** tab, change **Index of Refraction** to **1.5**. In the **Single** tab, select the **Enabled** check box. In the **Multiple** tab, change **Mode** to **Direct** and **Minimum Threshold** to **0.01**.

**Parameter: Index of Refraction**
The **Index of Refraction** parameter controls the refraction index corresponding to the **SSS** effect. Higher the value you specify, darker the **SSS** effect will be.

**Parameter: Single mode**
The **Single** check box turn on the **Single** mode. There are two types of modes for **SSS**: **Single** and **Multiple**. In the **Single** mode, light is dispersed once and then continue travelling in a straight line. The angle at which light enters in has major influence on the **SSS** effect. This is the reason that you need actual light sources in the scene when the **Single** mode is used. **Global Illumination** alone cannot produce the effect.

**Parameter: Multiple mode**
In the **Multiple** mode, the light is dispersed multiple times until it reaches to the surface at some other point on the surface. In this case, direction of the light does not matter. The **Direct** mode does not create a cache and calculate illumination for each pixel. This method is specifically suited for the short **Path Length** values. If you use this mode with large **Path Length** values, the process will be slow. Also, this mode does not work with **Global Illumination**. In the **Cache** mode, points are spread out on the surface of the object as uniformly as possible and then they are cached. Then, light dispersion is calculated on each point and then spread across the whole surface.

25. In the **Attribute Manager > matSSSPlastic > Luminance** tab, change **Mix Mode** to **Multiply**. In the **Reflectance** tab, change **Type** to **GGX**, **Attenuation** to **Average**, and **Roughness** to **100**. Now, create a **Layer** shader for the **Roughness** parameter as done earlier when you created shiny plastic material. Change **Specular Strength** to **0** and **Reflection Strength** to **100**. In the **Layer Fresnel** area, change **Fresnel** to **Dielectric** and **IOR** to **1.5**.

26. In the **Normal** tab, click **Texture > Triangle** button and then choose **Effects > Normalizer** from the popup menu. Click on the **Normalizer** button. In the **Normalizer Shader** properties area, click **Texture > Triangle** button and then choose **Load Image** from the popup to open the **Open File** dialog box. Select **noise.jpeg** and then click **Open**. Now, change **Strength** to **3** and **Filter** to **Sobel 4x**. Render the scene [see Fig. E16]. You need to increase the value of the **Subsurface Scattering Subdivision (Max)** parameter in the **Render Settings** window to get noise free SSS.

27. Double-click in the **Material Manager** to create a new material. Rename the material as **matPlasticGrid**. Apply the material to the **Geo2** and **Geo3** objects in the **Object Manager**. Select the material in the **Material Manager** and then in the **Attribute Manager > matPlasticGrid > Basic** tab, select the **Bump** and **Alpha** checkboxes.

28. In the **Attribute Manager > matPlasticGrid > Color** tab, change **Color** to white and **Brightness** to **20**. In the **Reflectance** tab, change **Type** to **Phong**, **Attenuation** to **Average**, **Roughness** to **28**, **Reflection Strength** to **35**, and **Specular Strength** to **0**. In the **Layer Fresnel** area, change **Fresnel** to **Dielectric** and **Preset** to **PET**.

29. In the **Attribute Manager > matPlasticGrid > Bump** tab, click **Texture > Triangle** button and then choose **Surfaces > Tiles** from the popup. Click on the **Tiles** button to open the **Tile Shader** settings. Change **Grout Color** to **white**. Change **Tiles Color 1**, **Tiles Color 2**, and **Tiles Color 3** to black. Change **Pattern** to **Circle 1**. Change **Grout Width** to **20**.

> ⊘ *What just happened?*
> *Here, I've added **Tiles** shader to create the patterns for the holes. You can use this shader to create different patterns. The **Grout Color** is the color between the tiles. The **Tiles Color 1**, **Tiles Color 2**, and **Tiles Color 3** parameters are the colors of the tiles. **Grout Width** defines the width of the grout as a percentage of tile.*

30. Select the texture tag corresponding to **Geo2** and then in the **Attribute Manager > Tag** tab, change **Length U** and **Length V** to **20** and **30**, respectively. each. Repeat the process for the **Geo3**'s texture tag. Render the scene [see Fig. E17].

31. In the **Attribute Manager > matPlasticGrid > Bump** tab, RMB click on **Texture** label and choose **Copy** from the popup. In the **Attribute Manager > matPlasticGrid > Alpha** tab, RMB click on **Texture** label and choose **Paste** from the popup menu. Render the scene [see Fig. E18].

## Exercise 2: Creating Abstract Materials

Let's now create different types of abstract materials, refer to Figs. E4, E12, and E18. The following table summarizes the exercise:

| Table E2 | |
|---|---|
| Difficulty level | Intermediate |
| Estimated time to complete | 30 Minutes |
| Topics | • Getting Started<br>• Creating Abstract Materials |

| Table E2 | |
| --- | --- |
| Resources folder | **unit-ct2** |
| Units | **Centimeters** |
| Start file | **shader-ball.c4d** |
| Final file | **abstract-finish.c4d** |

### Getting Started

Open the **shader-ball.c4d** file.

### Creating Abstract Materials

Let's start by creating a two sided color material. Follow these steps:

1. Double-click on the **Material Manager** to create a new material. Rename the material as **matAbs1**. Apply the material to the **Geo2** and **Geo3** objects in the **Object Manager**. Select material in the **Material Manager** and then in the **Attribute Manager** > **matAbs1** > **Basic** tab, clear all checkboxes except the **Transparency** check box. In the **Transparency** tab, change **Refraction** to **1.6**.

*What just happened?*
*Here, the **Transparency** channel is used to define the transparency. If the material has color and you enable this channel, the color of the material is reduced to incorporate transparency. If a material has **100%** transparency, there will be no color.*

**Parameter: Refraction**
The **Refraction** parameter controls the index of refraction of the material. Later, we will reduce the color by **40%** and remaining **60%** we will use for the **Transparency** channel to produce the effect we are looking for.

2. Click **Texture** > **Triangle** button and then choose **Effects** > **Normal Direction** from the popup. Click on the **Normal Direction** button. In the **Normal Direction Shader** settings, change **Color 1** to HSV[ 228, 76, 97] and **Color 2** to HSV [128, 78, 66]. In the **Attribute Manager** > **matAbs1** > **Transparency** tab, change **Mix Mode** to **Multiply**. Render the scene [see Fig. E1].

*What the Normal Direction shader does?*
*It colors an object based on the direction of the surface normals. The area on the surface whose normals points towards the rendering ray takes **Color 1**, rest of the surface takes **Color 2**.*

3. In the **Attribute Manager** > **matAbs1** > **Basic** tab, select the **Reflectance** check box. In the **Reflectance** tab > **Default Specular** layer, change **Type** to **Beckmann**, **Roughness** to **35**, **Reflection Strength** to **7**, and **Specular Strength** to **45**. In the **Layer Color** area change **Color** to HSV[128, 78, 66]. Render the scene [see Fig. E2].

> **What just happened?**
> *Here, I've changed the color [filter color of the layer] to green from the default white. This green color will affect reflection colors.*

4.  In the **Attribute Manager > matAbs1> Basic** tab, select the **Color** check box. Copy the **Normal Direction** shader from the **Transparency** tab and then paste on the **Texture** parameter in the **Color** tab. Change **Mix Mode** to **Multiply**. Render the scene [see Fig. E3].

> **What just happened?**
> *Notice in Fig. E3, although you are able to see two colors but they are not prominent. Most of the look that you got through the **Transparency** channel is obscured by the **Color** channel. Next, we will fix it.*

5.  In the **Color** tab, change **Brightness** to **40%** and render the scene [see Fig. E4].

> **What next?**
> *Now, let's create a material with stripes.*

6.  Double-click on the **Material Manager** to create a new material. Rename the material as **matStripe**. Apply the material to the **Geo2** and **Geo3** objects in the **Object Manager**. Select material in the **Material Manager** and then in the **Attribute Manager > matStripe > Color** tab, change **Color** to HSV [44, 73, 100]. Click **Texture > Triangle** button and then choose **Layer** from the popup. Click on the **Layer** button.

7.  In the **Layer Shader** settings, click **Shader** and then choose **Gradient** from the popup. Click **Gradient** swatch to open the **Gradient Shader** settings. Change **Type** to **2D-U** and then change the **Gradient** as shown in Fig. E5. Render the scene [see Fig. E6].

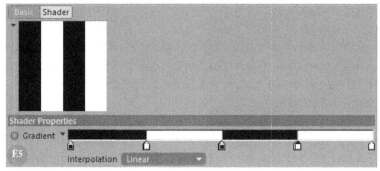

 *What just happened?*
*Notice that **Gradient** has taken over the color settings. Next, you will fix it.*

8. In the **Attribute Manager** > **matStripe** > **Color** tab, change **Mix Mode** to **Multiply**. Render the scene [see Fig. E7].

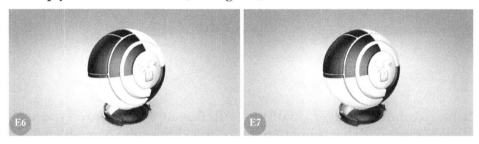

 *What just happened?*
*On changing **Mix Mode** to **Multiply**, the color will show where there is white in the gradient. As a rule of thumb, remember **Multiply** kills white and **Screen** kills black.*

9. Switch to the **Layer Shader** setting area in the **Attribute Manager**. Click **Shader** and then choose **Effects** > **Lumas** from the popup. Click on the **Lumas** swatch to open the **Lumas Shader** settings.

 *What just happened?*
*Here, I've created a **Lumas** shader layer. This shader is an illumination shader that has settings for simulating three specular highlights as well as ability to simulate anisotropic highlights.*

10. In the **Shader** tab, change **Color** to **black**. In the **Specular 1** tab, change **Glare** to **100**. In the **Specular 2** tab, change **Color** to **HSV [103, 5, 77]**, **Size** to **10%**, and **Glare** to **100%**. In the **Specular 3** tab, change **Color** to **HSV [233, 13, 53]**. In the **Anisotropy** tab, select the **Active** check box and then change **Projection** to **Planar** and **Y Roughness** to **200%**. Render the scene [see Fig. E8].

*What just happened?*

*In the **Shader** tab, black color is specified for the **Color** parameter which controls the base diffuse color of the surface. All three **Specular** tabs share the same settings. The **Glare** parameter affects the **Intensity** by using an edge falloff. The **Projection** parameter is used to define disproportional scaling of the specular highlights.*

11. Switch to the **Layer Shader** properties in the **Attribute Manager** and then change blending mode to **Soft Light** for the **Lumas** layer. Render the scene [see Fig. E9]. Notice that we need to reduce the effect of the **Lumas** layer so that more color is visible. To do so, change mix strength of the **Lumas** layer to **30%** and render the scene [see Fig. E10].

12. In the **Attribute Manager > matStripe > Reflectance** tab, change **Type** to **GGX**, **Roughness** to **5**, **Reflection Strength** to **10**, and **Specular Strength** to **0**. In the **Layer Fresnel** area, change **Fresnel** to **Conductor** and **Preset** to **Chromium**. Render the scene [see Fig. E11].

13. In the **Attribute Manager > matStripe > Basic** tab, select the **Bump** check box and then in the **Attribute Manager > matStripe > Bump** tab, click **Texture > Triangle** button and then choose **Noise** from the popup. Click the **Noise** button to open the **Noise Shader** properties. Change **Color 1** to **HSV [0, 0, 50]**, **Noise** to **Turbulence**, **Global Scale** to **2**, and **Delta** to **50**. In the **Attribute Manager > matStripe > Bump** tab, change **Strength** to **5**. In the **Attribute Manager > matStripe > Color** tab, change **Brightness** to **80**. Render the scene [see Fig. E12].

E.12

**Parameter: Delta**

It **Delta** parameter is a scaling factor and is used in sampling the noise. It is used to evaluate the slope that to be used in the **Bump** channel. It allows you to create sharp bumps with minute details.

*What next?*
*Now, let's create a little more complex stripe material.*

14. Double-click on the **Material Manager** to create a new material. Rename the material as **matStripe1**. Apply the material to the **Geo2 and Geo3** objects in the **Object Manager**. Select material in the **Material Manager** and then in the **Attribute Manager > matStripe1 > Color** tab, change **Color** to HSV[44, 0, 100] and **Brightness** to 80. Click **Texture > Triangle** button and then choose **Layer** from the popup.

15. Click on the **Layer** button. In the **Layer Shader** settings, click **Shader** and then choose **Layer** from the popup. Click on **Layer** color swatch to switch to the **Layer Shader** properties. Click **Shader** and then choose **Gradient** from the flyout. Create a gradient, as shown in Fig. E13. In the **Gradient** settings, change **Type** to **3D - Linear, Start** to **[-100, -40, 0]**, and **End** to **[100, 75, 0]**.

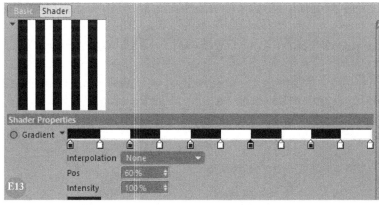

E13

*What just happened?*
*The **Start** and **End** parameters work with 3D gradients. They define the start and end points of the gradient. You can use these parameters to rotate the gradient.*

16. In the **Layer Shader** settings, RMB click on the **Gradient** layer as you created earlier and then choose **Copy Shader** from the popup. Now, RMB click and then choose **Paste Shader** from the popup menu to create another gradient layer.

17. Click **Folder** to create folder and then move the upper **Gradient** layer inside it [see Fig. E14]. Select the **Gradient** layer which is inside the **Folder** and then click **Effect** and then choose **Transform** from the popup. In the **Transform** layer, change **Scale** to **0.1, 0.1**, and **0.1**.

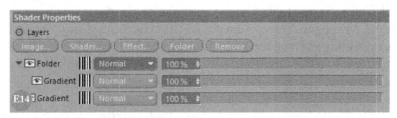

*What Transform effect does?*
*The **Transform** effect is used to transform [move, scale, and rotate] the output of the layers underneath. Here, I've scaled the **Gradient** layer to make many vertical strips. Next, we will merge it with the other **Gradient** layer with the **Soft Light** blending mode to create variations in the final gradient.*

18. Change **Folder's** blending mode to **Soft Light** and strength to **25** [see Fig. E15].

19. In the **Attribute Manager > matStripe1 > Color** tab, change **Mix Mode** to **Multiply** and render the scene [see Fig. E16].

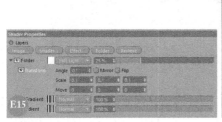

20. Click the **Layer** button to open the **Layer Shader** settings. Click **Effect** and then choose **Shader > Effects > Lumas** from the popup menu. Drag the **Lumas** layer at the bottom of the stack. Now, specify the settings for the **Lumas** layer as done earlier. Disable **Anisotropy** from the **Lumas** layer. Change blending mode to **Add** for the **Layer** layer that you created initially [see Fig. E17].

21. Now, specify the **Reflectance** settings as done earlier and render the scene [see Fig. E18].

## Exercise 3: Creating Effects Using Materials

Let's now create different kinds of effect materials, refer to Figs. E1, E5, and E9. The following table summarizes the exercise:

| Table E3 | |
|---|---|
| Difficulty level | Beginner |
| Estimated time to complete | 30 Minutes |
| Topics | • Getting Started<br>• Creating Effects Using Materials |
| Resources folder | **unit-ct2** |
| Units | **Centimeters** |
| Start file | **shader-ball.c4d** |
| Final file | **effects-finish.c4d** |

### Getting Started

Load the **shader-ball-2.c4d** file.

### Creating Effects Using Materials

Follow these steps:

1. Choose **Create > Shader > Cheen** from the **Material Manager** to create a new material. Rename the material as **matEffect1**. Apply the material to the **Geo1** object in the **Object Manager**.

 *When to use the Cheen shader?*
*The **Cheen** shader is specifically used to create the microscopic look. This shader has an additional **Gradients** channel to create different effects.*

2. Select material in the **Material Manager** and then in the **Attribute Manager** > **matEffect1** > **Basic** tab, clear the **Diffuse** and **Roughness** checkboxes and select the **Transparency** check box. In the **Attribute Manager** > **Transparency** tab, change **Refraction Index** to **1**.

3. In the **Gradients** tab, create an additional knob for the **Opacity** gradient at **65%** and change its color to black. Change **Interpolation** to **Cubic**.

**Parameters: Color and Opacity**

The **Color** gradient defines the base color of the object based on the angle between camera and the surface normals. The left side of the gradient affects the edge of the object whereas the right side of the gradient affects the center of the object. The **Opacity** gradient controls the opacity of the object depending on the angle between camera and the surface normal. The black knots are transparent whereas the white knots are opaque. The left side of the gradient affects the edge of the object whereas the right side affects the center of the object.

4. Render the scene [see Fig. E1].

*What next?*
*Now, let's create the X-Ray look.*

5. Double-click on the **Material Manager** to create a new material. Rename the material as **matEffect2**. Apply the material to the **Geo1** object in the **Object Manager**. Select material in the **Material Manager** and then in the **Attribute Manager** > **matEffect2** > **Basic** tab, clear the **Color** check box and select the **Luminance** and **Alpha** checkboxes.

6. In the **Attribute Manager** > **matEffect2** > **Luminance** tab, change **Color** to **HSV** **[229, 15, 100]** and **Brightness** to **50**. Click **Texture** > **Triangle** button and then choose **Fresnel** from the popup menu. Click the **Fresnel** button to open the **Fresnel Shader** settings. Change first knob of the gradient to **HSV [175, 28, 91]**. Render the scene [see Fig. E2].

*Note: Fresnel Shader*

The **Fresnel** shader reacts according to the camera viewing angle of each polygon on a 3D object. The **Gradient** parameter calculates the angle or falloff between the surface normals and viewing angle and then uses this information to attenuate the output.

The left of the gradient affects the edges of the objects whereas the right side of the gradient affects the center of the object. The **Render** parameter affects how the effect of the shader will be rendered. Here's the quick rundown:

- **Front Only**: Calculates the falloff for the front of the object and then change back of the object to **black**, if it can be seen.
- **Front Trans**: Calculates the falloff for the front of the object and then change back of the object to **white**, if it can be seen.
- **Back Only**: Calculates the falloff for the back of the object and then change front of the object to **black**, if it can be seen.
- **Back Trans**: Calculates the falloff for the back of the object and then change front of the object to **white**, if it can be seen.
- **Front and Back**: Calculates falloff for the intercepted surface.

7. Select the **Transparency** check box in the **Attribute Manager > Basic** tab. In the **Transparency** tab, change **Brightness** to **65** and clear the **Total Internal Reflection** check box. Select the **Additive** check box. Click **Texture > Triangle** button and then choose **Fresnel** from the popup menu.

8. Click the **Fresnel** button to open the **Fresnel Shader** settings and then set the gradient, as shown in Fig. E3.

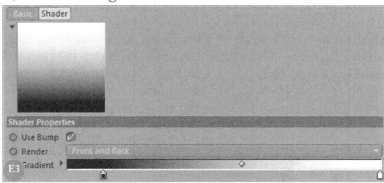

9. In the **Transparency** tab, change **Mix Mode** to **Multiply** and **Blurriness** to **10**. Render the scene [see Fig. E4]. In the **Alpha** tab, click **Texture > Triangle** button > **Effects** and then choose **Normal Direction** from the popup menu. Render the scene [see Fig. E5].

*What next?*
*Now, let's create the involution effect.*

10. Double-click on the **Material Manager** to create a new material. Rename the material as **matEffect3**. Apply the material to the **Geo1** object in the **Object Manager**. Select material in the **Material Manager** and then in the **Color** tab, change **Color** to HSV [**120, 4, 100**] and **Brightness** to **80**. Click **Texture > Triangle** button and then choose **Fresnel** from the popup menu. Click the **Fresnel** button to open the **Fresnel Shader** settings.

11. Create a gradient, as shown in Fig. E6. In the **Color** tab, change **Mix Mode** to **Multiply**. Render the scene [see Fig. E7].

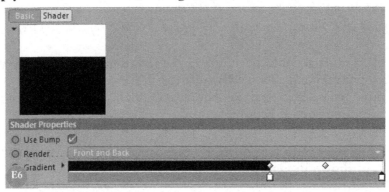

12. Select the **Luminance** check box in the **Basic** tab. In the **Luminance** tab, click **Texture > Triangle** button and then choose **Fresnel** from the popup menu. Click the **Fresnel** button to open the **Fresnel Shader** settings. Change color of the second knob to **HSV [0, 0, 22]**. In the **Luminance** tab, change **Mix Mode** to **Multiply** and **Brightness** to **70**. Render the scene [see Fig. E8].

13. Select the **Transparency** check box in the **Basic** tab. In the **Transparency** tab, change **Brightness** to **30, Refraction** to **2,** and the clear the **Total Internal Reflection** check box. Render the scene [see Fig. 9].

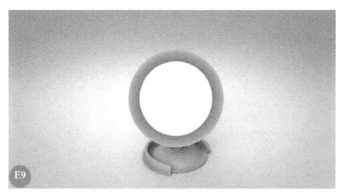

## Exercise 4: Creating Various Materials

Let's now create different kinds of materials, refer to Figs. E5, E6, E8, and E12. The following table summarizes the exercise:

| Table E4 | |
|---|---|
| Difficulty level | Intermediate |
| Estimated time to complete | 60 Minutes |
| Topics | • Getting Started<br>• Creating Materials |
| Resources folder | **unit-ct2** |
| Units | **Centimeters** |
| Start file | **shader-ball.c4d** |
| Final file | **varmat-finish.c4d** |

### Getting Started
Load the **shader-ball.c4d** file.

### Creating Materials
Let's start by creating the roman aqua glass material. Follow these steps:

1.  Double-click on the **Material Manager** to create a new material. Rename the material as **matRomanAqua**. Apply the material to the **Geo2 and Geo3** objects in the **Object Manager**. Select material in the **Material Manager** and then in the **Attribute Manager > Basic** tab, turn off all checkboxes except **Color**.

2.  In the **Color** tab, change **Color** to HSV [120, 17, 47] and **Diffuse Falloff** to **80**. Click **Texture > Triangle** button and then choose **Fresnel** from the popup menu. Click the **Fresnel** button to open the **Fresnel Shader** settings. Change color of the second knob to **HSV [0, 0, 65]**. In the **Color** tab, change **Mix Mode** to **Multiply**. Render the scene [see Fig. E1].

3.  In the **Basic** tab, select the **Diffusion** check box. In the **Diffusion** tab, click **Texture > Triangle** button and then choose **Noise** from the popup menu. In the

**Noise Shader** settings, change **Noise** to **Cell Voronoi**, and **Global Scale** to **5**. In the **Diffusion** tab, change **Mix Strength** to **50%**. Render the scene [see Fig. E2].

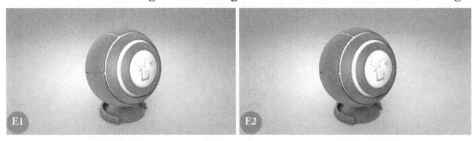

4. In the **Basic** tab, enable the **Transparency** channel and then in the **Transparency** tab, change **Color** to HSV [201, 27, 100] and **Refraction** to **1.5**. Clear the **Exit Reflections** check box and then change **Fresnel Reflectivity** to **70**. Render the scene [see Fig. E3].

*How transparency works?*

*If you increase transparency of a material, the color is automatically reduced to compensate for the transparency. The equation is as follows:* **Color % + Transparency% = 100%**. *So, if a white material has* **0%** *transparency, its color will be white. If you increase transparency to* **50%**, *color of the material will be gray. If you increase transparency to all the way upto* **100%**, *the material will have no color. This is the default behavior. However, if you want to prevent this behavior, select the* **Additive** *check box.*

**Parameter: Exit Reflections**
When reflection rays meet a surface after being refracted, two types of reflections can be calculated: one when rays enter the medium and the other when they exit the medium. A single reflection is visually more appealing than the double reflection. To achieve single reflection, clear the **Exit Reflections** check box.

**Parameter: Fresnel Reflectivity**
The **Fresnel Reflectivity** parameter controls the strength of the fresnel reflections.

**Parameters: Absorption Color and Absorption Distance**

 A glass is rarely completely colorless. When light enters in a transparent medium and as it travels through the medium it changes color to a certain degree. You can create such effects using the **Absorption Color** and **Absorption Distance** parameters. The **Absorption Color** parameter defines a color that is multiplied by the **Color** value when a light rays travelled a certain distance defined by the **Absorption Distance** parameter. You can blur the transparency using the **Blurriness**, **Min Samples**, **Max Samples** and **Accuracy** parameters.

*Tip: Absorption*
*The absorption algorithm works best with closed volumes. If there are holes in the geometry, unexpected results may be produced by Cinema 4D.*

*Tip: Glass filled with fluid*
*Model the glass and fluid separately. The fluid object should slightly extend to glass object to get predictable results.*

5. Click **Texture > Triangle** button and then choose **Noise** from the popup menu. In the **Noise Shader** settings, change **Noise** to **Luka**, **Octaves** to **8**, **Global Scale** to **500**, **Color 1** to **HSV [0, 0, 53]**. In the **Transparency** tab, change **Mix Mode** to **Multiply**, **Absorption Color** to **HSV [195, 20, 81]**. Render the scene [see Fig. E4].

6. Select the **Reflectance** check box in the **Basic** tab. In the **Reflectance** tab, select **Type** to **GGX**, **Roughness** to **0**, **Reflection Strength** to **45**, and **Specular Strength** to **0**. In the **Layer Fresnel** area, select **Dielectric** from the **Fresnel** drop-down list and **Glass** from the **Preset** drop-down list.

7. In the **Basic** tab, select the **Bump** check box. In the **Bump** tab, Click **Texture > Triangle** button and then choose **Noise** from the popup menu. In the **Noise Shader** settings, change **Texture** to **Stupl**, **Global Scale** to **500**, and **Color 1** to **HSV [0, 0, 53]**. Render the scene [see Fig. E5].

*What next?*
*Now, lets create the stained glass material.*

8. Double-click on the **Material Manager** to create a new material. Rename the material as **matStainedGlass**. Apply the material to the **Geo2 and Geo3** objects

in the **Object Manager**. Select material in the **Material Manager** and then in the **Attribute Manager** > **Basic** tab, clear the **Color** check box and select the **Transparency** check box. In the **Transparency** tab, change **Color** to HSV [94, 57, 65] and **Refraction** to 1.5.

9. Clear the **Exit Reflections** check box and change **Fresnel Reflectivity** to 50. Change **Absorption Color** to HSV [147, 17, 100] and change **Absorption Distance** to 50. In the **Reflectance** tab, select **Type** to GGX, **Roughness** to 11, **Reflection Strength** to 100, and **Specular Strength** to 20. In the **Layer Fresnel** area, select **Dielectric** from the **Fresnel** drop-down list and **Glass** from the **Preset** drop-down list.

10. In the **Basic** tab, select the **Bump** check box. In the **Bump** tab, click **Texture** > **Triangle** button and then choose **Noise** from the popup menu. In the **Noise Shader** settings, change **Noise** to **Turbulence**, **Global Scale** to 5, **Delta** to 50, and **Color 1** to HSV [0, 0, 50]. Render the scene [see Fig. E6].

*What next?*
*Now, lets create the tinted glass material.*

11. Double-click on the **Material Manager** to create a new material. Rename the material as **matTintedGlass**. Apply the material to the **Geo2** **and Geo3** objects in the **Object Manager**. Select material in the **Material Manager** and then in the **Attribute Manager** > **Basic** tab, clear the **Color** check box and select the **Transparency** check box. In the **Transparency** tab, change **Brightness** to 80 and **Refraction** to 1.55.

12. Clear the **Exit Reflections** check box and change **Fresnel Reflectivity** to 60. In the **Reflectance** tab, select **Type** to GGX, **Attenuation** to **Average**, **Roughness** to 0, **Reflection Strength** to 90, and **Specular Strength** to 3. In the **Layer Fresnel** area, select **Dielectric** from the **Fresnel** drop-down list and **Glass** from the **Preset** drop-down list.

13. Enable the **Color** channel in the **Basic** tab. Click **Texture** > **Triangle** button and then choose **Layer** from the popup menu. In the **Layer Shader** settings, click **Shader** and then choose **Shader** > **Effects** > **Falloff**. In the **Falloff** shader settings, change the gradient, as shown in Fig. E7.

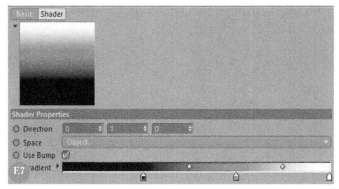

14. In the **Layer Shader** settings, click **Shader** and then choose **Fresnel** from the popup menu. Change the blending mode to **Multiply**. In the **Color** tab, change **Model** to **Oren-Nayar, Diffuse Falloff** to **-21**. Render the scene [see Fig. E8].

What next?
Now, lets create a ground material.

15. Double-click on the **Material Manager** to create a new material. Rename the material as **matGround**. Apply the material to the **Geo2 and Geo3** objects in the **Object Manager**. In the **Color** tab, change **Color** to HSV **[200, 0, 100]**. Click **Texture > Triangle** button and then choose **Layer** from the popup.

16. Click on the **Layer** button. In the **Layer Shader** settings, click **Shader** and then choose **Layer** from the popup. In the **Layer Shader** settings, click **Shader** and then choose **Noise** from the popup menu. In the **Noise Shader** settings, change **Color 1** to HSV **[18, 68, 38]**, **Color 2** to HSV **[22, 56, 46]**, **Noise** to **Wavy Turbulence**, **Octave** to **6**, and **Global Scale** to **85**.

17. In the **Layer Shader** settings, click **Shader** and then choose **Noise** from the popup menu. Change blending mode to **Multiply**. In the new **Noise Shader** settings, change **Noise** to **Blistered Turbulence**, and **Global Scale** to **10**. In the **Layer Shader** settings, change strength to **64** for the top noise layer. In the **Color** tab, change **Mix Mode** to **Multiply**. Render the scene [see Fig. E9].

18. Add another **Noise** layer on the **Layer Shader** settings and then in the **Noise Shader** settings, change **Noise** to **Naki**, **Octave** to **7**, and **Global Scale** to **600**.

In the **Layer Shader** settings, change blending mode to **Multiply** and strength to **33**. Render the scene [see Fig. E10].

19. In the **Layer Shader** settings, click **Shader** and then choose **Fresnel** from the popup menu. In the **Fresnel Shader** settings, change second gradient knob color to **HSV** [**0, 0, 46**]. In the **Layer Shader** settings, change blending mode to **Dodge** and strength to **22** for the **Fresnel** layer.

20. In the **Layer Shader** settings, click **Shader** and then choose **Noise** from the popup menu. In the **Noise Shader** settings, change **Noise** to **Nutous**, **Global Scale** to **2000**, and **Octave** to **8**. In the **Layer Shader** settings, change blending mode to **Soft Light** and strength to **28**.

21. In the **Color** tab, change **Model** to **Oren-Nayar**, **Diffuse Falloff** to **28**, and **Roughness** to **40**. In the **Basic** tab, clear the **Reflectance** channel and then select the **Diffusion** channel. In the **Diffusion** tab, click **Texture > Triangle** button and then choose **Noise** from the popup. In the **Noise Shader** settings, change **Global Scale** to **2**. In the **Diffusion** tab, change **Mix Strength** and to **19**. Render the scene [see Fig. E11].

22. Enable the **Bump** channel and then on the **Bump** tab, click **Texture >** **Triangle** button and then choose **Noise** from the popup. In the **Noise Shader** settings, change **Noise** to **Turbulence** and **Global Scale** to **125**. In the **Bump** tab, change **Strength** to **73**. Render the scene [see Fig. E12].

# Quiz

**Multiple Choice**
Answer the following questions:

1. Which of the following components is not available with the **HSV** model?

    [A] Hue                      [B] Saturation
    [C] Brightness               [D] Value

2. Which of the following components defines the brightness of the color?

    [A] Hue                      [B] Saturation
    [C] Brightness               [D] Value

3. Which is the following modes is available for the **Subsurface Scattering** shader?

    [A] Multiple                 [B] Duel
    [C] Singular                 [D] Additive

4. Which of the following shader colors an object based on the direction of the surface normals?

    [A] Surface Direction        [B] Normal Direction
    [C] Vector                   [D] Up Vector

**Fill in the Blanks**
Fill in the blanks in each of the following statements:

1. In the _____ technique, a detailed texture is applied to a low-poly object thus reducing the render time.

2. The _____, _____, and _____ channels are the most important aspect of creating a material.

3. The **Global Illumination** function takes values from the _____ channel not from the **Reflectance** channel.

4. The _____ is a powerful shader that is used to combine other shaders and bitmaps.

5. The _____ parameter controls the refraction index corresponding to the SSS effect.

6. The _____ channel is used to define the transparency.

7. The _____ shader is specifically used to create the microscopic look. This shader has an additional _____ channel to create different effects.

8. The _____ shader reacts according to the camera viewing angle of each polygon on a 3D object. The _____ parameter calculates the angle or falloff between the surface normals and viewing angle and then uses this information to attenuate the output.

## True or False
State whether each of the following is true or false:

1. When you apply a material to an object, a texture tag is automatically assigned to the object.

2. For normal use, you should use **Backmann** as it produces physically accurate results and it is computed faster than other types.

3. Fresnel reflections do not depend on the angle of view and index of refraction.

4. The render time decreases if you use a high value for the **Roughness** setting.

5. The **Oren-Nayar** shading model is suitable for creating matte materials.

6. If you increase transparency of a material, the color is automatically reduced to compensate for the transparency.

7. In the **Cheen** shader, the left side of the gradient affects the edge of the object whereas the right side of the gradient affects the center of the object.

## Summary
This unit covered the following topics:

- Material Manager
- Material Presets
- Channels
- Creating Different Materials
- Blending Modes

- Various Materials
- Reflectance Model

# Unit CT3: Creating Materials

In the last unit, we explored some of the built-in material presets in Cinema 4D. In this unit, we will create materials from scratch.

## Hands-on Exercises

### Exercise 1: Creating Denim Fabric Material

In this exercise, we will create the denim fabric material using Photoshop [refer to Fig. E5]. The following table summarizes the exercise:

| Table E1 | |
|---|---|
| Difficulty level | Intermediate |
| Estimated time to complete | 30 Minutes |
| Topics | • Getting Started<br>• Creating the Material |
| Resources folder | **unit-ct3** |
| Units | **Centimeters** |
| Start file | **shader-ball.c4d** |
| Final file | **denim-finish.c4d** |

### Getting Started

Open **shader-ball.c4d** in Cinema 4D.

### Creating the Material

Follow these steps:

1. Start **Photoshop**. Create a **1000 x 1000 px** document and fill it with **RGB [41, 67, 102]**. Create a new layer and fill it with **50%** gray. Press **D** to switch to the default background and foreground colors.

2. Choose **Filter Gallery > Sketch > Halftone Pattern** from the **Filter** menu and then change the parameters as shown in Fig. E1 and then click **OK**. Choose **Pixelate > Mezzotint** from the **Filter** menu and then change the parameters as shown in Fig. E2. Click **OK**.

3. Duplicate the layer and rotate/scale the duplicate layer [see Fig. E3]. Choose **Blur > Gaussian Blur** from the **Filter** menu and then apply a blur of radius **1**. Change blending mode to **Multiply**. Also, change the blending mode of the middle layer [**Layer 1**] to **Softlight** [see Fig. E4].

4. Save the file as **denimFebric.jpg**.

5. Choose **Flatten Image** from the **Layer** menu to flatten the image. Now, press **Ctrl+Shift+U** to desaturate the image. Apply **Levels** to bring back some contrast and then save it as **denimFebricBump.jpg**.

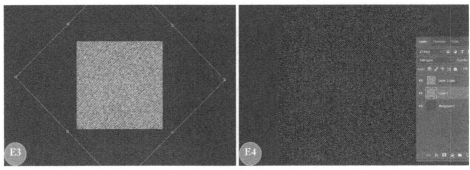

6. Now in Cinema 4D, double-click on the **Material Manager** to create a new material. Rename the material as **matDenim**. Apply the material to the **Geo2** and **Geo3** objects in the **Object Manager**. Select material in the **Material Manager** and then in the **Attribute Manager > matDenim > Basic** tab, clear the **Reflectance** check box. In the **Color** tab, change **Color** to HSV [213, 42, 89].

7. Click the **Texture > Triangle** button and then choose **Load Image** from the popup menu to open the **Open File** dialog box. In this dialog box, navigate to **denimFebric.jpg** and then click the **Open** button. Change **Mix Mode** to **Multiply**, **Model** to **Oren-Nayar** and **Diffuse Falloff** to **21**.

8. In the **Attribute Manager > matDenim > Basic** tab, select the **Bump** check box. In the **Bump** tab, click the **Texture > Triangle** button and then choose **Load Image** from the popup menu to open the **Open File** dialog box. In this dialog box, navigate to **denimFebricBump.jpg** and then click the **Open** button. Change **Strength** to **57** in the **Bump** tab.

9. In the **Attribute Manager > matDenim > Basic** tab, select the **Diffusion** check box. In the **Diffusion** tab, click the **Texture > Triangle** button and then choose **Noise** from the popup menu. Click the **Noise** button to open the **Noise** shader settings. Change **Color 1** to white, **Color 2** to black, **Noise** to **Stupl**, **Octaves** to **20**, **Global Scale** to **500**, **Low Clip** to **57**, **High Clip** to **38**, **Brightness** to **-1**, and **Contrast** to **-18**.

> ✎ *Note: Noise clipping*
> *The **Low Clip** and **High Clip** parameters control the clipping value of the noise. Noise values less than the value specified for the **Low Clip** parameter will clipped to **0**. Similarly, noise values greater than the value specified for the **High Clip** parameter will clipped to **100**.*

10. In the **Diffusion** tab, change **Mix Mode** to **Add** and then render the scene [see Fig. E5].

## Exercise 2: Creating Denim Fabric Material using Reflectance Model

In this exercise, we will create the denim fabric material using Cinema 4D's reflectance model [refer to Fig. E3]. The following table summarizes the exercise:

| Table E2 | |
|---|---|
| Difficulty level | Intermediate |
| Estimated time to complete | 30 Minutes |
| Topics | • Getting Started<br>• Creating the Material |
| Resources folder | **unit-ct3** |
| Units | **Centimeters** |
| Start file | **shader-ball.c4d** |
| Final file | **fabric-finish.c4d** |

### Getting Started

Start Cinema 4D and open the **shader-ball.c4d** file.

### Creating the Material

Follow these steps:

1. Double-click in the **Material Manager** to create a new material. Rename the material as **matDenim2**. Apply the material to the **Geo2** and **Geo3** objects in the **Object Manager**.

2. Select material in the **Material Manager** and then in the **Attribute Manager** > **matDenim2** > **Basic** tab, clear all checkboxes except the **Reflectance** check box. In the **Reflectance** tab, change **Type** to **Irawan (Woven Cloth)**. Render the scene; notice that pattern appears in the render [see Fig. E1].

E1

*Note: Irawan (Woven Cloth)*

**Irawan (Woven Cloth)** *is a cloth mode in Cinema 4D that allows you to simulate characteristic anisotropic specular highlights/reflections that are found on the real-world cloth objects. You can select a predefined cloth preset from the* **Preset** *drop-down list or you can apply your own customized settings.*

3. In the **Layer Cloth** area, make sure **Preset** is set to **Blue Gabardine (Suits)** and then change **Pattern** to **Cotton Denim**. Change **Scale U** and **Scale V** to **30** each. Change **Diffuse Warp, Diffuse Weft, Specular Warp,** and **Specular Weft** to HSV [221, 46, 48], HSV [242, 23, 42], HSV [208, 21, 20], and HSV [207, 13, 61], respectively. Change **Scattering - Uniform** and **Scattering - Forward** to **0.02** and **7**, respectively. Render the scene [see Fig. E2].

4. In the **Attribute Manager > matDenim2 > Basic** tab, select the **Color** check box. In the **Color** tab, change **Color** to HSV [217, 54, 95], **Brightness** to **20**, **Model** to **Oren-Nayer**, and **Diffuse Falloff** to **21**. Render the scene [see Fig. E3].

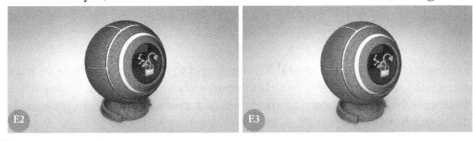

E2    E3

*What are diffuse and warp settings?*
*You can use these settings to specify separate diffuse and specular colors for the warp and weft threads.*

*Caution: Specular and diffuse colors*
*To get good results out of the cloth reflectance model, you need to make sure that the specular color should be always brighter than the diffuse color so that both colors fall in same tone. You can also plug a texture to define the color. This texture will be multiplied with the color. If you want to define the color using a texture, change color to white. The* **Scattering – Uniform** *parameter defines the overall specular and reflection strength. The higher the value you specify for*

*this parameter, the more brighter/reflective cloth will be. The **Scattering - Forward** parameter affects the bright regions of the specular highlight of the fabric.*

## Exercise 3: Creating an Abstract Material - 1

In this exercise, we will create an abstract material [refer to Fig. E5]. The following table summarizes the exercise:

| Table E3 | |
|---|---|
| Difficulty level | Intermediate |
| Estimated time to complete | 30 Minutes |
| Topics | • Getting Started<br>• Creating the Material |
| Resources folder | **unit-ct3** |
| Units | **Centimeters** |
| Start file | **shader-ball.c4d** |
| Final file | **abs1-finish.c4d** |

### Getting Started

Start Cinema 4D and open the **shader-ball.c4d** file.

### Creating the Material

Follow these steps:

1. Double-click in the **Material Manager** to create a new material. Rename the material as **matAbs1**. Apply the material to the **Geo2** and **Geo3** objects in the **Object Manager**.

2. Select **matAbs1** in the **Material Manager** and then in the **Attribute Manager** > **matAbs1** > **Basic** tab, clear the **Reflectance** check box. In the **Color** tab, click **Texture** > **Triangle** button and then choose **Layer** from the popup menu. Click the **Layer** button to open the **Layer** shader settings.

3. Click **Shader** and then choose **Filter** from the popup menu. Now, in the **Filter** shader settings, click **Texture** > **Triangle** button and then load **granite-texture.jpg**. Change **Hue** to 305 and **Contrast** to 39. Render the scene [see Fig. E1].

   *Note: Filter shader*
   *The **Filter** shader is used to adjust hue, brightness, contrast, saturation, gamma, and gradient curves of a bitmap or another shader. The **Gamma** parameter affects the midtones. The higher the value you specify for this parameter, the brighter the midtones will be. Lesser values darkens the midtones. If you select the **Colorize** check box, Cinema 4D converts texture to grayscale and then you can use the **Hue** and **Saturation** parameters to color the grayscale image.*

4. In the **Layer** shader settings, click **Shader** and then choose **Color** from the popup menu. In the **Color** shader settings and then change **Color** to HSV [229, 91, 100]. In the **Layer** shader settings, change blending mode **Luminance** and **Strength** to 88. Render the scene [see Fig. E2].

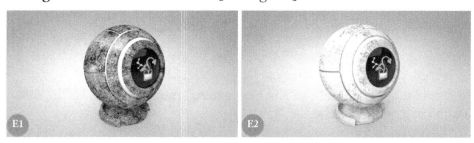

5. Select the **Reflectance** check box in the **Attribute Manager > Basic** tab. In the **Reflectance** tab, change **Type** to Beckmann, **Attenuation** to **Average**, **Roughness** to 10, **Reflection Strength** to 15, and **Specular Strength** to 0.

6. Copy the texture from the **Color** tab and then paste it on the **Reflectance** tab > **Layer Color** area > **Texture** parameter [see Fig. E3]. Change **Brightness** to 7 and then render the scene [see Fig. E4].

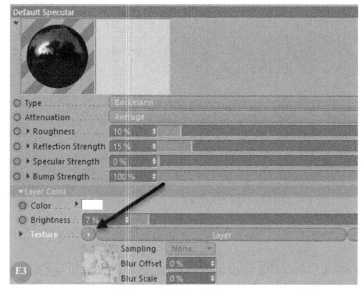

7. Select the **Bump** check box in the **Attribute Manager > Basic** tab. Copy the texture from the **Color** tab and then paste it on the **Bump** tab > **Texture** parameter. In the **Layer** shader settings, delete the **Color** layer and then switch to the **Filter** shader settings.

8. Change **Hue** to 0, Saturation to -100, and **Contrast** to 26. In the **Bump** tab, change **Strength** to 100 and then render the scene [see Fig. E5].

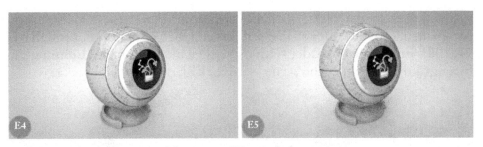

## Exercise 4: Creating an Abstract Material - 2

In this exercise, we will create an abstract material [refer to Fig. E4]. The following table summarizes the exercise:

| Table E4 | |
| --- | --- |
| Difficulty level | Intermediate |
| Estimated time to complete | 30 Minutes |
| Topics | • Getting Started<br>• Creating the Material |
| Resources folder | **unit-ct3** |
| Units | **Centimeters** |
| Start file | **shader-ball.c4d** |
| Final file | **abs2-finish.c4d** |

### Getting Started
Start Cinema 4D and open the **shader-ball.c4d** file.

### Creating the Material
Follow these steps:

1. Double-click in the **Material Manager** to create a new material. Rename the material as **matAbs2**. Apply the material to the **Geo2** and **Geo3** objects in the **Object Manager**.

2. In the **Color** tab, click the **Texture > Triangle** button and then choose **Gradient** from the popup menu. In the **Gradient** shader settings, change **Type** to **2D-V** and then change the **Gradient** using the red and white colors, as shown in Fig. E1. Now, change **Angle** to **45**.

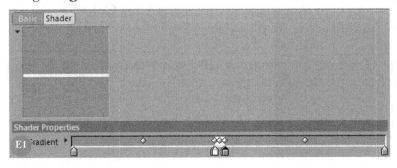

3. Select the **Displacement** check box in the **Attribute Manager > Basic** tab. In the **Displacement** tab, click the **Texture > Triangle** button and then choose **Filter** from the popup menu.

 *What just happened?*
*Here, I have enabled the **Displacement** channel. Unlike the **Bump** channel, the **Displacement** channel is used to actually deform the object. The **Height** parameter defines the height of the displacement. The **Strength** parameter can be used to adjust the maximum displacement defined by the **Height** parameter. If you select **Intensity** from the **Type** drop-down list, the displacement takes place in the positive direction. The black parts of the map produce no displacement whereas the white parts produce maximum displacement. The **Intensity Centered** type produces displacement in both directions. A gray value of **50%** on the map produces no displacement. White area on the map produces maximum positive displacement whereas the black area produces maximum negative displacement.*

4. In the **Filter** shader settings, click the **Texture > Triangle** button and then choose **Gradient** from the popup. In the **Gradient** shader settings, load the **Pattern 6** preset and then change **Angle** to **45**.

5. In the **Filter** shader settings, change **Saturation** to **-100** and **Contrast** to **6**. Render the scene [see Fig. E2]. In the **Displacement** tab, select the **Sub Polygon Displacement** check box and then render the scene [see Fig. E3].

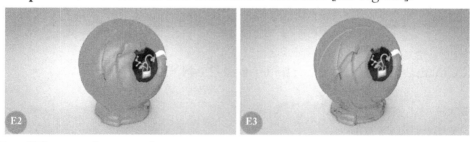

 *What just happened?*
*The **Sub Polygon Displacement** option allows you to render detailed render without actually subdividing the geometry.*

6. Select the **Round Geometry** check box and then render the scene [see Fig. E4].

*What just happened?*
*When you select the **Round Geometry** check box, a special algorithm similar to that of the **Subdivision Surface** object is used to ensure that the object is rounded before the sub-polygon displacement is calculated. This algorithm is used because the sub-polygon displacement can not calculate normal **Phong** shading.*

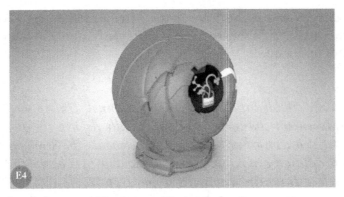

## Exercise 5: Creating an Abstract Material - 3

In this exercise, we will create an animated abstract material [refer to Figs. E1 and E2]. The following table summarizes the exercise:

| Table E5 | |
|---|---|
| Difficulty level | Intermediate |
| Estimated time to complete | 35 Minutes |
| Topics | • Getting Started<br>• Creating the Material |
| Resources folder | **unit-ct3** |
| Units | **Centimeters** |
| Start file | **shader-ball-2.c4d** |
| Final file | **abs3-finish.c4d** |

### Getting Started
Start Cinema 4D and open the **shader-ball-2.c4d** file.

### Creating the Material
Follow these steps:

1. Double-click in the **Material Manager** to create a new material. Rename the material as **matAbs3**. Apply the material to the **Geo1** object in the **Object Manager**. Select the **Luminance, Displacement,** and **Alpha** checkboxes in the **Attribute Manager > Basic** tab. Clear the **Color** check box.

2. In the **Alpha** tab, click the **Texture > Triangle** button and then choose **Noise** from the popup menu. Click the **Noise** button to open the **Noise** shader settings. Change **Noise** to **Cranal, Octaves** to **10**, and **Global Scale** to **1530**.

3. Change **Movement Z** to **0.001, Animation Speed** to **0.1, Brightness** to **3**, and **Contrast** to **94**. In the **Alpha** tab, select the **Invert** check box. Render the scene [see Fig. E1].

*What just happened?*

*In order to animate noise, you need to specify a value for the **Animation Speed** parameter in the **Noise** settings. This parameter defines the rate at which noise animates in cycles per second. To move the noise, you need to define a directional vector using the **Movement [XYZ]** parameters.*

4. Copy the texture from the **Alpha** tab and then paste it on the **Displacement** tab > **Texture** parameter. Select the **Sub Polygon Displacement** check box and then change **Height** to **15**. Also, select the **Round Geometry** check box. Render the scene [see Fig. E2].

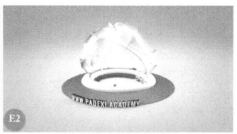

*Note: Rendering the animation*

*To render the animation, you need to specify a frame range in the **Render Settings** window > **Output** area using the **From** and **To** parameters. To save rendered animation to a file, select **Save** from the left pane of the **Render Setting** window [see Fig. E3]. In the right pane, click **Browse** button corresponding to the **File** parameter to open the **Save File** dialog box.*

*In this dialog box, navigate to the location where you want to save the file and then click **Save**. Select the file type from the **Format** drop-down list. To render a movie, you can choose **QuickTime Movie** or **AVI Movie** from the drop-down list. If you are rendering a still image and wants alpha channel in it, select the **Alpha Channel** check box. When selected, Cinema 4D calculates a pre-multiplied alpha channel that will be calculated during rendering.*

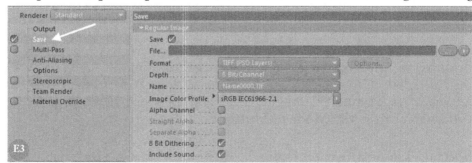

> **?** *What is pre-multiplied alpha?*
> *In computer graphics, there are two common representations of the alpha channel in an image: straight and pre-multiplied. When straight alpha is used in an image, the RGB components represent the color of the pixels in the image ignoring its opacity whereas in pre-multiplied alpha opacity is controlled using multiplication. Pre-multiplied alpha is more accurate than the straight alpha when filtering images or compositing different layers.*

## Exercise 6: Creating an Abstract Material - 4

In this exercise, we will create an abstract material [refer to Fig. E4]. The following table summarizes the exercise:

| Table E6 | |
|---|---|
| Difficulty level | Intermediate |
| Estimated time to complete | 35 Minutes |
| Topics | • Getting Started<br>• Creating the Material |
| Resources folder | **unit-ct3** |
| Units | **Centimeters** |
| Start file | **shader-ball-2.c4d** |
| Final file | **abs4-finish.c4d** |

### Getting Started
Start Cinema 4D and open the **shader-ball.c4d** file.

### Creating the Material
Follow these steps:

1.  Double-click in the **Material Manager** to create a new material. Rename the material as **matAbs4**. Apply the material to the **Geo1** object in the **Object Manager**.

2.  In the **Attribute Manager > Color** tab, change **Color** to HSV [33, 90, 74]. Click **Texture > Triangle** button and then choose **Filter** from the popup menu. Click the **Filter** button to open the **Filter** shader settings. Now, in the **Filter** shader settings, click **Texture > Triangle** button and then load **IMG-06.JPG**. In the **Color** tab, change **Mix Mode** to **Multiply**.

3.  Select the **Luminance** check box in the **Attribute Manager > Basic** tab. Copy the texture from the **Color** tab and then paste it on the **Luminance** tab > **Texture** parameter. Change **Color** to HSV [33, 90, 74] and **Mix Mode** to **Multiply**. Render the scene [see Fig. E1].

4. Select the **Transparency** check box in the **Attribute Manager > Basic** tab. In the **Transparency** tab, change **Refraction Preset** to **Beer**.

5. Click the **Texture > Triangle** button and then choose **Noise** from the popup menu. Click the **Noise** button to open the **Noise** shader settings. Change **Noise** to **Luka**, **Octaves** to **6**, and **Global Scale** to **1569**. Change **Movement Z** to **0.001**, **Animation Speed** to **0.1**, **Brightness** to **3**, and **Contrast** to **94**. Change **Low Clip** to **7**, **High Clip** to **62**, and **Contrast** to **79**. Render the scene [see Fig. E2].

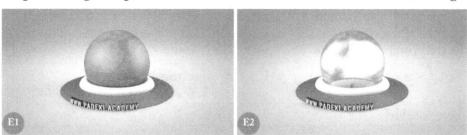

6. Select the **Bump** check box in the **Attribute Manager > Basic** tab. Copy the texture from the **Color** tab and then paste it on the **Bump** tab > **Texture** parameter. Change **Strength** to **61**.

7. In the **Filter** shader settings, select the **Colorize** check box and then change **Brightness** to **-7** and **Contrast** to **16**. Render the scene [see Fig. E3].

8. Select the **Displacement** check box in the **Attribute Manager > Basic** tab. Copy the texture from the **Transparency** tab and then paste it on the **Displacement** tab > **Texture** parameter. Select the **Sub Polygon Displacement** check box and then change **Subdivision Level** to **2**. Change **Height** to **12**.

9. In the **Reflectance** tab, change **Type** to **Beckmann**, **Attenuation** to **Average**, **Roughness** to **0**, **Reflection Strength** to **69**, and **Specular Strength** to **0**. In the **Layer Fresnel** area, change **Fresnel** to **Dielectric** and **Preset** to **Beer**. Render the scene [see Fig. E4].

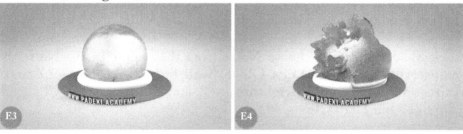

*Tip: Primitive Sphere*

*If you are applying material to a primitive sphere, in order to see the displacement effect on the sphere, select sphere and then in the **Attribute Manager > Object** tab, clear the **Render Perfect** check box. A prefect sphere looks round and smooth and it renders faster than the polygon sphere. Select* *the check box when you are using sphere as base for other effects such as displacement or hair.*

## Exercise 7: Creating an Abstract Material - 5

In this exercise, we will create an abstract material [see Figs. E5 and E6]. The following table summarizes the exercise:

| Table E7 | |
| --- | --- |
| Difficulty level | Intermediate |
| Estimated time to complete | 35 Minutes |
| Topics | • Getting Started<br>• Creating the Material |
| Resources folder | **unit-ct3** |
| Units | **Centimeters** |
| Start file | **shader-ball.c4d** |
| Final file | **abs5-finish.c4d** |

### Getting Started
Start Cinema 4D and open the **shader-ball.c4d** file.

### Creating the Material
Follow these steps:

1. Double-click in the **Material Manager** to create a new material. Rename the material as **matAbs5**. Apply the material to the **Geo1** object in the **Object Manager**.

2. In the **Color** tab, click the **Texture > Triangle** button and then choose **Layer** from the popup menu. In the **Layer** shader settings, click **Folder** to create a new folder. Rename it as **Noise Folder**. Click **Shader** and then choose **Fresnel** from the popup. In the **Fresnel** shader settings, change **Value** of the first knob to **57**.

3. Click **Shader** and then choose **Noise** from the popup. In the **Noise** shader settings, change **Noise** to **Luka**, **Global Scale** to **1526**, **Movement Z** to **0.001**, **Animation Speed** to **0.1**, **Brightness** to **3**, and **Contrast** to **94**. Change **Low Clip** to **23** and **High Clip** to **89**.

4. In the **Layer** shader settings, change blending mode to **Screen** and strength to **25** for the **Noise** layer [see Fig. E1]. Render the scene [see Fig. E2].

5. Click **Shader** and then choose **Noise** from the popup. In the **Noise** shader settings, swap **Color 1** with **Color 2**. Change **Noise** to **Nutous**, **Global Scale** to **1562**, **Movement Z** to **0.001**, **Animation Speed** to **0.1**, **Brightness** to **1**, and **Contrast** to **94**. Change **Low Clip** to **0**, **High Clip** to **38**, and **Contrast** to **76**.

6. In the **Layer** shader settings, change blending mode to **Overlay** and **Strength** to **25** for the **Noise** layer. Render the scene [see Fig. E3].

7. Click **Effect** and then choose **Colorize** from the popup. Make sure the **Colorize** layer is at the top of the stack. Load the preset **Heat3** for the **Colorize** effect.

8. Select the **Luminance** check box in the **Attribute Manager > Basic** tab. Copy the texture from the **Color** tab and then paste it on the **Luminance** tab > **Texture** parameter. Render the scene [see Fig. E4].

9. Select the **Transparency** check box in the **Attribute Manager > Basic** tab. Copy the texture from the **Color** tab and then paste it on the **Transparency** tab > **Texture** parameter. In the **Layer** shader settings, delete the **Colorize** layer. Render the scene [see Fig. E5].

10. Select the **Glow** check box in the **Attribute Manager > Basic** tab. Clear the **Reflectance** check box. In the **Glow** tab, change **Inner Strength** to **200**, **Outer Strength** to **300**, **Radius** to **5**, **Random** to **78**, and **Frequency** to **5**. Render the scene [see Fig. E6].

*How the Glow channel works?*
*The **Glow** channel is used to add glow to the pixels. The glow cannot be seen through reflections and transparent objects. Also, it does not act as a light and any part of the scene will not be lit by it. It also does not cast shadows. The maximum resolution glow can affect is **4000 x 4000** pixels. The **Inner Strength** and **Outer Strength** settings define the strength of the glow over the surface of*

*the material and on the edges, respectively. The **Radius** setting defines how far glow can extend outside the boundary of the surface. If you define a **Random** percentage, the intensity of the glow increases or decreases at each animation frame. The **Frequency** setting defines how often the glow radius changes. This setting works in conjunction with the **Random** setting.*

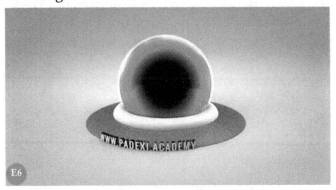

## Exercise 8: Creating Rust Material

In this exercise, we will create rust material [refer to Fig. E3]. The following table summarizes the exercise:

| Table E8 | |
|---|---|
| Difficulty level | Intermediate |
| Estimated time to complete | 30 Minutes |
| Topics | • Getting Started<br>• Creating the Material |
| Resources folder | **unit-ct3** |
| Units | **Centimeters** |
| Start file | **shader-ball.c4d** |
| Final file | **rust-finish.c4d** |

### Getting Started

Start Cinema 4D and open the **shader-ball.c4d** file.

### Creating the Material

Follow these steps:

1. Double-click in the **Material Manager** to create a new material. Rename the material as **matRust**. Apply the material to the **Geo2** and **Geo3** objects in the **Object Manager**.

2. In the **Color** tab, click **Texture > Triangle** button and then choose **Layer** from the popup menu. Click the **Layer** button to open the **Layer** shader settings.

3.  In the **Layer** shader settings, click **Shader** and then choose **Fusion** from the popup. In the **Fusion** shader setting, click **Blend Channel > Triangle** button and then load the **rustPaint.jpg** using the **Load Image** option. Click **Base Channel > Triangle** button and then load the **rust.jpg** using the **Load Image** option.

4.  Change **Mode** to **Darken** and then select the **Use Mask** check box. Click **Mask Channel > Triangle** button and then choose **Filter** from the popup. Now, in the **Filter** shader settings, click **Texture > Triangle** button and then load **scratchesMask.jpg**. Change **Contrast** to 72. In the **Fusion** shader settings, select the **Invert Mask** check box. Render the scene [see Fig. E1].

 *What Fusion shader does?*
*The **Fusion** shader allows you to combine two textures using one of the blending modes [standard in any image editing application such as Photoshop]. You can adjust the opacity of blend channel to control the mix between two textures. It also allows you to mask the blend using the **Mask Channel** setting. The **Base Channel** setting is used to specify a texture for the bottom layer and the **Blend Channel** setting specifies the top layer in the fusing.*

5.  In the **Layer** shader settings, click **Shader** and then choose **Noise** from the popup. In the **Noise** shader settings, change **Noise** to **Nutous**, **Octaves** to 6, and **Global Scale** to 1319. Change **Movement Z** to **0.001**, **Animation Speed** to **0.1**, **Brightness** to **0**, **Contrast** to **48**, **Low Clip** to **0**, and **High Clip** to **62**.

6.  Change **Color 1** to HSV [31, 74, 85] and **Color 2** to HSV [31, 74, 30]. In the **Layer** shader settings, change blending mode to **Multiply** and **Strength** to 30 for the **Noise** layer. Render the scene [see Fig. E2].

7.  Select the **Bump** check box in the **Attribute Manager > Basic** tab and clear the **Reflectance** check box. In the **Bump** tab, click **Texture > Triangle** button and then choose **Filter** from the popup menu. Copy the texture from the **Color** tab and then paste it on the **Filter** shader settings > **Texture** parameter.

8. In the **Filter** shader settings, select the **Colorize** check box and then change **Contrast** to **48**. In the **Bump** tab, change **Strength** to **40**. Render the scene [see Fig. E3].

## Exercise 9: Creating Brown Leather Material

In this exercise, we will create brown leather material [refer to Fig. E1]. The following table summarizes the exercise:

| Table E9 | |
|---|---|
| Difficulty level | Intermediate |
| Estimated time to complete | 30 Minutes |
| Topics | • Getting Started <br> • Creating the Material |
| Resources folder | **unit-ct3** |
| Units | **Centimeters** |
| Start file | **shader-ball.c4d** |
| Final file | **leather-finish.c4d** |

### Getting Started
Start Cinema 4D and open the **shader-ball.c4d** file.

### Creating the Material
Follow these steps:

1. Double-click in the **Material Manager** to create a new material. Rename the material as **matLeather**. Apply the material to the **Geo2** and **Geo3** objects in the **Object Manager**.

2. In the **Color** tab, click the **Texture > Triangle** button and then load the **brownLeather.jpg** using the **Load Image** option.

3. In the **Reflectance** tab, change **Type** to **Beckmann**, **Attenuation** to **Average**, **Roughness** to **10**, **Reflection Strength** to **23**, and **Specular Strength** to **0**. In the **Layer Fresnel** area, change **Fresnel** to **Dielectric** and **IOR** to **3.5**.

4. Select the **Bump** check box in the **Attribute Manager > Basic** tab. In the **Bump** tab, click the **Texture > Triangle** button and then choose **Filter** from the popup menu. In the **Filter** shader settings, click **Texture > Triangle** button and then load the **brownLeather_bump.jpg** using the **Load Image** option. Now, change **Contrast** to **39**. In the **Bump** tab, change **Strength** to **27**. Render the scene [see Fig. E1].

## Exercise 10: Creating Concrete Material

In this exercise, we will create concrete material [refer to Fig. E1]. The following table summarizes the exercise:

| Table E10 | |
|---|---|
| Difficulty level | Intermediate |
| Estimated time to complete | 30 Minutes |
| Topics | • Getting Started<br>• Creating the Material |
| Resources folder | **unit-ct3** |
| Units | **Centimeters** |
| Start file | **shader-ball.c4d** |
| Final file | **concrete-finish.c4d** |

## Getting Started

Start Cinema 4D and open the **shader-ball.c4d** file.

## Creating the Material

Follow these steps:

1. Double-click in the **Material Manager** to create a new material. Rename the material as **matConcrete**. Apply the material to the **Geo2** and **Geo3** objects in the **Object Manager**.

2. In the **Color** tab, click the **Texture > Triangle** button and then choose **Filter** from the popup menu. In the **Filter** shader settings, click **Texture > Triangle**

button and then load the **concreteBare_Diffuse.jpg** using the **Load Image** option. Now, change **Contrast** to **8**.

3. In the **Color** tab, change **Mode** to **Oren-Nayar**, **Diffuse Falloff** to **-20**, and **Roughness** to **27**.

4. In the **Reflectance** channel, change **Type** to **Oren-Nayar (Diffuse)**. Change **Roughness** to **0**, **Reflection Strength** to **27**, and **Specular Strength** to **0**. In the **Layer Color** area, click **Texture > Triangle** button and then load the **concreteBare_Reflection.jpg** using the **Load Image** option.

5. Select the **Normal** check box in the **Attribute Manager > Basic** tab. In the **Normal** tab, click **Texture > Triangle** button and then load the **concreteBare_Normal.jpg** using the **Load Image** option.

6. Select the **Displacement** check box in the **Attribute Manager > Basic** tab. In the **Displacement** tab, click **Texture > Triangle** button and then load the **concreteBare_Displacement.jpg** using the **Load Image** option. Change **Strength** to **19** and **Height** to **2**. Also, select the **Sub Polygon Displacement** check box. Render the scene [see Fig. E1].

## Exercise 11: Creating Red Brick Material

In this exercise, we will create red brick material [see Fig. E1]. The following table summarizes the exercise:

| Table E11 | |
|---|---|
| Difficulty level | Intermediate |
| Estimated time to complete | 30 Minutes |
| Topics | • Getting Started<br>• Creating the Material |
| Resources folder | **unit-ct3** |
| Units | **Centimeters** |
| Start file | **shader-ball.c4d** |
| Final file | **brick-finish.c4d** |

Start Cinema 4D and open the **shader-ball.c4d** file.

## Creating the Material

Follow these steps:

1. Double-click in the **Material Manager** to create a new material. Rename the material as **matBrick**. Apply the material to the **Geo2** and **Geo3** objects in the **Object Manager**.

2. In the **Color** tab, click the **Texture > Triangle** button and then load the **redBrick.png** using the **Load Image** option. Change **Model** to **Oren-Nayar**, **Diffuse Falloff** to **-24**, and **Roughness** to **52**.

3. In the **Reflectance** tab, change **Type** to **Beckmann**, **Attenuation** to **Average**, **Roughness** to **0**, **Reflection Strength** to **20**, and **Specular Strength** to **0**.

4. In the **Layer Color** area, click the **Texture > Triangle** button and then choose **Filter** from the popup menu. In the **Filter** shader settings, click **Texture > Triangle** button and then load the **redBrickGray.jpg** using the **Load Image** option. Now, change **Brightness** to **-39** and **Contrast** to **0**.

5. Select the **Bump** check box in the **Attribute Manager > Basic** tab. In the **Bump** channel, click the **Texture > Triangle** button and then choose **Effects > Normalizer** from the popup menu. In the **Normalizer** shader settings, click **Texture > Triangle** button and then load the **redBrickGray.png** using the **Load Image** option. In the **Bump** tab, change **Strength** to **94**. Render the scene [see Fig. E1].

## Exercise 12: Creating Leather Material - 2

In this exercise, we will create leather material [see Fig. E1]. The following table summarizes the exercise:

| Table E12 | |
| --- | --- |
| Difficulty level | Intermediate |
| Estimated time to complete | 30 Minutes |
| Topics | • Getting Started<br>• Creating the Material |
| Resources folder | **unit-ct3** |
| Units | **Centimeters** |
| Start file | **shader-ball.c4d** |
| Final file | **leather2-finish.c4d** |

### Getting Started
Start Cinema 4D and open the **shader-ball.c4d** file.

### Creating the Material
Follow these steps:

1. Double-click in the **Material Manager** to create a new material. Rename the material as **matLeather2**. Apply the material to the **Geo2** and **Geo3** objects in the **Object Manager**.

2. In the **Color** tab, click the **Texture > Triangle** button and then load the **Leather_Texture.jpg** using the **Load Image** option.

3. Select the **Diffusion** check box in the **Attribute Manager > Basic** tab. In the **Diffusion** tab, click the **Texture > Triangle** button and then choose **Noise** from the popup menu. Click the **Noise** button to open the **Noise** shader settings. Change **Noise** to **Gaseous**, **Octaves** to 8, and **Global Scale** to 1600. Change **Brightness** to 42, and **Contrast** to 4.

4. In the **Diffusion** tab, change **Mix Mode** to **Multiply** and **Mix Strength** to 72 and also select the **Affect Reflection** check box.

*What just happened?*
*In the **Color** channel, I have multiplied the **Noise** shader with the color values but it only affects the color values. It does not affect channels such as **Reflectance**. You can use the **Diffusion** channel to give material a used look. Make sure that you select the **Affect Specular** and **Affect Reflection** checkboxes for the **Diffusion** channel.*

5. In the **Reflectance** tab, rename the **Default Specular** layer to **HighLights**. Change **Type** to **GGX**, **Attenuation** to **Average**, **Roughness** to **56**, **Reflection Strength** to **0**, and **Specular Strength** to **90**. In the **Layer Fresnel** area, change **Fresnel** to **Dielectric** and **IOR** to **1.3**.

6. In the **Layer Color** area, change **Color** to HSV[0, 39, 100]. Create a new **GGX** layer and then rename it as **Reflections**. Change **Attenuation** to **Additive**, **Roughness** to **37**, **Reflection Strength** to **23**, and **Specular Strength** to **11**. In the **Layer Fresnel** area, change **Fresnel** to **Dielectric** and **IOR** to **1.3**.

*What just happened?*
*I have also used two reflection layers for creating realistic diffuse reflection of the leather. The **HighLights** layer controls the highlight properties whereas the **Reflections** layer controls the reflective properties.*

7. Select the **Bump** check box in the **Attribute Manager > Basic** tab. In the **Bump** tab, click the **Texture > Triangle** button and then choose **Noise** from the popup menu. Click the **Noise** button to open the **Noise** shader settings. Change **Noise** to **Gaseous**, **Octaves** to **8**, and **Global Scale** to **350**. In the **Bump** tab, change **Strength** to **16**.

8. Select the **Normal** check box in the **Attribute Manager > Basic** tab. In the **Normal** tab, click the **Texture > Triangle** button and then choose **Effects > Normalizer** from the popup menu. In the **Normalizer** shader settings, click **Texture > Triangle** button and then load the **Leather_Texture.jpg** using the **Load Image** option. In the **Normalizer** shader settings, change **Filter** to **Sobel 4x** and **Strength** to **190**. Render the scene [see Fig. E1].

## Exercise 13: Creating Car Paint Material

In this exercise, we will create car paint material [see Fig. E2]. The following table summarizes the exercise:

| Table E13 | |
| --- | --- |
| Difficulty level | Intermediate |
| Estimated time to complete | 30 Minutes |

| Table E13 | |
|---|---|
| Topics | • Getting Started<br>• Creating the Material |
| Resources folder | **unit-ct3** |
| Units | **Centimeters** |
| Start file | **shader-ball.c4d** |
| Final file | **car-paint-finish.c4d** |

## Getting Started

Start Cinema 4D and open the **shader-ball.c4d** file.

## Creating the Material

Follow these steps:

1. Double-click in the **Material Manager** to create a new material. Rename the material as **matCarPaint**. Apply the material to the **Geo2** and **Geo3** objects in the **Object Manager**.

2. Clear all checkboxes except the **Reflectance** check box in the **Attribute Manager > Basic** tab. In the **Reflectance** tab, rename **Default Specular** layer to **Layer 1**. Change **Type** to **Lambertian (Diffuse)**, **Attenuation** to **Average**, **Reflection Strength** to **24**, and **Specular Strength** to **32**. In the **Layer Fresnel** area, change **Fresnel** to **Dielectric** and **IOR** to **2.3**.

3. In the **Layer Color** area, change **Color** to HSV [5, 93, 56].

4. Add a new **Ward** reflectance layer and change blending mode to **Add** [see Fig. E1]. Change **Attenuation** to **Average**, **Roughness** to **64**, **Reflection Strength** to **22**, and **Specular Strength** to **22**. In the **Layer Fresnel** area, change **Fresnel** to **Dielectric** and **IOR** to **2.3**.

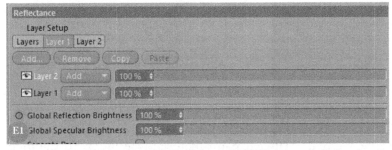

5. In the **Layer Color** area, change **Color** to HSV [5, 93, 70]. In the **Layer Mask** area, click the **Texture > Triangle** button and then choose **Noise** from the popup menu. Click the **Noise** button to open the **Noise** shader settings. Change **Noise** to **Cell Voronoi** and **Global Scale** to **2**.

6. Add a new **Beckmann** reflectance layer. Change **Attenuation** to **Average**, **Roughness** to **0**, **Reflection Strength** to **100**, and **Specular Strength** to **0**. In the **Layer Fresnel** area, change **Fresnel** to **Dielectric** and **IOR** to **1.52**. Render the scene [see Fig. E2].

*What just happened?*
*Generally, a car paint material is made of three reflection layers: base coat, metallic particles, and clear coat. In this exercise, I have used three reflectance layers to simulate the car paint material. We have used **Lambertian (Diffuse)** for the base coat which is used for smooth surfaces. If you are simulating a rough surface, use the **Oren-Nayer (Diffuse)** type. The **Roughness** parameter is only available for the **Oren-Nayer (Diffuse)** type.*

*The **Color** parameter in the **Layer Color** area provides color for this layer. By setting **IOR** of **2.3** for this layer, I have reduced the contrast from center to the edges. The second reflectance layer is masked with the noise shader to create effect of metallic particles. Third reflectance layer is used to create the clear coat effect. An **IOR** value **1.52** creates a perfect reflective surface.*

## Exercise 14: Creating Rubber Material

In this exercise, we will create rubber material [see Fig. E1]. The following table summarizes the exercise:

| Table E14 | |
| --- | --- |
| Difficulty level | Intermediate |
| Estimated time to complete | 30 Minutes |
| Topics | • Getting Started<br>• Creating the Material |
| Resources folder | **unit-ct3** |
| Units | **Centimeters** |
| Start file | **shader-ball.c4d** |
| Final file | **rubber-finish.c4d** |

## Getting Started
Start Cinema 4D and open the **shader-ball.c4d** file.

## Creating the Material
Follow these steps:

1. Double-click in the **Material Manager** to create a new material. Rename the material as **matRubber**. Apply the material to the **Geo2** and **Geo3** objects in the **Object Manager**. In the **Color** tab, change **Color** to HSV [38, 2, 17]. Change **Model** to **Oren-Nayar**, **Diffuse Falloff** to **30** and **Roughness** to **25**.

2. Select the **Normal** check box in the **Attribute Manager** > **Basic** tab. In the **Normal** tab, click the **Texture** > **Triangle** button and then choose **Effects** > **Normalizer** from the popup menu. In the **Normalizer** shader settings, click **Texture** > **Triangle** button and choose **Layer** from the popup menu.

3. In the **Layer** shader settings, click **Shader** and then choose **Surfaces** > **Tiles** from the popup menu. In the **Tiles** shader settings, change **Tiles Color 1** and **Tiles Color 2** to white. Change **Grout Width** to **9**, **Bevel Width** to **86**, and **Global Scale** to **8**.

4. In the **Layer** shader settings, click **Effect** and then choose **Transform** from the popup menu. In the **Transform** shader settings, change **Angle** to **42**. In the **Normalizer** shader settings, change **Filter** to **Sobel 4x** and **Strength** to **242**. In the **Normal** tab, change **Strength** to **72**.

5. In the **Reflectance** tab, rename **Default Specular** layer to **Layer 1**. Change **Type** to **Phong**, **Attenuation** to **Additive**, **Roughness** to **66**, **Reflection Strength** to **100**, and **Specular Strength** to **100**. In the **Layer Fresnel** area, change **Fresnel** to **Dielectric** and **IOR** to **1.52**. Change **Layer 1**'s strength to **12**.

6. Create another **Phong** layer and set its blending mode to **Add**. Change **Attenuation** to **Average**, **Roughness** to **30**, **Reflection Strength** to **18**, and **Specular Strength** to **20**. In the **Layer Fresnel** area, change **Fresnel** to **Dielectric** and **IOR** to **2**. Change **Layer 1**'s strength to **10**. Change **Layer 2**'s strength to **13**. Render the scene [see Fig. E1].

## Exercise 15: Creating Wood Material

In this exercise, we will create wood material [see Fig. E1]. The following table summarizes the exercise:

| Table E15 | |
|---|---|
| Difficulty level | Intermediate |
| Estimated time to complete | 30 Minutes |
| Topics | • Getting Started<br>• Creating the Material |
| Resources folder | **unit-ct3** |
| Units | **Centimeters** |
| Start file | **shader-ball.c4d** |
| Final file | **wood-finish.c4d** |

### Getting Started

Start Cinema 4D and open the **shader-ball.c4d** file.

### Creating the Material

Follow these steps:

1.  Double-click in the **Material Manager** to create a new material. Rename the material as **matWood**. Apply the material to the **Geo2** and **Geo3** objects in the **Object Manager**. In **Basic** tab, clear the **Color** check box.

2.  In the **Reflectance** tab, change **Type** to **GGX** and **Attenuation** to **Average**. Expand the **Roughness** area and then click the **Texture > Triangle** button and then choose **Layer** from the popup menu.

3.  In the **Layer** shader settings, click **Image** and then load the **scratch - 2.jpg**. Click **Shader** and then choose **Fresnel** from the popup menu. Change mode to **Multiply** and then change strength to **31**.

4.  In the **Reflectance** tab, change **Roughness** to **20**, **Reflection Strength** to **100**, and **Specular Strength** to **5**. In the **Layer Color** area, change **Brightness** to **59**.

5.  In **Basic** tab, select the **Color** check box. In the **Color** tab, click the **Texture > Triangle** button and then load the **woodCabinetDiff.png** using the **Load Image** option.

6.  In the **Reflectance** tab, expand the **Bump Strength** area and then change **Mode** to **Custom Normal Map**. Click the **Custom Texture > Triangle** button and then choose **Effects > Normalizer** from the popup menu. In the **Normalizer** shader settings, click **Texture > Triangle** button and then load the

**woodCabinetBump.png** using the **Load Image** option. In the **Normalizer** tab, change **Strength** to **250**.

7. In the **Reflectance** tab, change **Bump Strength** to **90**. In the **Layer Color** area, click the **Texture > Triangle** button and then choose **Layer** from the popup menu. In the **Layer** shader settings, click **Image** and then load the **woodCabinetGloss.png**. Click **Shader** and then choose **Fresnel** from the popup menu. Change blending mode to **Lighten** and strength to **29**. In the **Reflectance** tab > **Layer Fresnel** area, change **Fresnel** to **Dielectric** and **IOR** to **1.5**. Render the scene [see Fig. E1].

## Quiz

**Fill in the Blanks**
Fill in the blanks in each of the following statements:

1. The _____ and _____ parameters of the **Noise** shader control the clipping value of the noise.

2. The _____ cloth mode in Cinema 4D allows you to simulate characteristic anisotropic specular highlights/reflections that are found on the real-world cloth objects.

3. The _____ shader is used to adjust hue, brightness, contrast, saturation, gamma, and gradient curves of a bitmap or another shader.

4. Unlike the **Bump** channel, the _____ channel is used to actually deform the object.

5. In the **Displacement** channel, the _____ option allows you to render detailed render without actually subdividing the geometry.

6. In computer graphics, there are two common representations of the alpha channel in an image: _____ and _____.

7. The _____ channel is used to add glow to the pixels.

8. The _____ shader allows you to combine two textures using one of the blending modes.

**True or False**
State whether each of the following is true or false:

1. In the **Noise** shader, values less than the value specified for the **Low Clip** parameter will clipped to **100**.

2. In the **Reflectance** channel, the diffuse and warp settings are used to specify separate diffuse and specular colors for the warp and weft threads.

3. To get good results out of the cloth reflectance model, you need to make sure that the specular color should be always brighter than the diffuse color so that both colors fall in same tone.

4. In the **Reflectance** channel, when you select the **Round Geometry** check box, a special algorithm similar to that of the **Subdivision Surface** object is used to ensure that the object is rounded before the sub-polygon displacement is calculated.

5. The sub-polygon displacement can calculate normal **Phong** shading.

6. In order to animate noise, you need to specify a value for the **Animation Speed** parameter in the **Noise** settings.

**Summary**
This unit covered the following topics:

- Various Materials
- Reflectance Model

- Node-based material system
- **Node Editor**

# Unit CT4 - Node-Based Materials

The node-based material system introduced in Cinema 4D R20 is a material system that you can use as a robust alternative for creating materials for the **Standard** and **Physical** material systems. This new system is seamlessly integrated into the old material system and can be used to define complex material properties that cannot be created using old material systems. When you use the new system, you will notice that many material channels no longer exist because nodes are based on a physically-correct concept. This system uses physically-based BSDF [**Bidirectional Scattering Distribution Function**] shading, which – comparable with a physical material – calculates diffuse shading using dispersed reflections.

 *Note: BSDF*
*The acronym **BSDF** stands for **Bidirectional Scattering Distribution Function** – a method that emulates the physically correct transmission and reflection behavior of surfaces, i.e., reflections and transparencies are physically accurate and rendered realistically.*

When using the node-based material system, keep the following in the mind:

- The **ProRender** renderer does not support the node-based system.
- The old material system cannot be combined with the node-based system. However, some of the important shaders such as **Fresnel, Gradient, Noise,** and so on are available.
- When applying materials to the **Sky, Floor, Background,** and **Foreground** objects, make sure that you use luminous properties. If you use only a diffuse property, these objects will render black.
- If you use an additional environment lighting using the **Environment** object, it has no effect on node-based materials.
- Physically-based Subsurface Scattering is not supported.
- Using **Global Illumination** as a render effect has no effect on node-based materials because they have no **Color** channel by default.

# Node Editor

The **Node Editor** is where material nodes are created and edited. You can open the **Node Editor** in one of the following ways:

- Double-clicking on a material node in the **Material Manager**.
- RMB clicking on the material node and then choosing **Node Editor** from the context menu. You can also press **Shift+Alt+F2** to execute this command.
- In the **Basic** tab of the **Attribute Manager**, click on the **Node Editor** button, see Fig. 1.
- In the **Material Editor**, click the **Node Editor** button, see Fig. 2.

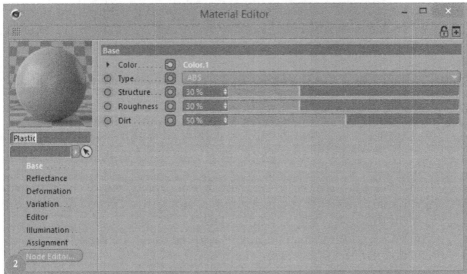

Fig. 3 shows the **Node Editor**'s elements. Table 1 summarizes these elements:

| No. | Name |
|-----|------|
| **Table 1: Node Editor** elements |
| **No.** | **Name** |
| 1 | Material History |
| 2 | Material or group name |
| 3 | Input and output group areas for outgoing ports |
| 4 | **Attribute Manager** |
| 5 | Connector icon |
| 6 | Navigator |
| 7 | **Node Editor** view |
| 8 | Info area |
| 9 | Asset list |
| 10 | Node list |
| 11 | Common commands as icons |
| 12 | Connection |

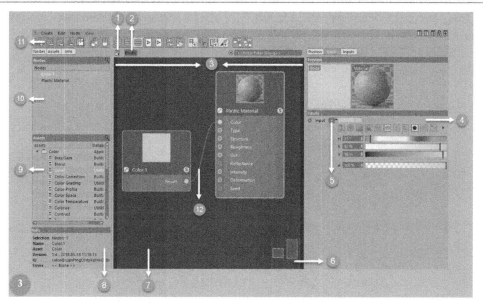

## Navigating Node Editor

To move in the **Node Editor**, press one of the following combinations and then drag the mouse: **MMB, 1+LMB,** or **Alt+MMB**. To zoom, press one of the following combinations and then drag the mouse: **Alt+RMB** or **2+RMB**. To frame all or selected nodes, press **H** or **S**.

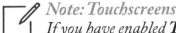

*Note: Touchscreens*
*If you have enabled **Touchscreen** in the **Preferences** window, you can move vertically by scrolling the mouse wheel. To move horizontally, use **Shift**+mouse wheel. Use **Ctrl**+mouse wheel for zooming in or out.*

## Creating Nodes

To create a node, drag the node from the **Asset** list to the **Node Editor** view; a new node with no connection will be created. You can also drag the node onto the input port of an existing node; ports will be connected directly. If you drag to a connection, the node will be added to the connection if it is a compatible port. Alternatively, you can choose **Edit > Nodes Commander** from the **Node Editor** menubar to open the **Nodes Commander** window and then drag nodes from there. The **C** hotkey can be used to invoke the **Nodes Commander** window. For both methods, if you drag a node onto an input port and then release the mouse button, a small menu will open, if multiple output ports are available. Then, you can select the output port of the first node to be connected.

You can also connect nodes using the connector ▣ icon. This connector is available for just about every input type in the **Attribute Manager**. Click on the connector to display a context menu, select the **Connect Node** option to display a list of all nodes and then select the desired node [see Fig. 4]. The context menu is also displayed when you RMB click on the connector. When you select a node, the node will be created and simultaneously connected with the input.

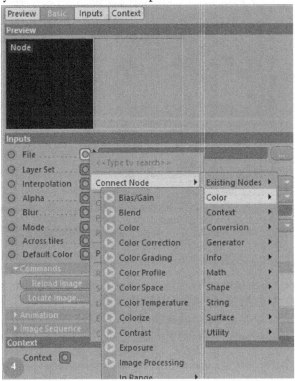

*Tip: Using bitmaps*
You can drag bitmaps from outside of Cinema 4D directly onto the **Node Editor** view or onto ports, **Image** nodes with a correspondingly linked bitmap will be created.

*Note: Connections*
When you make connections, Cinema 4D gives you clue whether connection is possible or not. If you hover over the port to which you want to connect, the potential connection will be either bright (possible) or dark (not possible).

*Caution: Connections*
Note that not all output ports can be connected with all input ports.

## Moving Nodes

You can move nodes by clicking and then dragging them. If you have selected multiple nodes, you can move them as whole. If you move the selection to any edges of the **Node Editor** view, the view will start to scroll correspondingly.

## Connecting Nodes

In order to let the data flow from one node to another, they must be connected. For this to work, outputs [available on the right side of the node] of one node should be connected to inputs [available on the left side of the node] of another node, see Fig. 5. To connect, click once on the output node and once on the input node (or vice-versa).

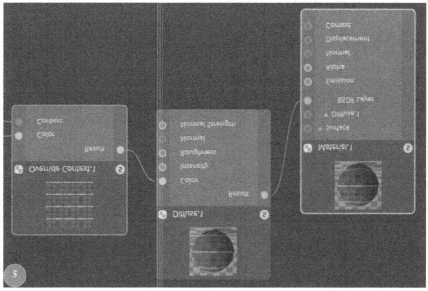

You can also click and drag from the first port to the second and then release the mouse button. You can also drop the connection onto the middle of a node; a list with all input and output ports will be displayed from which you can make a selection. If you drop the connection on the empty area of the **Node Editor** view, input/output ports for groups can be created [see Fig. 6].

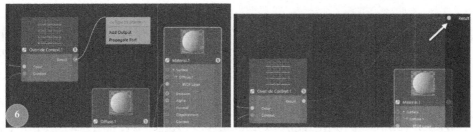

 *Tip: Connection mode*
*When you click on the first port to be connected, you are in the connection mode. You can disable this mode by pressing **Esc**.*

## Selecting/Deleting Nodes

You can select nodes by clicking on them or by dragging a rectangle around them. You can use the **Shift** and **Ctrl** keys to add and remove nodes from the selection, respectively. Other editing commands are available in the **Edit** menu of the **Node Editor** menubar. To delete selected nodes, press **Backspace** or **Del**.

## Node Editor Title

At the top of the **Node Editor** view you will find the **Node Editor** title [see Fig. 7]. You will find the following items from left to right:

- **Material History:** Click on this icon to open a list of the most recently opened node materials. Select a material from the list to display it in the **Node Editor**.
- **Material or Group Name:** Next to the **Material History** icon you will find the name of the material. If nested groups are available, their hierarchy will be displayed here. Clicking on a group higher up in the hierarchy will let you jump to that group. The **Edit Asset** mode will also be displayed here, which can be exited by choosing the **Quit Edit Asset Mode** option from the **Create** menu of the **Node Editor** menubar.
- **Filter:** You can type a series of characters in this field that affects the nodes displayed. Nodes whose names contain these characters will be displayed more prominently by fading all other nodes.

## Navigator

You will find navigator at the bottom-right corner of the **Node Editor** view. It is especially useful when you are working on a complex node network. It allows you to quickly navigate in the **Node Editor** view. The light gray triangle shows the visible part of the **Node Editor** view. You can move this section by clicking and dragging in the view.

The following nodes have a special display in the **Navigator** [see Fig. 8]:

- If you have specified a custom color for a nodes from the **Attribute Manager >
  Basic** tab, these colored nodes will be displayed in identical colors [see arrow
  marked as 1 in Fig. 8].
- Selected nodes also appear selected in the **Navigator** [see arrow marked as
  2 in Fig. 8].
- Group nodes will be displayed with a diagonal element [see arrow marked
  as 3 in Fig. 8].

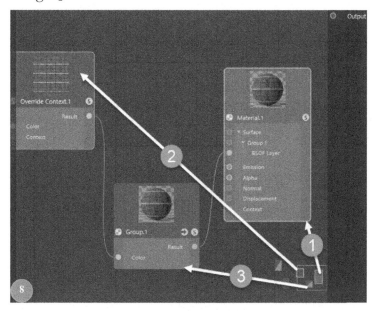

## Getting Around in the Node Editor

Before we dive deep into the **Node Editor**, let's first learn some of the basics of the
working with the **Node Editor**. Follow these steps:

1. Create a new scene in Cinema 4D and then
   choose **Create > New Node Material** from
   the **Material Manager** menubar [see
   Fig. 9]; a new node material with the name
   **Node** is created in the **Material Manager**.
   Alternatively, you can press **Ctrl+Alt+N**.
   If you select the node in the **Material
   Manager**, its parameters will be displayed
   in the **Attribute Manager** [see Fig. 10].

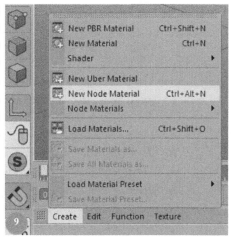

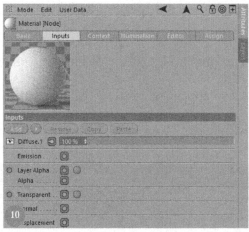

2. Double-click on the **Node** material swatch in the **Material Manager** or press **Shift+Alt+F2**. This action opens the **Node Editor** with two nodes displayed in the **Node Editor** view: **Diffuse.1** and **Material.1** [see Fig. 11]. Also, notice in Fig. 11 that parameters shown in Fig. 10 are also available in the **Node Editor**'s **Attribute Manager**. Close the **Node Editor**.

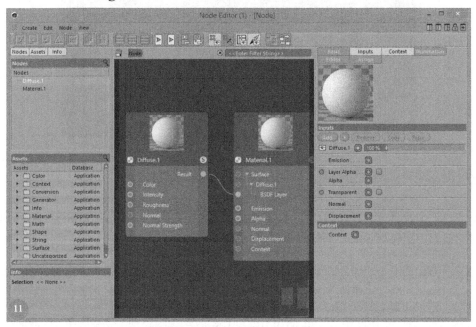

3. Choose **Create > New Uber Material** from the **Material Manager** menubar; a new material with the name **Uber** will be created in the **Material Manager**.

 *What is Uber material?*
*The **Uber** material is a node-based asset material which is controlled by nodes. The configuration of these nodes therefore often be done via the **Attribute Manager** or even via the **Material Editor** without having to open the **Node Editor**. The **Uber** material is very well suited for getting familiar with the working of node materials. Other than with the standard or physical materials, each new **Material Node** can be combined with the **Uber** material.*

4. Double-click on the **Uber** node in the **Material Manager**; the **Material Editor** will be displayed [see Fig. 12]. The **Uber** material can be edited in the **Node Editor** but you can also easily edit the material in the **Material Editor**.

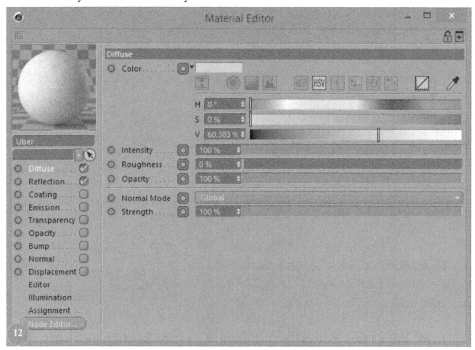

5. Make sure the **Diffuse** channel is selected and then in the right pane, click the **Color** connector and then choose **Connect Node > Generator > Checkerboard** from the popup menu [see Fig. 13]; the **Checkerboard.1** node is connected to the **Color** parameter [see Fig. 14]. Click on **Checkerboard.1** to open the **Checkerboard** settings [see Fig.15].

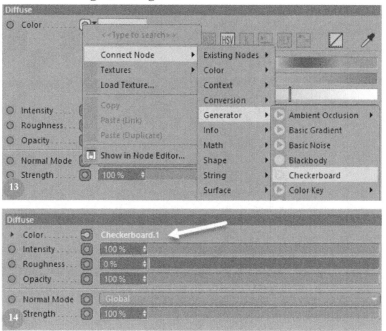

6. Select the **Diffuse** channel; notice the shape of the connector icon has changed [refer to Fig. 16]. Click on the icon; a popup menu will be displayed [see Fig. 16]. Now, you can use the options available in the menu to farther edit the **Color** channel. For example, to replace the node, choose the **Replace Node** option, for deleting the node, choose the **Remove** option, and so on.

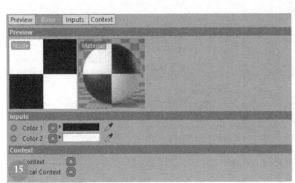

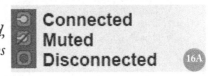

*Note: Shape of the connector icon*
*A connector icon can have three states: connected, muted, and disconnected. Fig. 16A shows these states.*

7. Click on the **Node Editor** button located at the bottom-left corner of the **Material Editor** to display the **Node Editor** [see Fig. 17]. Notice that the **Uber Material.1** and **Checkerboard.1** nodes are connected and displayed in the **Node Editor** view. Close the **Node Editor** followed by the **Material Editor**.

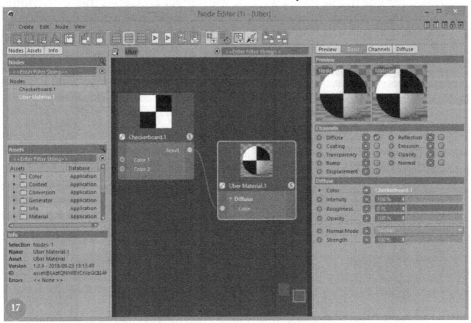

8. Choose **Create > Node Materials** from the **Material Manager** menubar to display a list of materials available [see Fig. 18]. Select **Plastic** from the list to create a plastic material.

9. Close the current scene and start a new scene.

10. Create a new node material by pressing **Ctrl+Alt+N**. Double-click on the node in the **Material Manager** to open the **Node Editor**. Click on the empty area of the **Node Editor** view to deselect all node. You can also choose **Edit > Deselect All** from the menubar or press **Ctrl+Shift+A**. All nodes can be selected using the **Ctrl+A** hotkeys.

11. Select **Material.1** in the **Node** list; the **Material.1** node is highlighted with orange border in the **Node Editor** view. Double-click on a node name in the **Node** list to enable an edit field that you can use to rename the node.

 *Tip: Renaming nodes*
*You can also rename a node by first double-clicking on the name of node in the **Node Editor** view and then typing a new name.*

12. **Alt+RMB** drag to zoom in or out in the view. Now, **MMB** drag to pan the view and move the nodes outside the visible **Node Editor** view. Select **Diffuse.1** in the **Nodes** list and then press **S** to frame the node at the center of the **Node Editor** view. Press **H** to frame both nodes.

13. Click on the **Material.1** node in the **Node Editor** view; the information about the node is displayed in the **Info** area [see Fig. 19]. Select the **Color** port of the **Diffuse.1** node in the view; its information will be displayed in the **Info** area [see Fig. 20].

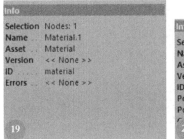

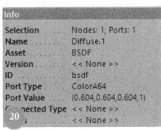

*Note: The Info area*

*The information pertaining to nodes, connections, and ports is displayed in the **Info** area.*

*For nodes:*

**Selection:** *The number and type of selected elements. For example, **Nodes: 1**, and **Ports: 2**.*
**Name:** *The name of the node as defined in the **Basic** tab.*
**Asset:** *The non-modifiable asset name as it is defined internally.*
**Version:** *The version of the asset, including date and time.*
**ID:** *A unique ID for internal use.*
**Errors:** *All errors are displayed here.*

*Additional information for connections:*

**Selection:** *The number of selected connections.*
**Port Type:** *The input data type that a port accepts or the data type it itself puts out.*
**Connected Type:** *The data type that flows through the connection.*

*Additional information for ports:*

**Port Value:** *If a port has no connection, the value defined in the **Attribute Manager** will be displayed here.*

14. Click on the magnifying icon in the **Assets** list to enable a search field. Type **che** in the field to filter the node whose names contain the series of character **che** [see Fig. 21]. Drag **Checkerboard** from **Assets** list to view. Now, click drag the **Result** port of the **Checkerboard.1** node; a wire appears. Now, drop the wire on the **Color** port of the **Diffuse.1** node to make a connection [see Fig. 22].

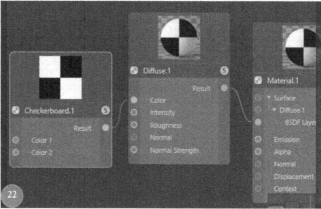

*Tip: Assets list*
*You can also open the floating **Assets** list at the location of the mouse pointer by pressing **C**. If you press the **Esc** key or click outside of the **Commander** window, it will close. Press the **Tab** key to switch from the **Assets** list to the filter field. Press **Shift + Tab** to switch from filter field to list.*

15. To delete the connection, drag and drop the wire on the empty area of the view. You can also delete the connection by first clicking on it and then pressing the **Delete** key. Another way to delete a connection is by double-clicking on the wire. Delete the connection between the **Checkerboard.1** and **Diffuse.1** nodes.

16. Click drag the **Result** port of the **Checkerboard.1** node and drop in the middle of the **Diffuse.1** node; a popup menu appears. Select **Color** from the menu to make the connection.

17. Delete the **Checkerboard.1** node from the view. Now, drag **Checkerboard** from the **Assets** list and drop it on the **Color** port of the **Diffuse.1** node to make a connection. Delete the **Checkerboard.1** node from the view.

18. **RMB** click on the **Color** port of the **Diffuse.1** node and then choose **Connect Node > Generator > Checkerboard** to make a connection.

*Tip: Connector icon*
*You can also connect nodes using the **Node Editor**'s **Attribute Manager**. Select the node in the view to display its attributes in the **Attribute Manager** and then use the connector icon of a parameter to connect a node to it.*

19. Create a **Cube** in the viewport and then assign the **Node** material from the **Material Manager** to the cube [see Fig. 23].

20. In the **Node Editor**, drag **Color > Color** from the **Assets** list to the **Color 1** port of the **Checkerboard.1** port. In the **Attribute Manager** change **Color** to red. Fig. 24 shows the result in the viewport.

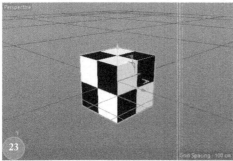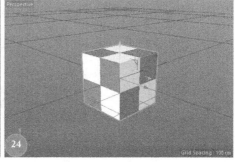

21. In the view, click on the **Set Solo Node/Port** icon of the **Color.1** node to activate the solo mode for the **Color.1** node. The icon is marked 2 in Fig. 25. Notice in viewport only red color is displayed on the cube [see Fig. 26]. Click on the icon again to clear the solo mode.

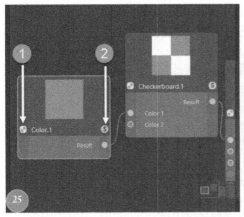

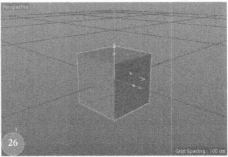

 *Tip: Solo mode and other options*
*You can also access the solo and other commands from the **Node** menu of the*
***Node Editor** menubar. These commands are also available in the contextual*
*menu which is displayed when you RMB click on a node in the view.*

22. Click on the **Preview** icon [marked with number 1 in Fig. 25] to hide the preview
of the **Color.1** node. Click again to show the preview. Select the **Color.1** node
in the view and then in the **Basic** tab of editor's **Attribute Manager,** select the
**Custom Node Color** check box and then change **Node Color** to yellow; the
color is displayed in the preview area of the node as well as in the **Navigator**
[see Fig. 27].

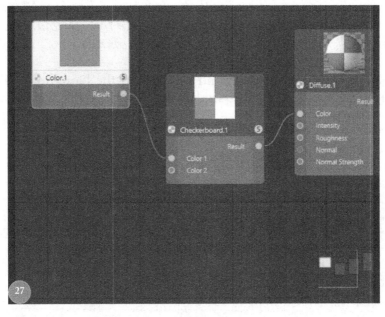

*Note: Data types and color*

*Notice in Fig. 27, the **Color** and **Normal** ports of the **Diffuse.1** node are displayed in yellow and violet color, respectively. These colors can be used to identify the data type associated with the ports:*

*Dark gray: Represents a container consists of various data types in a complex setting.*
*Light gray: Represents a number integer or float value.*
*Yellow: Represents color values [RGB vectors] or textures.*
*Blue: Represents Boole data type, the matrices are also represented by this color.*
*Violet: Represents vectors.*
*Green: Reserved for **BSDF** layers, which can be used to define physical shading and reflectance information.*

23. Select the **Color.1** node in the view and then choose **Edit > Duplicate** from the editor's menubar to create a copy of the node with the name **Color.2**. Change the **Color** parameter to green in the **Attribute Manger** and then connect **Color.2 > Result** to **Checkerboard.1 > Color.2**.

24. Select the **Color.1** and **Color.2** nodes by drawing a rectangle around them and then choose **Create > Group Nodes** from the menubar or press **Alt+G**, See Fig. 28. Double-click on group's name and then type the new name as **color-group**. Similarly, rename the **Result** ports of the group as **Red** and **Green**, respectively [see Fig. 29].

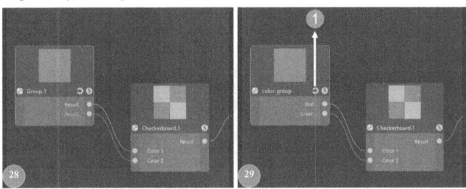

25. Click on the icon marked with the number 1 in Fig. 29 to expand the group [see Fig. 30].

📝
*Note: Input and Output Group Areas*

*Notice in Fig. 30, each side of the view you will see a dark edge. Notice the **Red** and **Green** ports are located on the right dark edge. You can connect ports with these areas by dropping a new connection into an empty region of the area. As a result, an outward connection is created. This makes little sense for individual nodes but if you combine different groups with one another, you can use this method to create ports for groups.*

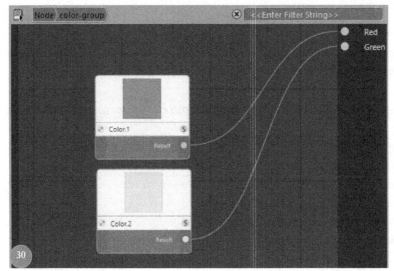

26. Click on the **Node** icon [see Fig. 31] in the **Node Editor** tile to switch back to the material nodes. Select the **color-group** node and then choose **Create > Ungroup Nodes** from the editor's menubar or press **Shift+G** to ungroup the nodes.

27. Drag the **Assets** list > **Color** > **Color Correction** node to the wire connecting the **Color.1** and **Checkerboard.1** nodes and drop when the solid square icon is displayed with the mouse pointer; the **Color Correction.1** node appears in between the **Color.1** and **Checkerboard.1** nodes [see Fig. 32].

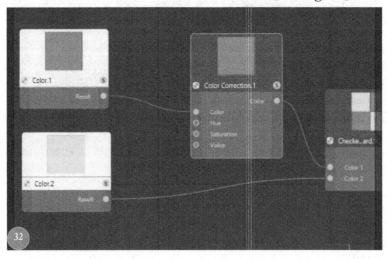

28. In the **Attribute Manager > Inputs** tab, change **Hue** to **220**. Drag the **Assets** list > **Color** > **Color Space** node to the wire connecting the **Color Correction.1** and **Checkerboard.1** nodes and drop when the solid square icon is displayed

with the mouse pointer; the **RGB > RGB.1** node appears in between the **Color Correction.1** and **Checkerboard.1** nodes. In the **Attribute Manager** > Inputs tab, change **Output Color Space** to **HSV**.

29. Select the **Color Correction.1** and **RGB > HSV.1** nodes and then press **Alt+G** to group nodes. Now, you if expand the node, you will notice that ports are now displayed in each dark edge in the view [see Fig. 33].

30. Switch back to the **Node** view and then ungroup the group we created in the last group by pressing **Shift+G**.

31. In the **Node Editor** tile, enter **color** in the **<<Enter Filter String>>** field; nodes whose names contain color will be displayed more prominently by fading all other nodes [see Fig. 34]. Click on the ⊗ icon to clear the filter.

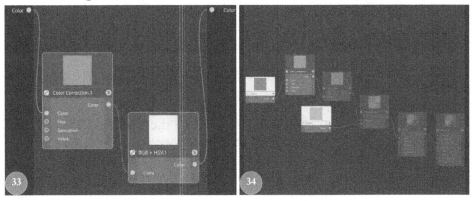

32. Click on the first icon ▥ located on the top-right corner of the **Node Editor** to hide the left column from the **Node Editor**. Click again to restore the left column that contains the **Node** and **Asset** lists as well as the **Info** area.

 *Note: Icons at the top-right*
*There are five icons on the top-right corner of the **Node Editor**, from left to right:*

> *__Left Column:__ See Step 32.*
> *__Right Column:__ Toggles the visibility of the right column.*
> *__Two Column View:__ Use this icon to display or hide the two-column view. The **Node** and **Asset** lists, the **Info** area, and the **Attribute Manager** will be placed on the right.*
> *__Lock Node view:__ The view shows the **Node Material** currently selected in the **Material Manager**. Use this icon if you want to lock the node view to the currently selected material in the **Material Manager**.*
> *__New Node Manager:__ Use this icon to open a new **Node Editor**. This is helpful if you want to see node network of two different materials or two different parts of the same material.*

33. Select the **Checkerboard.1** and **Diffuse.1** nodes and then **RMB** to open the context menu. Now, select the **Horizontal Layout** from the menu; the input and output ports do lie next to each other [see Fig. 35]. Similarly, select the **Vertical Layout** to change the arrangement of ports on the nodes [see Fig. 36].

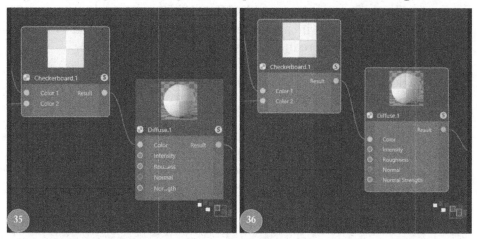

34. Double-click on a node to hide all ports of the node. Double-click again to show all ports.

35. Select all nodes except the **Material.1** node and then press **Alt+G** to group the nodes. Now, expand the group. Select the **Intensity** and **Roughness** ports of the **Diffuse.1** node and then choose **Create > Propagate Port** from the menubar to create two propagate ports [see Fig. 37]. These ports are denoted by a filled square icon. You can also drag ports to the left dark edge of the view to create propagated ports.

36. Move one level up to the group node and notice the propagated nodes appear on the group node [see Fig. 38].

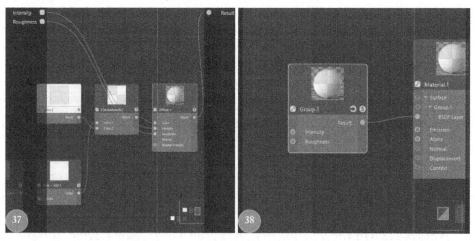

The **Node Editor** menubar consists of four menus: **Create**, **Edit**, **Node**, and **View**. The commonly used commands are also available from the toolbar [located below menubar, see Fig. 39] and contextual menu [see Fig. 40].

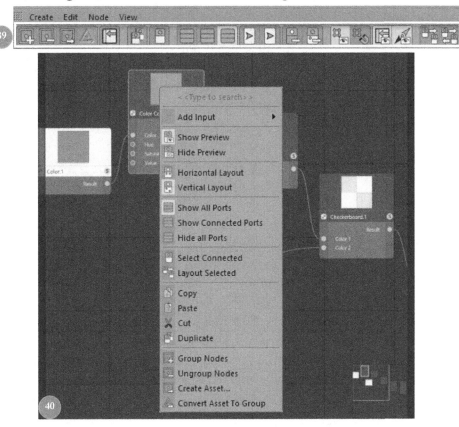

The following table summarizes the menus:

| Table 1: Node Editor menus | | |
|---|---|---|
| **Name** | **Hotkey** | **Description** |
| | Create menu | |
| New Node Material | Ctrl+ Alt+N | Creates a new node material. |
| Create Empty Group | | Creates an empty group for the current material. Click on the arrow icon located on the node to expand the node. |
| Group Nodes | **Alt+G** | Groups selected nodes. The groups can be converted and passed on as assets. |
| Ungroup Nodes | **Shift+G** | Ungroups grouped node and deletes the group node, the connections are maintained. |

| Table 1: Node Editor menus | | |
|---|---|---|
| **Name** | **Hotkey** | **Description** |
| Create In Port | | Creates a new input port. This is useful for nodes within the groups. |
| Create Out Port | | Creates a new output port. |
| Propagate Port | | Use this command to create parameter input ports for all selected ports. |
| Create Asset | | Opens the **Save Asset** dialog box that you can use to save the asset. Assets are generally created from group nodes. |
| Convert Asset to Group | | As discussed, asset nodes are created from groups. This command can be used to convert assets nodes back to groups. |
| Save new Version | | Saves a new version of the asset. |
| Save as new asset (Copy) | | Saves a new copy of the asset without implementing versioning. |
| Quit Edit Asset Mode | | When you open an asset using the **Edit Asset** command, you invoke the **Edit Asset** mode. Use this command to exit the mode. |
| | **Edit** menu | |
| Undo | Ctrl+Z | Use these commands to undo/redo changes. Contrary to the XPresso Editor, moving or expanding nodes is not affected by these commands. |
| Redo | Ctr+Y | |
| Cut | Ctrl+X | Use these commands for clipboard functions. |
| Copy | Ctrl+C | |
| Paste | Ctrl+V | |
| Duplicate | | This command duplicates the selected nodes, excluding existing connections. |
| Delete | BS, Del | Deletes selected nodes. |
| Select All | Ctrl+A | Selects all nodes. |
| Deselect All | Ctrl+Shift+A | Deselects all nodes. |
| Select Connected | U-W | Selects all nodes connected to the selected node. |
| Nodes Commander | C | This command works if the **Node Editor** is active. It allows to access a floating list of assets. |

| Table 1: Node Editor menus | | |
|---|---|---|
| **Name** | **Hotkey** | **Description** |
| | Node menu | |
| Show Preview  Hide Preview | | These commands are used to show or hide the node's preview. You can control default behavior from the **Preferences** window > **Material** category > **Node-based Materials** area. |
| Horizontal Layout | | When you select this option, the input and output nodes lie next to each other. |
| Vertical Layout | | When you select this option, the input and output nodes do not lie next to each other. |
| Hide all Ports/ Show All Ports | | The **Hide all Ports** option hides the port area of the selected nodes. The **Show all Ports** command will make these ports visible again. |
| Show Connected Ports | | This command allows you to show only ports with connections will be shown for the selected node. All others ports will be hidden. To show all ports, execute the **Show all Ports** command. |
| Set Solo Node/ Port | | This command allows you to solo the output of the selected node. |
| Clear Solo | | Use this command to exit the solo mode. |
| Set as Start Node | | A complex node network can consists of hundreds of nodes. If you want to make minor changes to the network without digging deep into the network, you can make one of the nodes as start node by executing the **Set as Start Node** command. Only this node's inputs will be displayed in the **Attribute Manager**. The start node appears with the green boundary. |
| Clear Start Node | | Use this command to remove the start node state. |
| Open in Material Editor | | Use this command to open the material in the **Material Editor**. |
| Select in Material Manager | | Selects the material's node in the **Material Manager**. |
| Remove Unused Nodes | | Use this command to remove unused nodes [nodes without connections] from the view. |
| Hide Unused Ports | | This command only works if at least one connection exists for each input or output port group |

| Table 1: Node Editor menus | | |
|---|---|---|
| **Name** | **Hotkey** | **Description** |
| | View menu | |
| Frame Selected | S | If nodes lie outside the **Node Editor**'s view, you can use this command to frame the selected nodes. The view will be scaled accordingly to ensure that all nodes are displayed. For the selected nodes, all ports without a connection will be hidden. |
| Frame All | H | Shows all nodes in the **Node Editor**'s view. The view will be scaled accordingly. |
| Center Selected | Alt+S | Shows selected nodes at the center of the view without changing the zoom factor. For multiple selections, the center of the selected nodes will be placed at the view's center. |
| Center All | | Shows all nodes at the center of the view without changing the zoom factor. |
| Zoom In/Out | +/- | Enlarges or reduces the **Node Editor** view. However, using the mouse with the **2** key is faster than using these commands. |
| Zoom 100% | | Sets the zoom to **100%**. |
| Show Grid | | Hides or shows the grid in the **Node Editor** view. However, this command does not affect the snapping. |
| Snap to Grid | Shift+S | Enables or disables the grid snapping. If enabled, node edges will snap to the grid lines. |
| Show Group Wires | | Toggles the visibility of group wires. |
| Bezier Wires | | This option is enabled by default. If you disable it, the connection appear linear in the view. |
| Show Navigator | | Toggles the visibility of the **Navigator**. |
| Show Errors | | If a node produces errors or is fed with invalid data types, a red frame will appear here. Once the frame appear you can look for error messages in the **Node** list or the **Info** area that can provide more information. To hide the frame, disable the **Show Errors** option. |
| Step Up | | This command is particularly useful when working with a group. Use it to move one level up in the hierarchy. |
| Layout Selected | L | Selected or all nodes will be arranged so they are visible in the current view - compact, arranged in order and positioned horizontally or vertically. |
| Layout All | Shift+L | |

# Assets

As discussed earlier, assets are accessed from the **Assets** list in the **Node Editor**. These assets are split in different groups and are discussed next:

## Shape

This group of nodes contains node that depict geometry shapes such as circle or polygon.

## Circle

The **Circle** node is used to create filled circle. The edge of the circle can be softened towards inside or outside. Follow these steps:

1.  Open **assets-start.c4d**. Choose **Create > New Node Material** from the **Material Manager** menubar to create a new node material. Rename the material as **mat-circle**. Apply this material to the **Cube, Geo2,** and **Geo3** objects, respectively.

2.  Double-click on **mat-circle** to open the **Node Editor**. Add a **Circle** node by navigating to **Assets > Shape**. Connect **Circle.1 > Result** to **Diffuse.1 > Color**.

3.  In the **Attribute Manager > Inputs** tab, change **Exterior** to red color and **Fill** to yellow color. Render the scene [see Fig. 41].

 *What just happened?*
*Here, I have defined the background color using the **Exterior** parameter on which the circle should be drawn. The **Fill** parameter defines the fill color for the circular shape. Notice the cube in Fig. 41, the circle is occupying only half of the area of a face because the **Scale** parameter is set to **50**. If you change the **Scale** parameter to **100**, it will occupy the whole face [see Fig. 42]. The **Scale** parameter defines the radius of the circle.*

4.  Change **Outer Softness** and **Inner Softness** to **15** and **35**, respectively to blur the outer edge and color filling, respectively. Render the scene [see Fig. 43]. Change **Outer Softness** and **Inner Softness** to **10** and **0**, respectively.

5. Add a **Basic Gradient** node by navigating to **Assets** > **Generator**. Connect **Basic Gradient.1** > **Result** to **Circle.1** > **Scale**; notice in the **Circle.1** preview that the effect of the **Scale** parameter is maximum where gradient is white. Select **Basic Gradient.1** node and then in the **Attribute Manager** > **Inputs** tab, change the gradient as shown in Fig. 44 and then render the scene [see Fig. 45]. Fig. 46 shows the node network. Also, refer to **circle.c4d**.

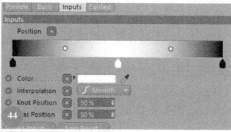

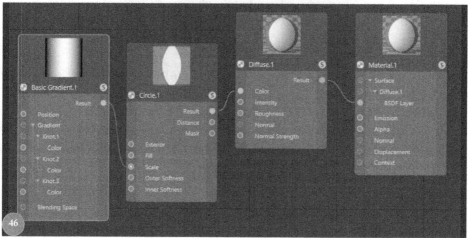

## N-Gon

The **N-Gon** node is used to create a filled N-Gon. The functioning of this node is similar to that of the **Circle** node. However, it has an additional parameter called **Sides** that you can use to define the number of sides for the n-gon. Large values will encroach increasingly on the result produced by the **Circle** Node. See Figs. 47 and 48. Also, refer to **ngon.c4d**.

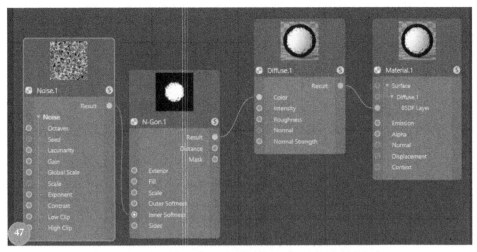

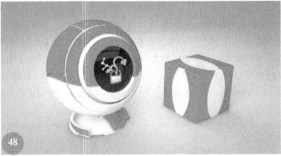

## Spiral

The **Spiral** node allows you to create a spiral shape by fanning out the lines from the center point of the texture tile. The progression of these lines can be curved to create the spiral effect. You can define the number of arms that will be filled with the **Fill** color using the **Arms** parameter. The **Scale** parameter controls the number of spiral arms. If **Scale** set to **0**, curvature will be created and the arms will run straight from the center outward, negative values invert the direction of the spiral. Follow these steps:

1. Open **assets-start.c4d**. Choose **Create > New Node Material** from the **Material Manager** menubar to create a new node material. Rename the material as **mat-spiral**. Apply this material to the **Cube, Geo2**, and **Geo3** objects, respectively.

2. Double-click on **mat-spiral** to open the **Node Editor**. Add a **Spiral** node by navigating to **Assets > Shape**. Connect **Spiral.1 > Result** to **Diffuse.1 > Color**.

3. In the **Attribute Manager > Inputs** tab, change **Scale** to **120**, and **Arms** to **3**. Render the scene [see Fig. 49].

→ *What next?*
   *Now, let's randomize the arms using the **Noise** node.*

4. Add a **Noise** node by navigating to **Assets > Generator**. Connect **Nosie.1 > Result** to **Spiral.1 > Arms**. Render the scene [see Fig. 50].

49 50

**What just happened?**

*Notice in Fig. 50, instead of getting random arms, we have got the circular spiral. The reason for this is that the **Noise** node is outputting a value between **0** [min value] and **1** [max value]. We need to find a way to remap this value to min/max **Arms** value. To remap the values and break the uniformity in the arms, let's use the **Range Mapper** node.*

5. Navigate to **Assets > Math > Range Mapper** and then drag **Range Mapper** onto the wire connecting the **Noise.1** and **Spiral.1** nodes to insert the **Range Mapper** node between them. Select the **Range Mapper.1** node and then in the **Attribute Manager > Inputs** tab, change **Data Type** to **Float** and **Output Max** to **5**. Render the scene [see Fig. 51]. Fig. 52 shows the node network. Also, refer to **spiral.c4d**.

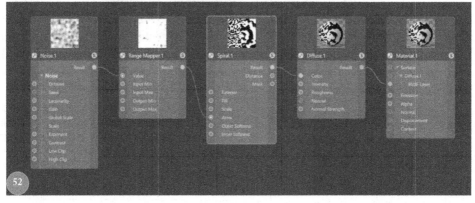

## Star

The **Star** node is used to create star-shaped structures with a variable number of spikes whose length can be defined. The **Spikes** parameter controls the number of spikes. The **Cutout** parameter can be used to define the distance from the center of the star to the tips of the spikes. The larger the value you specify, the wider the spikes will be. Fig. 53 shows the result when the node network shown in Fig. 54 is used.

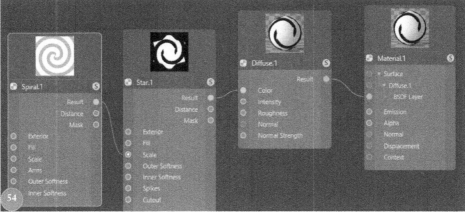

## Color

The nodes in the **Color** group are used to modify input color values, adjust brightness, contrast, and gamma curves. The nodes in this category are discussed next:

## Exposure

The **Exposure** node is used to adjust the brightness of the input data and compress dark or light values. Keep in mind that this node can output a brightness value in excess of **100%**. The **Exposure** parameter is used to darkens or brightens the input. The **Offset** parameter adds to the **Exposure** value by adding the given offset value. The **Gamma** parameter can be used to modify gamma curve to adjust the brightness of primarily mid-range colors.

The parameters in the **Mask** tab are used to restrict the effect of the node to a specific color portion(s). Color portions that you can affect are **Red, Green, Blue**, and **Alpha**. The **Blend** parameter can be used to steplessly blend between the input color and the color value modified by the **Exposure** node. Fig. 55 shows the result when no exposure was applied. Fig. 56 shows the result with the **Exposure** effect. Refer to Fig. 57 and **exposure.c4d**.

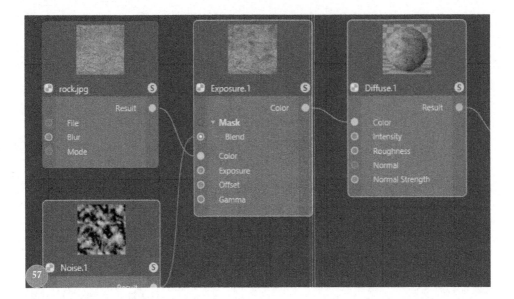

## Bias/Gain

The **Bias/Gain** node is used to re-calculate color values relative to the brightness of the colors. In other words, this node brightens or darkens specific colors whose brightness lies in the middle range or extreme range. This node breaks down the input colors into red, green, and blue parts and then set the color intensity in relation to a value range between **0%** and **100%**. As a result, a re-calculation of the RGB values will take place.

The **Bias** parameter reduces [value < **0.5**] the color portions that have a mid-range brightness. Values greater than **0.5** brightens the color portions with mid-range intensity. A value of **0.5** will cause no change in the colors. Like **Bias**, the **Gain** parameter will also brighten the three color portions but mid-range brightness will be less affected. Refer to Fig. 58 and **bias-gain.c4d**.

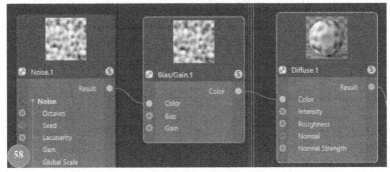

## Color Grading

The **Color Grading** node allows you a wide variety of functions that you can use for color correction and adjusting saturation and coloring of the textures. You can adjust hue, color, brightness, exposure, and so on using this node. Refer to Fig. 59 and **color-grading.c4d**.

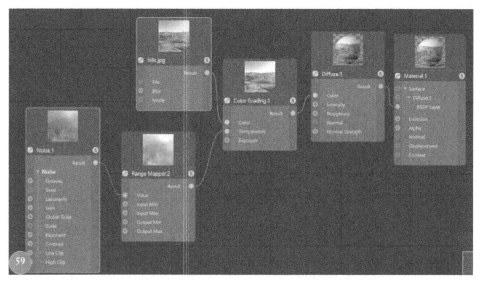

## Layer

The **Layer** node mostly resembles to the **Layer** shader of the standard material system. You can use this node to layer and mix any number of layers. The alpha portion of the layers is also considered when you use this node. Refer to Fig. 60 and **layer.c4d**.

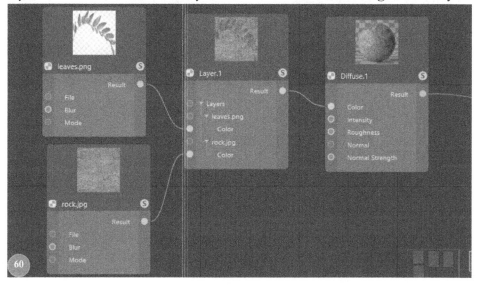

## Shuffle

The **Shuffle** node allows you to rearrange the red, green, blue and alpha components of the input color. You can use it to switch the **Color** and **Alpha** channels with one another. Refer to Fig. 61 and **shuffle.c4d**.

## Shuffle Combine

The **Shuffle Combine** node rearranges the red, green, blue and alpha components from two color inputs into a single color. Refer to Fig. 62 and **shuffle-combine.c4d**.

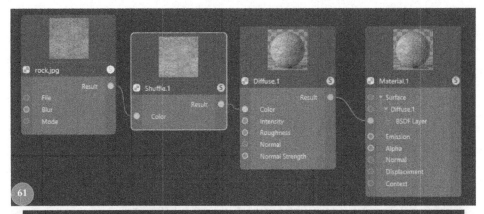

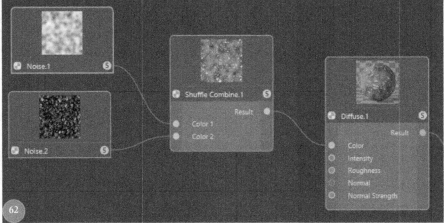

## Color

The **Color** node is used to select a color value or alpha portion.

## Invert Color

The **Invert Color** node is used to invert the color values of the input.

## Color Correction

The **Color Correction** node is used to recolor textures. You can also use it to color grayscale images. This node replaces the input color while maintaining the saturation and brightness. Refer to Fig. 63 and **color-correction.c4d**.

## Color Profile

The **Color Profile** node is used to convert a pre-defined color profile in another profile. By default, Cinema 4D uses the linear workflow to covert brightness values. Refer to Fig. 64 and **color-profile.c4d**.

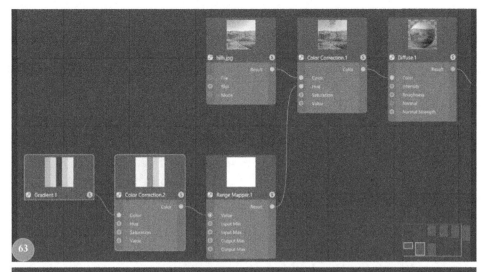

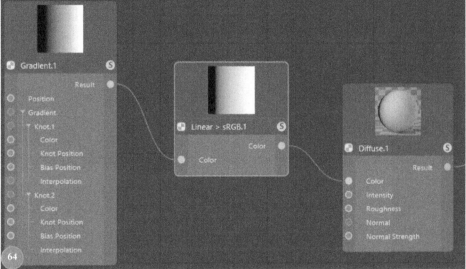

## Color Space

The **Color Space** node is used to convert one color space into another. This node works with the following color spaces: **RGB, HSV, HSL, XYZ,** and **CMY**.

## Color Temperature

The **Color Temperature** node is used to make a color or texture warmer. Normally, the green and violet colors are not included in the typical color range of color temperatures, a separate **Tint** value can be used to add these colors. Refer to **temprature.c4d**.

## Colorize

The **Colorize** node is used to replace colors. For example, you can use this node to transfer the brightness of to a gradient, you can also define the colors of the gradient. The functioning of this node is similar to that of the standard **Colorizer** shader. This node can also be used to convert color images to grayscale. Refer to **colorize.c4d**.

## In Range

The **In Range** node is used to calculate the distances between positions or between color components. You can also use this node to convert a pre-defined color value to vectors or colors. Use the **Value** parameter to define the position values to be checked or a RGB component of a color. The minimum and maximum values can be defined using the **Min** and **Max** parameters, respectively. Refer to **in-range.c4d**.

## Contrast

The **Contrast** node is used to sharpen or soften the transition from light to dark areas. In other words, it defines the difference between the brightest and darkest image colors. If the contrast is increased sharply, details in the lighter and shaded regions can be lost. Refer to **contrast.c4d**.

## Blend

The functionality of the **Blend** node is almost similar to that of the standard **Layer** shader. If you compare this node with the **Layer** node discussed earlier, here you can mix two color layers in conjunction with the optional mask. One other difference is here you can only blend two layers whereas using the **Layer** node you can mix any number of color layers.

## Premultiply

The **Premultiply** node is used to modify the color values according to the opacity of the alpha channel. This node multiplies the brightness in the alpha channel with individual RGB values. If no alpha channel is present in the input, color values will remain unchanged. Refer to **premultiply.c4d**.

## Selective Color

The **Selective Color** node is used to modify the hue, saturation, and brightness of the predefined color ranges. If you have worked with the Photoshop's RAW converter or have edited Lightroom photos, you will already be familiar with this function. Using this node, you can modify the hue, saturation, and luminance for the **Red**, **Orange**, **Yellow**, **Green**, **Aqua**, **Blue**, **Purple**, and **Magenta** color groups. Refer to **selective-color.c4d**.

## Transform

The **Transform** node is used to move, rotate, or scale the input individually. It also allows you to control the repetition of colors/textures within the UV space. Refer to **transform.c4d**.

## Un-premultiply

The **Un-premultiply** node is a reversal of the **Premultiply** node.

## White Balance

Most of the light sources in nature do not emit perfect white light but a slightly colored light. As a result, white surfaces appear slightly colored. Depending on the light source, the emitted color might appear to the human eye as yellow to orange, white, or blue. To ensure the most precise reproduction of surface colors with colored lights, a white balance value can be used to correct coloring of the rendered image. The **White Balance** node allows you to define that value. Refer to **white-balance.c4d**.

## Generator

The nodes in the **Generator** group are used to create patterns and color gradients. They are also used to create special shading effects. These nodes are discussed next:

## Falloff

The **Falloff** node is used to place gradients in front or backside of an object based on the angle of view. The functioning of this node is comparable to a combination of the standard **Falloff** shader with the **Fresnel** effect. Refer to **falloff.c4d**.

## Ambient Occlusion

Ambient Occlusion is a technique used to calculate how exposed a given sample point is to an imaginary ambient light source surrounding the entire scene. This approach is used in one of two ways: for calculating the diffuse lighting coming from an overcast sky and for enhancing contact shadows in interior renderings. This node allows you to calculate the ambient occlusion.

You can also reverse the sampling direction. In such a case, the rays will be traced in the opposite direction of the surface normal. This produces darkening effect on the edges and corners. You can use the **Invert Color** node to approximate the simple subsurface scattering effect.

## Basic Gradient

The **Basic Gradient** node is like the **Gradient** shader of the standard material system. However, this node provides a percentage **Position** value that can be used to output a color sample at any location.

## Basic Noise

The **Basic Noise** node allows you to create various noise patterns as grayscales. This node provides minimal parameters to create noise patterns. The functioning of this node is similar to that of the **Noise** shader in the standard material system. If you need more advanced settings to create noise, you can use the **Noise** node.

## Image

The **Image** node is used to load bitmaps and videos into the **Node Editor** and output their color values.

 *Tip: Bitmaps*
*If you drag bitmaps from **Explorer/Finder** or **Content Browser** to the **Node Editor**, the **Image** node will be created automatically.*

## Color Key

The **Color Key** node is used to filter a color from the input and interpret as mask. This node is especially useful if the input has homogenous colors in the background. Refer to **color-key.c4d**.

## Thin Film

In nature, when light refracts in a very thin layer of surfaces such as oil and soap, it bounces around and light interference occurs. Due to this interference and multiple wavelengths, some wavelengths cancel each other out [destructive interference] and /or boost each other [constructive interference]. Depending on the thickness, index of refraction and viewing angle, the characteristic colors of this effect will appear on the surfaces. The **Thin Film** node is used to simulate this effect.

## Gradient

The functioning of the **Gradient** node is similar to that of the **Gradient** shader in the standard material system. A **Position** value can be used to extract a color sample from any location and output it. Compared to **Basic Gradient** node, it offers additional controls for repetition and distortion.

## Flakes

The **Flakes** node is used to create tiny particles like the ones in the metallic car paint.

## Fresnel Dielectric

The **Fresnel Dielectric** node allows you to create the fresnel effect. The fresnel effect is already part of the BSDF nodes that you can use to simulate conductive and dielectric materials. However, if you want to simulate effect such as color change, depending on the angle of view, you can use the **Fresnel Dielectric** node which outputs a simple grayscale gradient. The **Presets** drop-down list allows you to select refractive index of typical dielectric materials, such as water or glass.

## Fresnel Conductor

Like the **Fresnel Dielectric** node, the **Fresnel Conductor** node generates fresnel effect but for conductor materials. You can use the **Presets** drop-down list to select values for simulating numerous common metals.

## Grid

The **Grid** node allows you to generate lines along the **X**, **Y**, and **Z** axes with individual density and thickness in each direction. It can generate uniformly spaced bands and grids. These elements can be separated from each other using the index numbers.

## Hash

The **Hash** node is used map data of an arbitrary size to data of a fixed size. It generates pseudorandom colors, floats, and vectors based on both the **Seed** and **Salt** values. The value of the **Seed** parameter is used for hash calculations, the resulting values remain identical for identical **Seed** values. The value of the **Salt** parameter farther influences the **Seed** value, you will get a different result even if the **Seed** value itself remain constant. Refer to **hash.c4d**.

## Scratches

The **Scratches** node is used to generate randomly placed, scaled, and rotated scratches. The scratches are created in form of randomly placed black lines on a white background.

## Checkerboard

The **Checkerboard** node is used to create a continuous tile pattern using two input colors.

## Noise

The functioning of the **Noise** node is similar to that of the **Basic Noise** node and the **Noise** shader of the standard material system. However, it offers additional settings for defining the repetition behavior and the orientation within the texture tiles.

## Blackbody

In physics, a black body is an object that absorbs all incident electromagnetic radiation. The **Blackbody** node can be used to assign temperatures of real colors. A color change is defined for certain temperatures, comparable to a piece of metal to which heat is applied. This produces colors that run from red to yellow, white and bright blue.

## Trace Ray

The **Trace Ray** node is used to trace a ray from a user-defined origin. If the ray hits an object surface, this node can output various data such as the distance to the collision point, its position, and its surface normals. In order to output the data, this node requires a point of origin and a direction to generate the ray.

## Voronoi Noise

The **Voronoi Noise** node is used to generate various voronoi patterns similar to the **Noise** node. The appearance of the pattern looks similar to the fragments created by the MoGraph's **Voronoi Fracture** object.

## Random

The **Random** node is similar to the **Hash** node since it also generates random colors, alpha values, and vectors. The random output is based on both the **Seed** and the **Salt** value. In addition, the random values will be recalculated for each modified animation time and for each calculated object surface point. When used as a surface color, each surface point will be assigned a random color that will also change with the temporal data.

## Rock Surface

The **Rock Surface** node is used to easily create common rock structures, including crystalline veins, and oxidizing effects. It combines various noise patterns to create the typical colors of a cliff or of stone.

## Wood

The **Wood** node is used to create a colored wood grain for planks or furniture. You can generate complex color transitions and structures of wood grain using this node.

## Edges Mask

The **Edges Mask** node is used to create masks that you can use to restrict properties to specific regions in the vicinity of edges. This functionality can be used to create a used or weathered look on objects with sharp edges.

## Landscape Mask

The **Landscape Mask** node can be used to convert specific heights and inclines of an object, for example a landscape, to grayscales. The result of this node then can be used to mask these regions. For example, you can use the result of this node to automatically create a change in material from a specific height on a terrain model.

## Metal Finish Surface

The **Metal Finish Surface** node can be used to create typical color gradients and patters for metallic surfaces, including embossing, dirt, and scratches.

## Multi Shader

The **Multi Shader** node is designed to use in conjunction with the MoGraph module of Cinema 4D. You can use this node to recolor clones sequentially based on their UVW coordinates or depending on their original color using the **Multi Shader** node.

## Patterns Generator

The **Patterns Generator** node is used to generate geometric patterns using lines and circles. Various geometric primitives such as triangles, circles, squares, or stars can be scaled, rotated or repeated freely using the **Pattern Generator** node to create complex patterns.

## Info

The nodes in the **Info** group are used to retrieve data from objects, tags, and scenes. These nodes are discussed next:

## Camera

The **Camera** node allows you to access the settings of the active render camera such as its position or settings such as focal length. By default, this node represents the active render camera of the scene. If there is no camera present in the scene, the viewport camera is used.

## Light

The **Light** node can be used to compute diffuse and specular shading based on the light sources in the scene. The result of this node is a fast approximation and not physically-based. This node works independently of the BSDF nodes.

## MoGraph

If you have applied a material on a MoGraph clone, the **MoGraph** node can output the clone colors, their internal index numbers or their UVW coordinates can be output.

## Render Object

The **Render Object** node collects information about the object currently being calculated to which the material was assigned. The position and size of the object can also be ascertained as well as the ID of the polygon at the current sample point.

## Ray

The **Ray** node allows you to query the ray type at the current sample position. You can ascertain if the ray computes a shadow, is used to create a reflection or even if it is used for Global Illumination.

## Scene

This **Scene** node lets you access information about the current scene available such as the render resolution, number of objects, or number of CPUs used.

## Scene Object

The **Scene Object** node can be used to read out specific objects in the scene. You can, for example, retrieve information about the position, scale, or distance of a given object.

## Vertex Color

If an object has a **Vertex Color** tag assigned to it, the **Vertex Color** node can be used to output the color values.

## Vertex Map

If a **Vertex Map** tag is assigned to the object, the **Vertex Map** node can be used read out its color values.

## Time

Whenever you want to make material properties or rendering dependent on the animation phase, the current time, or frame number within the animation can be valuable information. The **Time** node makes this and other information available.

## Conversion

The nodes under the **Conversion** group are used to separate colors and vectors into individual components. You can also use these nodes to combine complex data types from individual values. Let's explore these nodes:

## Compose Vector2D

The **Compose Vector2D** node is used to combine two individual values to create a two-dimensional vector. These vectors can be used to define the position of the local pivot within the texture file, output the width and height of a texture, UV coordinates, or the position of a pixel in a bitmap.

## Compose Vector3D

The **Compose Vector3D** node is used to create three-dimensional vectors from three individual values: **X**, **Y**, and **Z**. These vectors can be used to generate colors, positions, directions, and UVW coordinates.

## Compose Vector4D

The **Compose Vector4D** node is used to create four-dimensional vectors from four individual values: **X**, **Y**, **Z**, and **W**. You can, for example, use these node to save a color with the alpha value.

## Set Alpha

If you already have a color and you want to add alpha to it, you can use the **Set Alpha** node to do so.

## Compose Color

The **Compose Color** node can be used to create color from three color components: **Red**, **Green**, and **Blue**.

## Compose ColorA

The functioning of the **Compose ColorA** node is similar to that of the **Compose Color** node. However, it lets you add alpha channel to the color.

## Split Color

The **Split Color** node is used to break a color into its individual components.

## Color To Float

A color can consists of upto four components: red, green, blue, and alpha. The **Color To Float** node can be used to convert a color into a single value based on its individual or combined component values.

## Matrix to Vectors

In Cinema 4D, a matrix is used to define position, rotation, and scale of an object and is made up four vectors. The **Matrix to Vectors** node can be used to output individual components of the matrix: **V1**, **V2**, **V3**, and **Offset**.

## Split Vector

The **Split Vector** node can be used to split values into individual components.

## Vector To Float

The **Vector To Float** node can be used to output the length, component sum, or individual components of a vector.

### Vectors to Matrix

The **Vectors to Matrix** node is opposite of the **Matrix to Vector** node and used to create a matrix from four 3D vectors.

### Angular Unit

The **Angular Unit** node is used to convert from one system to the another [radians to degrees and visa-versa].

### Math

The nodes in the **Math** group are used to execute the mathematical calculations. These nodes are discussed next.

### Transform 2D

The **Transform 2D** node can be used to move, scale, and rotate vectors such as colors, UV coordinates, and position vectors.

### Absolute

The **Absolute** node is used to convert an input value to a positive value.

### Distance

The **Distance** node can be used to measure the distance between two positions in 3D space.

### Arithmetic

The **Arithmetic** node is used to calculate the basic mathematical operations such as addition, subtraction, division, and multiplication. It supports the following data types: **Float, Int, Color, Vector2d, Vector,** and **Vector4d**.

### Atan2

The **Atan2** node evaluates the atan2 function.

### If

The **If** node is used to evaluate the incoming condition and returns the value **True** or **False**. This node supports the following data types: **Float, Int, Id, Internedld, String, Url, Color, ColorA, Matrix, Vector2d, Vector, Vector4d, ShadingContext,** and **UInt**.

### Clamp

The **Clamp** node is used to restrict input values to a defined range using the **Minimum** and **Maximum** parameters.

### Range Mapper

The **Range Mapper** node is used to remap an input value to another arbitrary range.

## Boolean Operator
The **Boolean Operator** node is used to perform boolean algebra.

## Average
The **Average** node is used to calculate the average value [sum of all input values divided by the number of values] of the variable input values.

## Any/All
Sometimes, a number **0** can be problematic, for example, when a value is divided by **0**. The **Any/All** node can be used to check input vectors for any components set to **0**.

## Inverse Matrix
The **Inverse Matrix** node allows you to convert global vectors to local vectors.

## Invert
The **Invert** node subtracts the incoming value from **1**, i.e. **1-x**. You can use this node for example to mirror UV coordinates.

## Reciprocal
The **Reciprocal** node is used to divide **1** by the value that is input, i.e., **1/x**.

## Cross Product
The **Cross Product** node uses two vectors to calculate a new vector that lies perpendicular to the plane that runs through both original vectors. This node is regularly used for calculating matrices.

## Length
The **Length** node is used to analyze the input values and then outputs the length of vectors or the sum of the vector components. It supports the following modes for calculation: **Euclidian, Squared, Sum,** and **Average**.

## Compose Matrix
An object's matrix is made up of four vectors. The first vector is easy to calculate since it's just the position of the object. The other vectors define the direction of the three spatial axes of the object axis system and are not easy to calculate. You can use the **Compose Matrix** node to simplify the process of creating these values.

## Decompose Matrix
The **Decompose Matrix** node is opposite to the **Compose Matrix** node.

## Transform Matrices
The **Transform Matrices** node is used to convert local matrices to global matrices. If local matrices are each multiplied by their parent matrix, a global matrix can be calculated. The order of the matrices is important here, the top-most input matrix should therefore always be used for the matrix that should be converted.

## Min/Max
The **Min/Max** node is used to input any number of values and determine the smallest or the largest values within the set.

## Mix
The **Mix** node is used to mix the two predefined limit values.

## Modulo
The **Modulo** node calculates the remaining amount of a whole number division. For example, if you want to divide a value of **5** by **3**, **2** will remain.

## Fraction
This **Fraction** node can be used to output the decimal portion of float comma values.

## Negate
The **Negate** node inverts the value's algebraic symbol. A positive value will be negative and vice-versa.

## Sample Noise
Like **Noise** material node, the **Sample Noise** node also generates patterns. However, with this node, you can use an input vector to define the position at which a value should be computed by the noise generator. As a result, you can create variation of an otherwise static pattern.

## Normalize
The **Normalize** node is used to normalize a vector i.e. restricting the length to a value of **1**. This kind of vector also referred to as a **Unit Vector**. The vector's original direction will be maintained.

## Power
This **Power** node can be used to exponentiate the base value.

## Dot Product
The **Dot Product** node is used to calculate the dot product of two vectors.

## Quantize
The **Quantize** node is used to reduce number of colors from a texture and bluriness. You can use this node to create stepped color values. This node is comparable with the **Posterizer** shader.

## Box Step
The **Box Step** node outputs a percentage value between **0** and **1**, which defines the position of an input value relative to two values, defined using the **Edge 1** and **Edge 2** parameters. If the input value is larger than the **Edge 1** and **Edge 2** values, **1** will always be output. If the value is smaller than the **Edge 1** and **Edge 2** values, **0** will be output.

## Reflect

This **Reflect** node can be used to ascertain the direction in which a vector will be reflected. The **Vector 1** parameter defines the direction of the incoming ray. The **Vector 2** parameter defines the direction of the surface normal from which the sample should reflect.

## Round

The **Round** node provides several rounding algorithms. The input values will result in integers.

## Step

The **Step** node can be used to easily check if an input value is smaller or larger than a predefined threshold value.

## Switch

This **Switch** node can be used to add any number of sequential inputs. The **Index** value then determines which of the input values will be returned.

## Scaling Matrix

The **Scaling Matrix** node is used to distort and scale matrices.

## Smooth Step

The **Smooth Step** node outputs a value between **0** and **100%**. The calculation, however, is not done linearly as is the case with the **Box Step** node but will be done as a Hermite interpolation. If values of less than **0.5** are used, a shift of smaller percent values in the direction **0%** will occur and a shift in the direction of **100%** will occur if values greater than **0.5** are used.

## Strength

This **Strength** node can be used to modify the brightness of a color value or a texture. This node controls the brightness of colors within a range of **0%** and **100%** [the original color]. You can achieve overbright colors by using a **Strength** value greater than **100**.

## Transform Vector

The **Transform Vector** node can be used to transform the vectors. This node provides three modes: **Transform Vector**, **Transform Normal**, and **Transform Point**.

## Trigonometry

You can use the **Trigonometry** node to perform trigonometric calculations. The following operations are available: **Sin, Cos, Tan, Sinh, Cosh, Tanh, Asin, ACos,** and **ATan**.

## Rotate Vector
The **Rotate Vector** node is used to calculate the rotation of a vector around a given axis. You can use this node, for example, to move UV coordinates or sample positions within a texture.

## Compare
The **Compare** node is used to compare the size relation of the two input values. It supports the following operations: **Greater Than, Lass Than, Greater or Equal, Less or Equal, Equal,** and **Not Equal**.

## Translation Matrix
The **Translation Matrix** node can be used to generate a neutral, non-rotated matrix with a size of **1, 1, 1**. The functioning of this node is comparable to that of the **Scale Matrix** and **Angle Matrix** nodes.

## Sign
The **Sign** node checks the existing algebraic symbols of the inputs and then outputs a fitting multiplier. Input values smaller than **0** will produce an output of **-1**, values greater than **0** will output **+1**. Only if the input value is **0**, the output will be **0**.

## Smooth Minimum
The **Sooth Minimum** node has three inputs: **a, b,** and **k**. It evens out the differences between the input values **a** and **b**. The intensity of the smoothing can be defined using the **k** parameter.

## Value
The functioning of the **Value** node is similar to that of the **Constant** node in XPresso. This node can be used to define any data type and value.

## Angle Between
The **Angle Between** node is used to calculate the angle between two direction vectors and then output the angle as a degree or radian value.

## Rotation Matrix
The **Rotation Matrix** node is used to freely define the rotation of a matrix.

## Root
The **Root** node is used to calculate the root [**Square Root** or **Cube Root**] of a number.

## String

The nodes in the **String** group are used for processing text, character, and letters. These nodes are discussed next:

## Print

The **Print** node is used to write the **Input** value into the console. You can open the console by choosing **Script > Console** from the menubar or by pressing **Shift+F10**.

## Letter Case

The **Letter Case** node is used to convert a **String** value to lower-case letters. upper-case letters, or to capitalize the first letter of the first word.

## Truncate

The **Truncate** node is used to delete characters at the end of a given **String** input.

## Length

The **Length** node is used to count the number of characters in a **String** value and output the resulting numeric value.

## Prefix/Suffix

The **Prefix/Suffix** node is used to add a series of characters to the front of a **String** value [**Prefix**] or after a String [**Suffix**] value.

## Search and Replace

The **Search and Replace** node can be used to delete or replace characters within a given **String** value.

## Part

This **Part** node separates a section of characters from a **String** value.

## Concatenate

The **Concatenate** node can be used to combine any number of **String** segments to a single new **String**.

## Surface

The nodes in the **Surface** group are used to define individual properties of a given material such as the emission, reflectivity, normal orientation, and so on. Let's explore these nodes.

## Material

The **Material** node is used to define all physically relevant properties of a given surface. It provides the **Emission, Alpha, Normal, Displacement,** and **Context Only** input ports to define the properties of a material. This includes in particular the **BSDF** layers with which the shading and the reflections of the surface are defined.

This node combines all of a material's information and its **Result** defines the object's surface to which it is assigned.

### BSDF

The **BSDF** node is automatically included in the node network when a node material is created and it defines the reflective properties of a surface. By default, this node computes render intensive indirect illumination in the form of diffuse reflections. While very realistic, the indirect illumination effect can often be too expensive to compute within a reasonable time frame, especially for interior scenes. To remedy this, you can select the **Use Color Channel for Node Material** check box in **Project Settings**. Then the **BSDF** node will be setup to work with the **Global Illumination** effect. You can open **Project Settings** by pressing **Ctr+D**.

### Emission

This **Emission** node is used to define the color and intensity of the self-illuminating properties of a material. A self-illuminating material also illuminates other surfaces that have diffuse reflectance or a diffuse **BSDF** layer.

### Displacement Map

The **Displacement Map** node is used to deform surfaces using a material. This node moves points on the surface.

### Normal Map

The **Normal Map** node is used to prepare a normal map texture to be used with the **Normal** input of the **Material** node.

### Bump Map

A bump map only contains grayscale values, it does not contain the angles of the surface. The **Bump Map** node can be used to affect surface normals and simulate minor surface irregularities and structures. This node only produces shading effect and does not alter the geometry of the object.

### Context

The node in the **Context** group are used with projecting color values onto the UVW texture space as well as with the creation or modification of UV coordinates. Since node materials are also assigned via the **Texture** tag in the **Object Manager,** you can also use tag's projection settings to adjust the mapping. The node in **Context** group can help, if you want to make custom adjustments in the mapping to individual elements of the material. Most of the nodes in the node material system has separate inputs for **Context** and **Local Context**.

*Note: Context input*
The **Context** input represents all UV coordinates of all color inputs used for calculating a given node. If no further modifications are made, the **Texture** tag's **Projection** function will otherwise be used. With the **Local Context** input on the other hand, only the UV coordinates used for that particular node will be modified. In both cases, the **Texture** tag has the last say and its **Offset** and **Length** settings can also be used to affect the projection of the material on a given surface.

*Note: Origin of the UV coordinates*
Please keep in mind that the UV coordinates for **Material** nodes start at [0, 0] in the UV space at the bottom-left corner whereas the **Texture** tag follows from an older location at which the origin of the UV coordinates lie in the top-left corner of a texture tile.

The nodes in the **Context** group are discussed next.

## Get Context
The **Get Context** node is used to read the context. It provides comprehensive access to data.

## Override Context
The **Override Context** node can be used to insert a custom shading context at any position within the node graph. This is particularly helpful when a node has multiple outputs and you would like to preview several of them at once.

## Projection
The **Projection** node can be used to create projection coordinates for materials with different coordinate systems. New UV coordinates will be created.

## Set Context
This node is opposite of the **Get Context** node.

## Triplanar
The **Triplanar** node can be used to project up to six shaders from six different directions and also be superimposed. This can make unwrapping UV coordinates for complex objects unnecessary.

## UV Reprojection
You can use the **UV Reprojection** node with different projection types to distort UV coordinates. It can be used to create different patterns. The following modes are available with this node: **Angular**, **Radial**, **Circular**, **Box**, **Star**, and **N-Angle**.

## UV Transform

The **UV Transform** node can be used to move, scale, and rotate UV coordinates within a given texture projection tile. You can also repeat UVs using this node.

## UV Distorter

The **UV Distorter** node can be used to transform the current UV coordinates according to the specified **Direction** vector.

## UVW Transform

Like the **UV Transform** node, this node can be used to move, scale, and rotate UV coordinates. This node generates a three-dimensional coordinate structure as is also used for volumetric materials. An additional **W** component will be generated in addition to the UV coordinates.

## Scatter

This **Scatter** node can be used to calculate distribution, rotation, and scaling of UV tiles. You can use it to create UV tiles with variable positions, sizes, and rotations.

## Utility

The nodes in **Utility** group are primarily used to create groups and get the information about rendering that can be displayed in the **Console**.

## Debug

The **Debug** node can be used to output various information about a specific part of the rendering to the console.

## Group

The **Group** node itself has no function, it is used as a container of other nodes that will be grouped.

## Group (with Ports)

The **Group (with Ports)** node is a group node that already has one input and one output. You can use this node to link grouped nodes with other nodes and settings outside of the group. Additional inputs and outputs can be added via the context menu

## Object Link

The **Object Link** node can be linked with any object in the scene whose link will then be made available at the output.

## Variadic Count

If there are variable number of inputs for ports [such as a color gradient's ports], you can use the **Variadic Count** node to ascertain the number of entries.

## Material

The materials in the **Material** group are called **Node Materials**. You can also use these materials as nodes. The following material are available in this group: **Uber Material, Emission Material, Cutout Material, Car Paint Material, Concrete Material, Rock Material, Gold Material, Granite Material, Wood Material, Ceramic Material, Marble Material, Metal Material**, and **Plastic Material**.

## Hands-on Exercises

### Exercise 1: Working with the Ambient Occlusion Node

In this exercise, we will measure the indentations in the surface of a **Landscape** object and then make the material luminous in the indentations [see Fig. E1]. We will use the **Ambient Occlusion** node to automatically calculate the indentations.

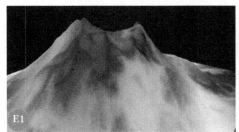
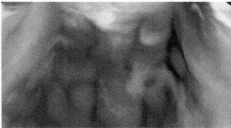

The following table summarizes the exercise:

| Table E1 | |
|---|---|
| Skill level | Intermediate |
| Time to complete | 20 Minutes |
| Topics | • Getting Started<br>• Working with the Node |
| Resources folder | **unit-ct4** |
| Units | **Centimeters** |
| Start file | **ao-glow-start.c4d** |
| Final file | **ao-glow-finish.c4d** |

#### Getting Started
Open **ao-glow-start.c4d**.

#### Working with the Node
Follow these steps:

1. Choose **Create > New Node Material** from the **Material Manager** menubar to create a new node material. Apply this material to the **Subdivision Surface** object. In the **Material Manager**, double-click on **Node** to open the **Node Editor**.

2. Select the **Diffuse.1** node and then in the **Attribute Manager > Inputs** tab, change **Color** to HSV [0, 38, 2]. Add an **Ambient Occlusion** node by navigating to **Assets > Generator**.

3. Connect **Ambient Occlusion.1 > Occlusion** to **Material.1 > Emission**. Select the **Ambient Occlusion.1** node and then in the **Attribute Manager > Inputs** tab, change **Max Ray Length** to **170** and **Accuracy** to **70**. Render the scene [see Fig. E2].

4. Navigate to **Assets > Color > Colorize** and then drag **Colorize** onto the wire connecting the **Ambient Occlusion.1** and **Material.1** nodes to insert the **Colorize** node between them. In the **Attribute Manager > Colorize.1** node > **Inputs** tab, click the **Load Preset** button and then select the **Heat 3** preset. Render the scene [see Fig. E3].

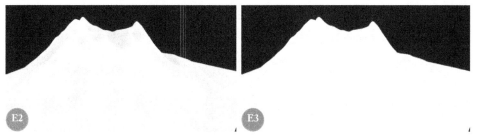

E2                                          E3

*What just happened?*
*Here, we have used the **Colorize** node to replace the colors generated by the **Ambient Occlusion.1** node. But, notice in Fig. E3, the emission is not occurring in the indentation. We need to fix it and we will do so by inverting the colors of the **Ambient Occlusion.1** node.*

5. Navigate to **Assets > Color > Invert Color** and then drag **Invert Color** onto the wire connecting the **Ambient Occlusion.1** and **Colorize.1** nodes to insert the **Invert Color** node between them. Render the scene [see Fig. E4].

*What next?*
*Now, let's add some details to the shading.*

6. Disconnect the **Colorize.1** and **Material.1** nodes. Add a **Noise** node by navigating to **Assets > Generator**. In the **Attribute Manager > Noise.1** node > **Inputs** tab, change **Noise Type** to **Wavy Turbulence**, **Octave** to **8** and **Global Scale** to **300**. Also, change **Low Clip** to **29**.

7. Add a **Arithmetic** node by navigating to **Assets > Math**. In the **Attribute Manager > Add.1** node > **Inputs** tab, change **Operation** to **Add** and **Data Type** to **Color**. Connect **Noise.1 > Result** to **Add.1 > Input 1**. Connect **Colorize.1 > Result** to **Add.1 > Input 2**. Now, connect **Add.1 > Result** to **Material.1 > Emission**. Render the scene [see Fig. E5]. Fig. E6 shows the node graph.

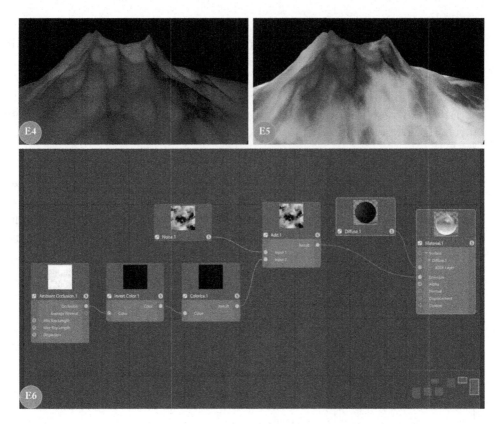

## Exercise 2: Working with the Basic Gradient Node

In this exercise, we will shade clones of a **Cloner** object using a gradient produced by the **Basic Gradient** node. We will use the **Render Object** node to read the index numbers of clones and then change the individual color values along the gradient's progression, see Fig E1.

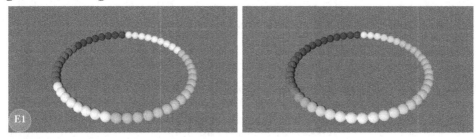

The following table summarizes the exercise:

| Table E2 | |
|---|---|
| Skill level | Intermediate |
| Time to complete | 15 Minutes |
| Topics | • Getting Started<br>• Working with the Node |
| Resources folder | **unit-ct4** |

| Table E2 | |
|---|---|
| Units | **Centimeters** |
| Start file | **bgrad-start.c4d** |
| Final file | **bgrad-finish.c4d** |

## Getting Started
Open **bgrad-start.c4d**.

## Working with the Node
Follow these steps:

1. Choose **Create > New Node Material** from the **Material Manager** menubar to create a new node material. Apply this material to the **Cloner** object. In the **Material Manager**, double-click on **Node** to open the **Node Editor**.

2. Add the **Basic Gradient** node by navigating to **Assets > Generator**. In the **Attribute Manager > Basic Gradient.1** node > **Inputs** tab, click the **Load Preset** button and then select the **Pattern 3** preset.

3. Add the **Render Object** node by navigating to **Assets > Info**.

*What next?*
*The **Position** input port of the **Basic Gradient** node expects values between **0** to **1** or **0%** to **100%**. Since, we have **50** clones in the **Cloner** object, we need to divide the value of the **Render Object.1 > Object Index** port by **50** in order to get **0** to **1** range for the **Position** port of the **Basic Gradient** node.*

4. Add the **Arithmetic** node by navigating to **Assets > Math**. In the **Attribute Manager > Add.1** node > **Inputs** tab, change **Operation** to **Divide**, **Data Type** to **Float**, and **Input 2** to **50**.

5. Connect **Render Object.1 > Object Index** to **Divide.1 > Input 1**. Connect **Divide.1 > Result** to **Basic Gradient.1 > Position**.

6. Connect **Basic Gradient > Result** to **Diffuse.1 > Color**. Render the scene [see Fig. E1], Fig. E2 shows the node graph.

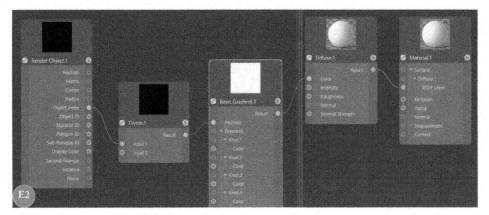

## Exercise 3: Working with the Thin Film Node

In this exercise, we will use the **Thin Film** node to simulate the surfaces like oil or soap, see Fig. E1.

The following table summarizes the exercise:

| Table E3 | |
| --- | --- |
| Skill level | Intermediate |
| Time to complete | 25 Minutes |
| Topics | • Getting Started<br>• Working with the Node |
| Resources folder | **unit-ct4** |
| Units | **Centimeters** |
| Start file | **thin-film-start.c4d** |
| Final file | **thin-film-finish.c4d** |

### Getting Started
Open **thin-film-start.c4d**.

### Working with the Node
Follow these steps:

1. Choose **Create > New Node Material** from the **Material Manager** menubar to create a new node material. Apply this material to the **Sphere** object. In the **Material Manager**, double-click on **Node** to open the **Node Editor**.

2. In the **Attribute Manager > Material.1** node > **Inputs** tab, select the **Transparent** check box and then change **IOR** to **2**.

> *What just happened?*
> *Here, we have selected the **Transparent** check box to get access to additional settings that we can use to define the transparency and refraction properties.*

3. Add the **Thin Film** node by navigating to **Assets > Generator**. Connect **Thin Film.1 > Result** to **Diffuse.1 > Color**.

4. In the **Attribute Manager > Thin Film.1** node > **Inputs** tab, change **Thickness** to **300**, **IOR** to **2**, and **Spectral Samples** to **15**. Render the scene [see Fig. E2].

> **Parameters: Thickness and Spectral Samples**
> The higher the value you specify for the **Thickness** parameter, the more spectral colors will appear in the result. The **Spectral Samples** parameter controls the quality of the render. If you specify a very low value for this parameter, you will get a monochrome output.

> *What just happened?*
> *Notice in Fig. E2, we are getting completely transparent result, there is not a hint of color we are after. It happened because we did not change the transparency color of the material. Let's change that.*

5. In the **Attribute Manager > Material.1** node > **Inputs** tab, change **Transparency** to **HSV [0, 0, 72]**. Render the scene [see Fig. E3].

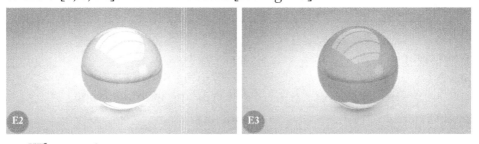

> *What next?*
> *Next, we will create variations in the film. To do so, we ill use a multiplied* **Noise** *node.*

6. Add the **Noise** node by navigating to **Assets > Generator**. In the **Attribute Manager > Noise.1** node > **Inputs** tab, change **Noise Type** to **Naki**. Add the **Arithmetic** node by navigating to **Assets > Math**. In the **Attribute Manager > Add.1** node > **Inputs** tab, change **Operation** to **Multiply** and **Input 2** to **20**.

7. Connect **Noise.1 > Result** to **Multiply.1 > Input 1**. Connect **Multiply.1 > Result** to **Thin Fim.1 > Variation**. Render the scene. Fig. E4 shows the node graph.

**Parameter: Variation**
This parameter is used to create variations in the color patterns.

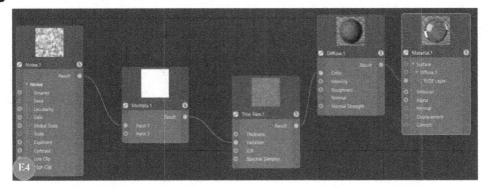

## Exercise 4: Working with the Gradient Node

In this exercise, we will distort a gradient using the brightness values of another gradient [see Fig. E1].

The following table summarizes the exercise:

| Table E4 | |
|---|---|
| Skill level | Intermediate |
| Time to complete | 20 Minutes |
| Topics | • Getting Started<br>• Working with the Node |
| Resources folder | **unit-ct4** |
| Units | **Centimeters** |
| Start file | **assets-start-01.c4d** |
| Final file | **grad-rot-finish.c4d** |

### Getting Started
Open **assets-start-01.c4d**.

### Working with the Node
Follow these steps:

1. Choose **Create > New Node Material** from the **Material Manager** menubar to create a new node material. Apply this material to the **Sphere1** and **Sphere2**

objects. In the **Material Manager**, double-click on **Node** to open the **Node Editor**.

2. Add a **Gradient** node by navigating to **Assets > Generator**. In the **Attribute Manager > Gradient.1** node **> Inputs** tab, click the **Load Preset** button and then select the **Pattern 3** preset.

3. Connect **Gradient.1 > Result** to **Diffuse.1 > Color**. In the **Attribute Manager > Gradient.1** node **> Inputs** tab, select the **Distortion** check box in the **Distortion** area. In the **Projection** area, change **Local Rotation** to **90**. Render the scene [see Fig. E2].

4. In the **Distortion** area, **Strength** to **70**. Render the scene [see Fig. E3].

> *What just happened?*
>
> *Here, we have selected the **Distortion** check box. As a result, we got access to the **Strength** and **Color** settings. You can use these settings to make color transitions in the gradient appear less uniform. The **Strength** setting is a multiplier for the intensity of the color distortion within the gradient. You can also specify a negative value to reverse the distortion.*
>
> *The **Color** setting allows you to define the color components and brightness that should be multiplied by the **Strength** value.*

5. Add a **Basic Gradient** node by navigating to **Assets > Generator**. Connect **Basic Gradient.1 > Result** to **Gradient.1 > Distortion > Color**. In the **Attribute Manager > Basic Gradient.1** node **> Inputs** tab, change the gradient, as shown in Fig. E4. Render the scene [see Fig. E5], Fig. E6 shows the node graph.

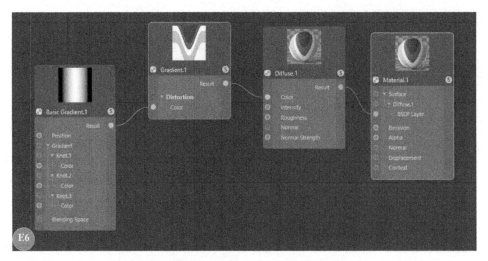

## Exercise 5: Create Flakes using the Flakes Node

In this exercise, we will create flakes on a surface using the **Flakes** node [see Fig. E1].

The following table summarizes the exercise:

| Table E5 | |
| --- | --- |
| Skill level | Intermediate |
| Time to complete | 40 Minutes |
| Topics | • Getting Started<br>• Working with the Node |
| Resources folder | **unit-ct4** |
| Units | **Centimeters** |
| Start file | **assets-start-01.c4d** |
| Final file | **flakes-finish.c4d** |

### Getting Started
Open **assets-start-01.c4d**.

### Working with the Node
Follow these steps:

1. Choose **Create > New Node Material** from the **Material Manager** menubar to create a new node material. Apply this material to the **Sphere1** and **Sphere2**

objects. In the **Material Manager,** double-click on **Node** to open the **Node Editor.**

→ *What next?*
*Here, we want to create a layered metallic paint material. To create it, we will use three layers: base layer, a layer for flakes, and a layer for clear coat at the top.*

2. Rename **Diffuse.1** as **Base Coat.** Add the **BSDF** node by navigating to **Assets > Surface.** Rename **Diffuse.1** as **Flakes.** Create another **BSDF** node and then rename it as **Clear Coat.**

3. In the **Attribute Manager > Material.1** node > **Inputs** tab, click the **Add** button to add a **BSDF** layer. Now, connect **Flakes > Result** to **BSDF Layer 2 > BSDF Layer.** Similarly, create another layer and connect **Clear Coat** with it [see Fig. E2].

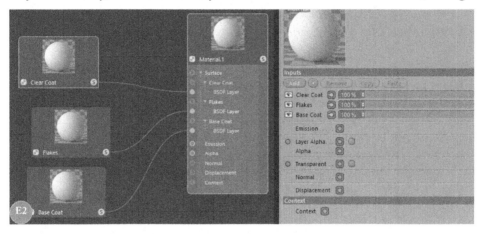

4. In the **Attribute Manager > Base Coat** node > **Inputs** tab, change **Color** to **HSV** [218, 97, 27]. In the **Attribute Manager > Flakes** node > **Inputs** tab, change **BSDF** type to **GGX, Fresnel** to **Dielectric,** and **Presets** to **PET.** In the **Attribute Manager > Clear Coat** node > **Inputs** tab, change **BSDF** type to **GGX, Fresnel** to **Dielectric,** and **Presets** to **PET.** Render the scene [see Fig. E3].

5. Add the **Flakes** node by navigating to **Assets > Generator.** Connect **Flakes.1 > Normal** to **Flakes > Normal.** Render the scene [see Fig. E4]. In the **Attribute Manager > Flakes.1** node > **Inputs** tab, change **Scale** to **0.05, Density** to **10,** and **Intensity** to **70.** Render the scene [see Fig. E5].

**Parameters: Scale, Density, and Intensity**
The **Scale** parameter defines the size of the flake structure. Higher values create larger but fewer flakes. The **Density** parameter allows you to define the individual size of the flakes and also the gap between the flakes. The **Intensity** parameter controls the contrast of the flakes.

6. Add the **Compose ColorA** node by navigating to **Assets > Conversion**. Connect **Flakes.1 > Mask** to **Compose ColorA.1 > Alpha**. Connect **Compose ColorA.1 > Result** to **Flakes > Color**. In the **Attribute Manager > Compose ColorA.1** node > **Inputs** tab, change **RGB** to white. Render the scene [see Fig. E6]. Fig. E7 shows the node graph.

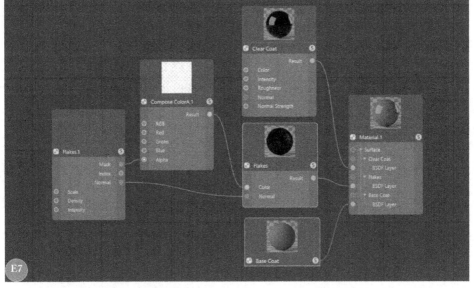

## Exercise 6: Working with the Grid Node

In this exercise, we will create a grid using the **Grid** node. We will use the same grid for the **Displacement** map [see Fig. E1]. The following table summarizes the exercise:

| Table E6 | |
|---|---|
| Skill level | Intermediate |
| Time to complete | 20 Minutes |
| Topics | • Getting Started<br>• Working with the Node |
| Resources folder | **unit-ct4** |
| Units | **Centimeters** |
| Start file | **assets-start-01.c4d** |
| Final file | **grid-finish.c4d** |

### Getting Started
Open **assets-start-01.c4d**.

### Working with the Node
Follow these steps:

1.  Choose **Create > New Node Material** from the **Material Manager** menubar to create a new node material. Apply this material to the **Sphere1** and **Sphere2** objects. In the **Material Manager**, double-click on **Node** to open the **Node Editor**.

2.  Add the **Grid** node by navigating to **Assets > Generator**. In the **Attribute Manager > Grid.1** node > **Inputs** tab, change Thickness to [**0.1, 0.3, and 0.1**], **Softness** to **0.05**, and **Frequency** to [**10, 4, 2**]. Create another **Grid** node. In the **Attribute Manager > Grid.2** node > **Inputs** tab, change Thickness to [**0.1, 0.3, and 0.1**], **Softness** to **0.05**, and **Frequency** to [**4, 4, 2**].

    *What next?*
    *Now, we want to change appearance of every other row. To do so, we will mask some area of the **Grid.2** result and then combine it with the result of **Grid.1**.*

3.  Add the **Compose ColorA** node by navigating to **Assets > Conversion**. Connect **Grid.2 > Color** to **Compose ColorA.1 > RGB**. Add the **Modulo** node by navigating to **Assets > Math**.

4.  Connect **Grid.2 > Index** to **Modulo.1 > Value 1**. In the **Attribute Manager > Modulo.1** node > **Inputs** tab, change **Value 2** to **2**. Connect **Modulo.1 > Result** to **Compose ColorA.1 > Alpha**.

5. Add the **Layer** node by navigating to **Assets > Color**. Connect **Compose ColorA.1 > Result** to **Layer.1 > Layer 1**. Connect **Grid.1 > Color** to **Layer.1 > Layer 2**.

6. Add the **Displacement** node by navigating to **Assets > Surface**. Connect **Layer.1 > Result** to **Displacement Map.1 > Value**. In the **Attribute Manager > Displacement Map.1** node **> Inputs** tab, change **Strength** to **40**. Connect **Displacement Map.1 > Result** to **Material.1 > Displacement**.

7. Add the **Invert Color** node by navigating to **Assets > Color**. Connect **Layer.1 > Result** to **Invert Color.1 > Color**. Connect **Invert Color.1 >** output **Color** to **Diffuse.1 > Color**. Render the scene, see Fig. E1. Fig. E2 shows the node graph.

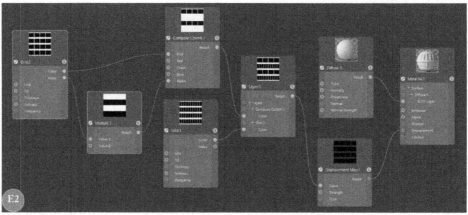

## Exercise 7: Working with the Scratches Node

In this exercise, we will create scratches on a surface using the **Scratches** node [see Fig. E6]. The following table summarizes the exercise:

| Table E7 | |
|---|---|
| Skill level | Intermediate |
| Time to complete | 35 Minutes |
| Topics | • Getting Started<br>• Working with the Node |
| Resources folder | **unit-ct4** |
| Units | **Centimeters** |
| Start file | **assets-start-01.c4d** |
| Final file | **scratches-finish.c4d** |

## Getting Started
Open **assets-start-01.c4d**.

## Working with the Node
Follow these steps:

1. Choose **Create > New Node Material** from the **Material Manager** menubar to create a new node material. Apply this material to the **Sphere1** and **Sphere2** objects. In the **Material Manager**, double-click on **Node** to open the **Node Editor**.

2. In the **Attribute Manager > Diffuse.1** node **> Inputs** tab, change **Color** to HSV [**234,93,93**]. Add a **BSDF** node by navigating to **Assets > Surface**. Add another layer in the **Material.1** node and then connect it with **Diffuse.2 > Result**.

    *What just happened?*
   *Here, I have added another **BSDF** layer that we will use to overlay scratches on the original **BSDF** layer.*

3. Add the **Gradient** node by navigating to **Assets > Generator**. In the **Attribute Manager > Gradient.1 node > Inputs** tab, change the gradient as shown in Fig. E1. In the **Projection** area, change **Rotation** to **90**.

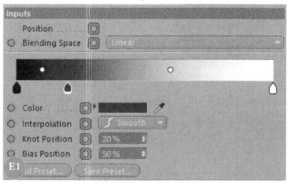

4. Add the **Scratches** node by navigating to **Assets > Generator**. Connect **Gradient.1 > Result** to **Scratches.1 > Depth**. In the **Attribute Manager > Scratches.1** node **> Inputs** tab, change **Scale** to **32.15**, **Rotation** to **66**, **Layers** to **3**, **Frequency Step** to **0.75**, **Bend** to **60**, and **Thickness** to **60**.

    *What just happened?*
   *Here, we have connected a gradient to the **Depth** port. The **Depth** value allows you to fade or darken the scratches. Increasing values will darken the scratches accordingly. The **Scale** parameter is used to scale the scratches. By default, the **Rotation** value creates the scratches perpendicularly. You can change this value to adjust the orientation. The **Layers** parameter defines the number of scratch layers. The **Frequency Step** value can be used to modify the scaling of each new scratch layer compared to the previous layer. The **Bend** parameter is used*

*to add curvature to the scratches and the **Thickness** parameter is used to define the maximum width for the scratches.*

→ **What next?**
*Now, we will use the **Invert Color** node to invert the result of the **Scratches.1** node. As a result, we will get white scratches on a black background. Next, we will use the **Compose ColorA** node to extract the alpha information to compose the scratches information on the surface.*

5. Add the **Invert Color** node by navigating to **Assets > Color**. Connect **Scratches.1 > Result** to **Invert Color.1 > Color**. Connect **Invert Color.1 > Color** to **Diffuse.2 > Color**. Render the scene, see Fig. E2.

6. Navigate to **Assets > Compose > Compose ColorA** and then drag **Compose ColorA** onto the wire connecting the **Invert Color.1** and **Diffuse.2** nodes to insert the **Compose ColorA.1** node between them. Re-route the connection to the Alpha port of the **Compose ColorA** node. In the **Attribute Manager > Compose ColorA.1** node > **Inputs** tab, change **RGB** to white. Render the scene, see Fig. E3.

7. Navigate to **Assets > Math > Arithmetic** and then drag **Arithmetic** onto the wire connecting the **Gradient.1** and **Scracthes.1** nodes to open a popup. Next, choose **Result:Multiply** from the popup.

8. In the **Attribute Manager > Multiply.1** node > **Inputs** tab, change **Data Type** to **Float** and **Input 2** to **3**.

9. In the **Attribute Manager > Gradient.1** node > **Inputs** tab, change the gradient, as shown in Fig. E4. Render the scene, see Fig. E5.

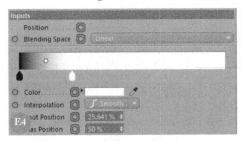

10. In the **AttributeManager** > **Scratches.1** node > **Inputs** tab, change **Scale** to **5**, **Rotation** to **66**, **Density** to **100**, and **Thickness** to **79**. Render the scene [see Fig. E6]. Fig. E7 shows the node graph.

## Exercise 8: Working with the Blackbody Node

In this exercise, we will use an **Ambient Occlusion** node to vary the blackbody temperature [see Fig. E2]. The following table summarizes the exercise:

| Table E8 | |
| --- | --- |
| Skill level | Intermediate |
| Time to complete | 35 Minutes |
| Topics | • Getting Started<br>• Working with the Node |
| Resources folder | **unit-ct4** |
| Units | **Centimeters** |
| Start file | **assets-start-01.c4d** |
| Final file | **blackbody-finish.c4d** |

### Getting Started

Open **assets-start-01.c4d**.

### Working with the Node

Follow these steps:

1. Choose **Create > New Node Material** from the **Material Manager** menubar to create a new node material. Apply this material to the **Sphere1** and **Sphere2** objects. In the **Material Manager**, double-click on **Node** to open the **Node Editor**.

2. In the **Attribute Manager > Diffuse.1** node > **Inputs** tab, change **Color** to HSV **[0, 0, 9]**. Add the **Ambient Occlusion** node by navigating to **Assets > Generator**.

3. Add the **Range Mapper** node by navigating to **Assets > Math**. Connect **Ambient Occlusion.1 > Occlusion** to **Range Mapper.1 > Value**. In the **Attribute Manager > Range Mapper.1** node > **Inputs** tab, change **Output Max** to **78**.

4. Add the **Blackbody** node by navigating to **Assets > Generator**. Connect **Range Mapper.1 > Result** to **Blackbody.1 > Temperature**. Connect **Blackbody.1 > Result** to **Material.1 > Emission**. Render the scene [see Fig. E1].

**?** *What just happened?*
*Here, we have remapped the result [float comma value, **0** to **1** range] of the **Ambient Occlusion** to a new range and then connected it with the **Temperature** port of the **Blackbody.1** node. The **Temperature** parameter is used to define the temperature with which the black body is heated. By connecting the result of the **Blackbody.1** node to the **Material.1 > Emission** port, we have ensured that the emission properties of the material will be controlled by ambient occlusion.*

**→** *What next?*
*Next, we will use an **Invert** node to affect the area which is in the proximity of the objects. The warmer colors will appear on those areas.*

5. Navigate to **Assets > Math > Arithmetic** and then drag **Arithmetic** onto the wire connecting the **Blackbody.1** and **Material.1** nodes to open a popup. Next, choose **Result:Multiply** from the popup.

6. Add the **Invert** node by navigating to **Assets > Math**. Connect **Ambient Occlusion.1 > Occlusion** to **Invert.1 > Value**. Connect **Invert.1 > Result** to **Multiply.1 > Input 2**. In the **Attribute Manager > Invert.1** node > **Inputs** tab, change **Data Type** to **Float**. Render the scene [see Fig. E2]. Fig. E3 shows the node graph.

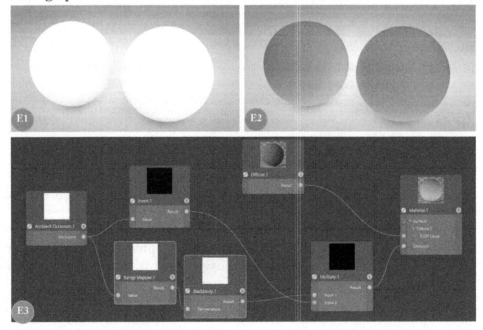

## Exercise 9: Working with the Light Node

In this exercise, we will use the **Light** node to read the **Light Color** data and then use it to control the luminance effect of the material [see Fig. E2]. The following table summarizes the exercise:

| Table E9 | |
| --- | --- |
| Skill level | Intermediate |
| Time to complete | 40 Minutes |
| Topics | • Getting Started<br>• Working with the Node |
| Resources folder | **unit-ct4** |
| Units | **Centimeters** |
| Start file | **assets-start-01.c4d** |
| Final file | **light-finish.c4d** |

### Getting Started
Open **assets-start-01.c4d**.

### Working with the Node
Follow these steps:

1. Choose **Create > New Node Material** from the **Material Manager** menubar to create a new node material. Apply this material to the **Sphere1** and **Sphere2** objects. In the **Material Manager**, double-click on **Node** to open the **Node Editor**.

2. Add the **BSDF** node by navigating to **Assets > Surface** and then connect it with the **Material.1** node using a new layer. In the **Attribute Manager > Diffuse.2** node > **Inputs** tab, change **BSDF Type** to **GGX**, **Fresnel** to **Dielectric**, and **Intensity** to **40**.

3. Load the **glass.jpg** to the **Node Editor** and then add the **Veins** node by navigating to **Assets > Generator**. In the **Attribute Manager > Veins.1** node > **Inputs** tab, change **Large Turbulence** to **30**, **Small Turbulence** to **5**, **Veins Gaps** to **26**, and **Contrast** to **20**.

4. Add the **Mix** node by navigating to **Assets > Math**. Connect **Veins.1 > Color** to **Mix.1 > Input 1**. Connect **glass.jpg > Result** to **Mix.1 > Input 2**. In the **Attribute Manager > Mix.1** node > **Inputs** tab, change **Data Type** to **Color**. Connect **Mix.1 > Result** to **Material.1 > Emission**.

 *What just happened?*
*Here, we have used the **Mix** node blend the result of the **glass.jpg** bitmap and the **Veins.1** node. The **Blend Factor** parameter can be used to blend between two values.*

*What next?*
*Now, we will use the result of the **Mix.1** node to affect the luminance properties of the material by connecting the node to the **Material.1 > Emission** port. Next, we will add a **Light** node and then use its **In Shadow** port to create shading via shadows.*

5. Add the **Light** node by navigating to **Assets > Info**. Add the **Color to Float** node by navigating to **Assets > Conversion**. Connect **Light.1 > In Shadow** to **Color to Float.1 > Color**.

*Why the Color to Float node is used?*
*The **In Shadow** port of the **Light.1** node outputs a boole value and the **Blend Factor** port of the **Mix** node accepts a float value. Therefore, we need the **Color to Float** node to convert the boole value to a float value.*

6. In the **Attribute Manager > Color to Float.1** node > **Inputs** tab, change **Mode** to **Length**. Render the scene [see Fig. E1].

*What just happened?*
*Notice in Fig. E1 the effect of **Mix** node is in the areas that lie in the shadow but it is too pronounced. We need to reduce this effect. Now, we will use the **Reciprocal** node for making the effect less pronounced.*

7. Add the **Reciprocal** node by navigating to **Assets > Math**. Connect **Color To Float.1 > Result** to **Reciprocal.1 > Input**. Connect **Reciprocal.1 > Result** to **Mix.1 > Blend Factor**. Render the scene, see Fig. E2. Fig. E3 shows the node graph.

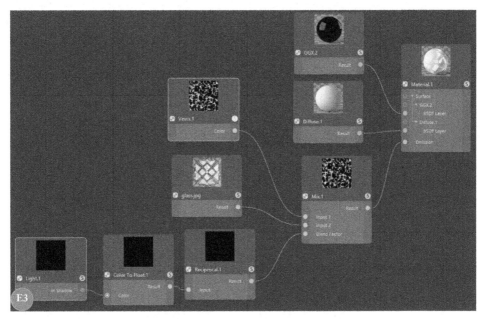

## Exercise 10: Working with the Quantize Node

In this exercise, we will use the **Quantize** node to reduce the number of colors using stepped values [see Fig. E1]. The following table summarizes the exercise:

| Table E10 | |
|---|---|
| Skill level | Intermediate |
| Time to complete | 15 Minutes |
| Topics | • Getting Started<br>• Working with the Node |
| Resources folder | **unit-ct4** |
| Units | **Centimeters** |
| Start file | **assets-start-01.c4d** |
| Final file | **quantize-finish.c4d** |

### Getting Started
Open **assets-start-01.c4d**.

### Working with the Node
Follow these steps:

1.  Choose **Create > New Node Material** from the **Material Manager** menubar to create a new node material. Apply this material to the **Sphere1** and **Sphere2** objects. In the **Material Manager**, double-click on **Node** to open the **Node Editor**.

2. In the **Attribute Manager > Diffuse.1** node > **Inputs** tab, change **Fresnel** to **Dielectric**.

3. Add the **Noise** node by navigating to **Assets > Generator**. In the **Attribute Manager > Noise.1** node > **Inputs** tab, change **Noise Type** to **Luka**, **Global Scale** to **2000**, **Low Clip** to **2**, and **High Clip** to **75**.

4. Add the **Quantize** node by navigating to **Assets > Math**. Connect **Noise.1 > Result** to **Quantize.1 > Value**. In the **Attribute Manager > Quantize.1** node > **Inputs** tab, change **Steps** to **15**. Connect **Quantize.1 > Result** to **Diffuse.1 > Color**.

5. Add the **UV Transform** node by navigating to **Assets > Context**. Connect **UV Transform.1 > Result** to **Noise.1 > Context**. In the **Attribute Manager > UV Transform.1** node > **Inputs** tab, change **Local Repetitions** to **50** each. Render the scene [see Fig. 1]. Fig. E2 shows the node graph.

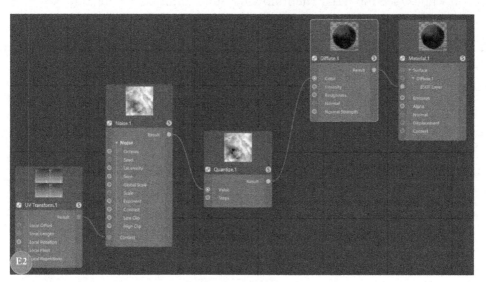

## Exercise 11: Working with the Override Context Node

In this exercise, we will use the **Override Context** node to override context of sub-graph [see Fig. E1]. The following table summarizes the exercise:

| Table E11 | |
| --- | --- |
| Skill level | Intermediate |
| Time to complete | 15 Minutes |

| Table E11 | |
|---|---|
| Topics | • Getting Started<br>• Working with the Node |
| Resources folder | **unit-ct4** |
| Units | **Centimeters** |
| Start file | **assets-start-01.c4d** |
| Final file | **override-finish.c4d** |

## Getting Started
Open **assets-start-01.c4d**.

## Working with the Node
Follow these steps:

1. Choose **Create > New Node Material** from the **Material Manager** menubar to create a new node material. Apply this material to the **Sphere1** and **Sphere2** objects. In the **Material Manager**, double-click on **Node** to open the **Node Editor**.

2. Add the **Noise** node by navigating to **Assets > Generator**. In the **Attribute Manager > Noise.1** node > **Inputs** tab, change **Noise Type** to **Voronoi3**. Add the **Override Context** node by navigating to **Assets > Context**.

3. Connect **Noise.1 > Result** to **Override Context.1 > Color**. Connect **Override Context.1 > Result** to **Diffuse.1 > Color**.

4. Add the **UV Reprojection** node by navigating to **Assets > Context**. Connect **UV Reprojection.1 > Result** to **Override Context.1 > Context**. In the **Attribute Manager > UV Reprojection.1** node > **Inputs** tab, change **Mode** to **Circular**. Render the scene, see Fig. E1. Fig. E2 shows the node graph.

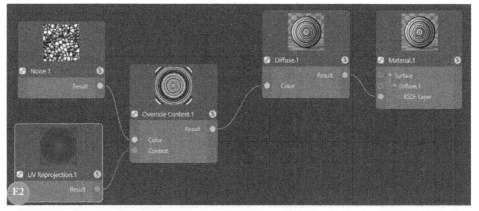

## Exercise 12: Working with the Projection Node

In this exercise, we will use the **Projection** node to alter the coordinate system [see Fig. E1]. The following table summarizes the exercise:

| Table E12 | |
|---|---|
| Skill level | Intermediate |
| Time to complete | 30 Minutes |
| Topics | • Getting Started<br>• Working with the Node |
| Resources folder | **unit-ct4** |
| Units | **Centimeters** |
| Start file | **assets-start-01.c4d** |
| Final file | **projection-finish.c4d** |

### Getting Started
Open **assets-start-01.c4d**.

### Working with the Node
Follow these steps:

1.  Choose **Create > New Node Material** from the **Material Manager** menubar to create a new node material. Apply this material to the **Sphere1** and **Sphere2** objects. In the **Material Manager**, double-click on **Node** to open the **Node Editor**.

2.  Add the **Grid** node by navigating to **Assets > Generator**. In the **Attribute Manager > Grid.1** node > **Inputs** tab, change **Frequency** to [2, 4, 2]. Connect **Grid.1 > Result** to **Diffuse.1 > Color**.

3.  Add the **Projection** node by navigating to **Assets > Context**. In the **Attribute Manager > Projection.1** node > **Inputs** tab, select the **Additional Transform** check box. Now, change **Rotation** to **45** each.

    ⟶  *What next?*
    *Now, we will scale the UVs of the **Grid.1** node. To do so, we will use the **Scale** parameter of the **Projection** node. This parameter scales the texture file. The values are multipliers of the value of the **Reference Size** parameter. We will use a **Gradient** node to drive the **Scale** value.*

4.  Add the **Gradient** node by navigating to **Assets > Generator**. In the **Attribute Manager > Gradient.1** node > **Inputs** tab > **Projection** area, change **Mode** to **Circular**.

5. Add the **Range Mapper** node by navigating to **Assets > Math**. Connect **Gradient.1 > Result** to **Range Mapper.1 > Value**. In the **Attribute Manager > Range Mapper.1** node > **Inputs** tab, change **Data Type** to **Color**, and **Output Max** to HSV [0, 0, 22].

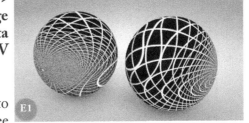

6. Connect **Range Mapper.1 > Result** to **Projection.1 > Scale**. Render the sene, see Fig. E1. Fig. E2 shows the node graph.

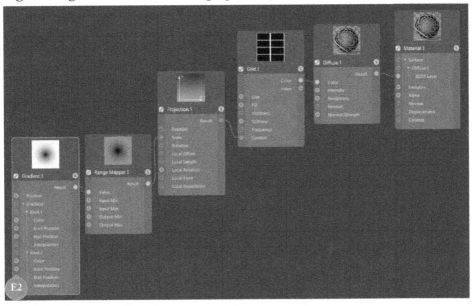

## Exercise 13: Working with the Scatter Node

In this exercise, we will use the **Scatter** node to scatter an image on a surface [see Fig. E1]. The following table summarizes the exercise:

| Table E13 | |
|---|---|
| Skill level | Intermediate |
| Time to complete | 15 Minutes |
| Topics | • Getting Started<br>• Working with the Node |
| Resources folder | **unit-ct4** |
| Units | **Centimeters** |
| Start file | **assets-start-01.c4d** |
| Final file | **scatter-finish.c4d** |

### Getting Started

Open **assets-start-01.c4d**.

## Working with the Node
Follow these steps:

1.  Choose **Create > New Node Material** from the **Material Manager** menubar to create a new node material. Apply this material to the **Sphere1** and **Sphere2** objects. In the **Material Manager**, double-click on **Node** to open the **Node Editor**.

2.  Load **Logo.png** and then connect its **Result** port with the **Diffuse.1 > Color** port. Create a copy of **Logo.png** and rename it as **Logo-Alpha**. Add the **Split Color** node by navigating to **Assets > Color**. Connect **Logo-Alpha > Result** to **Split Color .1 > Color**.

3.  Add the **Scatter** node by navigating to **Assets > Context**. Connect **Split Color.1 > Alpha to Scatter.1 > Shape**. In the **Attribute Manager > Scatter.1** node > **Inputs** tab, change **Max Splat Count** to **50, Density** to **30**, and **Scale** to **0.5** and **0.5**.

4.  Connect **Scatter.1 > Context** to **Logo. png > Context**. Render the scene, see Fig. E1. Fig. E2 shows the node graph.

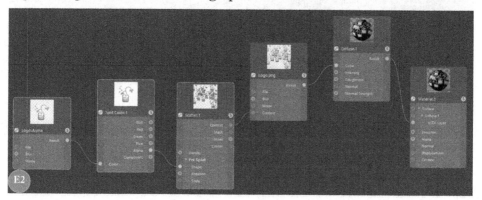

## Exercise 14: Working with the UV Distorter Node
In this exercise, we will use the **UV Distorter** node to create distortion directly in the projection [see Fig. E3]. The following table summarizes the exercise:

| Table E14 | |
|---|---|
| Skill level | Intermediate |
| Time to complete | 35 Minutes |
| Topics | • Getting Started<br>• Working with the Node |
| Resources folder | **unit-ct4** |

| Table E14 | |
|---|---|
| Units | **Centimeters** |
| Start file | **assets-start-01.c4d** |
| Final file | **distortion-finish.c4d** |

## Getting Started
Open **assets-start-01.c4d**.

## Working with the Node
Follow these steps:

1. Choose **Create > New Node Material** from the **Material Manager** menubar to create a new node material. Apply this material to the **Sphere1** and **Sphere2** objects. In the **Material Manager**, double-click on **Node** to open the **Node Editor**.

2. Add the **Grid** node by navigating to **Assets > Generator**. In the **Attribute Manager > Grid.1** node > **Inputs** tab, change **Frequency** to [5, 5, 4]. Connect **Grid.1 > Color** to **Diffuse.1 > Color**.

3. Add the **UV Distorter** node by navigating to **Assets > Context**. Connect **UV Distorter.1 > Result** to **Grid.1 > Context**.

⊕→ *What next?*
*Now, we will use the **Basic Gradient** nodes to drive the **Direction** of the distortion. Also, we will use the **Noise** node to drive the **Strength** of the distortion. We can define the direction using vectors. The X component of the linked vector is responsible for the movement in the U direction. The Y color component can be used to define the movement in the V direction. The W coordinates can be moved using the Z component of the vector. The **Strength** value is a multiplier for the linked direction vectors.*

4. Add the **Basic Gradient** node by navigating to **Assets > Generator**. In the **Attribute Manager > Basic Gradient.1** node > **Inputs** tab, change the gradient, as shown in Fig. E1.

5. Add the **Basic Gradient** node by navigating to **Assets > Generator**. Add the **Compose Color** node by navigating to **Assets > Conversion**. Connect **Basic Gradient.1 > Result** to **Compose Color.1 > Red**. Connect **Basic Gradient.2 > Result** to **Compose Color.1 > Green**. Connect **Compose Color.1 > Result** to **UV Distorter.1 > Direction**. Render the scene [see Fig. E2].

6. Add the **Noise** node by navigating to **Assets > Generator**. In the **Attribute Manager > Noise.1** node > **Inputs** tab, change **Noise Type** to **Box**. Connect **Noise.1 > Result** to **UV Distorter.1 > Strength**. Render the scene [see Fig. E3]. Fig. E4 shows the node network.

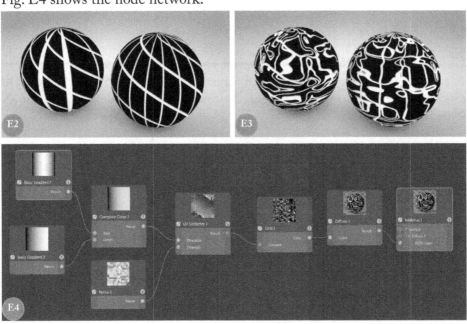

## Quiz

Evaluate your skills to see how many questions you can answer correctly.

**Multiple Choice**
Answer the following questions:

1. Which of the following keys is used to open the **Nodes Commander** window?

   [A] N                          [B] C
   [C] W                          [D] S

2. Which of the following hotkeys is used to create group of nodes?

   [A] Alt+G                      [B] Shift+G
   [C] Ctrl+G                     [D] Shift+Alt+G

3. Which of the following hotkeys is used to frame the selected nodes in the **Node Editor**?

[A] N                          [B] S
[C] F                          [D] K

4. Which of the following hotkeys is used to snap to grid in the **Node Editor**?

[A] Shift+S                     [B] Ctrl+S
[C] Alt+S                       [D] Shift+Ctrl+S

**Fill in the Blanks**
Fill in the blanks in each of the following statements:

1. Using Global Illumination as a render effect has no effect on node-based materials because they have no _____ channel by default.

2. In the **Material Manager**, you can create a new node material using the _____.

3. The _____ hotkey is used to frame all nodes in the **Node Editor**.

4. The _____ hotkey is used to show selected nodes at the center of the view without changing the zoom factor.

5. The _____ node is used to create a filled N-Gon.

6. The _____ node is used to adjust the brightness of the input data and compress dark or light values.

7. The _____ node mostly resembles to the **Layer** shader of the standard material system.

8. The _____ node can be used to compute diffuse and specular shading based on the light sources in the scene.

9. The _____ node is used to calculate the basic mathematical operations such as addition, subtraction, division, and multiplication.

10. The _____ node is automatically included in the node network when a node material is created and it defines the reflective properties of a surface.

**True or False**
State whether each of the following is true or false:

1. The **ProRender** renderer supports the node-based system.

2. You can open the **Node Editor** by double-clicking on a material node in the **Material Manager**.

3. You can drag bitmaps from outside of Cinema 4D directly onto the **Node Editor** view or onto ports, **Image** nodes with a correspondingly linked bitmap will be created.

4. The **Uber** material is a node-based asset material which is controlled by nodes.

5. The **Split Color** node is used to break a color into its individual components.


**Summary**
This unit covered the following topics:

- Node-based material system
- Node **Material Editor**

# Unit CAN: Understanding Animation and Keyframes

Animation is an act of giving life to a 3D object or character. The **4D** in **Cinema 4D** stands for the 4th dimension, the time. To animate an object, you need to change and record properties over time. As a result, an animation is created. On playing an animation, all frames are displayed one after the other in quick succession to create an illusion of movement. In this unit, you will learn about the 4th dimension.

## Animation Palette

The **Animation** palette is located below the view. It consists of three main elements: The **Timeline Ruler** [labelled as A in Fig. 1], the **Powerslider** [labelled as B in Fig. 1], and the **Animation Toolbar** [labelled as C in Fig. 1].

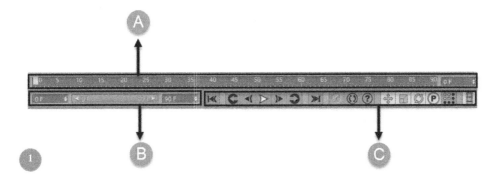

The following table summarizes these elements:

| Table 1 | |
|---|---|
| **Element** | **Description** |
| Timeline Ruler | The **Timeline Ruler** consists of two halves. Click on the top half to view the current image in the view. The lower half of the **Timeline Ruler** displays the keys of the active objects and selections. You can scale or move the ruler using the **1** and **2** hotkeys, respectively. |
| Powerslider | The **Powerslider** is located at the lower-left corner of the **Animation** palette. You can use it to quickly navigate along the timeline. The length of the **Powerslider** can be varied by dragging the triangles at its left or right ends [see Fig. 2]. You can also define a preview range by double-clicking the grayed-out frame numbers at each end of the **Powerslider**. In Fig. 2, these grayed-out frame numbers are **10** and **50**, respectively. You can extend the **Powerslider** to the entire length of the project by clicking on the timeline and simultaneously pressing **Ctrl+A**. You can toggle between the previous and current state of the **Powerslider** by double-clicking on it. Simultaneously pressing the **Alt** key while dragging on one end of the slider will scale the slider at both ends. To jump to a specific point in animation, click on the top half of the **Timeline Ruler**. You can click-drag in the top half of the **Timeline Ruler** to play the animation. If you don't want animation to play, drag with the **Alt** key. |
| Animation Toolbar | The **Animation Toolbar** consists of navigation and mode icons. You can use these icons to play an animation, define the recording mode, and so on. |

## Setting Animation Preferences

But, before we explore ways to record animation, let's first talk about animation settings. To open these settings, press **Ctrl+D**; the animation settings will be displayed in the **Project Settings** and **Key Interpolation** tabs of the **Attribute Manager**. These tabs are discussed next:

## Project Settings Tab

The **FPS** parameter controls the frame rate for the current document. This value is applied to all animations created in the scene.

The **Project Time** parameter, this is the time (frame) at which the **Timeslider** is currently positioned. The **Minimum Time** parameter controls the starting point of the animation tracks. You can also use a negative value for this parameter. The **Maximum Time** parameter defines the end time for the animation. The **Preview Min Time** and **Preview Max Time** parameters represent the start and end time of the preview range displayed in the **Powerslider**, respectively.

## Key Interpolation Tab

The options in the **Interpolation** tab are used to define the interpolation between the active key and the next key. Cinema 4D provides three options for interpolation:

- **Spline:** This is the default and most used interpolation type [see first image in Fig. 3] in Cinema 4D. You can use it to create animations in which objects accelerate and decelerate.
- **Linear:** This interpolation type [see middle image in Fig. 3] does not change the value i.e. the value remain constant.
- **Step:** When you select this type [see last image in Fig. 3], no interpolation takes place. A key value remain unchanged until the next value is reached.

You can select the interpolation type from the **Interpolation** drop-down list in the **Interpolation** tab. If the **Overdub** check box is selected and a keyframe already exists, the existing keyframe's interpolation type will be maintained when a new keyframe is recorded [only the value key will be overwritten].

You can use the options in the **Quaternion Interpolation** drop-down list to temporally affect the Quaternion interpolation [the rotational values saved in the keyframes will remain unchanged]. The **Linear (SLERP)** option animates temporally in a linear fashion [i.e., with identical velocity] whereas as the **Cubic** option casus the velocity near a keyframe to decelerate.

## Recording keyframes in CINEMA 4D

Cinema 4D offers several ways to create keys/tracks and animation.

Follow these steps:

1. Open **animation-start.c4d** and then invoke the **Scale** tool. Select **Aeroplane** in the **Object Manager** and then switch to the **Attribute Manager > Coord** tab. Scale the object; notice that scale values are not changing in the **Coord** tab.

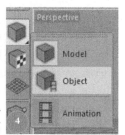

2. Choose the **Object** tool from the **Tools** palette [see Fig. E4]. Next, scale the object; notice now the scale values are changing in **Coord** tab.

3. Undo to changes you made or reopen **animation-start.c4d**.

*What just happened?*
*Here, we have enabled the **Object** mode. In this mode, when you scale an object, its axis system is scaled. This in contrast to the **Model** mode in which the surfaces are scaled. The **Object** mode is suited when you are working with an animation. When you scale an object using the **Scale** tool, only the object axes are scaled not the surfaces themselves. If you scale an object non-uniformly, the child objects get squashed and stretched when you rotate them. You can avoid this problem by working in the **Object** mode. The rule of thumb is when modeling, use the **Model** mode, use the **Object** mode for animation.*

4. In the **Animation** toolbar, click on the **Scale** , **Rotation** , and **Parameter** icons to disable them.

*What just happened?*
*Here, I have kept the **Position** icon  enabled and disabled the rest of the icons. As a result, only the position of the object will be recorded for animation. The **Position**, **Scale**, and **Rotate** modes are used to record the position, scale, and orientation values of the object, respectively. In the **Parameter**  mode, in conjunctions with the key selections, only the selected parameters will be applied when recording keyframes. This does not apply to **Position**, **Scale**, and **Rotation** settings.*

*What next?*
*Now, we will animate the position of the **Aeroplane** from blue cube to red cube.*

5. Make sure the timeslider is at frame **0** [see Fig. 5] and then click on the **Record Active Objects**  icon in the **Animation Toolbar** to create a keyframe.

6. Move the timeslider to frame **30** [see Fig. 6]. Invoke the **Move** tool, select **Aeroplane**, and then move it along the x-axis to the green cube [see Fig. 7]. Click on the **Record Active Objects** ⊘ icon in the **Animation Toolbar** to create a keyframe. Notice at frames **0** and **30**, we have created two position keyframes[see Fig. 8].

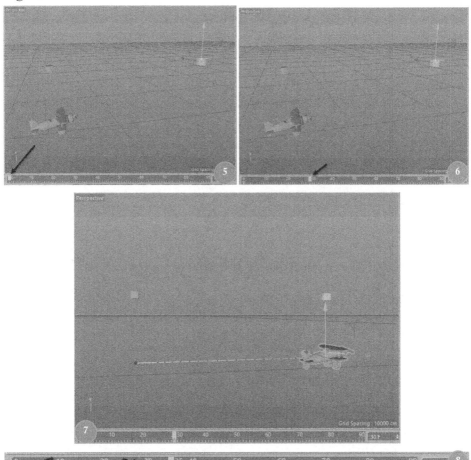

*What just happened?*

*Here, we have animated the position of the **Aeroplane** along the x-axis. The dotted line in the viewport shows the trajectory of the animation. The larger dots in the line represent keyframes [at frame **0** and **30**] and the smaller dots represent spacing.*

*Note: Record Active Objects*

*This mode allows you to create key for each selected object at the current time in the animation using the settings defined in the **Animation** palette.*

7. Click on the **Play Forwards** button to play the animation. You can also scrub the timeline to see the animation.

**What next?**
*If you play the animation, you will notice that the object is moving slowly from frame red cube to green cube. Next, we will reduce the spacing to speed up the animation.*

8. In the lower half of the **Animation Ruler,** click on the keyframe which is at frame **30**; it turns orange [see Fig. 9]. Now, drag the keyframe to frame **15** [see Fig. 10].

 **What just happened?**
*Notice in Fig. 10 the spacing between the smaller dots have increased. As a result, the animation will speed up.*

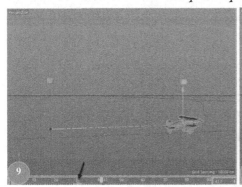

9. Move the keyframe back to frame **30**. Select **Aeroplane** in the **Object Manager** and then switch to **Coord** tab. Notice there are red circles next to position parameters: **P.X, P.Y,** and **P.Z**. See Fig. 11, also refer to **animation-finish-01.c4d**.

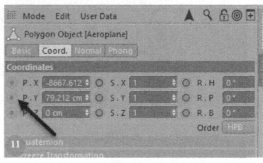

 *Note: Circles*
*Any parameter that can be animated in Cinema 4D has a black circle with the gray background next to it in the **Attribute Manager**. Click on the black circle with the gray background to create a keyframe for that particular setting. A track will also be created automatically. The following describes more about the circles and their colors:*

*__Solid red circle:__ A key exists at the current location in the animation.*
*__Empty red circle:__ An animation track exists at the current location in the animation but no keyframe.*
*__Solid yellow circle:__ a key exists at the current location but a different value exists in the **Attribute Manager**.*
*__Empty yellow circle:__ An animation track exists but the value at the current location is a different one.*

*Tip: Hotkeys for creating keys*
*Click on a circle to create a key, click again to delete key. **Shift+Ctrl+Click** on a circle to delete the track including all keys. Keyframes can be created or deleted by clicking on a keyframe circle and immediately dragging the cursor along the column of circles while continuing to press the mouse button. This also works for deleting tracks using the keyboard shortcuts described above.*

10. In the lower half of the **Timeline Ruler**, click on the right of frame **30** and drag the mouse to frame **0** to select the two keyframes [see Fig. 12]. Now, RMB click on the **Timeline Ruler** and then choose **Edit > Reverse Sequence** from the context menu [see Fig. 13].

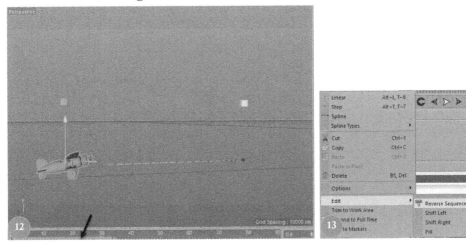

11. Play the animation; notice the direction of transition has changed i.e., the animation will run in reverse. Reverse the sequence again to restore the previous state.

 *Tip: Keys selection*
*You can also slide they keys by dragging the selection. Notice there are two dark gray handles [boxes] on each side of the selection [see Fig. 14]. You can use these handles to scale the animation [see Fig. 15]. You can use this technique to slow down or speed up the animation. You can double-click on the lower half of the **Animation Ruler** to clear the selection.*

12. Clear the keyframe selection by double-clicking on the on the lower half of the **Animation Ruler**. Move the keyframes to frame **0** and **50**. Move to timeslider to frame **44** and then click on the upper half of the **Timeline Ruler** at frame **55** with **Ctrl** held down to create a frame [see Fig. 16]. Play the animation; notice that the animation moves back little bit at the end of the animation. Also, refer to **animation-finish-02.c4d**.

**What just happened?**
*Here, we have used a non-traditional way of animating an object. If you want to make changes on a frame but want to key pose on a different frame you can use this method.*

13. Click and drag one of the larger dots in the viewport to change the position of the keyframe [see Fig. 17]. Undo the change by pressing **Ctrl+Z**.

14. Move to the frame **25** and then click on the **Autokeying** icon in the **Animation Toolbar** to enable autokeying. Invoke the **Move** tool and then move the **Aeroplane** along the y-axis, as shown in Fig. 18.

*Note: Autokeying*
*The **Autokeying** mode is an special recording mode that allows you to record keyframes without having to manually click on the record button. All changes made to a given item will be automatically saved. When you are in the autokeying mode, the viewport will be framed in red.*

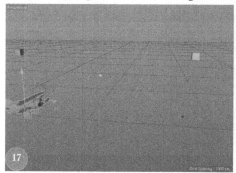

15. Select the keyframe dot in the viewport, refer to Fig. 19; the **Key Properties** are displayed in the **Attribute Manager** [see Fig. 20]. In the **Attribute Manager**, expand the **Key Preset** area and then clear the **Auto Tangents** check box; notice that the tangents appear on the key in the viewport [see Fig. 21].

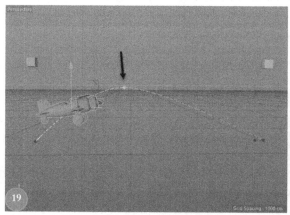

*Note: Auto Tangents*

*When **Auto Tangent**s is enabled, Cinema 4D automatically sets tangent length and angle to a soft interpolation. The tangents will run horizontally from the first key to the last key. To move tangents independently, hold **Shift** and then move a tangent. To unify the tangents again, select the **Auto Tangents** check box in the **Attribute Manager**.*

*Tip: Hiding Motion Paths*

*To hide the motion trajectory from the viewport, choose **Mode > View Settings** from the **Attribute Manager**'s menubar and then clear the **Animation Path** check box in the **Display** tab.*

16. Make sure the **Aeroplane** object is selected and then RMB click in the viewport. Now, select **Show FCurves** from the context menu to open the **Timeline** window [see Fig. 22].

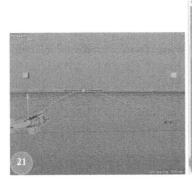

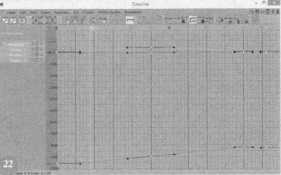

17. Choose **Functions > Position Track to Spline** from the **Timeline** menubar to create a spline out of the position FCurve [see Fig. 23]. Also, refer to **animation-finish-03.c4d**.

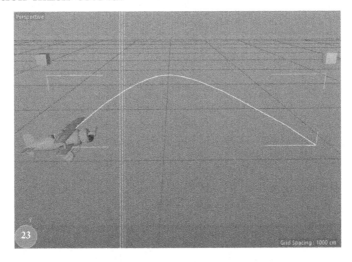

*What next?*

Notice in the **Timeline Ruler** we have keys at frame **0**, **25**, **50**, and **56** for the **Aeroplane** object. Now, if you want to accelerate the motion from frame **0** to **25** but want to keep the distance between rest of the keys, you can use the **Ripple Edit** feature. Let's explore this feature next.

18. Delete the **Spline**. RMB click on the **Timeline Ruler** and then choose **Options > Ripple Edit** from the context menu. Drag the keyframe at frame **25** to **15**; notice that all keyframes on the right of the selected frame move with it maintaining the distance between them. Now, disable the ripple edit mode by choosing **Options > Ripple Edit** from the context menu.

*What next?*

Now, we will animate the rotation of the object. Notice that we are in the **Autokeying** mode. We need to first create a keyframe for the rotation in order to create rest of the keyframes automatically for rotation.

19. Make sure **Aeroplane** is selected. Move the timeslider at frame **0** and then enable the **Rotation** ⊘ icon from the **Animation Toolbar**. Click the **Record Active Objects** ◉ icon on the **Animation Toolbar**. Move to frame **8** and then rotate the object [see Fig. 24]. Similarly, create other rotation keys. Refer to **animation-finish-04.c4d**.

*Caution: Keys in the Timeline Ruler*

If you do not see the keys in the **Timeline Ruler** for a track, it might be possible that track is not selected in the **Timeline** window. To show the keys of a track in the **Timeline Ruler**, you need to select the track in the window. Fig. 25 shows the keys if the **Position.X** track. To select all keys of an animated object, select the object in the **Timeline** window. If you have selected a track in the **Timeline** window and you want to see rest of the keys in the **Timeline Ruler**, RMB click in the **Timeline Ruler** and then choose **Options > Show Inactive Keys** from the context menu.

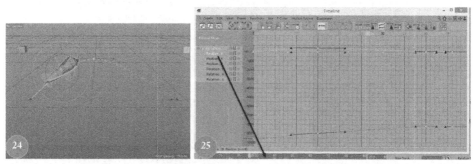

20. RMB click on the **Timeline Ruler** and then choose **Options > Advanced Mode** from the context menu; notice each key has lengthen to the height of the **Timeline Ruler** [see Fig. 26].

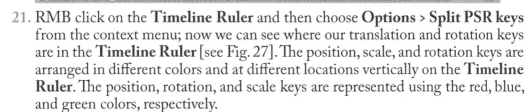

21. RMB click on the **Timeline Ruler** and then choose **Options > Split PSR keys** from the context menu; now we can see where our translation and rotation keys are in the **Timeline Ruler** [see Fig. 27]. The position, scale, and rotation keys are arranged in different colors and at different locations vertically on the **Timeline Ruler**. The position, rotation, and scale keys are represented using the red, blue, and green colors, respectively.

*Tip: Advanced Mode*

*In the **Advanced Mode**, you can offset keys by first selecting the keys using **Shift** and then dragging the gray bar to offset the keys. You can also use the handles located on either side of the bar to scale the animation. **Shift**+click on the **Timeline Ruler** to clear the selection. You can also MMB drag to offset the keys. You can double-click on the **Timeline Ruler** to play the animation. Double-click again to stop the animation.*

*Tip: Quantize function*

*The **Quantize** function is available in the **Edit** menu of the **Timeline Ruler** context menu. Enabling this function lets you set keys that do not lie entirely on a full frame [e.g., on frame **25.5**] to the nearest full frame [in this example to frame **25**].*

22. RMB click on the **Timeline Ruler** and then choose **Options > Split Vector keys** from the context menu; now Cinema 4D will show the position, scale and rotation keys' X, Y and Z components. The X, Y and Z components occupy the upper $3^{rd}$, middle $3^{rd}$, and lower $3^{rd}$ of the **Timeline Ruler**.

23. RMB click on the **Timeline Ruler** and then choose **Options > Advanced Mode** from the context menu to turn off the **Advanced Mode**. Refer to **animation-finish-05.c4d**.

*Note : Frame Rate*

*By default, Cinema 4D uses the frame rate defined in the **Project Settings**. However, you can define a different rate by pressing and holding the mouse button on the **All Frames** icon ▓ in the **Animation Toolbar** and then selecting the desired frame rate from the popup menu. When the **All Frames** option is selected, Cinema 4D actually shows each individual frame when the animation is played.*

*Tip: Keyframe selection*

When you record a key, all sub-channels of the parameter are keyed. For example, if you create a key for the rotation of an object; keys will be created for all three sub-channels: **R.H**, **R.P**, and **R.B**. Now, if you want to restrict recording to a particular channel, for example **R.B**, RMB click on it and then choose **Animation > Add Keyframe Selection** from the context menu. You can select multiple parameters as well. The selected parameter names will be colored to indicate that they belong to a keyframe selection. When you use Cinema 4D's **Autokeying** mode, only parameters in the keyframe selection will be recorded [provided their values actually change].

*Tip: Selection Object*

When recording keys in autokeying mode, you can restrict the recording to specific objects by using a **Selection** object. Then, only those objects that are assigned to the **Selection** object can be animated. To assign an object, select it and then choose **Select > Selection Filter > Create Selection Object** from the menubar; the **Selection** object will be created in the **Object Manager**. Select it and then switch to the **Attribute Manager > Object** tab. Here, you will find the selected object in the **List** box. From here, you can add or remove objects from the list. Click on the **Keyframe Selection** icon ⊚ in the **Animation Toolbar** and make sure the selection object is active here.

Clicking the **Record Active Objects** button in the **Timeline** will create a keyframe for all objects contained in a **Selection** object [position, scale, rotation, etc.]. Select the **Hierarchy** icon in the **List** box for each object whose children should be recorded in auto-keying mode as well.

*Tip: Selecting objects*

Drag the **Selection** object from the **Object Manager** into the editor view. A HUD element will be created. Double-clicking this HUD element will select all objects contained in that object's hierarchy.

*Tip: Link XYZ Sub-channels*

This option is available in the **Animate > Record** sub-menu. If this option is disabled in the **Autokeying** mode, only the vector keys [**position**, **size**, **rotation**, and **color**] that have actually changed will be recorded, i.e., if an object only moves in the **X**-direction a key for only the **X**-direction will be recorded.

The **Play Mode** options in the **Animate** menu allows you to control the playback in the timeline:

**Simple:** *The animation will play through once.*
**Cycle:** *The animation will cycle endlessly until stopped.*
**Ping-Pong:** *The animation will play forward and backward between start and end frames until stopped.*
**Preview Range:** *This option allows you to play only the defined preview range of the animation instead of playing through the entire length of the scene.*

The following table summarizes the hotkeys associated with the commands available in the **Animate** menu:

| Table 2 | | |
| --- | --- | --- |
| **Command** | **Hotkey** | **Description** |
| Record Active Objects | F9 | Creates a key for each selected object. |
| Autokeying | Ctrl+F9 | Enables the **Autokeying** mode. |
| Play Forwards | F8 | Play the animation forwards. |
| Play Backwards | F6 | Play the animation backwards. |
| Stop | F7 | Stops the animation. |
| Go to Start | Shift+F | Jumps to the start of the animation. |
| Go to End | Shift+G | Jumps to the end of the animation. |
| Go to Next Frame | G | Jumps to the next frame. |
| Go to Previous Frame | F | Jumps to the previous frame. |
| Go to Next Key | Ctrl+G | Jumps to the next key. |
| Go to Previous Key | Ctrl+F | Jumps to the previous key. |

## Timeline

The **Timeline** window is a powerful tool that you can use to edit and play the animation. You can use the **Timeline** in three modes: **Dope Sheet**, **FCurve** and **Motion** modes. You can use **Spacebar** to play or stop the animation in the **Timeline**. Use the **Tab** key to switch between these modes. Fig. 28 and Table 3 shows the main elements of the **Timeline**. Fig. 28 shows the **FCurve Mode**. To switch to the **Dope Sheet Mode**, click on the **Dope Sheet** icon on the toolbar [see Fig. 29]. Similarly, click on the **Motion Mode** icon to switch to the **Motion Mode** [see Fig. 30].

| Table 3 | |
|---------|---------|
| Number | Element |
| A | Menubar |
| B | Toolbar |
| C | Objects area |
| D | Layer column |
| E | Timeline Ruler |
| F | Keys area |

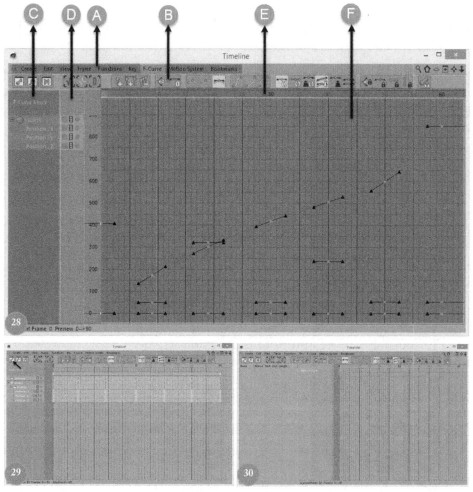

Let's first discuss the **Dope Sheet Mode**. The tracks are shown in the **Objects** area. Tracks are used to differentiate what is currently being animated. Each track represents the temporal change of one object property. Each track has its own curve that is displayed in the **Keys** area. This curve controls the interpolation between keys. The controls in the **Layer** column work similar to that of the **Object Manager** controls. You can use these controls to specify a layer/layer color, lock track, and solo a track. You can also on/off the animation using these controls. You can resize the **Objects** and **Keys** areas by dragging the separation line. Double-click on the line to reset the size.

*Note: Navigating in the Timeline*
*You can use the controls on the top-right corner of the window to navigate in the timeline. Alternatively, you can use **1** and **2** keys + click drag to move and scale, respectively.*

## Objects Area

In the **Objects** area you will find all objects, tags, materials, shaders, post effects, XPresso, and material nodes and their corresponding animation tracks. You can rename almost all items in this area. Simply, double-click on the item and then type the new name. You can also press **F2** to enable the edit field. The **Objects** area presents a hierarchial view. All animated properties belonging to a given object are displayed in this hierarchy, as well as any tags assigned to that object. You can click the + or - icons to open and close hierarchies.

*Tip: Shader and post effects*
*The shader and post effects will appear in the hierarchy of the corresponding material or render settings. Materials and render settings only displayed in the **Document** path. To display the current path, choose **View > Bars > Show Path Bar** from the menubar.*

*Caution: Number of tracks*
*An item in the **Timeline** can have any number of tracks. If any items has two tracks, only the first one will be used and the second track will be ignored.*

*Tip: Selecting entire hierarchy*
*Click on an item to select all child animation tracks [also those of child objects within the hierarchy], including all corresponding keys will be selected.*

Items in the **Timeline** can be selected using one of the following methods:

- Click on an track, use arrow keys to move up or down. The **Page Up** and **Page Down** keys let you jump to the first or last object, respectively.
- Drag a selection box around the items you want to select.
- Use the **Shift** key to select multiple consecutive items.
- Use the **Ctrl** key to select/deselect individual items that do not lie next to each other.
- **ALT** click on a track to select the track and all similar tracks of child objects. For example, clicking on **Position** X will select this track and all **Position** X tracks of the child objects.
- **ALT + Shift** click on a track to select this track and all similar tracks throughout the entire scene.

*Tip: Copying and moving tracks*
*You can transfer the selected tracks, including keys to another object via drag and drop. Simply drag a track onto another track to transfer the values. Simultaneously pressing the **Ctrl** key will copy, not move, the tracks.*

*Caution: Transferring values*
*You should only move/copy tracks that can be red by the target object. For example, you can not transfer a sphere's radius to a cube.*

*Caution: Tags/materials*
*You can not transfer track selection containing tags, materials, etc. to another object, even objects of the same type. This only works object to object, tag to tag, or material to material.*

## Timeline Ruler

The **Timeline Ruler** is located at the top of the **Key** area. Here, you can resize the preview area by dragging each end [see Fig. 31]. The top half of the **Timeline Ruler** shows the numeric location within the animation range. Normally, this information is displayed in frames. However, it can also be displayed in seconds or SMPTE. Simply click on a given location on the **Timeline Ruler** to snap the timeslider to that location. If you press **Shift** and then drag the timeslider the animation will not play in the editor view. Double-clicking on the timeslider will open a small edit field that you can use to enter precise location to which you want to jump.

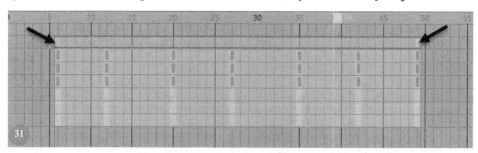

You can also create markers in the **Timeline**. Markers are visual reference points that can be placed at specific locations in the animation. Keys can also be snapped to markers. Markers can also be hidden in the **Layer Manager**. You can also exchange markers by merging the scene containing markers with the current scene. To create a marker, **Ctrl** click on the middle third of the **Timeline** [see Fig. 32].

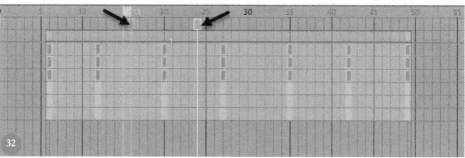

To delete a marker, simply drag it away vertically. Multiple markers can be selected by dragging a box around them. To rename a marker, double-click on it to enable an edit field and them type the new name. If you select a marker, its properties will be displayed in the **Attribute Manager**.

 *Tip: Markers*
*To create markers in the **Timeline Ruler** located below the editor view,*
***Ctrl+Shift** click.*

If you click on **Summary** in the **Objects** area, all tracks and corresponding keys will be selected. If you want to see a function curve for a track in the **Dope Sheet Mode**, twirl open the triangle located next to the track's name [see Fig. 33].

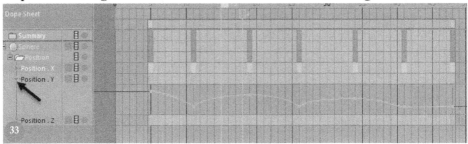

## Keys Area

All keys are displayed in the **Keys** area in chronological order. You can change value of a key without having to got the **Attribute Manger,** by double-clicking on a real key and typing the new value. A new key can be created by **Ctrl** clicking on a given track. If you click on a master track, a key will be created on all child tracks as well. Notice in Fig. 32 there are hollow or outlined keys at the top. These keys themselves have no key value and serve only as handles and selection assistants. When you select a master key, all keys of child hierarchies located at the exact same time in the animation will also be selected. Selecting individual keys automatically selects the corresponding master keys.

You can select keys using **Shift** and **Ctrl**. Select a key and then **Shift** click on another key. All keys that lie between these two keys, both horizontally and vertically, will be selected. Keys within this selection can be deselected or (re)selected via **Ctrl** click. You can also drag a selection around the keys you want to select. You can **Ctrl** drag a selected key to create a copy of it. You can also copy keys from one track to another, by using **Shift+Ctrl**. Cinema 4D will show an icon whether or not the selected keys can be copied to a desired location. If a copy icon appears, the operation is possible. If prohibition sign appears, you can not copy the keys.

FCurve represents the interpolation between keys. The **F** in the **FCurve** stands for fuction, **FCurve** stands for **Function Curves**. The **Timeline** provides lots of functions that you can use to easily control the animation. Tangents are displayed on the FCurves that you can use to accelerate or de-accelerate animation.

The following keys can be used with tangents:

- **Shift:** You can use this key to edit individual tangents. The left and right tangents are broken and can be edited separately.
- **Ctrl:** Tangent ascension remains constant; only tangent length can be edited.
- **ALT:** Tangent length remains constant; only tangent rotation can be edited.

You can select an entire FCurve by clicking on its track in the **Objects** area. A key can be added to an FCurve via **Ctrl** click. Double-clicking on an existing key lets you change its value right then and there. The following table summarizes the hotkeys associated with the **Timeline** window:

| Table 4 | |
|---|---|
| **Command** | **Hotkey** |
| Record Current State | Q |
| Region Tool | R |
| Ripple Edit | Alt+R |
| Enable Frame Snapping | X |
| Timeline Preferences | Ctrl+E |
| Automatic Mode | Alt+A |
| Go to Previous Key | Ctrl+F |
| Go to Next Key | Ctrl+G |
| Go to First Key/Motion Clip | Ctrl+P |
| Go to Last Key/Motion Clip | Ctrl+O |
| Go to Previous Marker | Shift+P |
| Go to Next Marker | Shift+N |
| Go to First Marker | Ctrl+Shift+P |
| Go to Last Marker | Ctrl+Shift+O |
| Frame Selected | S |
| Frame All | H |
| Go to Current Frame | O |
| Go to Start | Alt+F |
| Go to End | Alt+G |
| Frame Preview Range | Alt+H |
| Linear | Alt+L, T~6 |
| Step | Alt+T, T~7 |
| Auto Tangents - Classic | A, T~1 |
| Break Tangents | B, T~2 |

| Table 4 | |
|---|---|
| Command | Hotkey |
| Clamp | C, T~5 |
| Zero Angle (Tangent) | 0, T~3 |
| Zero Length (Tangent) | L, T~4 |

## Exploring the Interpolation Types

We have already discussed the interpolation options found in the **Project Settings**. These option define how the interpolation between the active key and the next key should be calculated. Follow these steps:

1. Open **simple-bounce.c4d**. Select the **Sphere** in the **Object Manager** and then RMB click in the viewport. Next, select **Show FCurves** from the context menu to open the **Timeline** window.

2. Choose **View > Grid > No Grid** from the **Timeline** menubar to hide the grid [see Fig. 34].

 *Note: Default interpolation*
*The default interpolation type is **Spline** which is shown in Fig. 34. Notice the **Spline** icon ⌁ is enabled in the **Timeline** toolbar. Also, notice that **Spline** option is selected in the **Key** menu.*

3. Make sure all keys are selected. You can also use **Ctrl+A** to select all keys and then choose **Key > Linear** from the menubar [see Fig. 35]. Alternatively, you can press **Alt+L** or click the **Linear** icon ⌁ in the **Timeline** toolbar. This type of interpolation is best suited for mechanical and robotic motion. Play the animation to see the result.

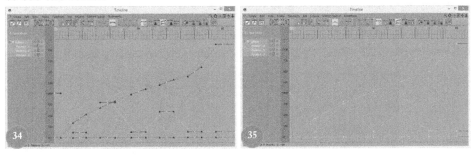

 *Tip: Keys hidden menu*
*You can press the **T** key to open the **Keys** hidden menu [see Fig. 36] and then access various commands from it. For example, to change interpolation to **Linear**, you can press **T** followed by **6**.*

Keys: T
1 ... Auto Tangents - Classic
2 ... Break Tangents
3 ... Zero Angle (Tangent)
4 ... Zero Length (Tangent)
5 ... Clamp
6 ... Linear
7 ... Step
8 ... Soft
9 ... Ease Ease
I ... Ease In
O ... Ease Out

4. Make sure all keys are selected. Choose **Key > Step** from the menubar [see Fig. 37]. Alternatively, you can press **Alt+T** or click the **Step** icon ⚐ on the **Timeline** toolbar. Play the animation; you will not see any change in the animation until you get to the next key. This type of interpolation is best suited for blocking the poses.

5. Click the **Spline** icon on the **Timeline** toolbar. Choose **F-Curve > Show All Tracks** from the **Timeline** menubar. Select the **Position.Y** track from the left pane of the **Timeline** window; the track function is displayed in the **Timeline** window [see Fig. 38].

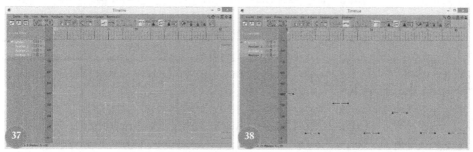

6. Select the keys as shown in Fig. 39 and then adjust the tangents using the **Shift** key [see Fig. 40]. Play the animation; now you will notice that sphere is realistically bouncing off the imaginary plane. Similarly, you can use the top keys to create ease in effect [see Fig. 41]. Play the animation to see the effect. Also, refer to **simple-bounce-finish.c4d**.

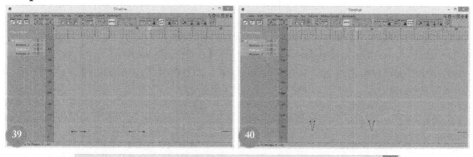

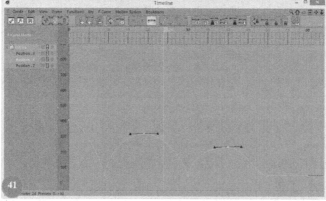

7. Open **simple-bounce-2.c4d**. Select **Sphere** and then open the **Timeline**. Select the **Position.Y** track and then select the key at frame **50** [see Fig. 42]. Choose **Key > Spline Type > Soft** from the menu bar. Alternatively, you can press **Alt+S** or **T~8** [see Fig. 43].

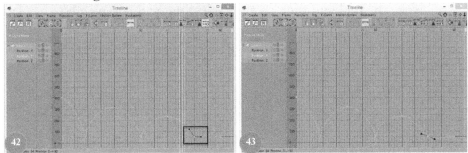

> **What just happened?**
> *Here, I have changed **Spline Type** to **Soft**. The functioning of the **Soft** type is similar to that of the **Auto Tangents** feature. However, there is one exception, when **Soft** is applied, the first and last keys' tangents will be aligned in accordance with a soft interpolation.*

8. Press **Alt+I** to change type to **Ease In** [see Fig. 44]. Press **Alt+O** to change type to **Ease Out** [see Fig. 45]. Press **Ctrl+Z** to undo last action and then press **Alt+E** to change type to **Ease Ease** [see Fig. 46].

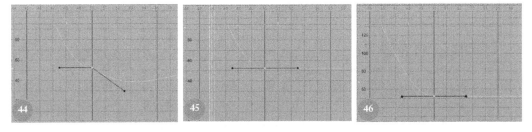

> **What just happened?**
> *Here, we have used different spline types that control the ease interpolations. These are used to make acceleration and/or deceleration more realistic. Given below is a summary of ease interpolation:*
>
> ***Ease In:*** *The tangents will be broken. The right tangent remains unchanged and the left tangent will be rotated horizontally.*
> ***Ease Ease:*** *The tangents will be placed horizontally. The FCurve will be assigned a local minimum / maximum, preventing the animation from over-rotating.*
> ***Ease Out:*** *The tangents will be broken. The left tangent remains unchanged and the right tangent will be rotated horizontally.*
>
> *The **Zero Angle Length** parameter changes the key tangents to defined basic state. The **Unify** function should be applied to broken tangents only. This parameter mirrors the right tangent and replaces the left tangent.*

## Working with the Region Tool

This tool creates a floating selection that you can change at any time. It allows edit key groups in either **Dope Sheet** mode or in **F-Curve** mode. The selection frame has handles at all corners and on each side with which it can be scaled. To make a selection, invoke the tool and then create a selection by dragging a box; a selection box is created [see Fig. 47].

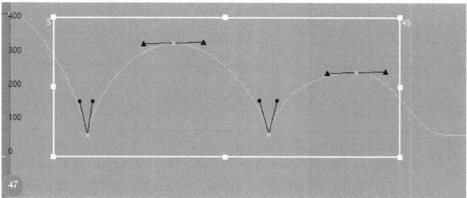

You can use the **Shift** key to select multiple regions. Every key within a given selection frame will be selected. Click and drag inside the box to move the selected keys. You can simultaneously create copies of the selected keys at another location on the tack. The selection frame has handles at all corners and on each side with which you can scale the box.

The following applies to this tool:

- Click and drag within a given region to move the region underneath the mouse pointer including keys.
- Click and drag with **Alt** held down to move all regions including keys.
- Click and drag with **Shift** held down within a given region to move the region underneath the cursor, without keys.
- Click and drag with **Shift+Alt** held down within a given region to move all regions, excluding keys.
- Click drag outside a region with **Shift** held down to create a new region.
- Click drag with **Ctrl** held down outside of a given region to remove regions or parts of regions.
- You can copy keys within a given region by using **Ctr+C** and then paste the keys using **Ctrl+V**.

## Ghosting Animation

Ghosting is a traditional animation aid that display animation states [hereinafter referred to as ghosts] prior to and following an animation frame. Depending on the proximity in the animation to the current frame the ghosts have an decreasing transparency value up to **0%**.

Follow these steps:

1.  Open **simple-bounce.c4d**. Select **Sphere** in the **Object Manager** and then RMB click. Choose **Cinema 4D Tags** > **Display** from the context menu.

2.  In the **Attribute Manager** > **Ghosting** tab, select the **Enable** check box to enable ghosting; the ghosts appear in the editor view [see Fig. 48].

3.  Play the animation. Notice that at the beginning of the animation the ghosts are spread farther apart [see Fig. 49]. It simply means that the object is moving fast in the beginning.

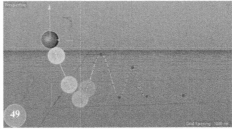

 *Tip: Ghosting in viewport*
*You can temporarily disable ghosting by choosing **Filter** > **Ghosting** from the*
***Menu in editor view**.*

4.  Make sure **Draw Mode** is set to **Object** and then change **Frames Before** and **Frames After** to **10** each. Also, change **Frames Step** to **1**. Play the animation [see Fig. 50].

 *What just happened?*
*Here, we are using **Object** as the **Draw Mode**. The options in the **Draw Mode** drop-down list are used to define how ghosts will be drawn in the viewport. When you select **Object** as **Draw Mode**, the ghosts are drawn in wireframes. Given below are other draw options available:*

*Point: Ghosts will be displayed as points at the object's origin.*
*Axis: Ghosts will be drawn as small axis shape.*
*Trail: The animation will be drawn as a trail along the animation path. The longer the trail the faster the movement.*
*Multi Trail: Each object point will be followed by a trail.*
*Velocity: Each object point's ghost point will be assigned a velocity vector.*

*The **Frames Before** and **Frames After** parameters control how many frames before and after the current frame should be included in the ghosting process. The color of the ghosts can be defined using the swatches to the right of these parameters. The **Frames Step** parameter defines the temporal interval between individual ghosts.*

5. Change **Frames Step** to **3** and then select the **Use Range** check box. Now, change **Start** and **End** to **30** and **60**, respectively. Play the animation; notice that now ghosts are only appearing within the specified range [see Fig. 51]. Clear the **Use Range** check box.

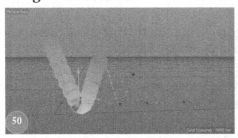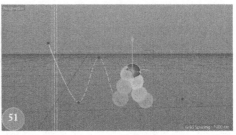

6. Select the **Use Custom** check box and then enter **20, 30, 50-60** in the **Custom Frames** field. Play the animation [see Fig. 52]. Also, refer to **ghosting-finish.c4d**.

*What just happened?*
*Here, we have used the **Custom Frames** parameter to display ghosts at specific time. Ghosts will be drawn at frame **20** and **30** as we as the frame range **50-60** [per frame of the animation for the range].*

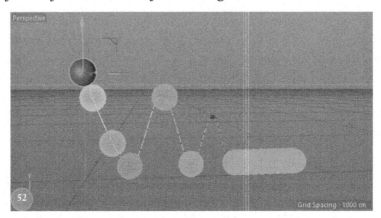

*Note: Caching ghosts*
*You need to calculate the cache in the following cases:*

*• A deformer object affects the object, for example, the **Skin** object.*
*• If generators are used for ghosting, for example, the **Subdivisions Surfaces** and **Sweep** objects.*
*• Expressions/Plugins affect the geometry.*

*You need to select **Use Cache** check box if you want cache to be used.*

*Caution: Cache size*
*Make sure to empty the cache by clicking on the **Empty Cache** button to avoid large file size. Therefore, delete the cache before saving the file.*

## Creating Animation Previews

To **Make Preview** option in the **Render** menu allows you to create preview of the rendered animation; the preview is displayed in the **Picture Viewer**. When you choose this option, the **Make Preview** dialog box is displayed. In this dialog box, select the options as per requirement and then click **OK** to start rendering. Once the rendering completes, the preview is loaded in the **Picture Viewer**. In the **History** tab of the **Picture Viewer**, select the render folder and then **RMB** click. Select **Save As** option from the context menu or press **Shift+Ctrl+S** to open the **Save** dialog box. Change **Type** as **Animation**. Select a video format such as **AVI** or **MP4** from the **Format** drop-down list and then click **OK** to save the file.

## Hands-on Exercises

### Exercise 1: Animating a Seamless Cycle

In this exercise, we will animate a seamless animation cycle. Table E1 summarizes the exercise.

| Table E1 | |
|---|---|
| Difficulty level | Beginner |
| Estimated time to complete | 25 Minutes |
| Topics | • Getting Started<br>• Creating the Animation |
| Resources folder | **unit-can** |
| Units | **Centimeters** |
| Start file | **seamless-cyele-start.c4d** |
| Final file | **seamless-cyele-finish.c4d** |

### Getting Started

Open **seamless-cyele-start.c4d**.

### Creating the Animation

Follow these steps:

1. Select **Aeroplane** in the **Object Manager** and then in the **Attribute Manager >**
   **Coord** tab > **Freeze Transformation** area, click **Freeze All**.

 *What just happened?*
   *Freezing transformations in Cinema 4D freezes [zero out, also referred to as dual transformation] the coordinates of all selected objects. When you freeze coordinates, the local position and rotation coordinates will each be set to 0 and scale to 1 without changing position or orientation of the object.*

*Freezing transformations is particularly useful in animations using parent-child relationships. When you rotate a child object around an axis, all three axes are affected because the parent object's coordinate system has a different orientation from the local coordinates. You can avoid this scenario by freezing the coordinates before animating.*

2. Press **Ctrl+D** to open the **Project Settings**. In the **Attribute Manger** > **Project Settings** tab, change **Maximum Time** and **Preview Max Time** to **32**. Now, select **Object** from the **Tools** palette to enable **Object** mode.

 *What just happened?*
   *Here, we have set **Maximum Time** to **32** that gives a nice mid point at frame **16** and two sub-midpoints at frame **8** and **24**. You can use even number for **Maximum Time** parameter.*

3. Make sure you at frame **0** and then click on the **Scale** and **Parameter** icons in the **Animation Toolbar** to disable them. Now, click on the **Record Active Objects** icon to record the keyframe.

4. Select the keyframe in the **Timeline Ruler** and then press **Ctrl+C** to copy the key. Now, move to frame **32** and press **Ctrl+V** to paste the key.

 *Tip: Copying frame*
   *You can also **Ctrl** click on frame **32** to create a copy of frame **0** because there are no other keys between frame **0** and **32**. You can also copy-paste keys in the **Timeline**.*

5. Move to frame **16** and then click the **Autokeying** icon in the **Animation Toolbar**. Make sure the **Aeroplane** is selected in the **Object Manager** and then in the **Attribute Manager** > **Coord** tab, change **P.Y** to **-20**. Play the animation; notice that now **Aeroplane** oscillates up and down because we have specified the same value for frame **0** and **32**.

6. Move to frame **8** and then in the **Attribute Manager** > **Aeroplane** > **Coord** tab, change **R.P** to **-5**. In the **Timeline Ruler**, copy the key at frame **8** and paste it on frame **24**.

7. **RMB** click in the viewport and then choose **Show FCurves** from the context menu to open the **Timeline** window [see Fig. E1]. Disable the **Show All Tracks** option by choosing **F-Curve** > **Show All Tracks** from the menubar.

8. Select the **Rotation.P** track from the **Objects** area and then press **S** to frame the selected function [see Fig. E2].

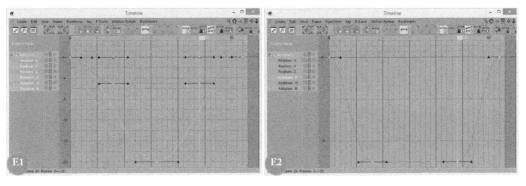

E1  E2

*Tip: Framing all curves*
*Press* **H** *to frame all curves in the* **Timeline**.

9. In the **Keys** area, double-click on the key at frame **24** and then enter **5** [type **5** and then press **Enter**] in the edit field. Press **H** to frame all keys [see Fig. E3].

→ *What next?*
*Play the animation; notice there a pause when timeslider moves from frame* **32** *to frame* **0**. *Next, we will fix it.*

10. Select the **Position.Y** and **Rotation.P** tracks in the **Objects** area and then select all keys in the **Keys** area by dragging a selection box.

11. Choose **Functions** > **Track Before** > **Repeat Before** from the menubar [see Fig. E4]. Choose **Functions** > **Track After** > **Repeat After** from the menubar [see Fig. E5].

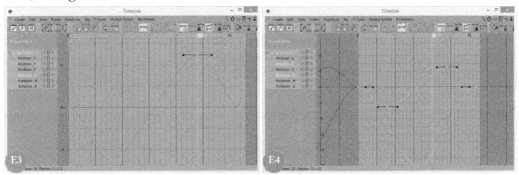

E3  E4

 **Parameters: Repeat Before/ Repeat After**
These two parameter define how the track animation should be calculated before the first and after the last key.

12. Select the **Rotation.P** track in the **Objects** area; notice the abrupt change in the curvature of the graph at frame **0** and **32** [see Fig. E6]. Select these two keyframes and then adjust the tangents, as show in Fig. E7. Play the animation.

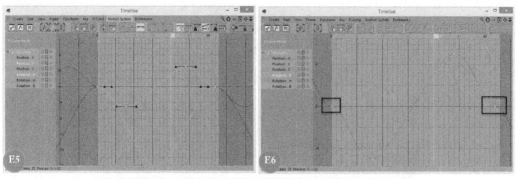

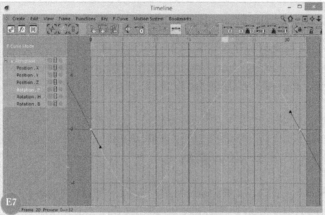

13. Using the **Powerslider** change range to **0** to **300**. Now, if you play the animation stops at frame **64**. It happens because animation is looping just once [**32+32=64**]. Next, we will fix it.

14. Select the **Rotation.P** track in the **Objects** area and then in the **Attribute Manager** > **Properties** tab, change **After** > **Repetitions** to **10**. Repeat the process for the **Position.Y** track. Play the animation.

## Exercise 2: Animating a Cube - I

In this exercise, we will animate a cube using the linear interpolation. Fig. E1 shows the cube at frame **13** and **65**, respectively. Table E2 summarizes the exercise.

| Table E2 | |
|---|---|
| Difficulty level | Intermediate |
| Estimated time to complete | 35 Minutes |
| Topics | • Getting Started<br>• Creating the Animation |
| Resources folder | **unit-can** |
| Units | **Centimeters** |
| Start file | **cube-1-start.c4d** |
| Final file | **cube-1-finish.c4d** |

## Getting Started
Open **cube-1-start.c4d**.

## Creating the Animation
Follow these steps:

1. Select **Cube** in the **Object Manager** and then in the **Attribute Manager** > **Coord** tab > **Freeze Transformation** area, click **Freeze All**.

2. Press **Ctrl+D** to open the **Project Settings**. In the **Attribute Manger** > **Project Settings** tab, change **Maximum Time** and **Preview Max Time** to **128** each. Now, select **Object** from the **Tools** palette to enable **Object** mode.

3. Make sure you at frame **0** and then click on the **Scale** and **Parameter** icons in the **Animation Toolbar** to disable them.

4. Select **Cube** in the **Object Manager** and then in the **Attribute Manager** > **Coord** tab, select the **R.P**, **P.Y**, and **P.Z** labels using **Ctrl**. RMB click and then choose **Animation** > **Add Keyframe Selection** from the context menu.

*What just happened?*
*Here, we have created a keyframe selection using the **Add Keyframe Selection** option. As a result, only these three parameters will be keyed when we will record keyframes.*

5. Click on the **Record Active Objects** icon in the **Animation Toolbar** to record the keyframe.

6. Move to frame **16** and then in the **Attribute Manager** > **Cube** > **Coord** tab, change **P.Z** to **-335** [see Fig. E2]. Move to frame **32** and then in the **Attribute Manager** > **Cube** > **Coord** tab, change **P.Y** to **-300**. Also, change **R.P** to **90** [see Fig. E3]. Press F9 to create a keyframe.

*What next?*
*Play the animation; you will notice that the cube is intersecting the base. To fix it, we need to move along the Y axis.*

7. Move to frame **16** which is the midpoint between the two keyframes we have created. In the **Attribute Manager > Cube > Coord** tab, change **P.Y** to **65** and then press F9 [see Fig. E4].

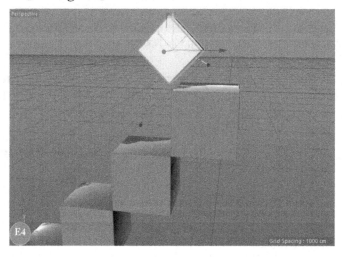

*What next?*
*Play the animation; notice that to create linear motion we need to make **R.P** and **P.Z** functions linear and also we need to give more air to the **Cube** along **P.Y**. We will do it in the **Timeline**.*

8. Make sure **Cube** is selected and then **RMB** click in the editor view. Next, choose **Show FCurves** from the context menu to open the **Timeline**.

9. Disable the **Show All Tracks** option by choosing **F-Curve > Show All Tracks** from the menubar. Also, choose **View > Grid > No Grid** from the menubar to hide the grid.

10. Select the **Position.Z** and **Position.P** tracks in the **Objects** area [see Fig. E5]. Now, press **Alt+L** to change interpolation to **Linear**.

11. Select the **Position.Y** track in the **Objects** area. Select the end points of the curve [see Fig. E6] and then choose **Key > Zero Length (Tangent)**. Alternatively, you can press **L** or **T~4**.

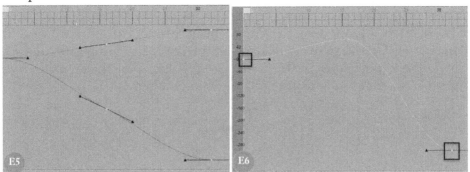

*What just happened?*

*Here, we have set the tangent length to zero, which prevents a kink in the curve. Two sequential keys with this property produces a linear interpolation between them. And, that's what we are looking for. The **Zero Angle (Tangent)** command also available in the **Key** menu, allows you to set the tangent to a horizontal position. In doing so, the animation near the key will not reach greater/lesser values than those defined in the key itself.*

*Tip: Tangents*

*You can also change the length of the tangents using **Ctrl** dragging.*

12. Select the middle key and then give it a nice curve by manipulating the tangents [see Fig. E7].

13. Select all keys in the **Keys** areas for all tracks. Choose **Functions > Track After > Offset Repeat After** from the menubar [see Fig. E8].

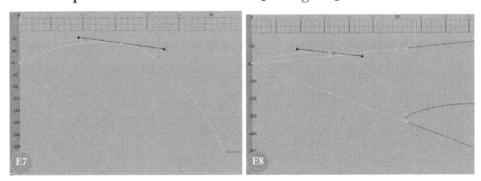

14. Select all tracks in the **Objects** area and then in the **Attribute Manager > Properties** tab, change **After > Repetitions** to **3**. Play the animation to see the result.

*What next?*

*Notice that the animation is little bit on the slower side. We need to increase the speed, we will do so by scaling the animation in the **Dope Sheet Mode**.*

15. Choose **View > Dope Sheet** from the menu bar to activate the **Dope Sheet Mode**. Press **Ctrl+A** to select all keys and then scale the **Timeline Ruler** so that the right end is anchored at frame **20** [see Fig. E9]. Play the animation; adjust the preview range and repetitions as per your requirement.

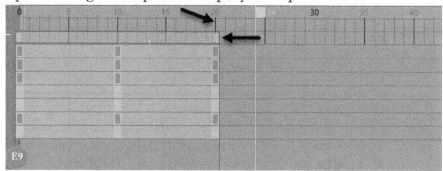

## Exercise 3: Animating a Cube - II

In this exercise, we will animate a cube using the **Null** object. Fig. E1 shows the animation at frame **5** and **25**, respectively.

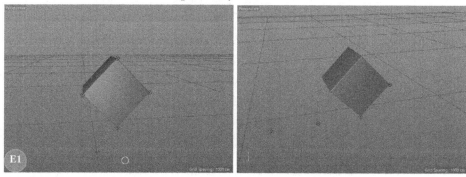

Table E3 summarizes the exercise.

| Table E3 | |
|---|---|
| Difficulty level | Intermediate |
| Estimated time to complete | 30 Minutes |
| Topics | • Getting Started<br>• Creating the Animation |
| Resources folder | **unit-can** |
| Units | **Centimeters** |
| Final file | **cube-2-finish.c4d** |

Follow these steps:

1. Create a **Cube** object. Select the **Cube** in the **Object Manager** and then in the **Attribute Manager** > **Coord** tab, change **P.Y** to **100** to place the **Cube** on the grid.

2. In the **Attribute Manager** > **Coord** tab > **Freeze Transformation** area, click **Freeze All**.

3. Create a **Null** object, press **Shift+S** to enable snapping, and then align the **Null** object, as shown in Fig. E2. Select **Null** in the **Object Manager** and then in the **Attribute Manager** > **Object** tab, change **Display** to **Diamond**.

4. Similarly, create three more **Null** objects [by **Ctrl** dragging] and align them, as shown in Fig. E3. Fig. E4 shows the objects in the **Object Manager**. Now, group the objects, as shown in Fig. E5. Also, refer to Fig. E6.

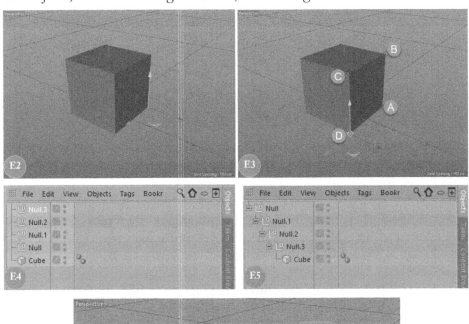

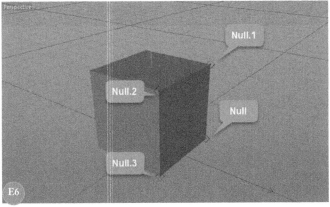

## Creating the Animation
Follow these steps:

1. Make sure you at frame **0** and then click on the **Scale** and **Parameter** icons in the **Animation Toolbar** to disable them. Select the **Null** object in the **Object Manager** and then press **F9** to record the key.

2. Move to frame **10** and then in the **Attribute Manager > Null > Coord** tab, change **R.P** to **-90** [see Fig. E7]. Press **F9** to record the key.

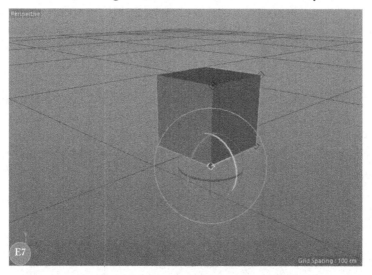

3. Select the **Null.1** object in the **Object Manager** and then press **F9** to record the key. Move to frame **20** and then in the **Attribute Manager > Null.1 > Coord** tab, change **R.P** to **-90**. Press **F9** to record the key.

4. Select the **Null.2** object in the **Object Manager** and then press **F9** to record the key. Move to frame **30** and then in the **Attribute Manager > Null.2 > Coord** tab, change **R.P** to **-90**. Press **F9** to record the key.

5. Select the **Null.3** object in the **Object Manager** and then press **F9** to record the key. Move to frame **40** and then in the **Attribute Manager > Null.3 > Coord** tab, change **R.P** to **-90**. Press **F9** to record the key. Press **F8** to play the animation.

## Exercise 4: Animating Along a Path
In this exercise, we will animate an object along a path. Fig. E1 shows the object at frame **23** and **64**, respectively. Table E4 summarizes the exercise.

| Table E4 | |
|---|---|
| Difficulty level | Beginner |
| Estimated time to complete | 15 Minutes |

| Table E4 | |
|---|---|
| Topics | • Getting Started<br>• Creating the Animation |
| Resources folder | **unit-can** |
| Units | **Centimeters** |
| Start file | **path-animation-start.c4d** |
| Final file | **path-animation-finish.c4d** |

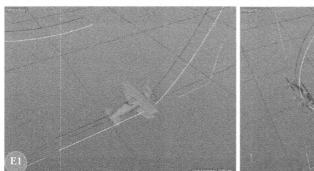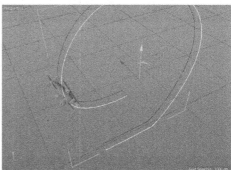

## Getting Started

Open **path-animation-start.c4d**. This scene contains an object and a spline [see Fig. E2] along which we will animate the object.

## Creating the Animation

Follow these steps:

1. Select **Aeroplane** in the **Object Manager** and then in the **Attribute Manager >  Coord** tab > **Freeze Transformation** area, click **Freeze All**.

2. Select the **Aeroplane** in the **Object Manager** and then **RMB** click. Choose **Cinema 4D Tags > Align to Spline** from the context menu.

3. Drag **Spline** from **Object Manager** to **Spline Path** field of the **Attribute Manager > Tag** tab.

4. Make sure you at frame **0** and then in the **Attribute Manager,** click on the **Position** circle to create a keyframe. Move to frame **90** and then change **Position** to **100**. Click on circle to create a keyframe and then play the animation.

 *What just happened?*
*Here, we have animated the **Position** parameter. As a result, the object is following the spline. This parameter uses the axis defined by the **Axis** parameter. If the object should follow, say, only the first half of the spline, animate **Position** from **0%** to **50%**.*

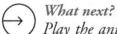

What next?
Play the animation; notice that the **Aeroplane** is not oriented correctly [see Fig. E3]. Next, we will fix it.

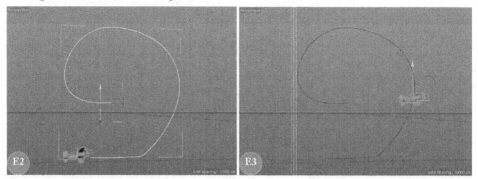

5. In the **Attribute Manager > Tag** tab, select the **Tangential** check box; notice the **Aeroplane** is facing in the wrong direction [see Fig. E4]. Change **Axis** to **X** to correct the direction.

What next?
If you play the animation, you will notice that the **Aeroplane** flips around frame **39** [see Fig. E5]. Next, we will fix it.

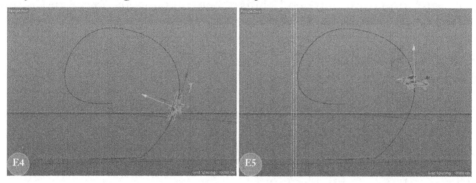

6. Create a copy of **Spline** and rename it as **Path-Rail**. Align it, as shown in Fig. E6. Select the tag in the **Object Manager** and then drag **Path-Rail** from the **Object Manager** to the **Rail Path** field in the **Attribute Manager > Tag** tab. Play the animation; notice that now the **Aeroplane** is correctly oriented along the path [see Fig. E7].

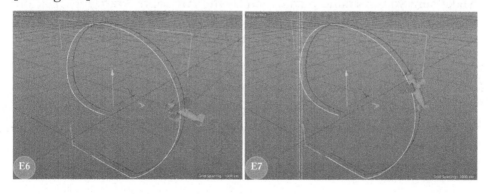

## Exercise 5: Driving Animation using XPresso

In this exercise, we will create an animation using the XPresso module of Cinema 4D.

> **Note: Learning XPresso**
> *If you want to learn the XPresso module of Cinema 4D in detail, please refer to our book, **Maxon Cinema 4D R20: A Detailed Guide to XPresso**.*

Table E5 summarizes the exercise.

| Table E5 | |
|---|---|
| Difficulty level | Beginner |
| Estimated time to complete | 15 Minutes |
| Topics | • Getting Started<br>• Creating the Animation |
| Resources folder | **unit-can** |
| Units | **Centimeters** |
| Start file | **gear-xpresso-start.c4d** |
| Final file | **gear-xpresso-finish.c4d** |

### Getting Started
Open **gear-xpresso-start.c4d**.

### Creating the Animation
Follow these steps:

1. Select the **Wheel** in the **Object Manager** and then **RMB** click. Choose **Cinema 4D Tags** > **XPresso** from the context menu to open the **XPresso Editor**.

2. Add a **Time** node by navigating to **New Node** > **XPresso** > **General**. Add the **Real** output port to the **Time** node. Drag **Wheel** from the **Object Manger** to

the **XPresso Editor**. Add the **Coordinate** > **Position** > **Position.X** input port to the **Wheel** node. Connect **Time** > **Real** to **Wheel** > **Position.X** [see Fig. E1].

*What just happened?*
*Here, we have used the temporal data generated by the **Time** node to drive the animation along the x-axis. The **Time** node gives access to various temporal data of an animation using various output ports. The **Real** port outputs the current time in seconds from the beginning of the animation. The **Time** port also outputs the current time in seconds from the beginning of the animation. However, internal calculations are more precise than the **Real** port. If you play the animation, you will notice the movement of the object is slow. Next, we will use a multiplier to increase the speed.*

3. Disconnect the **Time** and **Wheel** nodes. Add a **Math** node by navigating to **New Node** > **XPresso** > **Calculate**. Connect **Time** > **Real** to **Math** > first **Input**. In the **Attribute Manager** > **Math** node > **Node** tab, change **Function** to **Multiply**. In the **Parameter** tab, change **Input [2]** to **10**. Connect **Math** > **Output** to **Wheel** > **Position.X** [see Fig. E2]. Play the animation.

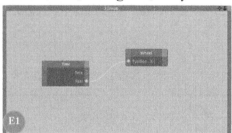
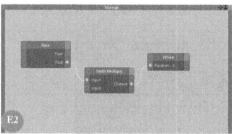

*What next?*
*Now, we will work on the rotation of **Wheel**.*

4. Add the **Rotation.B** input port to the **Wheel** node. Add a **Degree** node by navigating to **New Node** > **XPresso** > **Calculate**. Create a copy of the **Math** node [see Fig. E3].

5. Connect **Time** > **Real** to new **Math** node > first **Input**. Connect new **Math** node > **Output** to **Degree** > **Input**. Connect **Degree** > **Output** to **Wheel** > **Rotation.B**. [see Fig. E4]. In the **Attribute Manager** > new **Math** node > **Parameter** tab, change **Input [2]** to **5**. Play the animation to see the result.

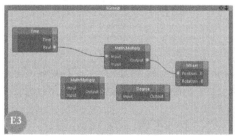
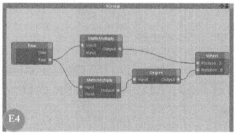

## Exercise 6: Working with Set Driven Keys

In this exercise, we will understand the concept of setting objects' parameter as driver or driven. The parameter that controls the attributes of the other object is called driver and the parameter that is being controlled is called driven. Table E6 summarizes the exercise.

| Table E6 | |
|---|---|
| Difficulty level | Intermediate |
| Estimated time to complete | 20 Minutes |
| Topics | • Getting Started<br>• Creating Set Driven Keys Setup |
| Resources folder | **unit-can** |
| Units | **Centimeters** |
| Start file | **driver-driven-start.c4d** |
| Final file | **driver-driven-finish.c4d** |

### Getting Started

Open **driver-driven-start.c4d**. Now, we will use **Capsule** as driver and **Cube** as driven object.

### Creating Set Driven Keys Setup

Follow these steps:

1. Choose the **Object** mode from the **Tools** palette. With **Capsule** selected in the **Object Manager,** select the **Coord** tab in **Attribute Manager. RMB** click on the **P.X** label and navigate to **XPressions > Set Driver** [see Fig. E1]. With **Cube** selected in **Object Manager,** choose the **Coord** tab in **Attribute Manager. RMB** click on the **R.H** label and navigate to **XPressions > Set Driven (Absolute).**

*What just happened?*
*Notice that **XPresso Expression** tag appears on the right of **Cube** in the **Object Manager** [see Fig. E2]. Click on the tag to select it and check its parameters in the **Attribute Manager**. The text in the **Name** field shows the relationship we have created by mapping parameters of **Capsule** and **Cube** [see Fig. E3].*

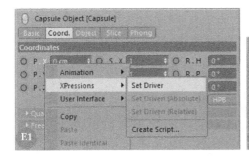

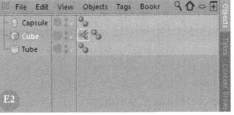

2. Move the **Capsule** in viewport along the **X** axis; notice that the driver **Capsule**'s movement is rotating driven **Cube**. Moving **Capsule** along the positive x-axis rotates the **Cube** anti-clockwise whereas the along the negative x-axis the **Cube** rotates clockwise.

3. Double-click on the **XPresso XPression** tag to open the **XPresso Editor** [see Fig. 4]; notice that the **Capsule** and **Cube** are connected via the **Range Mapper** node which is converting input real values to degrees. Now, you can use any XPresso node you want to farther edit the node graph.

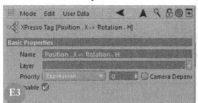
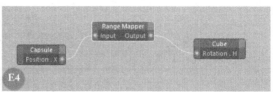

## Exercise 7: Working with the Animation Layers

In this exercise, we will modify an animation non-destructively using Cinema 4D's animation layers. Table E7 summarizes the exercise.

| Table E7 | |
| --- | --- |
| Difficulty level | Intermediate |
| Estimated time to complete | 25 Minutes |
| Topics | • Getting Started<br>• Working with Animation Layers |
| Resources folder | **unit-can** |
| Units | **Centimeters** |
| Start file | **animation-layer-start.c4d** |
| Final file | **animation-layer-finish.c4d** |

### Getting Started
Open **animation-layer-start.c4d**.

### Working with Animation Layers
Follow these steps:

1. Select **Sphere** in the **Object Manager** and then **RMB** click. Next, choose **Cinema 4D Tags > Motion System** from the context menu. Fig. E1 shows the properties of the tag in the **Attribute Manager**.

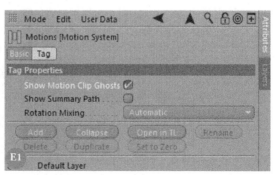

**What just happened?**

*Here, we have applied the **Motion System** tag to the object. This tag allows you to work with animation layers. It allows you to add animation on top of the existing animation in nondestructive way.*

**Caution: Motion System tag**

*If a **Motion System** tag is assigned to an object that is part of a hierarchy that already has a **Motion System** tag assigned to it, you might get unwanted results. Therefore, avoid such setup. You should also avoid modifying a hierarchy to which a **Motion System** tag has been assigned.*

**Note: Motion System tag**

*This tag affects not only the object to which it is assigned but the entire object's hierarchy as well. This tag is automatically assigned to the active object once you execute the **Add Relative Animation Layer**, **Add Absolute Animation Layer**, **Add Motion Clip**, or **Add Empty Motion Layer** command from the **Animate** menu.*

**What next?**

*Notice there are two options available for adding animation layer: **Add Relative Animation Layer** and **Add Absolute Animation Layer**. These options create a new absolute or relative animation layer, respectively, for the object(s) currently selected in the **Object Manager**. Normally, relative animation layers are used; the active animation layer is added to the one below it. When recording the keyframes, only the relative offset to the underlying animation layer will be recorded. For example, if an object is positioned at **Y=100** and you record on an animation layer at **Y=110**; the keyframe on this animation layer will be assigned a value equal to the difference: **10**. If you record this keyframe on an absolute animation layer, the difference would be animated as an absolute value of **Y=210**. Next, we will use the **Add Relative Animation Layer** command to add the **Motion System** tag.*

**Note: Tags menu**

*When you add the **Motion System** tag from the **Tags** menu, a relative animation layer is added. To add an absolute layer, you need to choose the **Add Absolute Animation Layer** option from the **Animate** menu.*

2. Delete the **Motion System** tag from the **Object Manager**. Choose the **Add Relative Animation Layer** option from the **Animate** menu to add the **Motion System** tag to the **Sphere** in the scene.

*What next?*

*The **Sphere** in the scene comes in contact with the ground on frame **9** and **30**. On frame **19**, the frame is at top of the first bounce. Let's now add animation layer to move the sphere little bit higher along the y-axis.*

3. Move to frame **9** and then in the **Attribute Manager** > **Sphere** > **Motion System** tab, make sure **Layer 0** is active and then click **Set to Zero** button to create a keyframe. Likewise, on frame **30** create another keyframe.

*What just happened?*

*Here, we have reset the coordinates of the **Sphere** to the values defined by the **Default** layer.*

4. Move to frame **19** and then move the **Sphere** little bit higher along the y-axis. Press **F9** to create a keyframe. Now, If you play the animation; you will notice that the layer we just created has been added on the animation that was there on the **Default Layer**. Fig. E2 shows the **Sphere** at frame **19**. Fig. E3 shows the original animation at frame **19**.

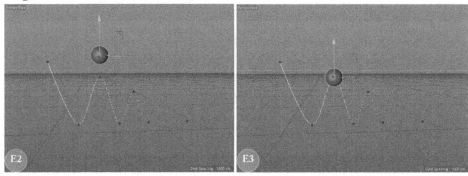

*Tip: Layer weight*

*You can adjust the weight of the layer by using the slider available to the right of layer's label.*

## Exercise 8: Working with the Motion System

The **Motion System** [also referred to as NLA: Non-linear animation system] is used to create animation clips. These clips allow you to work non-linearly and non-destructively. You can also use this system to create animation layers. In this exercise, we will use the Cinema 4D's **Motion System**. Table E8 summarizes the exercise.

| Table E8 | |
|---|---|
| Difficulty level | Intermediate |
| Estimated time to complete | 30 Minutes |
| Topics | • Getting Started<br>• Working with the Motion System |

| Table E8 | |
|---|---|
| Resources folder | **unit-can** |
| Units | **Centimeters** |
| Final file | **motion-system-finish.c4d** |

## Getting Started
Follows these steps:

1. Start a new scene and then set **Units** to **Centimeters**. Create a **Cube**. Now, select **Object** from the **Tools** palette to enable **Object** mode.

2. Make sure you at frame **0** and then click on the **Scale, Rotation,** and **Parameter** icons in the **Animation Toolbar** to disable them.

3. Select **Cube** in the **Object Manager** and then in the **Attribute Manager** > **Coord** tab, select the **P.Y** and **P.Z** labels using **Ctrl. RMB** click and then choose **Animation** > **Add Keyframe Selection** from the context menu. Now, click on the **Record Active Objects** icon to record the keyframe.

4. Move to frame **90** and then in the **Attribute Manager** > **Cube** > **Coord** tab, change **P.Z** to **200**. Next, press **F9** to create keyframe.

## Working with the Motion System
Follow these steps:

1. Make sure **Cube** is still selected and then choose **Animate** > **Add Motion Clip** from the menubar to open the **Add Motion Clip** dialog box [see Fig. E1]. In this dialog box, type **src_pos_x** and then make sure that the **Position** check box is selected in the **Include** area. Next, click **OK**.

*What just happened?*
*Here, we have created a motion clip. You can mix clips [motion segments] in various ways. You can fade them in or out, or you can loop them any number of time. You can move and scale them as well as modify via curves.*

*Notice that the **Cube** has been assigned a new **Motion System** in the **Object Manager**. If switch to the **Coord** tab, you will notice that the red circles that usually denote an animated parameter in the **Attribute Manager** have been removed. As a result, the cube itself no longer contains an animation. If you are in the **Animation** layout, you will notice that the **Timeline** has switched to the **Motion Mode**. A blue line also appears in editor view that denotes the clip path [see Fig. E2].*

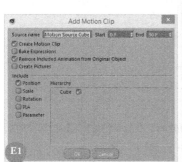

2. **RMB** click on the **Cube** in the **Object Manager** and then choose **Show Motions** from the context menu to open the **Timeline** [see Fig. E3]. Notice at the left of the **Timeline**, you will see a new **Motion Source** and cube's saved animation with the name [**src_pos_x**] we had assigned. At the right you will see a **Motion Clip** that is linked to this **Motion Source** and transfers the saved animation back to the cube. If you select the clip, you can use the bar at the top to offset the clip. You can also scale the clip using bar handles like you do in the **Dope Sheet** mode.

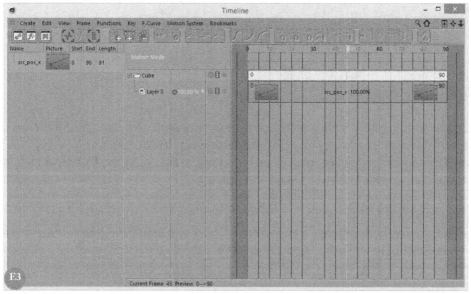

💡 *Tip: Switching between modes*
*You can use the **Tab** key to quickly switch between the **Dope Sheet**, **FCurve**, and **Motion Mode**. You can also click on the icons located at the left of the **Timeline** to switch the modes. Simultaneously pressing the **Ctrl** key while clicking the mode change icon will maintain an active selection in the new mode. As a result, the same selected keys will also be selected in the new mode. Key selections will otherwise be handled independent of one another.*

**?** *What's the difference between a motion clip and motion source?*
*A **Motion Source** contains the previously created animation. In this case, an invisible copy of the animated cube. A motion clip is an instance of this **Motion Source** with which the animation contained in the **Motion Source** can be transferred back to the cube. The animation in the **Motion Clip** can be modified in many different ways, whereby the **Motion Source** remains unaffected. A **Motion Source** can be assigned to a **Motion Clip** at any time. The **Motion Clip** itself contains no animation. In this case, the animation of the cube was moved into the motion source and then assigned to a new motion clip that now affects the cube.*

3. Move to frame **0**. In the **Timeline**, click on the **Animation** icon next to **Layer 0** name to deactivate the clip [see Fig. E4].

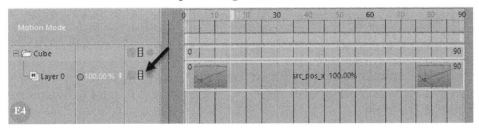

**?** *What just happened?*
*Here, we have disabled the motion clip. As a result, this clip no longer affects our **Cube** and we can animate it as we would a newly created object.*

4. Switch to the **Attribute Manager** > **Cube** > **Coord** tab. Press **F9** to create a frame. Move to frame **30** and then in the **Attribute Manager** > **Cube** > **Coord** tab, change **P.Y** to **200**. Press **F9** to create a keyframe.

5. Move to frame **60** and then in the **Attribute Manager** > **Cube** > **Coord** tab, change **P.Y** to **600**. Press **F9** to create a keyframe. Move to frame **90** and then in the **Attribute Manager** > **Cube** > **Coord** tab, change **P.Y** to **1000**. Press **F9** to create a keyframe [see Fig. E5].

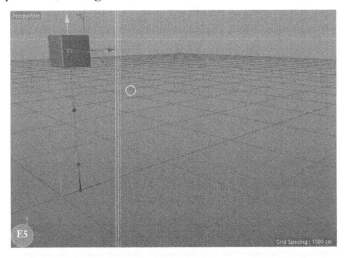

6. Switch to the **Timeline** and enable **Layer 0** animation icon. Play the animation; notice that the animation contained in the motion clip is given priority ignoring the **Position Y** animation we created in last two steps.

7. Disable the animation icon again. Choose **Animate > Add Motion Clip** from the menubar to open the **Add Motion Clip** dialog box. In this dialog box, type **src_pos_y** and then make sure that the **Position** check box is selected in the **Include** area. Next, click **OK**; a vertical motion path appears in the editor view and new layer with the name **Layer 1** is added in the **Timeline** [see Fig. E6].

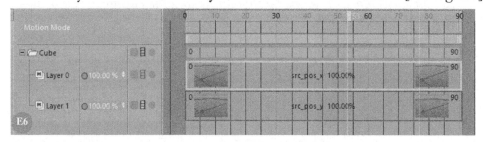

8. Enable the animation icon for **Layer 0** and play the animation in the editor view, you will see how both animations are mixed with each other. Fig. E7 shows the **Cube** at frame **56**.

 *Tip: Solo Animation*
*You can use the solo icon located to the right of the animation icon to solo an individual layer. Click again to disable the solo mode. The* **Solo** *and other options also appear in the* **Attribute Manager** *when you select a* **Motion Clip** *in the* **Timeline***.*

 *What next?*
*Suppose, you want to offset an animation or interactively move, scale, and rotate an animation within the* **Motion Clip***. How would you do it? Well, there is feature in Cinema 4D called* **Pivot Object** *that you can use to do exact same task. To use the* **Pivot Object** *it must be assigned to a motion clip. Next, we will explore the* **Pivot Object***.*

9. Save the scene as **motion-system-finish.c4d**. In the **Timeline**, Select **Cube > Layer 1** in the middle column and then press **Delete** to remove motion clip. Select **src_pos_y** in the left column and then **RMB** click. Choose **Delete Unused Motion Sources** from the context menu to delete the empty source. As a result, we are now left with only one layer that contains the forward Z motion.

10. In the **Timeline**, select the clip and then in the **Attribute Manager > Advanced** tab, click **Create Pivot** to create a **Pivot Object** with the name and assign it to the clip we have selected.

11. Select **Cube Pivot Object** in the **Object Manager** and then in the **Attribute Manager > Object** tab, change **Radius** to **60** [see Fig. E8]. Move the **Pivot Object** in the editor view; the whole animation moves with it. Now, you can animate the **Pivot Object** and the animation stored in the clip will follow it. Save the file with the name **motion-system-finish-02.c4d**.

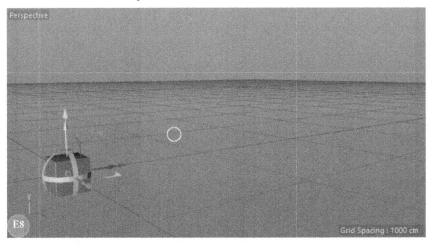

## Exercise 9: Blending the Motion Clips

In this exercise, we will blend two motion clips to create seamless motion. We will also learn to bake the animation created using the **Motion System**. Table E9 summarizes the exercise.

| Table E9 | |
|---|---|
| Difficulty level | Intermediate |
| Estimated time to complete | 35 Minutes |
| Topics | • Getting Started<br>• Blending Clips<br>• Baking the Animation |
| Resources folder | **unit-can** |
| Units | **Centimeters** |
| Start file | **blending-clips-start.c4d** |

| Table E9 | |
| --- | --- |
| Final file | **blending-clips-finish.c4d** |
| | **blending-clips-finish-baking.c4d** |

## Getting Started

Open **blending-clips-start.c4d**.

## Creating Something

Follow these steps:

1. Select **Aeroplane** and then choose **Animate > Add Motion Clip** from the menubar to open the **Add Motion Clip** dialog box. Change **Source name** as **src_aero_cycle** and then click **OK**.

2. **RMB** click on the **Aeroplane** in the **Object Manager** and then choose **Show Motions** from the context menu to open the **Timeline**. Set weight to **0** for **Layer 0** so that we can create a new animation in the editor view from the starting point.

3. Create a path using the **Pen** tool [see Fig. E1]. Now, animate the **Aeroplane** along the path as discussed earlier. You can also open **blending-clips-start-02.c4d**.

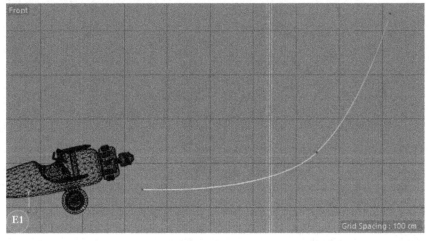

4. Select **Aeroplane** and then choose **Animate > Add Motion Clip** from the menubar to open the **Add Motion Clip** dialog box. Change **Source name** as **src_aero_spline** and then make sure the **Bake Expressions** check box is selected. Next, click **OK**. Now, delete the **Spline** object and the **Align to Spline** tag.

*What next?*

*Notice in the **Timeline** window, we have two motion clip [see Fig. E2]. Next, we will offset and blend the clips.*

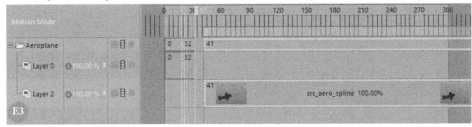

5. Set **Layer 0** weight to **100** and then offset the clips, as shown in Fig. E3.

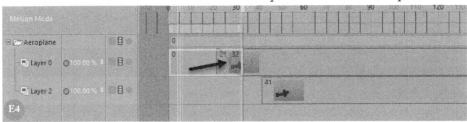

*What next?*
*Play the animation in the editor view; notice that we can now jump from one clip to another but there is not blending at all. Cinema 4D provides the following ways to blend the clip:*

• *Drag a source to the same layer in which the clip you want to blend with is located. Next, drag to overlap the two clips; a transition will atomically be created [see Fig. E4].*
• *You can manually animate the weights of the layers to create blending.*
• *You can use the **Make Transition** option.*

*Next, we will use the **Make Transition** option to blend the clips.*

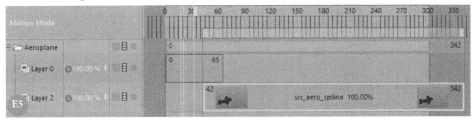

6. Select the **Layer 0** clip and then in the **Attribute Manager > Basic** tab, change **Loops** to **1** to loop the animation one more time. Now, overlap the layers, as shown in Fig. E5.

7. Choose **Motion System > Make Transition** from the **Timeline**'s menubar and then drag from **Layer 0** clip to **Layer 1** clip to create transition. Now, play the animation, you will notice that both clips have been blended smoothly and there is not pop in the animation. If you play the animation in the **Timeline**, you will notice that Cinema 4D has automatically created weight keyframes for you [see Fig. E6].

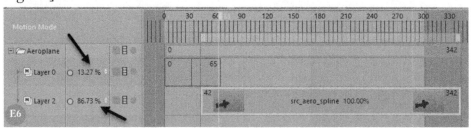

*Tip: Layer Curves*
*If you select the **Motion System** tag in the **Object Manager** and then switch to the **FCurves Mode** in the **Timeline**, you will notice that we have two curves [see Fig. E7] that you can use to farther edit the animation.*

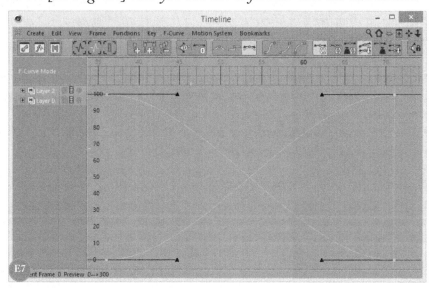

## Baking the Animation

The **Bake Objects** function is used to you can bake the position, scale and rotation values that were not necessarily made using the **P, S,** and **R** keys but using an expression or object. This function is useful when you want to export the animation to another application or for rendering using **Team Render**. Regardless of how the animation was created, this function will create one key per animation frame. Follow these steps:

1. Move to frame **0** and then select the **Aeroplane** object. Open the **FCurves Mode** in the **Timeline**. Notice that there are no keys in the **Timeline**. Press **F9** to create keyframes at frame **0**; now the position and rotation tracks appear in the **Timeline** [see Fig. E8].

2. Select **Aeroplane** in the **Objects** area. Choose **Functions > Bake Objects** from the **Timeline** menubar to open the **Bake Objects** dialog box. In this dialog box, make sure the **Bake Expressions** check box is selected and then clear the **Create Copy** check box. Next, click **OK** to start the baking process. On completion of the baking process the keys will be displayed in the **Timeline** [see Fig. E9].

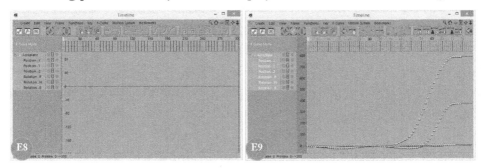

 *Tip: Cancelling baking process*
*The baking process can be cancelled by pressing the **Esc** key on your keyboard.*

 *Tip: Optimizing curves*
*There are several commands in the **Functions** menu to optimize the curves created after the baking process:*

**Delete Unused Tracks:** *All tracks with no keys will be deleted.*
**Clean Tracks:** *The **Clean Tracks** command deletes neighboring keys with the same value on a selected track. Such keys are redundant because no interpolation will take place between them and deleting them will have no effect on the animation itself.*
**Delete Every nth Frame:** *Opens the **Delete every nth frame** dialog. Type 2 in the **Time** field and then click **OK** to delete every 2nd frame, 5 to delete every 5th frame and so on.*
**Simplify:** *This command is useful when working with the motion capture files. Applying the **Simplify** command will make editing your motion capture files much easier. You can also use the **KeyReducer** command to achieve the same result.*

 *Tip: Snapshot*
*You can also use the snapshot functions available in the **F-Curves** menu to optimize the curves. First, take a snapshot of the curve that you want to fix. Next, view the snapshot and optimize the curve using the **KeyReducer** or **Simplify** commands. Now, view adjust the keys manually to match the snapshot.*

## Exercise 10: Animating with Constraints

In this exercise, we will animate objects using constraints. Table E10 summarizes the exercise.

| Table E10 | |
| --- | --- |
| Difficulty level | Beginner |
| Estimated time to complete | 25 Minutes |
| Topics | • Getting Started<br>• Creating the Animation |
| Resources folder | **unit-can** |
| Units | **Centimeters** |
| Start file | **constraint-start.c4d** |
| Final file | **constraint-finish.c4d** |

### Getting Started

Open **constraint-start.c4d**. This scene is has two objects: **Sphere** and **Capsule**. The animation of the **Sphere** is created using keyframe animation whereas the **Capsule** is animated using temporal data in **XPresso**. We will first attach the **Capsule** to the **Sphere** using a constraint. Later, we will break the relationship and then animate the **Capsule** independently.

### Creating the Animation

Follow these steps:

1.  Select **Capsule** in the **Object Manager** and then **RMB** click. Next, choose **Character Tags > Constraint**; the **Constraint** tag is added to the **Capsule** object in the **Object Manager** and its properties are displayed in the **Attribute Manager** [see Fig. E1].

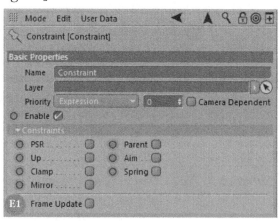

**Note: Constraints**

*Constraints in Cinema 4D allows you to limit how far an object can move during the animation relative to another object or objects. You can activate multiple constraint on an object. The constraints are evaluated in the following order: **Parent**, **PSR**, **Mirror**, **Clamp**, **Spring**, **Aim**, and **UP Vector**. If a constraint has more than one target, the targets are evaluated from top to bottom. The **Constraint** tag is not only useful for character animation but also for the object animation.*

**Note: Parent and PSR constraints**

*The **Parent** constraint makes the object behaves as if the target were its parent. If you change the target's coordinates, the object will behave as if it were a child of the target in the **Object Manager**. The **PSR** constraint controls whether the target affects position, scale, rotation, or any combination of the three.*

**Note: The Constraint tag vs XPresso**

*Much of the functionality of the **Constraint** tag can be achieved using **XPresso**. However, this tag is computed faster than the **XPresso XPressions** and also it is easy to setup. Last but not least, a few of the tag's constraints are simply not possible to achieve using **XPresso**.*

2.  In the **Basic** tab, choose the **Parent** check box. In the **Parent** tab, drag the **Sphere** object from the **Object Manager** to the **Target** field in the **Local Offset** area. Play the animation; notice that the **Capsule** object is now constraint with the **Sphere** object.

3.  Move to frame **50** and then create a keyframe for the **Strength** parameter. Move to frame **60**, change **Strength** to **0**, and then create a keyframe. Play the animation; notice that the constraint effect is vanishing on frame **60**.

4.  Move to frame **50** and create a position keyframe for the **Capsule**. Move to frame **90** and then position the **Capsule** around origin. Record a position keyframe. Play the animation see the effect.

# Quiz

Evaluate your skills to see how many questions you can answer correctly.

**Multiple Choice**
Answer the following questions:

1. Which of the following key combinations is used to open the **Project Settings**?

   [A] Ctrl+P                     [B] Ctrl+D
   [C] Alt+P                      [D] Shift+D

2. Which of the following interpolations types are available in Cinema 4D to define the interpolation between the active key and the next key?

   [A] Spline                     [B] Linear
   [C] Bezier                     [D] Step

3. Which of the following hotkey is used to delete the track including keys in the **Attribute Manager**?

   [A] Shift+Ctrl+LMB-Click       [B] Shift+Ctrl+MMB-Click
   [C] Alt+Ctrl+LMB-Click         [D] Alt+Ctrl+MMB-Click

4. Which of the following keys is used to move tangents handles independently?

   [A] Shift                      [B] Ctrl
   [C] Alt                        [D] Shift+Alt

5. Which of the following modes are available in the **Timeline** to edit and play animation?

   [A] Dope Sheet                 [B] FCurve
   [C] Motion                     [D] All of these

**Fill in the Blanks**
Fill in the blanks in each of the following statements:

1. The _____ and _____ parameters represent the start and end time of the preview range displayed in the **Powerslider,** respectively.

2. The _____ mode is an special recording mode that allows you to record keyframes without having to manually click on the record button.

3. When _____ is enabled in the **Keys Properties** settings, Cinema 4D automatically sets tangent length and angle to a soft interpolation.

4. To hide the motion trajectory from the viewport, choose _____ from the **Attribute Manager**'s menubar and then clear the **Animation Path** check box in the **Display** tab.

5. If you have selected a track in the **Timeline** window and you want to see rest of the keys in the **Timeline Ruler**, RMB click in the **Timeline Ruler** and then choose _____ from the context menu.

6. In the **Advanced** Mode, you can offset keys by first selecting the keys using _____ and then dragging the gray bar to offset the keys. _____ on the **Timeline Ruler** to clear the selection.

7. You can use the _____ key to switch between modes in the **Timeline**.

8. To create a marker, _____ click on the middle third of the **Timeline**.

9. To create markers in the **Timeline Ruler** located below the editor view, _____ click.

10. You can copy keys from one track to another by using _____.

11. Much of the functionality of the **Constraint** tag can be achieved using _____.

12. There are several commands in the **Timeline**'s _____ menu to optimize the curves created after the baking process.

13. The _____ command in the **Timeline**'s **Motion System** menu is used to automatically blend two clips.

14. When you add the **Motion System** tag from the **Tags** menu, a _____ animation layer is added.

15. If you want to reverse the animation along a spline path, you can do so by first selecting the spline and then choosing _____ from the menubar.

**True or False**
State whether each of the following is true or false:

1. You can toggle between the previous and current state of the **Powerslider** by double-clicking on it.

2. Simultaneously pressing the **Alt** key while dragging on one end of the slider will scale the slider at both ends.

3. When recording keys in autokeying mode, you can restrict the recording to specific objects by using a **Selection** object.

4. You can use the **Tab** key to quickly switch between the **Dope Sheet, FCurve,** and **Motion Mode**.

5. The **Parent** constraint makes the object behaves as if the target were its child.

**Summary**
This unit covered the following topics:

- Keyframe Animation
- Timeline
- Interpolation Types
- Animation Previews
- Animating Along a Path
- Animating using XPresso
- Set Driven Keys
- Animation Layers
- Motion System
- Non-linear Animation
- Constraints

# Appendix CMA: Quiz Answers [Modeling]

## Unit CM1: Introduction to Cinema 4D R20

**Multiple Choice**
1. B, 2. B, 3. A, 4. C, 5. B

**Fill in the Blanks**
1. lock, unlock, 2. C, 3. Shift+S, 4. Ctrl+D, 5. MMB, 6. Shift+C, 7. Shift+F4, 8. Shift+G

**True/False**
1. T, 2. T, 3. T, 4. T, 5. F

## Unit CM2: Tools of the Trade

**Multiple Choice**
1. A, 2. A

**Fill in the Blanks**
1. Workplanes, 2. Center, 3. Transfer, 4. Lens Distortion, 5. Doodle

**True/False**
1. F, 2. T, 3. T, 4. T, 5. F

## Unit CM3: Spline Modeling

**Multiple Choice**
1. D, 2. C, 3. A, 4. C, 5. D

**Fill in the Blanks**
1. C, 2. Spine Arch Tool, 3. Intermediate Points

**True/False**
1. T, 2. T

**Multiple Choice**
1. A, 2. B, 3. B, 4. A

**Fill in the Blanks**
1. Points, Edges, and Polygons, 2. C, 3. Set Selection

**True/False**
1. T, 2. F

# Appendix CVA: Quiz Answers [Volumes]

## Unit CV1: Volumes - I

**Fill in the Blanks**
**1.** Volume Builder, Volume Mesher, **2.** Union, Subtract, Intersect, **3.** Voxels, **4.** Signed Distance Field, **5.** Volume Builder, **6.** Voxel Size

**True/False**
**1.** T, **2.** T, **3.** F, **4.** T, **5.** T, **6.** T

## Unit CV2: Volumes - II

**Fill in the Blanks**
**1.** voxel, **2.** Smooth Filter, **3.** Strength, **4.** Voxel Distance, **5.** Reshape Filter, **6.** Volume Group, **7.** Volume Loader

**True/False**
**1.** T, **2.** T, **3.** F, **4.** F

This page is intentionally left blank

# Appendix CRA: Quiz Answers [Rendering]

### Unit CR1: Standard Renderer

**Multiple Choice**
1. B, 2. B, 3. C, 4. B

**Fill in the Blanks**
1. Render Region, 2. Copy from IRR, 3. Tokens, 4. Anti-Aliasing, 5. Compositing, 6. Textures, 7. Cel Renderer, 8. Color Correction, 9. Cylindrical Lens, 10. Compare > Swap Vert./Horiz.

**True/False**
1. T, 2. F, 3. F, 4. T, 5. T, 6. F, 7. T, 8. T, 9. F, 10. F

### Unit CR2: Physical Renderer

**Multiple Choice**
1. C, 2. D, 3. D

**Fill in the Blanks**
1. Vignetting, 2. Physical, Standard, 3. Fixed

**True/False**
1. F, 2. F, 3. F, 4. F, 5. T, 6. T, 7. T

# Unit CR3: Lighting

**Multiple Choice**
1. C, 2. D

**Fill in the Blanks**
1. Intensity, 2. Infinite, 3. Visible Light, 4. No Illumination, 5. Separate Pass, 6. Object/Spline, 7. Show in Render, 8. Visibility Multiplier, 9. Density, 10. Clipping Influence

**True/False**
1. T, 2. F, 3. T, 4. F, 5. F, 6. T, 7. F, 8. T, 9. T, 10. F

# Appendix CTA: Quiz Answers [Texturing]

## Unit CT1: Introduction to UV Mapping

**Fill in the Blanks**
1. BP - UV Edit, 2. Relaxing, 3. Texture

**True/False**
1. F, 2. T, 3. T

## Unit CT2: Material Presets

**Multiple Choice**
1. C, 2. D, 3. A, 4. B

**Fill in the Blanks**
1. Normal Mapping, 2. Color, Specular, Reflection, 3. Color, 4. Layer Shader, 5. Index of Refraction, 6. Transparency, 7. Cheen, Gradients, 8. Fresnel, Gradient

**True/False**
1. T, 2. T, 3. F, 4. F, 5. T, 6. T, 7. T

## Unit CT3: Creating Materials

**Fill in the Blanks**
1. Low Clip, High Clip, 2. Irawan (Woven Cloth), 3. Filter, 4. Displacement, 5. Sub Polygon Displacement, 6. Straight, Pre-multiplied, 7. Glow, 8. Fusion

**True/False**
1. F, 2. T, 3. T, 4. T, 5. F, 6. T

## Unit CT4: Material Nodes

**Multiple Choice**
1. B, 2. A, 3. B, 4. A

**Fill in the Blanks**
1. Color, 2. Ctrl+Alt+N, 3. H, 4. Alt+S, 5. N-Gon, 6. Exposure, 7. Layer, 8. Light, 9. Arithmetic, 10. BSDF

**True/False**
1. F, 2. T, 3. T, 4. T, 5. T

# Appendix CAA: Quiz Answers [Animation]

## Unit CAN: Understanding Animation and Keyframes

**Multiple Choice**
1. B, 2. A, B, D, 3. A, 4. A, 5. D

**Fill in the Blanks**
1. Preview Min Time, Preview Max Time, 2. Autokeying, 3. Auto Tangents, 4. Mode > View Settings, 5. Options > Show Inactive Keys, 6. Shift, Shift+click, 7. Tab, 8. Ctrl, 9. Ctrl+Shift, 10. Shift+Ctrl, 11. XPresso, 12. Functions, 13. Make Transition, 14. relative, 15. Mesh > Spline > Reverse Sequence

**True/False**
1. T, 2. F, 3. T, 4. T, 5. F

This page is intentionally left blank

# Index

**Index**

# Other Publications by
# PADEXI ACADEMY

*Visit **www.padexi.academy** to know more about the books, eBooks, and video courses published by PADEXI ACADEMY.*

## Cinema 4D

- MAXON Cinema 4D R20: Modeling Essentials
- MAXON Cinema 4D R20: A Detailed Guide to Texturing, Lighting, and Rendering
- MAXON Cinema 4D R20: A Detailed Guide to XPresso
- Exploring 3D Modeling with Cinema 4D R19
- Exploring MoGraph with Cinema 4D R19
- Exploring XPresso With Cinema 4D R19

## 3ds Max 2019

- Autodesk 3ds Max 2019: A Detailed Guide to Arnold Renderer
- Autodesk 3ds Max 2019: A Detailed Guide to Modeling, Texturing, Lighting, and Rendering
- Autodesk 3ds Max 2019: Arnold Essentials
- Exploring 3D Modeling with 3ds Max 2019
- MAXON Cinema 4D R20 and Autodesk 3ds Max 2019: Modeling Essentials

## Photoshop

- Exploring Filters With Photoshop CC 2017

**Coming Soon:**

- MAXON Cinema 4D R20: A Detailed Guide to MoGraph
- Autodesk 3ds Max 2020: Modeling Essentials
- Autodesk 3ds Max 2020: A Detailed Guide to Modeling, Texturing, Lighting, and Rendering
- Autodesk 3ds Max 2020: A Detailed Guide to Arnold Renderer

Made in the USA
Columbia, SC
08 February 2020